LIVING TOGETHER

Living Together

ESSAYS ON ARISTOTLE'S ETHICS

Jennifer Whiting

Oxford University Press is a department of the University of Oxford. It furthers the University's objective of excellence in research, scholarship, and education by publishing worldwide. Oxford is a registered trade mark of Oxford University Press in the UK and certain other countries.

Published in the United States of America by Oxford University Press
198 Madison Avenue, New York, NY 10016, United States of America.

Library of Congress Cataloging-in-Publication Data
Names: Whiting, Jennifer, author.
Title: Body and soul : essays on Aristotle's hylomorphism / Jennifer Whiting.
Description: New York, NY, United States of America : Oxford University Press, [2023] |
Includes bibliographical references and index. |
Contents: v. 1. Body and soul—v. 2. Living together |
Identifiers: LCCN 2023004938 (print) | LCCN 2023004939 (ebook) |
ISBN 9780197666005 (v. 1 ; hb) | ISBN 9780199969678 (v. 2 ; hb) |
ISBN 9780197666029 (v. 1 ; epub) | ISBN 9780197666036 |
ISBN 9780197682708 (v. 2 ; epub) | ISBN 9780190063160
Subjects: LCSH: Hylomorphism. | Aristotle.
Classification: LCC BD648 .W45 2023 (print) | LCC BD648 (ebook) |
DDC 128/.1—dc23/eng/20230501
LC record available at https://lccn.loc.gov/2023004938
LC ebook record available at https://lccn.loc.gov/2023004939

DOI: 10.1093/oso/9780199969678.001.0001

Printed by Integrated Books International, United States of America

To my father Douglas,

and my sisters Harriet and Emily,

in loving memory of our mother Charlotte

ἐν τούτῳ γνώσονται πάντες ὅτι ταύτῃ μαθηταί ἐσμέν,
ἐὰν ἀγάπην ἔχωμεν ἐν ἀλλήλοις

Contents

Preface

THIS IS THE second of three volumes that collect essays drafted between 1980 and 2011. I have made small changes here and there, especially in punctuation, to make individual sentences easier to read. And I have added, in square brackets, cross-references to essays in the other two volumes along with a few notes. The essays are otherwise unchanged. I have arranged those within each volume in the order in which they were first drafted, since this best displays the evolution of my thought. But I have assigned the essays to their respective volumes primarily along thematic lines.

The single most important idea in Volume I—the one that ties the essays together—is Aristotle's conception of the ideal friend as an "other self." But the essays in that volume, though inspired by my reading of Aristotle, are concerned less with what Aristotle himself actually thought than with the ways in which views inspired by his might allow us to address contemporary questions about, for example, the nature of personal identity; the rationality of concern for our future selves; the nature of love and friendship; and ideal versus non-ideal forms of psychic structure. In Volumes II and III, I turn to the precarious task of attempting to determine what Aristotle himself thought on these and related issues.

The first two essays of the present volume (henceforth II.1 and II.2) are relics of the dissertation I was attempting to write when I met Rogers Albritton—a dissertation, to borrow a phrase from Terence Irwin, on "the metaphysical and psychological basis of Aristotle's ethics." In two relatively brief but fateful conversations, Rogers persuaded me that what I had to say about Aristotle's metaphysics was more interesting than what I had to say about ways in which Aristotle's ethics was based on his metaphysics. Eight months later I submitted a dissertation—*Individual Forms in Aristotle,* Cornell

1984—whose central arguments appear in Volume III (Chapters 1–4). The remaining essays in that volume return to some of the questions about the metaphysical and psychological basis of Aristotle's ethics that first engaged my interest. But by the time I was writing them, I had come to see that claims about the connections between metaphysics and psychology on the one hand, and ethics on the other, are far less straightforward than I had once been disposed to think, not just in fact but also in Aristotle. I am thus grateful to Rogers for having slowed me down in ways such that I was able to benefit from conversations with John Rawls during the years when he was articulating his "political not metaphysical" ideas and from conversations with John McDowell about Aristotle's respect for the autonomy of ethics.

But the greatest windfall of slowing down came from teaching together with Steve Engstrom for an entire year relatively early in my career. We spent 1993–1994 teaching a graduate seminar on the ethics of Aristotle and Kant in preparation for a National Endowment for Humanities Conference on Aristotle, Kant, and the Stoics. It was then that I drafted "Self-Love and Authoritative Virtue," which is Chapter 4 of the present volume but first appeared in the conference volume I co-edited with Steve: *Aristotle, Kant, and the Stoics: Rethinking Happiness and Duty* (Cambridge, 1996). The seeds of Steve's salutary influence can be detected in this essay, but the fruits are more evident elsewhere. They can be seen by comparing Chapters 1–3 of the present volume with Chapters 6–7 of this volume, and by comparing Chapters 1–4 of Volume III with Chapters 5–7 of that volume. In each case, the method of the earlier essays is somewhat scattershot: I cite a wide range of texts, drawn from various bits of Aristotle's corpus, in support of this or that claim about what Aristotle thought. The method of the later essays is, thanks to Steve's influence, more dialectical. For it was primarily through following Steve's example, working gradually through single texts, that I came to appreciate both how dialectical and how carefully composed Aristotle's texts tend to be, despite their reputation as something like lecture notes with various layers of revision coinhabiting the extant manuscripts.

My aim here is not to disavow the conclusions of the earlier essays, but rather to call attention to the ways in which Aristotle is ill-served by the idea that what remains of his corpus are largely lecture notes—his, not his students'—in various states of revision. This idea, though it may have some basis in reality, leads too many commentators to support their readings of Aristotle by appeal to individual lines drawn from this or that passage, without paying adequate attention to the dialectical context in which the relevant lines are found. I am not referring simply to the common failure to observe whether the context is "endoxic" or "aporetic." Even when Aristotle is developing his own views, he may—as Martin Pickavé and I argue in "*Nicomachean Ethics* 7.3 on Akratic Ignorance" (III.7)—articulate them progressively. And the idea that what we have are incompletely revised lecture notes makes it too easy for commentators to mistake apparent repetition for multiple drafts of the same material where it is more plausible to see what Pickavé and I call the "progressive articulation" of Aristotle's considered views.

The importance of reading Aristotle dialectically, and of not assimilating apparently similar lines of text too quickly to one another, plays an important role in the final chapter of the present volume: "The Pleasures of Thinking Together" (which is a commentary on *Eudemian Ethics* VII.12). This is the only chapter aimed primarily at a specialist reader. But I summarize the overall argument in section 3, which can be read together with the first two sections by nonspecialist readers. And not just read but, I hope, appreciated. For the phenomenon to which Aristotle appeals to defend his claim that even the maximally self-sufficient person will want to live together with others is *familiar*. Readers should *easily* recognize the ways in which the pleasures we all take in dining together are enhanced by the ways in which conversation over dinner allows us to "think together" (on which see *Eudemian Ethics* VII.12). I have experienced many such pleasures in the company of Steve, especially during the year we co-taught and enjoyed post-seminar dinners every week with Michael Thompson and Tom Berry (two other colleagues to whom I am indebted for far more than I can say).

Acknowledgments

THIS VOLUME IS dedicated to my parents and sisters, with whom I first experienced the pleasures of thinking together, often over family dinners, much of the time with inspiring guests: missionaries from far and wide; seminarians who interned with Douglas (not entirely coincidentally, during the war in Vietnam); and seminarians who stuck around to enjoy the company and wisdom of Charlotte, who learned Greek while I was in graduate school and went on, as one of her students put it, to "love them into learning Greek." My sisters and I were always free to invite our friends, some of whom are now family and gather several times a year: Harriet with John and Pilot; Emily with Neil, Caroline, Charlotte, and Nate; and my beloved Tom and Ethan.

The pleasures of thinking together are plentiful among those of us who study ancient texts and make a regular practice of reading together and continuing our discussions over a meal. I am grateful to Verity Harte and M. M. McCabe for including me, despite my lack of track record, in the group that read Plato's *Republic*, one book per summer, over ten summers. The group's successor, in which we are reading Aristotle's *Parva Naturalia* with David Charles and Brad Inwood on board, is the intellectual highlight of my summer, one of the few events for which I am willing to leave my lakeside retreat. My fruitful collaborations with Dan Ferguson, along with Iain Petrie's hospitality and unmatched conviviality, were sorely missed for the second consecutive summer, as it was wisely decided that zooming just isn't the same as *sunhêmereuin* (my favorite word in Aristotle).

My debts to David and Brad are especially wide-ranging. David's invitation, back in 1983, to his *Posterior Analytics* group introduced me to the world of reading groups and made me feel at home among Oxford Aristotelians, and David has ever since been a sympathetic interlocutor. Brad was my go-to classicist in Toronto, where we collaborated on all fronts: in reading groups and workshops, supervising Ph.D. students, and co-teaching Toronto's year-long survey of ancient philosophy, which remains my most rewarding experience teaching undergrads. There can be no adequate compensation for losing Brad as a colleague, but I look forward to the week every summer when Brad and Jen are together again, enjoying, as always, a meal with Niko Scharer.

I focused more on ancient philosophy during my years in Toronto than during my years elsewhere because the historical company was so rich, including early modernists Donald Ainslie and Marleen Rozemond. I also co-taught the work of Michael Thompson and Philippa Foot with neo-Aristotelian Phil Clark, and a seminar on Aristotle and his commentators on *akrasia* with Martin Pickavé. The fruits of the collaboration with Martin include a co-authored paper (III.7) and Toronto's first graduate-faculty Workshop in Ancient Philosophy. But the greatest fruit by far is the friendship of Martin and his wife Fabienne Michelet, who are now "family."

Few readers of Plato are as well-equipped as Rachel Barney to appreciate his work in all its complexity: the literary aspects, the sophistic background and political context, the philosophical innovation. She goaded me into writing about Plato and then insisted that I not just attack prevailing interpretations but also construct a positive account of my own (see "Psychic Contingency in the *Republic*," I.8). I am immensely grateful to her for all that. She also hosted real symposia with visiting speakers. I have fond memories of evenings at her place with two people from whose written work and companionship, at various times and places, I have always benefited: Sarah Broadie and Myles Burnyeat.

One of the last times I saw Myles, he, Sarah, and I were sitting on the ground in Venice, enjoying bottle of wine. He had been, on and off, a visiting colleague at Pittsburgh, where, at a critical point in my career, he read everything I had written and encouraged me to move forward with the nonhistorical work now collected in Volume I, on which he then provided constructive feedback. And it was during a walk along Lake Cayuga that he suggested I make use in "Trusting 'First' and 'Second' Selves" of the story I was then describing to him in response to an objection he had raised (Susan Glaspell's "A Jury of Her Peers"). It should be clear from the end of the Introduction that follows how important his questions have always been for me. Sarah too has been a constant presence and her expressions of confidence in me have sometimes kept me afloat. I continue to read and re-read her work, both on my own and with my students, and am always finding something new in it. I am grateful for all she has shared and was deeply saddened by the news of her death only weeks after she participated constructively in yet another workshop with my students.

Another person who has always been there is Gisela Striker. Many of the thoughts in the Introduction that follows stem from what I learned from attending her seminar on Hellenistic ethics and then commenting on her "Plato's Socrates and the Stoics" at a Cornell conference devoted to the work of Gregory Vlastos. The conference was organized by Phil Mitsis, who made my time in graduate school a little less miserable and my life since then a lot more pleasant, most recently when he and his daughter

Alexandra hosted me and Ethan on their balcony just beneath the Acropolis. Phil's combination of intellectual breadth and generosity in all domains is unmatched.

I have benefited over the years from quasi-colleagues, people from other universities with whom I converse and from whom I learn on a regular basis: Chris Bobonich, Ursula Coope, John Cooper, Christine Kosgaard, Aryeh Kosman, Richard Kraut, Hendrik Lorenz, Alexander Nehamas, Susan Sauvé Meyer, Ben Morison, Richard Moran, Jessica Moss, David Sedley, Tom Tuozzo, and Christian Wildberg. Christian is now at Pitt, where ancient philosophy is flourishing thanks to the arrivals of Sara Magrin and Jacob Rosen. I have always been fortunate in ancient colleagues here at Pitt. I arrived in 1986 simultaneously with John McDowell, whose profound influence on my work is manifest in each of these volumes. James Allen arrived in 1987, brightening countless evenings with conversation about everything from Aristotle to jazZ. But it was Steve Strange who first welcomed me, nodding encouragement during my APA interview and then attending my seminars, always following up with additional texts to bolster what I was saying. His own courses were nutrient-dense and his departure from Pitt was a serious loss to me. His premature death was an even more serious loss to ancient scholarship and I count myself lucky to have bumped into him, shortly before his death, in Alexanderplatz, where we unwittingly enjoyed a few last drinks together.

That year in Berlin combined pleasure and productivity in ways hitherto unimagined by me. Thanks to the unflagging assistance of Marta Jimenez, I did much of the work on the later papers in these volumes (I.7; Chapter 7, this volume; and III.6–8). And thanks to Sally McConnell and Carl Ginet, who have been there for me since I wrote the first of these essays, Tom and I celebrated my fiftieth birthday with lunch at the Reichstag. I am grateful to the Royal Society of Canada and the Humboldt Stiftung for awarding me the Adenauer Fellowship, and to Christof Rapp and Dominik Perler for including me in their circles at the Humboldt University. Thanks to them, I made friends who indulged my desire to converse in German, especially Klaus Corcilius and Christoph Helmig. I was fortunate early on to discover Gesine Voeste-Scherer, Goethe Institute teacher par excellence. But I owe most on that front to Jakub Krajczynski, who decided late in the year that I should coordinate eyes, ears, and tongue by reading Sebastian Haffner's biography of Churchill aloud to him while he sat in the sun and smoked. We started in Berlin and finished in Toronto, where he spent the following year working with me on Aristotle and Alexander of Aphrodisias.

Living in Berlin allowed me to make new friends and to spend more time with old ones: André Laks, whose support made the year possible and with whom I discussed "The Pleasures of Thinking Together" when he and Michel Crubellier (to whom III.9 is dedicated) invited me to address the Paris Aristotle seminar; Dorothea Frede, whose company I have enjoyed in countless settings from Pittsburgh to Berlin (where she gave regular seminars during my visit); and Pieter Sjoerd Hasper. It is a sign of the value I place on my friendship with Marko Malink that I chose to spend my last evening in Berlin dining with him rather than hearing Barack Obama speak in Tiergarten.

Karel Thein, as conversant in early modern as in ancient philosophy, in film as in literature, has hosted me more than once in Prague, introducing me to its vibrant jazz scene and keeping me up to date with fresh releases on his visits to North America. And Gabor Betegh, a kindred (to Karel) spirit, has introduced me to many things: Budapest (with jazz); the Derveni Papyrus; and Jean-Michel Basquiat's *Jawbone of an Ass*, on which he recently gave a spectacular talk at Pitt's Humanities Center. Thanks to my beloved Tom, Gabor's talk was followed by what proved to be a kind of "last supper" with Jonathan Arac, Founder and (until recently) Director of Pitt's Humanities Center. Jonathan's sudden retirement, in the face of COVID-19, is a serious loss: I miss his and Susan Balee's companionship but am grateful for the space he gave me, through the Center, to spread my wings. Gabor was visiting Pittsburgh en route to Ithaca, to which it seems I am always trying to get back. So I drove him there, enjoying the fall foliage while catching up, but only after stopping at the Warhol Museum to see some of the Basquiat-Warhol collaborations.

Ithaca is home, where I most enjoy the pleasures of thinking and playing together with friends, especially Hayden Pelliccia and Charles Brittain. Our pleasures were increased by the recent arrival of Rachana Kamtekar. Two significant others are the late Sydney Shoemaker, with whom I enjoyed weekly lunches whenever I was in town; and the late Richard Boyd, an exemplary cheerleader/coach all in one enthusiastic bundle. Though I only audited his courses at Cornell, Richard spent countless hours talking philosophy with me. He also served, de facto, as placement officer when I was left on my own at the APA. He then phoned before and after every campus visit and coached me, again by phone, through my first few years of teaching. And though his own lectures set a standard to which I could not myself aspire, he helped me to find my own way. He was in that respect an ideal mentor and I hope only that I succeed in honoring his memory in my own work with students.

I was as an undergraduate so averse to standing in front of a class that I had to be talked into graduate school by my prime mentor, Leon Galis. I had no idea then how much one learns from teaching or how rewarding it is to teach the kinds of students with whom I have been blessed. Teaching grew on me, thanks, I am sure, to the benefaction of Richard Boyd. And while I cannot begin to acknowledge all that I have learned from students, I am conscious of debts, reflected here, to Alessandro Bonello, David Bronstein, Bridget Clarke, Robert Howton, Marta Jimenez, Doug Lavin, Larkin Philpot, Juan Piñeros Glasscock, Max Tegtmeyer, Laura Tomlinson, Tamar Shapiro (starting as a high school student at Cornell's summer school), Iakovos Vasiliou, and Daniel Warren (who served as my TA at Harvard). Special thanks are due to Larkin and Max—and to Victor Gonçalves de Sousa—for their assistance in preparing these volumes. And I am extremely grateful to my editor, Peter Ohlin, for his confidence in the three-state solution, his patience, and always cheerful guidance.

Last but not least, I want to thank my poetic but no less philosophical friends Jody Gladding and David Hinton for their friendship and intellectual sustenance over several decades. Jody was my classmate at Franklin and Marshall and then housemate at

Cornell, where we met David, who was always up for philosophical conversation and has devoted his life to his own and others' appreciation of the work of ancient Chinese philosophers and poets. Jody was around when I was, in one and the same month, dancing to the Dead in Barton Hall and drafting "Aristotle's Function Argument: A Defense." Only she knows what a long, strange trip it's been.

Introduction

THE ESSAYS IN this volume revolve around Aristotle's conception of *eudaimonia*, especially the roles played in it by the activities of theoretical and practical intellect and by the quality of our relationships with one another.[1] These concerns come together in the final chapter, where I discuss the importance Aristotle attaches to friendship, not just in a prototypically "political" life but even among those who are privileged to live a "contemplative" one. Aristotle grappled, at least theoretically, with the choice between these lives—but not, I think, just theoretically. Though he was not a citizen of Athens or any other polis in which he lived and worked, his association with Alexander the Great sufficed to make politics a practical concern for him—so much so that late in life, fearing anti-Macedonian sentiment in the wake of Alexander's death, he abandoned the Lyceum and retreated to his mother's estate in Chalcis lest he allow the Athenians, as he put it, "to sin twice against philosophy."

It seems that the choice between these lives was for Aristotle an existential question, in part no doubt because he witnessed in real time Plato's own struggles with it. He cites, in his (probably early) *Eudemian Ethics* (*EE*), Anaxagoras' response to the question "why one would choose to be born rather than not": namely, "for the sake of contemplating the heavens and the whole order of the universe," an activity to which Aristotle himself devoted the bulk of his life [*EE* 1216a11–14]. But he also says in his *Nicomachean Ethics* (*EN*) that he is inquiring not (as in other works) for the sake of

[1] For reasons explained in section 1, I have chosen simply to transliterate 'eudaimonia' which is most often rendered 'happiness' in English.

Living Together. Jennifer Whiting, Oxford University Press. © Oxford University Press 2023.
DOI: 10.1093/oso/9780199969678.003.0001

contemplation [*theôria*] but in order that he and his audience might become good [*EN* 1103b26–30].

The Nicomachean discussion of this choice is the focus of Chapter 2 below, "Human Nature and Intellectualism in Aristotle," where I argue against John Cooper's view that *EN* X.7 represents a relatively late, "intellectualist" stage in Aristotle's thoughts about the human good, the result of his mature reflections, articulated in *De Anima*, about the nature of human intellect.[2] I am now more sympathetic to an intellectualist reading of *EN* X, but this is not a function of any change in thought about the relationship between views expressed in *De Anima* and those expressed in *EN* X. The shift, which is subtle and regrettably inconclusive, is due primarily to changes in my thoughts about how to read *EN* I's account of the "formal" conditions that must be satisfied if an end (or set of ends) is to count as the highest good for a human being. The seeds of this shift were planted early on, when I commented in 1986 at an APA symposium on what became the "Inclusivism" chapter of Richard Kraut's *Aristotle on the Human Good* (Princeton, NJ: Princeton University Press, 1989). Chapter 2 was, alas, already on its way into print. But I did not then rush to change what I had said: it took time for the seeds to sink in and to bear the fruit I seek to pluck in this Introduction.

The "formal" conditions can be traced to the comparison [*parabolê*] of lives in Plato's *Philebus*, where Socrates pits his preference for a life devoted exclusively to intellectual activity against Protarchus' preference for a life devoted exclusively to pleasure. Each eventually concedes that his own candidate does not fully satisfy these conditions and they agree that some form of "mixed" life constitutes the highest good for a human being. This "backstory" shaped Chapter 2's reading of *EN* X as committed to a "bipartite" conception of this good as consisting in some combination of contemplative and political activity, each valued at least partly for itself and apart from any contribution it makes to the other. But the *Philebus* background reveals a glaring omission in my initial talk of a choice *between* lives. It is really a choice *among* lives. For in *EN* I.5 (as in *EE* I.5) Aristotle introduces the life devoted to pleasure alongside the other two. He does of course abruptly dismiss the life of sensual pleasure. But this has in my view misled countless readers, who fail as a result to fully appreciate the role played by pleasure in Aristotle's conception of philia and so, ultimately, in his conception of eudaimonia. My increased appreciation of this role, which is due largely to my increased appreciation of the *Philebus* background, is reflected in the title of Chapter 7 below: "The Pleasures of Thinking Together."

That chapter is a commentary on *EE* VII.12, where the *Philebus* looms large, especially in VII.12's claim that we should not allow ourselves to be misled by the comparison [*parabolê*] of the most *eudaimôn* human being to a god. Aristotle seeks in VII.12 to reconcile (a) *the manifest fact* that the maximally self-sufficient (and so most godlike) among us choose to have friends with (b) *an argument*, based on the assimilation of such persons to gods, concluding that they *should not*. As usual, Aristotle honors fact

[2] John Cooper, *Reason and the Human Good* [*RHG*], Cambridge, MA: Harvard University Press, 1975.

[*ergon*] over argument [*logos*]. And, to make a long story short, his view is essentially this: (1) because we are by nature social animals, each of us takes pleasure, in a way a god does not, in engaging together with like-minded others in the best activities of which we are capable; and (2) because of these pleasures, it makes sense that even someone able to live a purely contemplative life will want to share that life with a like-minded friend or two.

But the long story is not the one sometimes suggested by intellectualist readers like Cooper. It is not because he takes contemplating with a friend to increase the quality and/or quantity of the contemplative activity in which the agent's own eudaimonia consists that Aristotle includes friendship in the contemplative life. For that would flout the requirement that we love and seek to benefit our friends "for themselves." The point is rather that Aristotle treats friendship among those living contemplative lives as an example of the sort of friendship on account of virtue that he distinguishes both from friendships on account of pleasure and from friendships on account of advantage: it is an example of what, thanks to Cooper, we call "character-friendship."[3] It is in connection—and only in connection—with such friendship that Aristotle speaks of the friend as an "other self." His idea, I submit, is that it is only virtuous agents, including those whose lives are organized around contemplation, who value their friends and their friends' activities in the same way that they value themselves and their own activities—namely, as being "in themselves" the *kinds* of people and *kinds* of activities they are, to be valued *as such* and apart from the ways in which they happen to please and/or benefit any particular agent on account of *her* particular tastes and/or needs.

This account of loving another "for herself" serves as the basis for my reading of Aristotle's parallel requirement that a genuinely virtuous agent value and engage in virtuous activity "for itself."[4] The idea here is that a genuinely virtuous agent values virtuous actions not because of the ways in which performing them pleases and/or benefits her, but on account of the features that make them the *kinds* of actions they are. And among these features are the states of affairs at which virtuous actions typically aim. A generous agent values generous action primarily on account of the benefits, such as food and shelter, it aims to provide *for others*; a just agent values just action on account of the ways in which it aims to promote a fair distribution, *as such*, of the benefits and burdens of living together; and so on. I present the case for this account in Chapter 3: "*Eudaimonia*, External Results, and Choosing Virtuous Actions for Themselves."

That chapter is devoted largely to the question how to reconcile these requirements with Aristotle's commitment to what Gregory Vlastos has dubbed "the eudaimonist axiom."[5] The label seeks to capture an assumption so widespread among ancient

[3] John Cooper, "Aristotle on Friendship," in A. Rorty (ed.), *Essays on Aristotle's Ethics* (Berkeley: University of California Press, 1980), 301–40.

[4] For this strategy, I am indebted to Richard Kraut, "Aristotle on Choosing Virtue for Itself," *Archiv für Geschichte der Philosophie* 58 (1976): 223–39.

[5] See "Happiness and Virtue in Socrates' Moral Theory," in Vlastos, *Socrates: Ironist and Moral Philosopher* (Ithaca, NY: Cornell University Press, 1991).

Greeks that Vlastos regarded it as more or less axiomatic—namely, that eudaimonia is the ultimate end of *all* human action. This is generally taken to refer to the agent's own eudaimonia, which tends, however, to be broadly construed: commentators usually allow that the agent's eudaimonia *depends* to some extent on the *eudaimonia* of her loved ones and some even say that the agent's eudaimonia *includes* that of her loved ones.

I began in "Impersonal Friends" [I.2] to criticize this latter move, with its appeal to what I call "colonizing ego" accounts of Aristotle's conception of the ideal friend as an "other self." But I was less concerned there with interpreting Aristotle than with responding to a misreading of my argument in "Friends and Future Selves" [I.1] as expressing a form of rational egoism. I had originally attempted to show how concern for my future self could be justified even if—as some think taking a person's identity over time to consist in psychological continuity entails—she is not strictly identical to me. My idea, which is "Aristotelian" in the sense that it was inspired by Aristotle's conception of character-friendship, was that that concern for my future self can be justified in the same way that Aristotle thinks concern for my friend is (in the ideal case) to be justified—namely, by appeal to her character. The crucial point is that on the Aristotelian view, even concern for my *present* self is (in the ideal case) to be justified by appeal to character. For as we read in the *Magna Moralia*, which I take to express genuinely Aristotelian views even if Aristotle did not himself write it, the virtuous agent loves herself *not because she is herself, but because she is good.*

I discuss this passage in Chapter 4: "Self-Love and Authoritative Virtue." Just as the virtuous agent loves herself primarily on account of her decent character, so too she can love others (including her future selves) primarily on account of their decent characters (as distinct from the relationships in which they *happen* to stand *to her*: for example, the fact that they are *her* kin, *her* friends, or *her* compatriots). Drawing on the Greek word for character [*êthos*], "Impersonal Friends" dubbed the relevant form of concern "ethocentric." Copy editors and auto-correct like to change this to "ethnocentric." But that undoes its point: eth<u>o</u>centric concern, both for oneself and for others, is an antidote to eth<u>n</u>ocentric and other forms of egocentric bias. It is in my view the form of concern that Plato's Socrates urges on his interlocutors when he encourages them to avoid doing injustice, even at the cost of suffering it, on the grounds that doing injustice harms what is (or at least should be) most important to us: namely, our souls.

There is, however, a common objection to making the condition of one's own soul, or one's own virtue, one's top priority: doing so seems to involve a problematic form of moral self-indulgence. I address this objection in Chapter 3, where I assume for the sake of argument *both* that the eudaimonist axiom refers to the agent's own eudaimonia *and* that her eudaimonia consists to a significant extent in activities in which her capacities for friendship and ethical virtue are actualized. The problem is this: how are we to reconcile these claims, taken together, with the requirement that a genuinely virtuous agent engage in virtuous activity "for itself"? A similar problem arises in connection with the parallel requirement that a true friend love and seek to benefit her friend "for himself": how are we to reconcile this with the idea that the agent aims in friendship at her *own* eudaimonia?

The answer lies in taking Aristotle to treat our capacities for friendship and virtuous action as by their very natures capacities that *cannot* be actualized by someone who aims primarily to actualize them. To actualize her capacity for virtue, an agent must choose to perform virtuous actions *for themselves*; to actualize her capacity for friendship, she must love and seek to benefit her friends *for themselves*. So even if it were coherent to speak of an agent as aiming at these things "for themselves" *in order to actualize the relevant capacities*, it would be uncharitable to interpret the axiom in this way. We should, if possible, interpret it as allowing that an agent who is making the sort of choices in which eudaimonia consists—an agent choosing to perform a virtuous action "for itself" or choosing to benefit her friend "for himself"—is *thereby* choosing these things for the sake of eudaimonia, but not in any sense that involves choosing them *because* she takes her own eudaimonia to consist in so choosing. On the account proposed in Chapter 3, eudaimonia consists in activities of soul that express the values an agent attaches to goods like the welfare of her loved ones, a fair distribution among fellow citizens of the benefits and burdens of living together, and so on: because she values these things "for themselves," her eudaimonia consists to a large extent in activities aimed at securing and maintaining them. But Chapter 3 does not take Aristotle to restrict these activities, as the Stoics do, to the agent's soul narrowly construed. It seeks to show how Aristotle can allow that success in achieving the sort of results at which virtuous actions typically aim renders the agent's activity—and with it her eudaimonia—"more complete" than it would otherwise be.

My readings of these parallel requirements and their relationships to the eudaimonist axiom are the twin pillars of my attack on the common tendency to read Aristotle's eudaimonism as a form of rational egoism. I commence the textual case for this attack in Chapter 4, but it is in Chapter 6, "The Nicomachean Account of *Philia*," that I start to tie the pieces together. My strategy there owes much to the work of John McDowell, which I discuss in Chapter 5: "Strong Dialectic, Neurathian Reflection, and the Ascent of Desire: Irwin and McDowell on Aristotle's Methods of Ethics." The strategy is to start with Aristotle's conception of philia and to interpret his eudaimonism in the light of it, rather than working (as many commentators do) the other way round, starting with a conception of eudaimonism as a form of rational egoism and then interpreting Aristotle's conception of friendship (especially his conception of the friend as an "other self") as making friendship "safe" for a rational egoist. Chapter 6 thus defends the reading of Aristotle that inspired the attack on rational egoism that I launched in "Impersonal Friends" [I.2].

This attack on rational egoism, both in its own right and as an interpretation of Aristotle's eudaimonism, is one of the themes that connect the essays in this volume with those in Volume I. "Impersonal Friends" is the linchpin, and the shortest bridge between the two volumes is between it and Chapter 6 below. But this bridge, which can be traversed in either direction, is not the only bridge. Questions about rational-egoist readings of Aristotle play prominent roles in Chapters 4 and 5 below. And there are important connections between the essays collected here and other essays in Volume I, especially "Love: Self-Propagation, Self-Preservation, or Ekstasis?" [I.7]. There are also connections between the essays collected here and those in Volume III, especially "Hylomorphic Virtue: Cosmology, Embryology, and Moral Development in Aristotle" [III.6], where the McDowellian aspects of my views are made more explicit. But I want to focus here on the essays in this volume, paying special attention to points on which I have had second thoughts (and often more).

1. *EUDAIMONIA*: INTRODUCTORY REMARKS

The term 'eudaimonia' is usually—though not entirely satisfactorily—rendered 'happiness' in English. Its etymology suggests the presence in a person's life of a well-disposed spirit [*eu-daimôn*]. So we might take it to refer to the condition of someone who lives what we would call a "charmed" life. But insofar as 'charmed' connotes good fortune—an outside benefactor and/or a sublime constitution—it runs the risk of obscuring the central role played in Aristotle's conception of eudaimonia by activities that are proper [*oikeion*] to the subject herself, activities for which she bears a special responsibility (discussed in Chapter 4).

The nature of eudaimonia seems to have been as hotly disputed in Aristotle's milieu as the nature of happiness is in ours. Just as many of our contemporaries take happiness to consist largely in subjective satisfaction, or in being content with whatever one has and does, so too many of Aristotle's contemporaries took eudaimonia to consist largely in such satisfaction. And just as some of our contemporaries insist that certain objective conditions must be satisfied if a person is to achieve genuine happiness—that, for example, she be engaged in meaningful activities and/or sincere relationships with loved ones—so too some of Aristotle's contemporaries counted a person eudaimôn only if her life satisfied some such conditions.

These parallels in semantic range are part of what makes 'happiness' the most common translation of 'eudaimonia.' Cooper's suggestion that we use 'flourishing,' which casts subjective satisfaction in an epiphenomenal role, may fit Aristotle's conception, according to which eudaimonia consists primarily in the excellent performance of our distinctively human work or function.[6] But insofar as 'flourishing' has objectivist connotations, using it to translate 'eudaimonia' risks making nonsense of the debate in which Aristotle rejects the Protagorean view according to which each person is the measure of all things, including what counts (at least for her) as eudaimonia. If there were among Aristotle's interlocuters subjectivists about eudaimonia—and I suggest that Protagoras [c. 490–420 BCE] might qualify—their view is not well served by 'flourishing.' We need a term whose semantic range allows us to represent objectivists and subjectivists as arguing about the nature of what *they* take to be one and the same

[6] Cooper, *RHG*, 89–90. For excellent discussion of these issues, see Richard Kraut, "Two Conceptions of Happiness," *Philosophical Review* 88 (1979): 167–97.

thing. So the subjectivist connotations of 'happiness' as we tend to use it are a liability. Hence my choice simply to transliterate 'eudaimonia.'

Most of Aristotle's contemporaries (broadly construed so as to include Greeks in the surrounding centuries) agreed that eudaimonia is the highest good for a human being, a good that is *both* absolutely final [*haplôs teleion*] in the sense that it is "such-as-to-be chosen always for itself and never on account of something else" [*EN* 1097a33–34] *and* "self-sufficient" [*autarkes*] in the sense that it "by itself makes a life such-as-to-be-chosen and lacking in nothing" [*EN* 1097b14–15].[7] But they disagreed about what a life needs to include in order to satisfy these "formal" conditions. In other words, they disagreed about the components of eudaimonia.

Aristotle classifies the candidates for inclusion in *EN* I.8. There are *bodily* goods, such as health, strength, and good looks; *psychic* goods, such as pleasure, virtue, and intelligence; and goods that are *external* to body and soul, goods such as friends, wealth, and political power. Aristotle himself took psychic goods to be goods in the most authoritative [*kuriôtata*] sense [*EN* 1098b14–15], by which I think he means that eudaimonia is measured primarily (perhaps even exclusively) in terms of the extent to which its subject achieves and sustains *them*. But Aristotle acknowledged the ways in which bodily and external goods contribute to psychic ones: we accomplish many things through friends, wealth, and political power, just as we do through various instruments [*kathaper di' organa*] [*EN* 1099a34–b1]. This, he says, is why some people go so far as to identify eudaimonia with good fortune [*eutuchia*] [*EN* 1099b7–8].

Aristotle himself rejects this identification. He identifies eudaimonia with some activity—or perhaps set of activities—of soul. But insofar he counts an agent as eudaimôn only to the extent that the relevant activities are unimpeded, he seems to allow that the presence of whatever bodily and external goods are required for unimpeded activity can contribute to an agent's eudaimonia, if not directly then at least by enhancing the relevant activities [*EN/EE* 1153b7–25]. It is, however, unclear whether Aristotle allows other goods to contribute *directly* to person's *eudaimonia,* and not simply by increasing the activity (or activities) in which it principally consists.

The Stoics, following the Cynics and perhaps also the historical Socrates, notoriously denied something like this possibility. (I say "something like" because they seem to have focused more on the *condition* of being virtuous than on the *activities* with which Aristotle was primarily concerned. But insofar as they would agree that genuine virtue will act whenever possible, we can bracket this difference for present purposes.) The Stoics identified eudaimonia exclusively with moral virtue and claimed that although health, wealth, and freedom from pain are to be "preferred" to sickness, poverty, and pain, these preferred items are nonetheless "indifferent" with respect to the eudaimonia of their respective subjects: a virtuous agent who is healthy, wealthy, and pain-free is no more eudaimôn than a virtuous agent who is sick, impoverished,

---

[7] Translations, unless otherwise noted, are my own. For the use of "such-as-to-be-chosen" to render '*haireton*,' see Chapter 4, section 1.

and being tortured "on the rack." In other words, equally virtuous agents are equally eudaimôn, no matter what else is going on in their lives.

The Stoics bit this bullet in order to protect the "sovereignty" of virtue.[8] It was the price they were willing to pay in order to justify their view that eudaimonia could never be promoted by trading virtue for other so-called goods, no matter how great and how many the other so-called goods might be. But there is a way—and I think Aristotle saw it—to protect the sovereignty of virtue without having to bite this bullet. For he too seems to think that a genuinely virtuous agent will never make such trades: he says in *EN* I.5 that only someone who was defending a thesis would say that a virtuous agent, unable to engage in virtuous activity and suffering the greatest misfortunes, is eudaimôn [*EN* 1095b31–96a2]. And though we might read these lines as focused simply on the way in which the lack of bodily and external goods interferes with eudaimonia by interfering with the exercise of virtue, there is considerable evidence that Aristotle took at least some bodily and external goods to contribute to *eudaimonia* in ways that transcend their contributions to the agent's own virtuous activity.

Some of the strongest evidence appears in *EN* I.10–11, where Aristotle discusses Solon's advice that we refuse to count an agent eudaimôn until after she has died.[9] He does not take Solon [c. 630–c. 560 BCE] to say that a person could actually *be* eudaimôn after her death: that would be absurd *both* on common conceptions according to which eudaimonia consists primarily in pleasure or some form of subjective satisfaction *and* on Aristotle's own conception according to which eudaimonia is to be identified primarily with some form (or forms) of activity. He interprets Solon as saying only that once a person has died it is safe to declare that she had been eudaimôn, since she is then outside the realm of harms and misfortunes. But he notes that there is dispute even about this and adds (apparently in his own voice), "it seems that <things are> bad or good for someone who has died, since <things are good or bad> for one who is alive but not aware of them: for example, honors and dishonors <in the lives> of their children and generally good actions and misfortunes <in the lives> of their descendants" [*EN* 1100a14–21].[10] Aristotle recognizes that there is a puzzle about how exactly to accommodate this, but he does not seem to be opposed in principle to the idea of including the welfare of at least some of one's descendants among the conditions for

---

[8] I take this term from Vlastos (cited above). Iakovos Vasiliou, in his highly illuminating *Aiming at Virtue* (Cambridge: Cambridge University Press, 2008), speaks instead of "the supremacy of virtue."

[9] This is a familiar trope, found in Aeschylus (*Agamemnon*, 928–29); and in Sophocles (*Oedipus Rex*, 1529–30), who (like Herodotus when he attributes the claim Solon) uses the adjective '*olbios*' rather than '*eudaimôn*.'

[10] Except where noted, translations are my own. I use square brackets to indicate the Greek for what precedes them; and angular brackets, as here, to indicate what I understand in spite of its not being explicitly stated. In some cases what I understand is implicit in the text, but this is not always the case. I tend to make liberal use of angular brackets so as to make it clear exactly how *I* fill in various gaps that one must *somehow or other* fill in. I am *not* thereby claiming that my way is the *only* way to fill them. My aim is twofold: to make it clear how as a matter of fact I understand what is to be filled in and to flag my interpretive decisions for the reader to make of what she will.

achieving eudaimonia: he simply wants to place some limits on how far removed the relevant descendants can be [*EN* 1100a21–31].

There are thorny questions about how (if at all) Aristotle can reconcile taking an agent's eudaimonia to be partly a function of how things go for her descendants after she has died with his conception of eudaimonia as an activity of soul. But (as I argue in Chapter 3) he might appeal here to the account of teaching presented in *Physics* III.3, where the teacher's capacity to teach is said to be actualized in the learning that takes place in the souls of her students: he could argue that at least some of the activities in which an agent's eudaimonia consists are completed in what comes about, as a result of these activities, in the lives of others, especially the agent's offspring and other descendants. This would extend the activities of soul in which an agent's eudaimonia consists beyond what are ordinarily thought to be the boundaries of her life, both bodily and chronological. And there is support for this (not just in *Physics* III.3 but) in *EN* IX.7's account of the relationship between benefactor and beneficiary (discussed in Chapter 6 below).

We can of course say that an agent who lives long enough to see the good fortune of her descendants is more eudaimôn than one who does not and we might chalk this up to the increase in subjective satisfaction that accompanies her longevity. But we should not assign too much weight to such satisfaction in Aristotle's general conception of eudaimonia. For he seems committed to a set of views from which it follows that, other things equal, the life of an agent who does not live to take subjective satisfaction in some great accomplishment on the part of her child may nonetheless be more eudaimôn than the life of an agent who lives to take repeated satisfaction in a series of modest accomplishments on the part of his child. I say this because Aristotle seems in fact to accept an intrapersonal analogue of this interpersonal point when he says at *EN* 1169b17–25 that the *kaloskagathos* (whom I discuss in Chapter 4 below) will choose one fine and great action over many small ones.

Even so, subjective satisfaction matters more to Aristotle than some commentators would allow. But its value is not independent of the value of that in which it is taken. This is clear from what Aristotle says about cases where the satisfaction is not (as Aristotle often treats pleasure) integral to the activity in which this agent is engaged. Consider, for example, the way in which (as I note in Chapter 6) Aristotle takes mothers as paradigmatic examples of those who love and seek to benefit others "for themselves." Because mothers tend to care so much about the welfare of their children they often are willing—in cases where it is best *for the children*—to forego the activities of mothering in which their own eudaimonia to a large extent consists and to allow someone else to take their place and so to receive in their places the affection and other goods proper to them as mothers [*EN* 1159a27–34]. Aristotle, who may well be thinking of Euripides' *Alcestis,* refers to the subjective satisfaction mothers will thereby take in seeing their *children* doing well. But his point assumes a degree of sacrifice that surely makes this pale by comparison with the forms of subjective satisfaction internal to the activity of mothering their own children.

In sum, it is striking but rarely noted that Aristotle's discussion of fortune is (a) focused less on goods like wealth and power than on the agent's relations to her loved ones; and (b) concerned not just with what an agent suffers when her loved ones die but also on how things go for those who live on after the agent herself has died. His willingness to take the degree of eudaimonia enjoyed by an agent to be partly a function of how things go for others, even after she herself has died, makes it clear that he does not take eudaimonia to consist primarily in subjective satisfaction: certain objective conditions must be satisfied—*whether or not an agent knows they are*—if her life is to count as eudaimôn. This not to say that subjective satisfaction, in the form of pleasure or desire-satisfaction, counts in Aristotle's view for nothing: he may (contra Antisthenes) include some degree of it among the objective conditions for a person or her life to count as eudaimôn.[11] It is in fact one on the central claims of Chapter 7 below that Aristotle seeks to explain the fact that the maximally self-sufficient (and so most godlike) among us have friends by appeal to the pleasure that those who live contemplative lives take in the success of their friends *simply as such* and apart from any contribution this success makes to the quantity and/or quantity of their own contemplative activity. I shall return to this point in section 4. We must first examine my early readings of *EN* I and X.

2. THE "CONDITIONAL" READING OF *EN* X.7–8

EN I.5 (like *EE* I.5) introduces three popular candidates for the highest good: a life filled with pleasure (especially bodily pleasure), a life filled with honor (especially the sort bestowed on those who succeed in military and political affairs), and a life filled with contemplative activity undertaken and enjoyed purely for its own sake. I shall focus here, as in Chapter 2, on the Nicomachean account.

Aristotle quickly dismisses the life of pleasure on the ground that its devotees, who "decide on" [*prohairoumenoi*] a life suited to fatted beasts, are "completely slavish" [*pantelôs andrapodôdeis*] [*EN* 1095b19–22].[12] Aristotle thinks that such a life, no matter how full of bodily pleasures it is, lacks distinctively human goods, goods without which no human life can count as "by itself such-as-to-be-chosen and lacking in nothing." Here, as elsewhere, Aristotle relies on the notorious idea that what is good for a human being is determined by some function or work [*ergon*] that is proper [*idion*] to human beings as such. It is sometimes assumed that he is referring here simply to something *peculiar* to members of the human kind and so that activities like prostitution and engaging in nuclear warfare are obvious counterexamples. But Aristotle is using '*idion*'

[11] Antisthenes (c. 445–365 BCE) was a "Cynic" and companion of Socrates; he is alleged to have said that he would rather go mad than suffer pleasure.

[12] It is interesting, given Aristotle's conception of *prohairesis* as a form of deliberative desire limited to relatively mature rational agents, that he uses '*prohairoumenoi*' here. The idea may be that the preferences of these subjects, unlike those of non-rational animals, are based in deliberation, perhaps even in views about what constitutes the highest good for a human being.

here in the special sense in which he uses it in *Topics* 101b26–30, to indicate something that belongs to the *essence* of the kind and not simply something peculiar to its members. He assumes of course that the human essence involves reason and so that the human *ergon* involves some form of rational activity, one that sets us apart from other animals and perhaps also from divine beings. And he assumes that it is *good for* a human being to engage in such activity. But many readers object that there is no such thing as a distinctively human *ergon,* or that even if there is some such thing, nothing follows from the *fact* of its existence about what sort of life a human being *ought* to live. I answer these and other common objections to Aristotle's view in Chapter 1, "Aristotle's Function Argument: A Defense."

Aristotle also criticizes those who identify eudaimonia with achieving the sort of honor that comes with military and political success. Such honor is, as he puts it, "too superficial" to count as the highest good for a human being. The highest good is supposed to be something that belongs to the agent herself and cannot easily be taken from her [*oikeion ti kai dusaphaireton*] [*EN* 1095b22–26]. Aristotle allows that a life of political activity and its characteristic ends, if chosen not for the sake of honor but *for themselves,* may satisfy this condition. (This is more or less the life I discuss in Chapter 3.) But Aristotle seems to think that even so construed the most successful political life will lack an important good if it fails to include some purely contemplative activity. For it is clear from *EN* X.7 that he takes purely theoretical activity to be the highest and most rewarding sort of activity in which a human being can engage. But X.7 *also* says that an individual who lives a contemplative life does so not insofar as she is human, but insofar as there is something divine in her. And X.7 transitions to X.8 in the following way:

> [end of X.7] . . . for what is *oikeion* to each by nature is best and most pleasant for each. And for a human being the life in accordance with *nous* <is best and most pleasant> if [*eiper*] a human being is above all this <sc., *nous*>. This <life> then is most eudaimôn. [start of X.8] Secondarily <most eudaimôn> is the <life> in accordance with the other virtue. For the activities in accordance with this <virtue> are human [*anthrôpikai*].

The superlative, which is clearly implied at the start of X.8, is puzzling. How can there be two "most eudaimôn" lives? What does it mean for a life to be *secondarily* "most eudaimôn"?

I now see two relatively natural ways to read this transition. One, which I did not see clearly when I wrote Chapter 2, is as assuming a distinction between two different types of human being: your average political animal, for whom an "active" life (perhaps involving some degree of contemplation) is the most eudaimôn possible; and those rare individuals whose nature somehow sets them apart, rendering them suited for a contemplative life in which activity in accordance with ethical virtue, though it may be required, makes no direct contribution to their eudaimonia, which is measured only by the quality and quantity of their contemplative activity. Thanks to my consideration of *Politics* I together with related passages in Aristotle's *History of Animals,* I now see a glimmer of plausibility in this reading (to which I return in section 5 below).

A more natural way to read the transition is as tacitly relying on something like Aristotle's distinction between what is *haplôs* good (i.e., good *without qualification*) and what is good *tini* (i.e., good *for some particular being*) and so contrasting the divine life, qua *haplôs* 'most eudaimôn,' with the life that is 'most eudaimôn' *for a human being.* When writing Chapter 2, I gravitated to this for a combination of reasons, the weightiest of which was this: in spite of taking ethically virtuous activity to require external goods that are sometimes impediments to contemplation [*empodia pros ge tên theôrian*], Aristotle says that "the contemplator, insofar as he is human [*hê(i) d' anthrôpos esti*] and lives together with many, chooses to act in accordance with <ethical> virtue" [*EN* 1178b3–7]. I took this as a sign that the contemplator qua human is supposed to attach some value to virtuous activity not just *apart from* any contribution it might make to her contemplative activity but even *at some cost to* that activity. So I rejected Cooper's suggestion that the contemplator's choice to act in accordance with virtue is merely instrumental, and that she chooses to act this way because doing so happens to be what, in the society in which she lives, best promotes contemplation. I took Aristotle to be saying that the contemplator values virtuous action "for itself" and I moved quickly—I now think too quickly—to the conclusion that Aristotle took virtuous action to be a *component* of the contemplator's eudaimonia, something that adds to whatever degree of eudaimonia she enjoys in the form of contemplative activity.

This move was abetted by my early attachment to an "inclusivist" reading of the "formal" conditions that must be satisfied if an end (or some combination of ends) is to count as the highest good for a human being. I shall say more in section 3 below about how inclusivist readings of these conditions work, but the idea is roughly that eudaimonia is the most desirable end possible in the sense that it includes at least some degree of any end that is worth achieving "for itself." For as long as any end worth achieving for itself fails to be included in a proposed candidate for eudaimonia, that candidate can be improved by the addition of what is left out and so is not itself the most desirable end possible.

Because I was disposed to read the formal conditions in this way *and* to read *EN* X.8 as saying that the contemplator values virtuous action for itself, I read *EN* X as endorsing a bipartite account of the substance of the contemplator's eudaimonia. So I read the end of X.7 (quoted above) as making only a conditional claim: *if* a human being is identified exclusively with theoretical intellect, *then* contemplation is the sole component of eudaimonia. And I argued that Aristotle not only fails to affirm the antecedent but effectively denies it when he goes on in X.8 to say that the contemplator qua human will choose to have the external goods that are required for virtuous activity in spite of their sometimes being impediments to contemplation. For it seemed to me then, as it still does, that Aristotle thinks the contemplator will at least sometimes choose to act in accordance with virtue at the expense of her contemplative activity. But the question, as I now see it, is whether this requires him to treat such action as a component of her eudaimonia.

It is admittedly possible to translate '*eiper*' in the conclusion of X.7 as 'since' rather than 'if.' But I favored 'if' largely because I thought that required in order to reconcile the arguments of *EN* X with several features of the *EN* I–IX: first, Aristotle's commitment to the "eudaimonist axiom," according to which *all* things are chosen (or at least *ought* to be chosen) for the sake of eudaimonia, presumably the agent's own; second, his requirement that a genuinely virtuous agent choose virtuous actions *for themselves;* and third, his requirement that we love and seek to benefit our friends *for themselves.* I did not at the time see how Aristotle could identify eudaimonia exclusively with contemplative activity without running afoul of these requirements. For embracing that identification would seem to require him to say that the contemplator chooses to perform virtuous actions for the sake of (her own) contemplation, and likewise that the contemplator, assuming she has friends, loves and seeks to benefit her friends for the sake of (her own) contemplation.

I also thought that identifying eudaimonia with contemplative activity threatened the plausibility of the eudaimonist axiom, even construed as a claim about that for the sake of which an agent *ought* to choose all things. I thought the easiest way to make sense of that axiom while honoring the two requirements was to read Aristotle as adopting an "inclusivist" conception of eudaimonia according to which choosing something "for itself" *just is* choosing it as a component of eudaimonia. For this renders the eudaimonist axiom plausible in a way that respects these requirements. On this account, every agent chooses whatever she chooses *either* (a) "for itself," in which case it is component of her eudaimonia (broadly construed so as to involve that of her loved ones), *or* (b) for the sake of something that contributes eventually to something that is chosen for itself, and so, ultimately, for the sake of something that is a component of her eudaimonia (again broadly construed); and the activities characteristic of friendship and virtue belong in (a).

It was this package of thoughts that supported the central thesis of Chapter 2—namely, that virtuous activity is a component of the contemplator's eudaimonia. But I have come, thanks to reflection on the work of Richard Kraut, to question some of the contents of the package, especially my inclusivist reading of the "formal" conditions. So let me turn to that.

3. THE "FORMAL" CONDITIONS: HOLISM AND THE "CONDITIONALITY THESIS"

There was, according to Aristotle, widespread agreement that any candidate for the highest good must satisfy two conditions. It must, as he claims in *EN* I.7, be both *teleion* and *autarkes.* When Aristotle introduces the first condition, he explains his use of '*teleion*' in a way that supports taking it to indicate the *terminus* in a series of ends, something chosen for itself and not for the sake of some *further* end, something for the sake of which the rest are themselves chosen. So 'final' seems an appropriate way to render it. This leads some commentators to read the conclusion of Aristotle's impending function argument as signaling that eudaimonia consists exclusively in contemplative activity enjoyed purely for itself. Such commentators take the first condition to anticipate the arguments of X.7, where Aristotle argues for the superiority of theoretical over practical activity on the ground that only theoretical activity is cherished only for itself: in practical matters we are always more or less concerned with something beyond the action itself (on which, see Chapter 3).

But in the lines that follow immediately on the conclusion of the function argument, Aristotle adds that eudaimonia also requires a *teleios bios*, since "one swallow does not make a spring, nor does one day; nor, similarly, does one day or a short time make us blessed and *eudaimôn*" [1098a18–20].[13] The point here is clearly to do with the length of life, perhaps because a certain length is required if one is to experience the full range of goods, practical as well as theoretical, that human life has to offer. So it seems appropriate to speak here, as most translators do, of a "complete life." How, then, should we read the conclusion of the function argument, sandwiched as it seems to be between talk of an end that is most *final* in the sense that is "such-as-to-be chosen always for itself and never on account of something else" [*EN* 1097a33–34] and talk of a life that is *complete* in the sense that it is inter alia long enough to allow for the full range of goods that human life has to offer?

Commentators go both ways here. Some go with 'final' and take the function argument to be recommending a life devoted primarily, perhaps even exclusively, to the single best activity of which the agent is capable. Such commentators tend to read *EN* X.7 as identifying eudaimonia, in the best-case scenario, with contemplative activity enjoyed purely for its own sake, and X.8 as identifying eudaimonia, in the second-best case, with political activity (perhaps aimed at promoting contemplative activity on the part of those who are capable of it). Others go with 'complete' and take the function argument to recommend a life that includes the full range of distinctively human goods, not just contemplative activity but also friendship and the sort of socially engaged activities that suit our nature as "political animals." Translators who adopt this view often use 'complete' to render Aristotle's statement of the first condition, thinking perhaps that the term should be rendered uniformly throughout I.7. Others go for something more neutral, such as 'perfect.' But 'perfect' does not connote temporal extension in quite the way 'complete' does.

I can think of no English term whose ordinary usage displays the range of connotations that '*teleion*' does, but 'ultimate' comes close. Though it most naturally connotes the end of some series, it can also be used as it is in talk of "Ultimate," aka "ultimate frisbee." This is of course the *highest* form of the sport, the end towards which early training leads, but it is also the *most complete* form in the sense that it includes *all* the things, offensive and defensive, that make frisbee so cool: the various strategies and ways of executing them, the assists, layouts, picks, hucks, skies, greatests! Here, however, it is important to note that Ultimate is not simply a collection of such things: it

[13] From T. Irwin's 1999 translation, *Aristotle: Nicomachean Ethics*, 2nd edn. (Indianapolis, IN: Hackett).

consists in such things standing in the appropriate relations to one another. When you have them *all*, at the *highest* possible level, you have frisbee at its "most ultimate." So when Aristotle allows that more than one activity may be *teleion* and says that in this case eudaimonia is the "most *teleion*" of these, he may mean *either* that eudaimonia consists in the single best (distinctively human) activity *or* that it consists in a properly structured complex of (distinctively human) activities. In other words, he may intend what is sometimes called a "dominant end" conception of the substance of eudaimonia or he may intend an "inclusivist" one.

I myself prefer to contrast "inclusivist" accounts of the substance of eudaimonia with "exclusivist" rather than "dominant end" ones. The crucial issue is whether Aristotle ends up identifying eudaimonia with a single activity for the sake of which everything else is chosen and to which everything else is in that sense subordinate, or whether he takes eudaimonia to consist in more than one type of activity each of which makes at least some non-instrumental contribution to the value of the whole and so is not simply subordinate to some single activity to which it (along with the others) contributes. The problem with the "dominant end" label is that it is compatible *both* with readings according to which the "dominant end" is a single activity for the sake of which *all* "the rest" are chosen, *and* with readings according to which eudaimonia consists in a plurality of ends hierarchically ordered in ways such that one of the plural ends "dominates" the others, not in the sense that all the others are chosen for the sake of it but in the sense that its value is lexically prior to the value of the others. If an end is dominant in this "lexical" way, then there is room for the sort of view I think Aristotle eventually adopts, one according to which no sacrifice in the amount of the dominant end an agent enjoys can be compensated for by any amount of the others *even though* some others (e.g., innocent pleasures) have a kind of independent value such that adding them to that amount of the dominant end can make an agent more eudaimôn than she would be with that amount of the dominant end taken by itself. To the extent that the goods added make an agent more eudaimôn without increasing the amount of the dominant end she enjoys, these other goods *may* be *included* among the components of her eudaimonia. Such a view might be called *either* a "dominant end" *or* an "inclusivist" view. So I prefer to dispense with the "dominant end" label and to focus instead on the question whether Aristotle takes eudaimonia to consist exclusively in a single activity such as contemplation or whether he takes it to consist in some (presumably structured) combination of activities each of which makes at least some direct contribution to the whole.

Two factors moved me early on toward an inclusivist reading of the substance of the contemplator's eudaimonia; first, the arguments advanced by J. L. Ackrill and T. H. Irwin in favor of an inclusivist reading of the "formal" conditions; and second, the way in which Aristotle's discussion of these conditions echoes the argument Socrates gives in Plato's *Philebus* for preferring a "mixed" life *both* to a life filled exclusively with pleasure (without including any sort of intelligence) *and* to a life filled exclusively with intelligent activity (without including any sort of pleasure) [*Philebus* 20b–22d]. This echo serves, I think, to explain much of the popularity enjoyed by inclusivist interpretations of Aristotle's substantive conception. It may even in the end justify some such interpretation, though a more nuanced form than the one that I, following the lead of Ackrill and Irwin, gave in Chapter 2.

Ackrill's interpretation rests heavily on his reading of the lines that follow Aristotle's presentation of the second condition. Aristotle explains straightaway that he is talking about what is sufficient "not for an individual himself, living a solitary life, but also for parents and children and wife and generally friends and fellow citizens, since *ho anthrôpos* is by nature *politikon*" [*EN* 1197b8–11]. This suggests that Aristotle in fact takes the human good to include friendship and the forms of virtue suitable to our nature as political animals. And this suggestion seems to be confirmed when he acknowledges the need to place some limit on the extent to which one's significant others must be provided for if one is to count as eudaimôn and then summarizes the "self-sufficiency" condition by saying (a) that he means by '*autarkes*' "what on its own makes a life choiceworthy and lacking in nothing" [*ho monoumenon haireton poiei ton bion kai mêdenos endea*]; and (b) that people believe *eudaimonia* to be such. Aristotle then adds the following lines (as Irwin's translation has them):

> Moreover, we think eudaimonia is most choiceworthy of all goods, [since] it is not counted as one good among many. [If it were] counted as one among many, then, clearly, we think it would be more choiceworthy if the smallest of goods were added; for the good that is added becomes an extra quantity of goods, and the larger of two goods is always more choiceworthy. Eudaimonia, then, is apparently something complete [*teleion*] and self-sufficient, since it is the end of the things achievable in action. [*EN* 1097b16–21]

The final sentence suggests that Aristotle aims here not so much to add a third condition as to elucidate the second. But however exactly we individuate the conditions, Irwin and Ackrill take the upshot to be that eudaimonia is a "comprehensive" end, one that (as Irwin puts it) includes "a sufficient number of tokens" of any type of good whose addition to a life makes that life better than it would be without tokens of the relevant type. *That*, according to Ackrill and Irwin, is why Aristotle says that *eudaimonia* is not counted as one good among others.[14] Here is Ackrill's account.

> Eudaimonia is the most desirable sort of life, the life that contains *all intrinsically worthwhile activities*. . . . For, Aristotle says, we regard it as the most worth while of all things *not* being counted as one good thing among others—for *then* (if it *were* simply the most worth while of a *number* of candidates) the addition of any of the others would make it better, more worthwhile—and it would not have been lacking in nothing. He is saying, then, that *eudaimonia*, being absolutely

[14] T. H. Irwin, "Permanent Happiness: Aristotle and Solon," *Oxford Studies in Ancient Philosophy* 3 (1985): 89–124. For Ackrill, see next note.

> final and genuinely self-sufficient, is more desirable than anything else in that it *includes* everything desirable in itself. It is best, and better than everything else, not in the way that bacon is better than eggs and than tomatoes (and therefore the best *of the three* to choose), but in the way that bacon, eggs, and tomatoes is a better breakfast than either bacon or eggs or tomatoes—and is indeed the best breakfast without qualification. [Ackrill's italics][15]

It is worth pausing here to note the way in which talk of a "comprehensive" good, one that "includes *all* intrinsically worthwhile activities," lends itself to a kind of atomistic approach: we ask about various types of good, which ones are worth having "for themselves," and we keep adding any that are to the hopper. Is a life of successful political activity *plus* contemplative activity more desirable than a life of successful political activity alone? Check: add contemplative activity. Is a life of successful political and contemplative activity *plus* the regular enjoyment of some sport more desirable than a life exhausted by political and contemplative activity? Check: add sport. Is a life of political, contemplative, and athletic activity *plus* aesthetic enjoyment more desirable than a life exhausted by political, contemplative, and athletic activity? Check: add aesthetic activity. Is a life of successful political, contemplative, athletic, and aesthetic activity *plus* the company of good friends more desirable than a life exhausted by the former? Check: add good friends. And so on.

But this is insane. Even if, as Irwin suggests, agents are to consider only various relatively determinate *types* of good, with the idea of including a "sufficient number of tokens" of each of the types added, an agent who proceeds in this way is likely to end up with a dog's breakfast—or in the loony bin. It is crucial to consider how the various types of good, and more especially individual tokens of them, interact with one another in the particular circumstances in which the agent finds herself.

This is especially true of goods like contemplation and virtuous activity. Consider the following "romantic" analogy, which seems to resonate with my students.

> Suppose that you finally meet the Partner of Your Dreams (*really*). If only you can be with PD, all sorts of things, including certain friends "with benefits," will cease to matter to you in the ways they have mattered in the past, the sorts of things you have always taken—and would in the absence of PD continue to take—to make your life more desirable than it would be without them. None of them by itself would make your life complete in quite the way being with PD would, but you have gradually accumulated them, and reasonably so, by thinking of each as it comes that adding it to whatever else you have will make your life more desirable. But now PD comes along and says "Yes"!

[15] J. L. Ackrill, "Aristotle on *Eudaimonia*," *Proceedings of the British Academy* 10 (1974): 339–59; reprinted in A. Rorty (ed.), *Essays on Aristotle's Ethics* (Berkeley: University of California Press, 1980), 12–33. Ackrill rejects the "reverse" reading of 1097b16–20 proposed by Anthony Kenny in "Happiness," *Proceedings of the Aristotelian Society* 66 (1965–1966): 92–102. So too do Irwin and Kraut: I concur.

> Enter your Philosophy Professor, an inclusivist reader of Aristotle who says, "but you always regarded the addition of your relationship to *x* to your relationship to *y* as yielding a better good than either relationship by itself: surely a relationship with PD *plus* either (or both) is more desirable than a relationship with PD alone."

Perhaps the Professor is distinguished (DP). The Professor is alert to the problems of applying Aristotle's argument to tokens of any given type and so works at the level of determinate types: "but you always took polyamory as making your life more desirable, so you should surely insist that PD agree to this, lest your life with PD lack goods whose addition would surely improve it." This is bad advice: it would be reasonable to reject this argument on the grounds that attempts to add to your life with PD types of good that you might reasonably value in the abstract will only screw things up. BTW: it is important never to mistake a DP for a PD!

The lesson here is that the inclusivist can and should attend to the ways in which any ingredient that is added to a life interacts with its other ingredients. And there is evidence that Aristotle himself is sensitive to the ways in which various so-called goods interact with one another in individual lives. This is clear from *EN* X.10, where he warns against attempting to have too many friends of *any* of the three kinds: even if you add relationships only with good exemplars of the relevant kind, there comes a point when adding one does not yield "an extra quantity of goods." It may threaten other relationships. In the case of utility friends, too many of whom are "impediments to living finely" [*empodia pros to kalôs zên*], one may end up burned out [*EN/EE* 1170b26–27]. In the case of "character" friends, the nature of the relationship makes it impossible to have more than a few [*EN/EE* 1170b28–71a16].

Aristotle's commitment to holistic consideration is perhaps clearest from what he says about the ways in which pursuing various "goods of fortune"—things like wealth, honor, and political office—can compromise an agent's virtue.

> Since the unjust person is greedy, he will be concerned about goods, not all goods but whatever ones are subject to good and bad fortune, those which are without qualification [*haplôs*] always good, but for a particular person [*tini*] not always <good>. Human beings pray for these things and pursue them, but they ought not: they should instead pray that the things that are without qualification goods also be good for them, but choose the things that are <in fact> good for them. [*EN/EE* 1129b1–6]

I take this as evidence that Aristotle is committed to a thesis for which Plato's Socrates argues both in the *Meno* and in the *Euthydemus*: namely, that virtue (aka wisdom) is the only unconditional good, the value of all other so-called goods being conditional on the virtue (or wisdom) of the one who possesses them.

I discuss this "conditionality thesis" in Chapter 4 below. It is relevant here because it points to the possibility of a non-atomistic form of inclusivism that allows various so-called goods to increase the degree of eudaimonia enjoyed by an agent in ways that go beyond simply increasing the amount of virtuous activity in which she engages, but does not open the door to weighing the value afforded by these goods against the value of virtue in a way that might seem to justify trading her virtue for enough such would-be goods. For any such trade would deprive the condition for their goodness of its satisfaction.

I said above that I thought Aristotle saw a way to avoid saying that a genuinely virtuous agent will contemplate the sort of trade-offs objections to which drove the Stoics to identify eudaimonia exclusively with virtue. The Stoics were concerned that allowing for the goodness of anything other than virtue opens the door to the possibility of situations in which it would be reasonable to sacrifice one's virtue for a *large enough* quantity of such goods. But the conditionality thesis allows other would-be goods, *when virtuously and wisely used*, to add to the degree of eudaimonia enjoyed by an agent and it allows this *without* permitting such trade-offs. For without virtue (aka wisdom), these so-called goods are not in fact good and so (pace Polus and his ilk) do not increase the eudaimonia of their possessor. But given the conditionality thesis, Aristotle can allow that goods of fortune contribute to eudaimonia in ways that go beyond their contribution to virtuous activity: such goods may increase eudaimonia by facilitating contemplation and other activities the agent values "for themselves."

So, for example, Aristotle can allow that a virtuous agent whose situation permits her to enjoy a certain amount of fine wining and dining with friends is more eudaimôn than a virtuous agent whose situation does not; and that a virtuous agent who sees her grown children flourishing on their own is more eudaimôn than one who sees her grown children suffering or making messes of their lives. But if the cost of wining and dining with friends—or worse yet of living to see her grown children flourish—is to commit or be complicit in the commission of injustice, then these things, though they may be good *haplôs*, will not be good *for her*. So *she* will not regard them as making *any* contribution to her eudaimonia in cases where securing them requires her to commit or be complicit in injustice.[16]

I conclude that a holistic form of inclusivism is the only form that can be plausibly ascribed to Aristotle should we decide in the end to read him in inclusivist terms. Let me turn, then, to what pushed me in Chapter 2 toward an inclusivist reading of the *substance* of Aristotle's conception—namely, the way in which Aristotle's "formal" conditions echo those used in the *Philebus* argument in favor of a "mixed life." For

---

[16] I take Aristotle's commitment to the conditionality thesis to lend plausibility to J. McDowell's claim that Aristotle takes "silencing" to distinguish the psychic economy of a genuinely virtuous agent from that of a merely continent one. But the role played by the conditionality thesis in my account renders my conception of "silencing" somewhat different from McDowell's: in situations where wealth or power or some other thing that is generally good is not in fact good, the virtuous agent does not (on my account) even see it as good, so she fails (unlike the merely continent agent) to have any desire for it. I touch on this issue briefly in Chapter 5 below and discuss it at length in "See the Right Thing: 'Paternal' Reason, Love, and Phronêsis," in Boyle and Mylonaki (eds.), *Reason in Nature: New Essays on Themes from John McDowell* (Cambridge, MA: Harvard University Press 2022), 243–384.

this argument—thanks to its relevance to *EE* VI.12—has come to play an increasingly prominent role in my reading of Aristotle.

4. THE *PHILEBUS* "BACKSTORY" AND A "NEUTRAL" READING OF ARISTOTLE'S FORMAL CONDITIONS

The *Philebus* is primarily a debate about what constitutes the highest good for a human being. Protarchus argues, on behalf of the indolent hedonist Philebus, that *the good* for a human being consists exclusively in enjoyment [*to chairein*] and pleasure [*hedonê*] and whatever is in accord with this *genos*, while Socrates argues that *the good* for a human being consists exclusively in thinking [*to phronein*], understanding and remembering [*to noein kai memnêsthai*], and whatever is akin to these [*Philebus* 11b]. Socrates proceeds by getting Protarchus to agree at the outset to what are essentially Aristotle's formal conditions: the good they seek must be both *teleon* (i.e., "final" or "complete") and *hikanon* (i.e., "adequate" or "sufficient"), and it must be without need of anything further in addition to itself [*mêden mêdonos eti prosdeisthai*] [*Philebus* 20d–e]. Socrates then gets Protarchus to concede that a life consisting exclusively of pleasure, without any form of intelligence, would not satisfy these conditions: without memory of past pleasures or awareness that one is experiencing pleasure when one is in fact doing so, and without the ability to calculate how to achieve future pleasures, one would not be living the life of a human being but rather the life of a jellyfish or some testacean [*Philebus* 21c]. We see hints here of the master premise of Aristotle's function argument: the human good must involve a distinctively human form of activity. So the life of pleasure, if it is to be adequate *for a human being*, must include some form or forms of intelligence [*nous*].

Protarchus then turns the tables on Socrates and argues that a life of pure intelligence, without any pleasure, *also* fails to satisfy the formal conditions: adding pleasure surely makes such a life more desirable. Plato's idea seems to be that each candidate is improved by the addition of at least some measure of the other, so that neither by itself makes a life, as Aristotle would put it, "choiceworthy and lacking in nothing." But note what happens at this point in the *Philebus*. In conceding that a life of intelligence without any pleasure is not the best and most choiceworthy life *for a human being*, Socrates insists that there is an important difference, when it comes to the life of *nous*, between the human and the divine form of it.

Socrates denies that the divine form can be improved by the addition of any pleasure [*Philebus* 22c–d]. For Socrates and Protarchus are at this point assuming a "restorative" account of pleasure, one according to which pleasure consists (roughly speaking) in the filling of some lack in a way that restores a creature to its natural (and hence proper) condition—as, for example, when a hungry animal eats (without overeating) or a thirsty one drinks (without overhydrating) [*Philebus* 31c–d]. They assume that a god, being perfect, will not suffer any of the forms of deficiency with whose correction pleasure is being identified. So there is no form of pleasure whose addition to the divine life of *nous* can improve that life: the divine good is, according to the *Philebus* Socrates, *beyond pleasure*.

But Aristotle departs from the *Philebus* on this point when he says in *Metaphysics* (*Met.*) XII.7 that divine contemplation is *itself* a pleasure [*Met.* 1073a14–16].[17] In building pleasure into divine contemplation, he retains Socrates' claim that a divine life, filled with contemplative activity, cannot be improved by the addition of any further good. But Aristotle need not conclude from this that a human life that is filled with contemplative activity (and any pleasure built into that) cannot improved by the addition of any further good. For he says explicitly that human nature is complex in a way divine nature is not.

> There is no one thing that is always pleasant because our nature is not simple . . . If <our> nature were simple, the same activity [*hê autê praxis*] would <always> be most pleasant. This is why God always enjoys one simple pleasure. . . . [*EN* VII.14/ *EE* VI.14, 1154b20–26]

This seems to support the conditional reading of *EN* X.7: because the human essence is not exhausted by theoretical intellect, a human life filled with contemplative activity *can* be improved by the addition of goods that are associated with our nature as "political animals." That would explain why Aristotle warns in *EE* VII.12 against comparing the maximally self-sufficient (and so most blessed) human being to a god: because human beings take pleasure in engaging together with loved ones in the activities in which they take their eudaimonia to consist, their lives *can* be improved by the company of loved ones in a way that divine lives *cannot*. Pleasure plays a role here in explaining why the contemplator prefers contemplating with a friend or two to contemplating alone, but this need not flout the requirement that she value her friends and their good "for themselves." For (as I argue in Chapter 7) the virtuous agent takes pleasure in seeing her *friend* enjoying the relevant activity, and this pleasure is not the end for the sake of which she pursues the friendship but a sign of the fact that she values her friend's activities "for themselves." One might even say that the disposition to take pleasure in seeing her friend enjoy the relevant activities is part of what it *is* to value her friends and their activities "for themselves." And to extent that such pleasures make her life more desirable than it would otherwise be, it seems reasonable to treat such pleasures as contributing directly to the degree of eudaimonia she enjoys.[18]

A similar argument might be run for activity in accordance with ethical virtue: because we are by nature "political animals," our lives can be improved, in a way divine lives cannot, by participation "for itself" in natural communities [*koinôniai*],

---

[17] For this passage, see [ST1][b] in Chapter 7 below. Aristotle builds here on the suggestion, made late in the *Philebus*, that there are some pleasures (such as those taken in beautiful sounds and colors) that do not consist in the correction of some deficiency and are thus "pure."

[18] For more on this idea, which I take from Bishop Butler (Preface to Fifteen Sermons, section 383), see the end of "Friends and Future Selves" [I.1].

from the household on up. See, for example, *Politics* (*Pol.*) III.6, where Aristotle says that human beings, even when they do not require one another's assistance, desire to live together [*oregontai tou suzên*, *Pol.* 1278b20–21]. The idea seems to be that human beings take pleasure in one another's company, simply as such. Here again, pleasure is not the end for the sake of which they form communities but rather a sign of the fact that they value participation in such communities "for itself." And to the extent that such pleasure makes a person's life more desirable than it would otherwise be, it seems reasonable to treat such pleasure as making a direct contribution to the degree of *eudaimonia* she enjoys.

If we put these arguments together, we might conclude (as I do in Chapter 2) that Aristotle adopts a bipartite conception of the highest good for a human being, a conception in which ethical activity (including the activities involved in friendship) figures as a component alongside of contemplative activity. And we might, in ascribing this conception to Aristotle, appeal to the *Philebus*' use of the formal conditions to support a "mixed" account of the substance of the highest good for a human being.

Here, however, caution is required. First, it is not clear that the *Philebus* argument is meant to address substantive questions about the roles played in *eudaimonia* by (for example) friendship and virtuous activity. I cannot now engage in a reading of that difficult dialogue and want to focus instead on what conclusions Aristotle might have drawn from it.[19] For there is clearly a close connection between his "formal" conditions and the *Philebus*' assumption that the human good is something *teleon* and *hikanon*. But it is a serious question whether we should take the fact that the *Philebus* explicitly deploys this assumption in favor of some form of "mixed life" as a sign that Aristotle took the formal conditions to support a bipartite account of the *substance* of our highest good. For even if the *Philebus* did move in that direction, the point Aristotle takes from that dialogue may be (as Kraut suggests) merely formal.

Kraut supports his suggestion by appeal to a passage in *EN* X.2 where Aristotle alludes to the *Philebus* argument. Aristotle is discussing various arguments offered by Eudoxus [c. 408–355 BCE] to show that pleasure is *the good*. His reply to Eudoxus turns, as Kraut notes, on the distinction between *a* good (as in one good among others) and *the* good (as in the *highest* good, in this case for a human being). With respect to Eudoxus' claim that whenever pleasure is added to any individual good, such as just or temperate action, that good is made more choiceworthy than it is on its own, Aristotle says:

> This argument, at any rate, seems to show that it [pleasure] is among the goods, and no more *a good* than any other; for every good is more choiceworthy with another good than it is by itself. In fact, it is with precisely this sort of argument that Plato makes a destructive case that pleasure is not *the good*; for the pleasant life is made more choiceworthy with wisdom than without, and if the mixture is

[19] For some discussion of this dialogue, see my contribution to the Festschrift for Gisela Striker, "Fools' Pleasures in Plato's *Philebus*," in M. Lee (ed.), *Strategies of Argument: Essays in Ancient Ethics, Epistemology, and Logic* (Oxford: Oxford University Press, 2014), 21–59.

better, pleasure is not *the good*; for *the good* does not come to be more choiceworthy by the addition of anything to it. It is obvious, then, that nothing else either would be *the good* if it comes to be more choiceworthy with [the addition of] any of the things that are good in themselves. [*EN* 1172b26–33][20]

The language used here is close to that used in *EN* I.7's presentation of the self-sufficiency condition. But this passage is neutral on the question whether the human good is to be identified with a single intrinsically good activity, or rather with some (perhaps structured) compound of such activities: the point is simply that *whatever* the human good turns out to be, it cannot be improved by the addition of anything else, not even something that is good in itself [*kath' hauto*].

In other words, the X.2 passage leaves open the possibility that there is a single good such that nothing, not even something good in itself, can be added to any amount of it to yield something even more choiceworthy than that amount of it taken by itself. And this was not for Aristotle simply a logical possibility. There were philosophers in the Socratic tradition who took virtue to be a good such that *nothing* could be added to it to yield an even more desirable compound. And it is clear from *EN* I.5 and VII.13 that Aristotle was familiar with an early version of this view: he ridicules the idea that a virtuous agent who is being tortured on the rack is no less eudaimôn than one who is not. So we cannot without begging the question take I.7's presentation of the self-sufficiency condition to provide direct support for an inclusivist account of the *substance* of Aristotle's conception of eudaimonia. It is possible that Aristotle regards contemplation in the way that Cynics and Stoics regarded ethical virtue—namely, as a good such that nothing could be added to any amount of it to yield something more desirable than that amount of it taken by itself. For Aristotle clearly takes contemplation to have this sort of value in the life of a *god*. So he might well take contemplation to play this role in the life of a *philosopher*, especially if (as he suggests in *Met.* XII.7) pleasure is built *into* contemplative activity.

There seems in fact to have been a tradition, predating Socrates and the Cynics, of taking contemplation to play exactly this role in the life of a philosopher. And there is reason to think that Aristotle was aware of it. Cicero relates a story told by Heraclides of Pontus, a student of Plato who was about as exact a contemporary of Aristotle as one could be. (Both died around 322 BCE.) Heraclides claimed that Pythagoras, when asked what his craft was, replied that he did not know any craft but was a "philosopher." Pythagoras then explained to his puzzled interlocutor that

> . . . the life of many seemed to him to resemble the festival which was celebrated with most magnificent games before a concourse collected from the whole of Greece; for at this festival some men whose bodies had been trained

[20] The translation (with my italics) is from p. 280 of R. Kraut, *Aristotle on the Human Good* (Princeton, NJ: Princeton University Press, 1989).

> sought to win the glorious distinction of a crown, others were attracted by the prospect of making gain by buying or selling, while there was on the other hand a certain *genus*, and that quite the best of the free-born men, who looked neither for applause nor gain, came for the sake of the spectacle and closely watched what was done and how it was done. So also we . . . entered upon this life, and some were slaves of ambition, some of money; there were a special few who, *counting all else as nothing*, closely scanned the nature of things; these men gave themselves the name of lovers of wisdom (for that is the meaning of the word 'philosopher'). And just as at the games the men of the truest breeding looked on without any self-seeking, so in life the contemplation and discovery of nature surpassed all other pursuits. [*Tusculan Disputations* V.iii.8–9; Loeb translation by J. F. King (slightly modified) Cambridge MA, 1927]

The three lives mentioned in *EN* I.5 are discernible here. The association between wealth and pleasure, entrenched in Plato's *Republic*, ties the first group to those who identify eudaimonia with pleasure. Those who compete correspond to those who identify eudaimonia with honor and/or that on account of which one is deserving of honor. But what interests me is that Cicero, in relating what Heraclides is supposed to have said, speaks of "the philosopher" as counting everything but the study of nature "for nothing" [*pro nihilo*]. This suggests that by the time Aristotle came along, there was an established tradition of taking "the philosopher" to embrace what is, logically speaking, a contemplative version of the Cynic, and eventually Stoic, identification of eudaimonia with virtue.

On this view, a philosopher may prefer to have rather than lack at least some so-called goods apart from contemplation. But she will not regard these things as making any direct contribution to her eudaimonia: contemplation is the only thing she counts towards that. Other things have at best the status of "preferred indifferents": although she prefers to have these things rather than lack them, she views them as standing in an "indifferent" relationship to the degree of eudaimonia she enjoys. She does not regard a life lacking such "goods" as deficient. Nor does she take the presence of such "goods" to make her life any more eudaimôn than it would be without them.[21]

The crucial question is how, on such a view, Aristotle would explain his claim that the contemplator qua human chooses to act in accordance with virtue. Chapter 2 considered only two options. *Either* (as Cooper suggests) it is simply in accordance with virtue and not as a genuinely virtuous agent that she acts, taking such action as the best way, given that she lives among others, to maximize her contemplative activity. *Or* (as I argued) she values virtuous action in the way a genuinely virtuous agent does

[21] For excellent discussion see Jacob Klein, "Making Sense of Stoic Indifferents," *Oxford Studies in Ancient Philosophy* 49 (2015): 227–81.

(namely, "for itself") and so takes virtuous action to be a component of her eudaimonia: she regards her life as, ceteris paribus, more eudaimôn with such activity than without it. But taking Aristotle to adopt a contemplative version of the Stoic identification of eudaimonia with virtue suggests a third possibility—one that reveals why Chapter 2's move from rejecting the instrumental option to accepting the component conclusion was too quick.

Aristotle may think that the contemplator values virtuous activity in something like the way a Stoic sage values so-called goods like health and wealth. She prefers engaging in such activity to not engaging in it even though she does not take engaging it to contribute directly to her eudaimonia, which she measures simply in terms of the quality and quantity of her contemplative activity. Aristotle might even think it an advantage that this allows him to explain the contemplator's attachment to virtuous activity *without* taking that activity to contribute directly to the degree of eudaimonia she enjoys: he might think it strengthens the case for saying that she values such activity "for itself."

It is worth noting how this fits Chapter 3's account of valuing virtuous action "for itself." The idea there is that choosing such action "for itself" consists largely in choosing it insofar as it is the *kind* of action it is, where what determines that is at least partly the fact that it aims at bringing about a certain kind of result. For example, what makes an action generous is at least partly the way it aims to provide benefits to others; what makes an action just is at least partly the way it aims to secure an equitable distribution of the benefits and burdens of living together with others; and so on. So someone who chooses to perform such actions "for themselves" chooses to do so at least partly because she values the ends at which they aim: the welfare of others, equitable distributions of benefits and burdens, and so on. But it is an open question whether she therefore takes activity aimed at promoting these ends to contribute directly to the degree of eudaimonia she enjoys. Inclusivist readings of the formal conditions suggest that she does. But if we adopt a neutral reading of these conditions, then the question remains open, at least in the case of those who choose the contemplative life. For if Aristotle ascribes to such agents a contemplative analogue of the Stoic identification of eudaimonia with virtue, he may think that they choose to perform virtuous actions "for themselves" while measuring their own eudaimonia simply in terms of the quality and quantity of their own contemplative activity.

Reading Aristotle this way would require us to address various questions, especially about how the contemplative life fits the eudaimonist axiom. One possibility, broached in my work on Aristotle's conception of friendship, is to drop the assumption that this axiom refers to the agent's own eudaimonia (even broadly construed). We might take actions aimed primarily at the eudaimonia of others to count. But I cannot now explore that option. The point here is that the possibility of the neutral reading reveals how little can be determined on the basis of the formal conditions alone. Much depends on the substance of Aristotle's views about other matters, especially about the nature and value of activity in accordance with virtue and the roles such activity plays in the lives of individual agents. If Aristotle takes such activity to play different sorts of roles in the lives of different sorts of agents, then there may be no simple answer to the question whether he thinks an agent who chooses to perform virtuous actions "for themselves" treats performing such actions as a component of her own eudaimonia. He may think that some do and some do not: those who go choose to live "active" lives may do so while those who choose to live contemplative lives may not.

5. DIVIDING THE HUMAN KIND: THE "POLITICAL" AND THE "SOLITARY"

I assumed in writing Chapter 2 that Aristotle's conception of human nature is for the most part univocal. There are of course defective members who fail in various ways and to various degrees to actualize that nature, but such failures are "accidental." They are due to the ways in which material-efficient causal mechanisms, both internal and external, can interfere with the proper development of a creature's form; they are products of chance [*tuchê*] as distinct from nature. But there is a single uniquely correct account of that human form or essence, whose components determine the components of eudaimonia.

I now see reason to question this. I am in fact tempted to take a striking passage from *Politics* I.2 together with passages from Aristotle's biological works as evidence that he "saw" differences due to nature, and not mere chance, between those suited for the contemplative life he recommends in *EN* X.7 and those suited for the political life recommended in X.8—differences on a par with the ones he "saw" between those suited by nature to be slaves and those suited by nature to be masters. Let me explain.

The point of the *Politics* passage is to establish that the polis is among the things that exist by nature. Because Aristotle views self-sufficiency for its citizens as part of the end that defines a polis, he views the polis as the form of community [*koinônia*] toward which prior, allegedly natural forms of community progress (e.g., the pairing of male and female for reproduction and the pairing of master and slave for the preservation of each): though a polis *comes to be* for the sake of mere living [*to zên*], it *exists* for the sake of living well [*to eu zên*, which Aristotle seems to use interchangeably with 'eudaimonia']. Aristotle argues from these and a few more or less axiomatic claims, such as "the final cause and the telos <of any coming to be> is best," that

> it is clear that the polis is among the things that exist by nature [*phusei*] and that *anthrôpos* is by nature [*phusei*] a political animal, and that one who is without a polis on account of nature and not mere chance [*ho apolis dia phusin kai ou dia tuchên*] is either base or better than human [*êtoi phaulos ê kreittôn ê anthrôpos*]. [*Pol.* 1253a1–4]

Aristotle characterizes the former (in Homer's words) as "tribeless, lawless, and without a hearth" and (in his own words) as "by nature [*phusei*] such and thirsting for war" [*Pol.* 1253a4–6]. When he returns to the point a few lines on, he says that "one who is *not able* to participate <in the life of the polis> or on account of self-sufficiency has *no need* <to do so> is either a beast or a god": such beings, unlike citizens but like allegedly natural slaves, are not part of any polis [*Pol.* 1253a27–29].

What strikes me here is Aristotle's suggestion, fast on the heels of his claim that *anthrôpos* is by nature [*phusei*] a political animal, that some human beings might be "on account of nature" [*dia phusin*] without a polis. How are we to understand *dia phusin*?

Some light may be shed on this by two passages in *EN* VII [= *EE* VI]. Aristotle begins, in VII.1, by identifying three forms of character to be avoided, each of which has a more desirable counterpart: vice, whose counterpart is virtue; lack of (self-) control [*akrasia*], whose counterpart is (self-) control [*enkrateia*];[22] and brutishness [*thêriotês*], whose counterpart is described as "beyond our [viz., human] virtue, something heroic and divine" [*ten huper hêmas aretên, hêrôikên tina kai theian*] [*EN* 1145a15–20]. Strictly speaking, this last condition is no more a kind of ethical virtue than its counterpart is a kind of vice. For neither virtue nor vice belongs to beast or god. Both conditions are rare and the latter, Aristotle says, "comes about especially among barbarians, and in some cases [presumably even among Greeks] on account of diseases and deformities" [*dia nosous kai pêrôseis*] [*EN* 1145a29–33].

Aristotle returns to brutishness in VII.5, where he distinguishes among the sources of pleasure (A) things that are pleasant by nature [*phusei*] and (B) things that are *not* pleasant *phusei* but come to be pleasant on account of (i) defects [*dia pêrôseis*], (ii) habits [*di' ethê*], or (iii) wicked natures [*dia mochthêras phuseis*]. What interests me here is the distinction Aristotle draws *within* (A), between (i) things that are pleasant simply or without qualification [*haplôs*] and (ii) things that are pleasant for certain kinds of animals and human beings [*ta de kata genê kai zô(i)ôn kai anthrôpôn*]. I take (A)(i) to refer to things that are categorically pleasant in the sense that they are pleasant to each (non-defective) member of some animal kind simply insofar as it is a member of that kind, for example, the pleasure of engaging in reproductive sex. In the case of human beings, Aristotle clearly includes (a) the pleasures of sight and the other senses, which are exercised both for themselves and for the sake of learning and understanding (see *Met.* I.1); (b) the sort of pleasure friends take in each other's company (discussed in Chapters 6 and 7 below); and (c) the pleasure taken in virtuous action, which is (according to *EN* I.8) *phusei* pleasant. This last claim, which follows the Nicomachean presentation of the function argument, strongly suggests that Aristotle in fact takes eudaimonia to consist at least partly in exercising our distinctively human capacity for virtuous action, a capacity shared by all non-defective members of our species.

But Aristotle seeks to distinguish such categorically pleasant things from (A)(ii), things that are pleasant by nature but *only* to the members of what I shall call different "sub-kinds." And it seems clear from what follows that Aristotle views men who enjoy sex with other men as falling into (at least) two groups: those to whom the relevant acts are by nature [*tois men phusei*] pleasant and those to whom the relevant acts

[22] For more on *akrasia* and the possibility of taking '*dia phusin*' to refer to the operation of material as distinct from formal causes, see "Akratic ignorance explained from the point of view proper to its nature: "*Nicomachean Ethics* VII.3 on Akratic Ignorance" (co-authored with Martin Pickavé), (III.7).

happen as a result of habit [*tois de ex ethous sumbainousin*] to be pleasant. Aristotle cites as examples of the latter, men who were abused as children [*tois hubrizomenois*, perhaps referring to acts of rape]. And his idea (however problematic) seems to be that what these men find pleasant is *dia tuchên* and not (as in the case of the former) *dia phusin*.

In sum, it seems to me plausible to suppose that Aristotle views this distinction, between what might be called "natural" and "chance" homosexuals, as parallel to the one he sees between individuals who are by nature suited to slavery and individuals who are not so suited but come to be slaves on account of some misfortune such as being captured in battle. He may well think that material-efficient causal mechanisms interfere in each sort of case with the "normal" processes of human development in something like the way in which material-efficient causal mechanisms interfere with a male animal's production of another little "himself," sex included. I discuss these issues in III.6: "Hylomorphic Virtue: Cosmology, Embryology, and Moral Development in Aristotle." What interests me here is Aristotle's apparent view that human nature admits of various sub-kinds that do not count as proper species of a genus: male and female (discussed, along with differences in pigment in *Met.* X.9), master and slave (discussed in *Politics* I), and heterosexual and natural (as distinct from chance) homosexuals. For this makes it plausible to read him as thinking that just as the "natural" constitution of some human beings is suited for heavy labor [*Pol.* I.5, 1254b25–30], so too the "natural" constitution of some human beings is suited for contemplation. The latter are self-sufficient in ways such that they find a purely contemplative life satisfying in a way your average political animal does not. As long as they are able to contemplate, they do not feel the *need* for anything else (though they do typically take pleasure in the company of their loved ones).

If Aristotle is committed to the existence of a contemplative sub-kind of the human species, then it is plausible to read the superlatives in the transition from *EN* X.7–8 not as contrasting the eudaimonia of a god with that of any and every non-defective free adult male, but rather as contrasting the eudaimonia of those human beings who are *dia phusin* suited for the contemplative life with the eudaimonia of your average political animal. And we might support this reading by suggesting that Aristotle is in *Politics* I.2 tapping into the Pythagorean tradition reported by Cicero and endorsing the idea that there is a special kind of human being whose members count nothing but contemplation as contributing to their own eudaimonia. They may, as X.7 suggests, perform actions in accordance with virtue, and such actions implicitly acknowledge the constitutive role played by activities other than contemplation in the eudaimonia of *others*. The question here is not just why they perform such actions but also whether or not their reasons for doing so commit them to treating their performance of such actions as a component of their *own* eudaimonia.

One might of course object on various grounds to the idea that there are different kinds of human beings for whom different ways of life are appropriate, some "masterly," some "slavish," and so on. One might treat such talk, common in Plato's *Republic*, as metaphorical and as serving simply to naturalize socially constructed differences, at best a "noble lie." But this is compatible with Aristotle's having taken such distinctions to be grounded in phenomena that allow them to do the sort of normative work he routinely assigns to them. And there is in fact some justification for reading him as assimilating his distinction between "the philosopher" and your average political animal to distinctions found in his biological works. For *Politics* I.2 is connected, via *Politics* I.8, to passages in the biological works where Aristotle suggests that the human kind resembles a few others in admitting sub-kinds, some whose members are solitary [*monadika*] and others whose members are gregarious [*agelaia*]. See *History of Animals* (*HA*) I.2, where Aristotle says that *anthrôpos* partakes of both [*epamphorizei*]; and *HA* IX.40, which is devoted to insects that produce honeycombs and identifies both gregarious and solitary sub-kinds. Bumblebees are solitary, drones, and queens gregarious.

My tentative suggestion, first presented at a conference honoring the late Allen Gottfhelf, is that Aristotle is thinking in the *Politics* passages of metic philosophers like Anaxagoras and himself, resident aliens in the poleis where they lived and worked. Recall Anaxagoras' response to the question "why one should choose to be born rather than not": "for the sake of contemplating the heaven and the order of the entire *kosmos*" [*EE* 1216a12–14]. He, like Pythagoras, may have "counted all else for nothing."

6. THE PRIORITY OF ETHICAL VIRTUE: THE CONDITIONALITY THESIS AND CONTEMPLATIVE ACTIVITY

In sum, it is not implausible to think that in writing *EN* X Aristotle understood the formal conditions in a way such that an exclusivist account of the substance of eudaimonia might satisfy them, at least for one sub-kind of human being. But I find it easier to think that he understood the substance of the contemplative life in exclusivist terms than that he understood the substance of a life devoted to ethical virtue in that way. For it seems clear from X.8 that he thinks *both* that virtuous activity is the dominant component of the distinctively human form of eudaimonia featured there *and* that contemplative activity renders those living "active" lives more eudaimôn than they would otherwise be, the more contemplative activity the better [*EN* 1178b25–32]. But it does not follow from this that he thinks a contemplative life is improved by the addition of ethically virtuous activity. He may see an asymmetry here: he may think that adding contemplative activity to a political life serves (ceteris paribus) to improve that life in a way in which adding political activity to a contemplative life does not serve (even ceteris paribus) to improve it. In other words, Aristotle may well endorse an inclusivist conception of the substance of "political" eudaimonia while endorsing an exclusivist conception of the substance of its contemplative counterpart. This possibility is afforded by a neutral reading of his formal conditions. But what could justify any such asymmetry? Isn't addition symmetrical?

It matters here, in ways touched on at the end of Chapter 2, how Aristotle conceives of ethical virtue and the demands it places on any given individual. Different forms of action are of course reasonably required of differently positioned subjects, as (for example) different forms of action are required of those who chose to parent and those who do not. Similarly, those with medical or other specialized training may find themselves in situations where more is required of them than of others who are present. So we cannot simply assume that what virtue requires of those living a contemplative life is the same across the board as what virtue requires of those living an active life.[23]

A responsible choice to live a contemplative life may consist largely in a kind of abstinence, in declining to enter the sorts of relationships that render the agent more rather than less obliged to others. Aristotle may in fact have this sort of abstinence in mind when he says in *EN* I.7's discussion of self-sufficiency that is not speaking there about what suffices for an "individual alone, one who is living a solitary life" [*autô(i) monô(i) tô(i) zônti bion monôtên*], but rather <about what suffices for one who lives> with parents, children, wives, and generally friends and fellow citizens, since *anthrôpos* is by nature political" [*EN* 1097b8–11]. But even so, it seems clear from X.7's claim that the contemplator who lives among others will choose to act in accordance with virtue that Aristotle does not take the choice to live a contemplative life to let an agent entirely off the human hook. The question is how X.7's contemplator is supposed to view her own virtuous activity: can she value it "in itself" in a way that does not commit her to treating it as a component of her eudaimonia?

Let us suppose for the moment that Aristotle regards many forms of virtuous action as fundamentally remedial and demanded by the less than ideal circumstances in which human beings tend to find themselves, often as a result of their own or others' misguided behavior. He is clearly worried about the dangers of imperialism and probably associates them with individual as well as collective failures to privilege contemplative activities over other more resource-intensive ones. *Politics* VII repays careful attention here, especially 1332a7–27, but I cannot now go into that. The important point is that the more remedial Aristotle takes virtuous actions to be, the more plausible it is for him to view the contemplator as performing whatever virtuous actions are required by her circumstances and performing them *simply as such*, without taking her performance of them to contribute directly to the degree of eudaimonia she enjoys.

He might lean here on what he says in *EN* X.7, where he treats the activities characteristic of a political life, by contrast with those of a contemplative life, as unleisurely [*ascholoi*]. The former, unlike the latter, always seek something beyond the action itself: "we are occupied in order that we may be at leisure, and we fight in order that we may have peace" [*EN* 1177b4–6]. The contemplator prefers of course to have peace and leisure without having to engage in the relevant activities. Who, among the sane, does not? The contemplator, like others, engages in such activities when they are required, but not simply because she thinks that necessary in order to secure the conditions

[23] If Aristotle rejects this assumption, then he may anticipate Stoic views (discussed in Book I of Cicero's *De Officiis*) about the various personae of an individual human being. For more on this issue, see Michael Frede, "A Notion of a Person in Epictetus," in T. Scaltsas and A. Mason (eds.), *The Philosophy of Epictetus* (Oxford: Oxford University Press, 2007), 153–77.

required for her preferred form of eudaimonic activity. She could perhaps free-ride, but insofar as virtuous actions serve to secure the conditions required for the activities in which she and others take their eudaimonia to consist, she may value performing such actions "for themselves" in the sense explained in Chapter 3. The more there are others about whom she cares (on which more in a moment), the more plausible this is. But it does not follow that she takes performing such actions as a component of her eudaimonia; she may measure that simply in terms of the quality and quantity of her contemplative activity.

But how exactly is this supposed to work? Surely honoring the requirements of virtue will sometimes require her to sacrifice some degree of contemplative activity. If she identifies eudaimonia with such activity, what in *her* view could justify any such sacrifice?

We might rely here on an assumption that Aristotle surely makes about those living the sort of "active" life that he says is more eudaimôn the more contemplation it involves [*EN* 1178b25–32, cited above]. He cannot mean to allow that *their* lives are made more eudaimôn by increasing *their* contemplative activity *at the expense of their virtue*. But he need not allow that if he takes the conditionality thesis to apply no less to contemplation than to the standard goods of fortune: any contemplative activity achieved at the expense of virtue will fail to count as good and so fail to add to the degree of eudaimonia enjoyed by the agent. But if Aristotle can say this about the contemplative activity of those who choose to live *active* lives, what prevents him from saying the same about those who choose to live *contemplative* lives?

We might appeal here to *EE* VIII.3, which is plausibly read in the way I am suggesting we read EN X—namely, as combining a contemplative version of the Stoic identification of eudaimonia with virtue with a version of the conditionality thesis according to which actual episodes of contemplative activity depend for their value to an agent (i.e., for their goodness *tini*) on her virtue (aka *phronêsis*). After saying that "*anthrôpos* is by nature constituted from something that rules and something that is ruled" and that "each ought to live with reference to his ruling <principle> [*pros tên hautou̧ archên*]," Aristotle explains that we speak of ruling in two ways: just as health rules by being that for the sake of which medicine gives commands and so that for the sake of which medicine rules *epitaktikôs*, so too God (or the sort of contemplative activity characteristic of God) rules by being that for the sake of which *phronêsis* rules by giving commands. Contemplative activity is clearly "that for the sake of which" in the sense that it is the end to be achieved. But the crucial point here is that it is *phronêsis* and not what *EE* V/EN VI.12 calls "cleverness" [*deinotês*] that gives the commands: for (as argued in *EE* V/EN VI.12–13) *phronêsis* presupposes virtue in the "strict" or "authoritative" [*kuria*] sense. Aristotle continues,

> Then whatever choice and acquisition [*hairesis kai ktêsis*] of natural goods will produce above all the contemplation of the divine—whether of bodily [goods] or money or friends or the other goods—this is best, and this standard [*horos*] is most fine [*kallistos*]. And whatever <choice and acquisition> either on account of

> deficiency or on account of excess hinders serving and contemplating the divine, this is base [*phaulos*]. Thus it is with the soul, and this is the best standard for the soul—whenever it perceives as little as possible the non-rational [*alogou*] part of the soul, insofar as it is such [*hê(i) toiouton*]. [*EE* 1249b16–23]

Given what he says here, Aristotle might well think that however necessary an agent's circumstances render virtuous activity, no amount of it can make her better off than she would have been had circumstances permitted her instead to enjoy contemplative activity without any such impediment.

Here, however, we should keep in mind what Aristotle said only a few chapters earlier, in *EE* VII.12: namely, that comparing the most eudaimôn human being to a god threatens to lead us astray. Even the maximally self-sufficient human being, the one most capable of living alone, will want to share her life with a good friend or two: she will take a contemplative life that *includes* time spent with friends to be more desirable than a life exhausted by solitary contemplation. And, as I argue in Chapter 7, this is not because she takes the time spent with friends to increase the quality and/or quantity of her own contemplative activity: it is rather because of the pleasure she takes in the company of her friends simply as such. Once again, this pleasure is not the end for the sake of which she engages in friendship, nor even in my view a condition for the persistence of the relationship once it is entrenched: it is a sign of the value she attaches to the existence of her friend and her friend's activities "for themselves." She will suffer on her friend's account if circumstances require her to do so and would regard her failure to aid her friend when her friend is in need as detracting from the value of whatever she thereby "achieves": even if she views contemplative activity as the best possible activity in which she can engage, as the activity in which her eudaimonia consists, she may still view contemplating when her friend really needs help as *no good at all*. This may even be Aristotle's point when he says at *EE* 1245a29–30 that the friend wants to be "another Heracles": she may want the capacity to provide aid, heroic if necessary, to her friend.

Aristotle relies here on premises about psychological tendencies that are associated with human nature as such, the sort of premises that are (as I explain in Chapter 6) appropriate [*oikeion*] to the explananda. And given the parallel he sees between the motivation of a genuine friend and the motivation of a genuinely virtuous agent, Aristotle may well take the contemplator to view virtuous activity in much the same way. He may think that she will value doing "for itself" whatever virtue requires in the circumstances in which she finds herself and that she would view failure to do so as detracting from the value of whatever she might "achieve" by neglecting to act as virtue requires. In other words, she might take the value even of contemplative activity to be conditional on its being virtuously exercised.

Readers of the previously quoted passage from *EE* VIII.3 may find it difficult to accept this view. But it fits common ethical intuitions or what Aristotle would call 'endoxa': "fiat contemplatio ruat caelum" is at least as disturbing as "fiat justitia ruat caelum." And there is much to be said for treating opportunities for contemplative activity as goods of fortune: living the contemplative life is a privilege even for those temperamentally suited to it. The result is close to that of the "superstructure view" cited at the end of Chapter 2: the contemplator maximizes *permissible* contemplative activity. But she will have arranged her life in a way such that contemplative activity is more often permissible for her than it is for those in positions that demand more rather than less of the cooperative activity in which the good of essentially political animals at least partly consists.

In sum, even the end of the *EE*, which I have always read as more intellectualist than *EN* X, seems to me to assign lexical priority to ethical virtue. And I see no reason to read the end of the *EN* in a different way: both texts can be read as allowing the contemplator to measure eudaimonia simply in terms of the quality and quantity of *permissible* contemplation she achieves.

7. CODA

I want to conclude by making a point due to the late Myles Burnyeat. When I presented an early version of Chapter 2 as my practice job talk at Cornell in 1982, Myles asked the first question.

> Why suppose that you *should* try to render Aristotle's views in this matter *consistent*? Why not read him in *EN* X as throwing up his hands in despair at the difficulty of combining devotion to contemplative activity with the demands of ethical virtue?

I was momentarily stunned and then, faute de mieux, asked whether he was looking for some reason apart from the fact that that was how we read Aristotle around there. The question went, as Myles's questions always did, straight to the heart of the matter. And it is a question to which I, now older than Myles was when he posed it, am increasingly attuned. I wish I could once again take it up with him.

1

Aristotle's Function Argument

A DEFENSE

ARISTOTLE THINKS IT is uncontroversial that eudaimonia is the highest good, or ultimate end, of human action [*Nicomachean Ethics* (*EN*) 1095a14–20].[1] He thinks that we all desire eudaimonia only for its own sake and not for the sake of anything else, and also that eudaimonia is that for the sake of which we do all things [*EN* 1097a30–b6, 1102a1–4]. But Aristotle also thinks that this is uninformative; it does not tell us what the components of eudaimonia are and this is something about which there is much dispute [*EN* 1095a20–28].[2]

Some of Aristotle's contemporaries (and many of ours) are so impressed by the fact that different people enjoy different things that they follow Protagoras and adopt a subjectivist conception of eudaimonia according to which what *seems* best to each person *is* best for him. Others adopt an objectivist conception according to which what is good for a person is at least partly independent of his beliefs about what is good for him. On this objectivist view (but not on the subjectivist one) a person can mistakenly believe that something is good for him. So within the objectivist camp there are further disputes about which particular conception of eudaimonia is correct—some

[1] Although I believe that 'happiness' is an appropriate translation of 'eudaimonia' in the sense that each refers to the ultimate end of human action and allows for both subjective and objective conceptions of that end, I leave 'eudaimonia' untranslated because I believe that contemporary conceptions of happiness tend to be subjectivist in a way in which Aristotle's conception of eudaimonia is not. On this point, see Kraut 1979b, 167–97.

[2] On Aristotle's distinction between the components of a thing and the necessary conditions for its existence, see *Eudemian Ethics* (*EE*) 1214b6–28; *Politics* (*Pol.*) 1328a21–b4 and 1239a34–39; and Greenwood 1909, 46–47.

Living Together. Jennifer Whiting, Oxford University Press. © Oxford University Press 2023.
DOI: 10.1093/oso/9780199969678.003.0002

objectivists identifying eudaimonia with pleasure, others identifying it with honor, and yet others with contemplation or some combination of these goods.[3]

Aristotle claims that we can resolve these disputes and give a clearer account of what eudaimonia is, if we appeal to the human ἔργον (or function). He argues that the good and the (doing) well [τἀγαθὸν καὶ τὸ εὖ] of a flute player or a sculptor or of anything that has a function is determined by that thing's function—a function that Aristotle says is peculiar [ἴδιον] to it [*EN* 1097b23–35]. A good flute player has the virtue or ability that enables him to perform well; a good knife is sharp and able to cut well.[4] Similarly, Aristotle thinks that a good human being has the virtues and abilities that enable him to do well whatever it is the function of a human being to do. Furthermore, Aristotle thinks that it is *good for* a human being to have these virtues and to do these things; in fact, an individual's eudaimonia depends on it [*EN* 1098a12–18].[5]

Many commentators have thought this argument obviously mistaken and wrongheaded—primarily on the grounds that human beings do not have functions, and that even if they did, nothing about their good or eudaimonia would follow from their having these functions. But I shall argue that these objections are based on misinterpretations of Aristotle, and that properly interpreted he presents an interesting and defensible (though admittedly controversial) account of the relationship between eudaimonia and human nature. If Aristotle's account *is* mistaken, it is mistaken in

---

[3] I include among objectivist conceptions of eudaimonia hedonism and others that identify eudaimonia with some subjective psychological state such as pleasure insofar as they claim that some subjective psychological state is good for us independently of our belief that it is so—that is, insofar as these conceptions allow that someone may (like Antisthenes) mistakenly believe that pleasure is not in fact good for him, and so mistakenly avoid pleasure. The fact that different things please different people does not undermine the claim that pleasure, whatever its source, is objectively good. [For further discussion of this issue in connection with Plato, see Whiting 2014.]

[4] Aristotle does not explicitly mention the function of a knife or of any other artifact in the Nicomachean version of the argument, but he argues by induction from the functions of artifacts to the function of the soul in the Eudemian version [*EE* 1219a 1–5]. This may support the view that the Eudemian version is earlier and that by the time he wrote the *EN* Aristotle was aware of, and sought to avoid, some of the objections discussed in this essay. But we must suspend judgment on this issue for now. (For a brief comparison of the Nicomachean and Eudemian versions of the function argument, see Cooper 1975, 145–46n.) I introduce the knife example at this point because many commentators believe that Aristotle is explicitly committed to it, and, indeed, relying on it.

[5] [Aristotle's term here is *'anthrôpos,'* which unlike our 'man' is not gendered. And though he is probably thinking primarily of men in the gendered sense, I do not think he is thinking exclusively of them. (See, for example, *EN* 1162a25–7, where Aristotle speaks of the possibility of the *philia* between husband and wife being "*dia* virtue if the parties are decent, for there is a virtue characteristic of each, and <each> will delight in such <virtue as the other has>.") But I shall sometimes use 'man,' which appeared in the original version, instead of 'human being.' [Unfortunately, for reasons made clear in various of the essays in Volume I—First, *Second, and Other Selves: Essays on Friendship and Personal Identity*—'person' (with its Lockean connotations) will not do. See also "The Lockeanism of Aristotle" (III.8).] It is also worth noting that the journal in which this essay appeared refused to accept my standard practice of varying my use of pronouns for anonymous subjects, sometimes masculine, sometimes feminine, on the grounds that it might be confusing for nonnative speakers of English: apparently such readers of philosophy could not yet be expected, in 1988, to deal with the feminine pronoun. I have left the pronouns here as originally demanded—with one salient exception at the very end (where I have restored what I was not allowed to print in the original).]

more interesting and ultimately more informative ways than commentators have traditionally thought.

1

In general, Aristotle attempts to argue from claims about what it is to be a human being (or from the function of a human being)[6] to conclusions about what is *good for* a human being. Because he does so by appeal to the notion of a *good human being*, commentators have often viewed his argument as consisting of two moves—first, the move from (a) what it is to be a *human being* (or the function of a *human being*) to (b) what it is to be a *good* human being; and second, the move from (b) what it is to be a *good* human being to (c) what is *good for* a human being.[7]

The legitimacy of these moves is typically challenged by appeal to the following sort of examples. From an understanding of the function of a knife, it *may* follow that being sharp and cutting well make something a *good knife*; but it does not follow that being sharp and cutting well is *good for* a knife. Similarly, from an understanding of what it is to be a flute player, it *may* follow that some things (e.g., perfect pitch and a sense of rhythm) make someone a *good flute player*; but it does not follow that these things are *good for* someone who plays the flute. In a depressed economy, an unemployed virtuoso may wish that he had been tone deaf and had instead become a doctor.

So the fundamental challenge to Aristotle runs as follows. From an understanding of what it is to be a human being, it *may* follow that a good human being is one who has the virtues and abilities that enable him to perform characteristically human activities (though even this much is doubted). But it does not follow that having these virtues or engaging in these activities is *good for* any given individual. Just as what makes someone a good flute player may fail to benefit him, so also what makes someone a good human being may not be good for him. Suppose, for example, that human beings are characteristically social or political animals. It does not follow that joining clubs or running for office is good for me, if I prefer to spend all my time reading Aristotle's *Metaphysics*.

Aristotle, however, does not agree. He thinks that *if* human beings are characteristically social or political animals, then my exclusive preference for reading his *Metaphysics* reflects a mistaken judgment about what is good for me.[8] Our current

---

[6] For the view that what a thing is is determined by its function, see *Meteorologica* 390a10–13, where, incidentally, Aristotle uses the example of a saw.

[7] Although I argue eventually that Aristotle thinks there is really only one move here, i.e., the move directly from (a) to (c), commentators have often represented Aristotle as making two moves here, and so have attacked the general move from (a) to (c) in different ways—some by attacking the move from (a) to (b), others by attacking the move from (b) to (c). So, for the sake of argument, I begin by speaking as if there were two distinct moves here, even though I doubt that Aristotle distinguished them in this way. On Aristotle's view, there is no real distinction between (a) and (b), because what it is to be an F (or the function of an F) and what it is to be a *good* F (or the function of a *good* F) are in an important sense the same.

[8] These examples are not intended to suggest that Aristotle takes the function argument to yield results at this level of specificity; the activities of joining clubs and reading the *Metaphysics* should be regarded

problem is to see whether Aristotle can defend this objectivist view against the foregoing challenge. That challenge rests on three common, but I think mistaken, objections to his argument.

The first objection attacks the move from (a) (the function of a human being or what it is to be human) to (b) (what it is to be a *good* human being) on the grounds that this requires that human beings, like bodily parts or craftsmen and their tools, have instrumental functions or virtues that presuppose their being good or useful for some further ends or purposes. But, the objection continues, human beings as such do not have instrumental functions or purposes, so the move from (a) to (b) is unwarranted.[9]

The second and third objections grant that human beings may have functions, not in the instrumental sense, but rather in the sense that there is some capacity (or set of capacities) that is peculiar to them and distinguishes them from other animals. The second objection then attacks Aristotle's moves from (a) to (b) and from (b) to (c) on the grounds that peculiarity is no recommendation. From the fact that some capacity (e.g., the capacity for prostitution) is peculiar to the human kind, it does not follow that a good human being is one who exercises that capacity. Nor does it follow that it is *good for* human beings to exercise that capacity.[10]

The third objection allows the move from (a) to (b), and so allows that there may be a distinctively human set of capacities (including, e.g., the capacities for courage and justice) that determine what makes someone a good human being. It then objects to the move from (b) to (c) on the grounds that *even if* a good human being is one who exercises these capacities, it does not follow that it is *good for* any individual human being to exercise these capacities; in situations of danger and scarcity, cowardly and unjust behavior may in fact benefit an individual. The idea is that what makes someone a good instance of his kind is not necessarily good for *him*.[11]

Behind these objections lies a more general worry—namely, that Aristotle is attempting to move from purely descriptive and non-evaluative claims about what the human function *is* to explicitly normative conclusions about what is good for human beings and about how human beings *ought* to live—very roughly, the worry that Aristotle attempts to move from an "is" to an "ought."

We have seen that these objections are typically supported by substituting references to things like knives and prostitutes for Aristotle's references to human beings in (a) to (c). The legitimacy of the moves from (a) to (c) in the human-instance is then challenged by appeal to their illegitimacy in these substitution instances. But these substitutions are unwarranted. Aristotle explicitly makes distinctions that rule out

as determinate examples of the more general determinable types of activity in which *eudaimonia* consists. On this point, see Irwin 1985, 98–99.

[9] See, e.g., Hardie 1980, 23–24. For statements (though not explicit endorsements) of this objection, see also Suits 1974, 23–25; and Siegler 1967, 37.

[10] See, e.g., Clark 1972, 273; Clark 1975, 14–17; and Nozick 1971, 288–89 (though Nozick does not explicitly discuss Aristotle.)

[11] See, e.g., Glassen 1957, 319–22; and Wilkes 1978, 555–56.

the inferences from (a) to (c) in the substitution instances while allowing them in the human-instance. Once we have seen how these distinctions rule out the illegitimate inferences, we shall see that the foregoing objections are based on misinterpretations of Aristotle's fundamental project. Aristotle does not suppose that human beings have instrumental functions or virtues. Nor does he attempt to move from a purely descriptive and non-evaluative account of the human function to normative conclusions. As we shall see, Aristotle's account is normative "all the way down."

2

First, Aristotle distinguishes two senses in which we say that one thing is for the sake of another [*De Anima* 415b20–21]. One is the *beneficial* sense in which *x*'s occurring benefits someone. The other is the *instrumental* sense in which *x* is instrumental (or a means) to bringing it about that *y*, and it is a further question whether or not anyone is benefited in the process; it is simply a matter of causal efficacy. For example, hemlock may be instrumental (or a means) to killing someone. If no one is benefited by his death, we can say that his taking hemlock is *merely instrumental* to bringing it about that he dies. But if someone is benefited by his death, we can say that his taking the hemlock is not merely instrumentally but also beneficially good for whomever it benefits.

This distinction between the merely instrumental and the beneficial senses in which we say that one thing is for the sake of another is important because Aristotle claims that the notion of benefit is appropriately applied *only* to living creatures. He explicitly distinguishes love for friends from love for inanimate objects and says that while it is a necessary condition of friendship that I wish good to another for his own sake, it would be ridiculous for me to wish good to a bottle of wine; it is only possible to wish that a bottle of wine be good in order to have it for oneself [*EN* 1155b29–31]. A certain kind of sugar may be instrumentally good for fermentation, and a lengthy aging process instrumentally good for producing a mellow wine. But unless we introduce reference to the desires and interests of living creatures, these things will be merely instrumentally, and not also beneficially, good.

Restricting the class of beneficiaries to the class of living things rules out the inferences from (b) to (c) in those substitutions involving inanimate objects such as knives. But this does not show that Aristotle will allow the inference in *all* substitutions involving animate creatures. He may want to rule out *some* inferences from (b) to (c) where living creatures are involved—for example, the inference from (b) what it is to be a good flute player (or a good prostitute) to (c) what is *good for* a flute player (or a prostitute).[12]

[12] Here Aristotle can allow that something is good for *x* qua flute player, but not good for *x* qua human being. So if *x* is essentially human and only accidentally a flute player, that thing will be only accidentally (and not essentially) good for x. In this case, *x* will belong to the class of what Aristotle calls goods τινί (i.e., goods for someone or in some respect) and distinguishes from goods ἁπλῶς (i.e., unqualified or

It is significant, I think, that the class of flute players and the class of prostitutes do not constitute natural kinds. Aristotle can thus rule out such inferences by claiming that the move from (b) to (c) is warranted only in substitutions involving natural kinds. But in order to show that this is not ad hoc, Aristotle must establish some connection between a thing's membership in a natural kind and what is beneficially good for that thing—or, since Aristotle takes membership in a natural kind to be an essential property [*Topics* 101b26–30], some connection between a thing's essential properties and what is beneficial for that thing. And this must be a connection that is lacking between a thing's membership in a nonnatural kind (or a thing's accidental properties) and what is beneficially good for it. In other words, Aristotle must show that my belonging *essentially* to the human species determines at least something about what is beneficially good for me in a way in which my belonging *accidentally* to the class of flute players does not.

It is not hard to see that nothing about what is beneficially good for me follows simply from my playing the flute. Whether or not the characteristics that make me a good flute player benefit me will depend upon on the other desires and interests I happen to have. These characteristics may in fact benefit me, not simply qua flute player but also qua human being, if playing is my sole source of support or personal fulfillment. But it will not follow *simply* from my being a flute player that these things benefit *me*. If I despise the flute, I may wish that I had been tone deaf so that my parents had not encouraged me to develop this talent and I were not now stuck giving music lessons when I would rather be doing philosophy instead. Because the potential benefits of playing the flute depend on what desires and interests I happen to have, they belong to the class of goods that Aristotle calls relative [τινί] and contrasts with unqualified or categorical [ἁπλῶς] goods.[13] And it is because the characteristics that make someone a good specimen of a nonnatural kind tend to confer only *relative* benefits that the inference from (b) to (c) is unwarranted in substitutions involving members of nonnatural kinds.

If this interpretation is correct, then Aristotle suggests a connection between something's membership in a natural kind (or its essential properties) and what is categorically good for that thing. These categorical goods are not fixed independently of the characteristics of the kind to which they are attached: they are fixed by characteristics that belong to each member of that kind simply in virtue of its being a member of that

categorical goods). See next note. [It is difficult to translate these terms and I have made what I think are slight improvements here over the original "conditional" (which I think should be reserved for Aristotle's talk of necessity *ex hupotheôs*) and "unconditional." I have stuck with the original "categorical," while dropping "unconditional," so as to indicate the connection with the sort of Aristotelian categoricals of which Michael Thompson speaks in Thompson 1995 and 2008.]

[13] See, e.g., *EN* 1152b26–27, 1155b23–27, and 1157b26–28 with 1148b15–19; *EE* 1235b30–34, and 1228b18–22. Cooper 1980, 317, describes this distinction as follows: "A thing is good absolutely if it is good for human beings as such, taken in abstraction from special and contingent peculiarities of particular persons: these peculiarities may provide additional interests, needs, and wants and on the basis of them one can speak of additional, possibly divergent, things as good for this or that particular person."

kind and *not* on characteristics (such as particular desires and interests) that may vary from one individual to another. These categorical goods are fundamental to Aristotle's project. Very roughly, his view is that for each species there is an ultimate end such that realizing that end (which Aristotle identifies with living a certain sort of life) is categorically good for any normal member of that species—that is, good for it whatever its actual interests and desires.[14]

Aristotle's account of friendship suggests that he regards these categorical goods as intrinsic and non-instrumental in a way in which relative goods are not. He claims that only virtuous persons wish well to one another for the other's own sake because only they wish one another well for the sake of what each is essentially, and not (as in friendships for advantage or pleasure) for the sake of what each is accidentally [*EN* 1156a10–19, b7–24].[15] This suggests that these categorical goods are independent of further ends and purposes, and so, intrinsically and non-instrumentally good in a way in which relative goods are not. This is certainly a controversial view. But it is not the easy target that our initial objections take it to be.

3

The first objection was that the inferences from (a) to (c) require that human beings have instrumental functions that presuppose their being good or useful for further ends or purposes. But we have just seen that this is not so. Aristotle can argue that the inferences from (a) to (c) hold only for individual members of (living) natural kinds to which categorical goods are attached. In other words, Aristotle can argue that these inferences depend upon there being some activities associated with each natural kind such that engaging in these activities is intrinsically and non-instrumentally beneficial for any normal member of that kind. So Aristotle's moves from (a) to (c) not only fail

[14] If Aristotle admits the possibility that there are members of natural kinds that are defective in the sense that they lack properties essential to the kind (e.g., mentally defective or non-rational members of the human species), then these categorical goods may not be good for *them*. He can say, as he does about pleasure at *EN* 1148b15–19, that because of such defects, what is good (or pleasant) for *them* does not coincide with what is categorically good (or pleasant). On the issue of essential properties that may fail to belong to some individual members of the species, see Irwin 1980, n. 5. [For more on these issues, see "Hylomorphic Virtue" (III.6), where I discuss the sort of explanatory asymmetries afforded by Aristotle's natural teleology; see also Thompson 1995 and 2008 on the character of "natural historical judgments."]

[15] [For more on Aristotle's conception of friendship, especially his understanding of the sense in which friends are to wish each other well for the sake of—or on account of—what each is essentially, see "The Nicomachean Account of *Philia*" (Chapter 6, this volume). Aristotle seems to think that this involves the friends wishing each other well on account of their virtues, which might seem puzzling since the realization of a virtue in any given individual seems contingent. But, as explained in "Hylomorphic Virtue" (III.6), Aristotle's essentialism seems to allow that, though it is only contingent that a first-actuality capacity such as a virtue comes to be, such an actuality is in cases in which it does come to be essential to its subject in the sense that it is an actualization of something belonging to the subject's nature or essence.]

to require that human beings be viewed instrumentally; they actually require that they *not* be viewed instrumentally.[16]

The inferences from (a) to (c) in those substitutions involving nonnatural kinds fail precisely because the goods involved are merely instrumental and dependent upon the further purposes and ends of the members of those kinds. So it is the notion of an intrinsic or categorical good associated with each species that allows Aristotle to say that my belonging to the human species determines something about what is good for me in a way in which my belonging to the class of flute players does not. Of course, other things besides categorical goods may in fact benefit me—either because I have essential properties additional to those belonging to me as a member of this kind or because of certain accidental features of my environment or constitution.[17] But the fact that *some* claims about what is beneficially good for an individual *do not follow* from her belonging to a certain kind is no counterexample to the view that *some* claims about what is good for an individual *do follow* from her belonging to that kind.

We can now see that the second objection—that peculiarity is no recommendation—is also based on a misunderstanding of the term 'ἴδιον' and its role in Aristotle's argument. In *Topics* I.4, Aristotle says that 'ἴδιον' is sometimes used to refer to the essence [τὸ τί ἦν εἶναι] of a thing, and sometimes to refer to the necessary but nonessential properties of a thing. Although Aristotle rarely uses 'ἴδιος' to refer to the essence of a thing, this seems to be how he uses it in the function argument. For in that argument he talks exclusively about activities (especially rational activities) of the human soul. And Aristotle takes the soul of an organism to be its *essence*, not simply one of its necessary but nonessential properties.[18] In any case, Aristotle is not using 'ἴδιος' as we would ordinarily use the word 'peculiar' to identify properties that are peculiar in the sense of being *unique* to the human species. If he were, he could not allow that contemplation is part of our good. For the capacity to contemplate is not unique to us; it belongs most of all to the gods. Similarly, he could not allow that *we too* share in contemplation, for then contemplation would also fail to be peculiar (in the ordinary sense of that word) to the gods.[19] Only if we interpret 'ἴδιος' as referring to the human essence as a whole can we allow that contemplation belongs both to human and to divine welfare. On this

---

[16] [Aristotle does of course argue in *Politics* I that those who are (in his view) suited by nature to be slaves (because they lack deliberative capacities and have bodies suited for labor) are benefited by serving as "living instruments" for those suited by nature to be rule over others. So he does defend the instrumental use of human beings. But he does not seem to take the benefits in question to follow directly from the fact that these individuals are human. In other words, his argument for "natural" slavery does not appeal to the sort of categorical goods on whose existence I take the function argument to turn.]

[17] It is worth noting that if Aristotle allows that there are qualitatively distinct individual essences that belong to a single kind, then he may be able to argue that individual members of a single species can be benefited in substantially different ways without abandoning the connection between a thing's essence and the ways in which it can be benefited. But nothing in my argument depends on taking Aristotle to allow for qualitatively distinct individual essences.

[18] Note that I am not claiming that 'ἴδιος' *means* 'essential'; I claim only that it is used here to *refer* to what is essential. Note also that 'proper' is arguably less misleading a translation than the common 'peculiar.'

[19] See Kraut 1979a, 469–71.

interpretation, human and divine welfare will differ insofar as each is determined by a different conjunction of essential properties. But any individual conjunct of one may be shared by the other as long as there is at least one conjunct that belongs to one and not to the other. And this interpretation of 'ἴδιος' as referring to the human essence as a whole enables Aristotle to rule out proposed counterexamples that involve capacities (like the capacity for prostitution) that are peculiar to us in the ordinary sense but are not parts of the human essence.[20]

I have now argued that Aristotle has the resources to rule out the illegitimate inferences from (a) to (c) in those substitutions involving inanimate objects and members of nonnatural kinds. But this does *not* show that the inferences from (a) to (c) *are* warranted in substitutions involving living members of natural kinds. Aristotle must defend his claim that something's membership in a natural kind at least partly determines what is beneficial for that thing; he must, that is, answer the third objection.

4

At this point, Aristotle might appeal to his view that membership in a natural kind is an essential property that an individual cannot lose without ceasing to exist. So the connection between membership in a natural kind and the capacity for benefit may simply be a consequence of Aristotle's view that there must be some stable and enduring entity that survives any change involved in coming to be benefited—i.e., something that sticks around to receive the benefit.[21] But Aristotle is not claiming simply that something must remain what it is essentially in order for it to be benefited. He is making the stronger claim that the *ways* in which a thing can be benefited are at least *partly determined* by the kind of thing it is and what its essential properties are.

Aristotle might defend this claim by appeal to the claim that the psychological structures and characteristic functions of a natural kind largely determine what is healthy

[20] At this point, someone may object that taking talk of what is ἴδιος to the human kind as referring to the human essence *as a whole* conflicts with Aristotle's explicit claim that nourishment and growth are not parts of our good. But Aristotle can deny that there is any conflict here, if he appeals to his distinction between necessary but nonessential properties on the one hand and essential properties on the other—or, alternatively, to his distinction between the necessary conditions and the components of a thing. (See note 2 above.) He can then argue that our nutritive and reproductive capacities are *necessary* but nonessential properties of us, while our capacities for moral virtue and contemplation are components of our essence. [For more on the question what things Aristotle *in fact* takes to be components (as distinct from necessary conditions) of our being, see "Human Nature and Intellectualism in Aristotle" (Chapter 2, this volume).]

[21] Aristotle clearly regards this point about change as relevant to the capacity for receiving benefit. For he argues that it is possible to wish someone well for his own sake and out of concern for what he is only on the condition of his remaining who (or what) he essentially is [οἷός ποτ' ἐστίν, *EN* 1159a8–12]. Just as one can wish the greatest goods for one's friend only insofar as he remains a man, one can wish goods for oneself only on the condition of remaining oneself. For no one would choose to possess all goods on the condition of becoming another—not even if he were to become a god [*EN* 1166a20–24]. For *he* would not himself survive that change and these goods would accrue rather to some newly existing deity.

for members of that kind. For example, the physiological structures and characteristic activities of a plant determine that exercising the capacity for photosynthesis is constitutive of a plant's health. So if we allow that healthy functioning is *good for* an individual, then these examples may show that at least *some* things about what is good for an individual are determined simply by the kind of thing it is. These things are what I have been calling the categorical goods associated with natural kinds. Aristotle wants to argue that just as the characteristic (physiological) structures and functions of plants determine that some things are categorically good for plants, so the characteristic (psychological) structures and functions of human beings determine that some things are categorically good for them.

At this point, however, we must read Aristotle's argument with care. For this is the point at which many commentators suspect that Aristotle attempts to move from a purely descriptive and non-evaluative account of the function of an organism to explicitly normative conclusions about what is good for that organism. But that is not Aristotle's move; he does not think that we can identify the characteristic structures and functions of an organism without introducing normative considerations. In other words, his argument does not assume that we can give an account of the essence or the function of a kind without introducing some notion of what is beneficial for members of that kind. This is what I had in mind when I said that Aristotle's account was normative "all the way down."

The primary evidence for this comes from Aristotle's teleology. As is well known, Aristotle distinguishes four types of cause—material, efficient, formal, and final—and argues that in the case of many things (especially natural ones) the formal and final causes coincide.[22] His idea here is not especially difficult.

The final cause of a thing is what that thing is for—the end [τέλος] for the sake of which it exists. This is usually some activity. For example, the final cause of an ax is the activity of chopping. The formal cause is the capacity (or set of capacities) that enables a thing to engage in whatever activity is constitutive of its final cause or end. In the case of an ax, this is the capacity to chop. This capacity is the essence of a thing or what makes that thing a thing of its kind. So the formal and final causes of a thing coincide in the sense that the formal cause of a thing is the capacity (or set of capacities) that enables that thing to perform the activities constitutive of its end—i.e., the capacity to perform those activities for the sake of which it exists. So we cannot say what the formal cause (or essence) of something is without reference to its final cause or end.

The fact that formal and final causes coincide in this way is important. For Aristotle generally associates the final cause with the *good* of the organism [*Met.* 983a30–b1, 1013b25–27] or with what is *better for* the organism [*Ph.* 198b4–9], and hence, with something explicitly normative. So if we cannot identify or define the formal cause (or essence) of a thing without reference to its end or final cause, we cannot identify or

[22] See *Physics* (*Ph.*) II.3; and *De Anima* II.4 where Aristotle argues that the soul is the formal, final, and efficient cause of the living body. [For more on the idea as the soul as the *essence* of the relevant sort of body, see "Living Bodies" (III.3).]

define the formal cause (or essence) of a thing without introducing explicitly normative considerations.[23] Such considerations will help to answer the question about which of our many characteristics (or sets of characteristics) constitute the human essence, and so help to determine what it is to be a good human being.[24] These will be whatever characteristics are essentially related to the activities constitutive of our end. But this serves only to relocate the problem to the point where we ask which of the many activities (or sets of activities) peculiar to men constitute our end. If Aristotle has no independent method of answering this question—independent, that is, of what seems best to each person—then he is going to have a tough time defeating the subjectivist. His strategy of appealing to an objectively determined essence to generate an objective end or good will be undermined if there is no objective essence and each person's end is just what it seems to him to be.

5

The fundamental claims on which Aristotle's position rests should by now be clear, even if controversial. They are first, that there are objective essences belonging to members of natural kinds, and second, that these essences (at least partly) determine what is beneficial for members of those kinds. In other words, Aristotle attempts to defeat the subjectivist by arguing that our essence is objective and not whatever it seems to us to be, and so, that our *eudaimonia* is objective and not whatever it seems to us to be. And Aristotle thinks that determining precisely what our essence is will also enable him to reject mistaken objectivist conceptions of *eudaimonia* such as hedonism and (I think) Strict Intellectualism.[25] It is because he thinks that we are neither beasts nor gods that Aristotle denies that our *eudaimonia* consists solely in the pursuit of pleasure or exclusively in contemplation.

An adequate defense of Aristotle's position thus involves three tasks. First, he must argue that there are objective essences belonging to members of natural kinds. Second, he must defend the alleged connection between the essence of a kind and what benefits members of that kind. And third, he must give an account of the human essence. Moreover, since Aristotle wants to appeal to that essence to resolve disputes about *eudaimonia* and human welfare, he must have some method for determining what our

---

[23] See Sorabji 1964, 289–302.

[24] [Here I have changed a sentence suggesting that these characteristics will be peculiar in the ordinary sense of *unique* to the human kind. But as noted in section 3 above, none of the characteristics (or capacities) that constitute the human essence *need* be peculiar in the ordinary sense of the word: each individual characteristic or capacity may belong to members of other kinds as long as there is some *package* of characteristics that is itself peculiar (in the ordinary sense) to the human kind.]

[25] Following Keyt 1978, 138–57, I take Strict Intellectualism to be the view that contemplation is the sole component (as opposed to necessary condition) for *eudaimonia*. In "Human Nature and Intellectualism in Aristotle" (Chapter 2, this volume), I argue that Aristotle rejects this view. [See also "The Pleasures of Thinking Together" (Chapter 7, this volume).] But nothing in my present argument depends on which particular objectivist conception of *eudaimonia* Aristotle adopts.

essence is and that method must be at least partly independent of our beliefs about human welfare.

Aristotle attempts his first task (that of defending essentialism) in several contexts—most notably, in *Metaphysics* IV.4 (where he attempts a dialectical argument against someone who denies the principle of noncontradiction), and also in his defense of the distinction between generation (or destruction) *simpliciter* and mere alteration in *Generation and Corruption*.[26] I cannot now evaluate the success of the arguments. Nor, barring the presence of a radically subjectivist opponent, do I think that necessary. The relevance of these arguments here is simply that they rest on *general* considerations about the possibility of rational discourse and change—considerations that are independent of our moral beliefs. So these arguments provide independent and nonmoral support for Aristotle's ethical argument.

I have already suggested that Aristotle can attempt his second task by appealing to the life sciences, where facts about the natures of various species are supposed to justify *some* claims about what is good or bad (in the sense of being healthy or unhealthy) for members of those species. For we are less inclined to be skeptical about biological benefit and harm. And even if we think that we must introduce *some* normative notions in order to determine what constitutes healthy functioning for a plant or animal, we need not deny the existence of a connection between the characteristic structures and activities of a living organism and what benefits and harms that organism. Here again, there is independent and nonmoral (though not necessarily non-evaluative) support for Aristotle's ethical conclusions.[27]

What I want to suggest now is that Aristotle can achieve some of the independence from our beliefs about *human* welfare that is necessary for his third task, if he applies to humans the *general* methods he uses to determine which of a plant's (or animal's) characteristics are essential to it, and which of a plant's (or animal's) activities constitute its end. In other words, Aristotle should apply to humans methods that are similar to (or the same as) those used to determine that, for example, photosynthesizing is constitutive of a plant's health. These methods will presumably include the observation of behavior and the attempt to explain such behavior within his general teleological framework, an attempt that admittedly appeals to beliefs about the ways in which such behavior is related to the welfare of the relevant organism.[28] *If* Aristotle can use these *general* methods to establish that the exercise of some capacities is essentially

---

[26] [For more on the latter argument, see "Aristotle on Form and Generation" (III.2).]

[27] This argument will not work against someone who rejects Aristotle's general teleological views. It will not, for example, convince someone who restricts the notion of benefit to rational evaluators and makes all benefits relative to the attitudes of such evaluators. But it does not follow that this is not Aristotle's view. There is no reason to assume that he expected his argument to convince opponents who rejected his teleological and essentialist premises. What is important for Aristotle is that some people do accept these premises and others can be persuaded to accept them on grounds that are independent of these people's views about morality. [For more on the importance to Aristotle of finding independent and nonmoral (though not necessarily non-normative) support for his ethical views, see "Strong Dialectic, Neurathian Reflection, and the Ascent of Desire" (Chapter 5, this volume).]

[28] See Irwin 1980, 35–53; and 1981, 193–223.

human, then he can claim that the exercise of these capacities is essentially related to human welfare or eudaimonia in much the same way that exercising the capacity for photosynthesis is related to a plant's health. These capacities may turn out to be rational, linguistic, social, or otherwise. But whatever they are, Aristotle can view the *method* of establishing what is good for rational beings as no less objective than that of establishing what is good for plants and non-rational animals.

So Aristotle need not rely on a mere analogy between a plant's health and a man's welfare. He can argue that each is a special case of the general notion of εὖ ζῆν (or living well). *Eudaimonia* is simply the εὖ ζῆν of essentially rational animals, and so, is strictly parallel to the εὖ ζῆν of any other plant or animal.[29]

6

At this point, someone might object to Aristotle's assimilation of *eudaimonia* to the εὖ ζῆν (or welfare) of plants and animals. She might object that we can derive an adequate conception of a plant's welfare simply from an understanding of its physiological structures and activities only because we *identify* a plant primarily—indeed exclusively—with the physiological structures and activities definitive of health; these things *exhaust* the essence of a plant. So contributing to (or damaging) the health of a plant is the *only* way to benefit (or harm) it. The same might be said of most animals. But we do not think that contributing to (or damaging) a man's health exhausts the ways in which we might benefit (or harm) him. That is because we do not *identify* human beings primarily with the physiological characteristics definitive of health and Aristotle may not identify human beings with these at all.[30] Something else is thought to be essential to human nature—namely, rationality.

So far, Aristotle agrees. He thinks that human beings are essentially rational animals whose characteristic activity or ἔργον is to pursue intentionally their own good—or at least their own apparent or conceived good. But Aristotle denies that this undermines his attempt to assimilate eudaimonia or human welfare to the welfare of plants and other animals. Given the connection between a thing's essence and the ways in which it can be benefited, Aristotle thinks that a man's rationality (at least partly) determines what is beneficial for him.

But someone who accepts the main points of Aristotle's argument *and* his characterization of human beings as essentially rational may still be dissatisfied. She may

[29] Aristotle sometimes seems to restrict the capacity for εὖ ζῆν to rational animals, or at least to higher ones. See *Parts of Animals* 656a5–10; and *Politics* 1280a31–34 (where he denies εὖ ζῆν even to slaves). If this is his considered view, then εὖ ζῆν is not a general conception of living well applicable to *all* living things. Nonetheless, there does seem to be some notion of what is beneficial for any living thing and *eudaimonia* can still be viewed as a special case of that—i.e., as a special case of the general notion of welfare applicable to any living thing.

[30] See Cooper 1975, 144–80 [discussed at length in "Human Nature and Intellectualism in Aristotle" (Chapter 2, this volume)].

object that this characterization is not sufficient to yield any interesting or substantive conclusions about human welfare, and so, will not help us to discover the components of eudaimonia. She may think that these components will be contingent on which goals and desires rational creatures happen to have, and that these goals and desires can vary from one individual to the next. She may say that whatever we think about the welfare of non-rational creatures, the welfare of rational ones is subjective in the sense that a rational agent's welfare is determined by the beliefs and desires an agent happens to have.

We have seen, however, that Aristotle does not entirely agree.[31] He thinks that there are objective components of eudaimonia that are determined by human nature without being entirely dependent on the particular goals and desires individuals happen to have. Aristotle might defend this claim by arguing that whatever goals and desires a man happens to have, he has reason to cultivate rational agency by developing those virtues which enable him to pursue his goals (whatever they are) most effectively. For example, practical wisdom or the ability to identify the best available means to his ends will contribute to the effective pursuit of his goals. And temperance or the capacity to control his appetites and passions will make a similar contribution. Just as someone *can* perform certain actions that undermine a heart or a kidney's capacity to function effectively (by, e.g., eating and drinking too much or exercising too little), so also someone can undermine his capacity to pursue his goals effectively if he fails to develop temperance and practical reason. And Aristotle is entitled to claim that establishing the connection between these virtues and effective rational agency is no less a matter of empirical inquiry than that of establishing the connection between the former actions and their effects on hearts and kidneys.

Similarly, Aristotle can appeal to the connection between a thing's essence and the conditions for its survival in order to argue that any essentially rational agent (whatever his actual goals and desires) has reason to preserve his capacity for rational agency. For remaining what he is essentially is a condition of *his* attaining those goals, or indeed, of *his* receiving any benefits *at all*. On Aristotle's view, someone who destroys his capacity for rational agency (by, e.g., taking excessive doses of hallucinogenic drugs) literally destroys *himself*. For even if someone else takes over and manages his life for "him," Aristotle would say that it is not *he*, but rather someone else, who receives the apparent benefits of this overseer's efforts.

This case—or the case of someone who becomes what we call "a human vegetable"—is analogous to the case in which my friend who "becomes" a god fails to survive that change, and so is not strictly the beneficiary of any goods accruing to that newly existing deity. This analogy is important if *practical* intellect is part of the

[31] Aristotle may allow that *some* of what benefits a rational agent may be contingent on what goals and desires she happens to have and that these goals and desires can vary from one creature to the next. This will presumably occur as our descriptions of what benefits individuals become increasingly specific and is, however, compatible with there being at higher levels of description things that benefit *any* rational agent.

human essence. For practical intellect is essentially concerned with psychophysical affections such as desire and anger. This means that even if my theoretical intellect could survive in a disembodied state, I (who am essentially human and so essentially composed of practical intellect) could not. So however single-mindedly Aristotle thinks I ought to pursue contemplation, he cannot recommend that I "become" a disembodied intellect in order to do so. For there is a sense in which *I* would be no better off "becoming" a god than if I were to "become" a beast or a vegetable. The general point is that *if* we are essentially rational agents, we have reason to preserve our rational agency simply as a necessary condition of attaining *any* of our goals, whatever they happen to be.

Of course this argument will not convince absolutely everyone. It will not convince a present-aim theorist whose goal is to live for the moment because he does not think of himself as existing over extended periods of time. Nor will it convince someone whose *goal* is to be intemperate or irrational. But Aristotle can reasonably reply that this goal is one that a rational agent, in so far as she thinks of herself as such, cannot coherently have. On Aristotle's view, each of these agents—the intemperate one and the present-aim theorist—makes a mistake about who or what he is, and so, about what is good for him. Of course, if these agents turn out to be right and Aristotle wrong about what we are, then Aristotle may have to abandon his own conception of eudaimonia. But the fact that he cannot convince people who do not think of themselves as rational agents existing over time that temperance and prudence are good for them is not an objection to Aristotle's view.

So far then, our objector may agree that any essentially rational agent has reasons to preserve and to cultivate his rational agency, whatever goals and desires he happens to have. But this shows only that temperance and practical wisdom are *instrumentally* valuable to any rational agent and these instrumental connections are not enough for Aristotle. For they do not show what the *components* of eudaimonia are. Nor do they justify the independent value Aristotle attaches to a man's rational pursuit of his *own* final good. In order to explain this, we must invoke Aristotle's conception of eudaimonia as a special case of the kind of welfare that we attribute to any plant or animal.

A merely instrumental connection between a heart's strength and its capacity to pump blood does not show why a heart is better off beating on its own if a pacemaker could be doing its work instead. Nor does a merely instrumental connection between practical wisdom and eudaimonia show why I am better off running my own life, if someone else could do it for me. Suppose that my powers of practical reasoning are modest and that I occasionally suffer from weakness of will. Why should I not turn my deliberations over to a highly efficient life-planning agency and then commit myself to the care of someone empowered to enforce its decisions? This might seem especially prudent, if I am thus able to satisfy a larger proportion of my first-order aims and desires than I would otherwise do—or than most of my admittedly more self-reliant friends do.

But Aristotle would not agree. He does not view eudaimonia (as we might view happiness) simply as the satisfaction of all (or of a reasonable portion) of a person's various first-order desires and aims. That person's role in bringing it about that his desires are satisfied or his aims attained is of fundamental importance.[32] We might put this point by saying that eudaimonia does not simply require that my desires *be* satisfied or that my ends *be* attained; eudaimonia requires that *I* satisfy my desires and that *I* attain these ends.[33] This explains why Aristotle says that eudaimonia is an *activity* of soul in accordance with virtue, and refuses to call a person eudaimôn if her various first-order ends and desires are satisfied simply as a matter of luck or chance.[34] While *we* might be willing to say that such a person is *happy* and perhaps even that she lives well, Aristotle's conception of eudaimonia as a special case of the welfare of living things shows why he would not agree.[35]

Aristotle is relying on a conception of attaining one's ends that is fundamentally natural. A heart that, owing to some deficiency in its natural capacities, cannot beat on its own but is made to beat by means of a pacemaker is not a healthy heart. For *it*, the heart, is not strictly performing its function. Similarly, a human being who, owing to some deficiency in his natural capacities, cannot manage his own life but is managed by means of another's deliberating and ordering him, is not eudaimôn—*not* even if he possesses the same goods and engages in the same first-order activities as one who is eudaimôn. For *he*, the man, is not strictly performing his function. This is part of why Aristotle refuses to call slaves, whom he takes to lack the capacity for deliberation, eudaimôn [*Pol.* 1260a12–14, 1280a31–35; *EN* 1177a8–9]. On this naturalistic view, the connection between eudaimonia and rational agency is not merely instrumental. Aristotle's claim that eudaimonia is an activity of soul in accordance with virtue shows that he takes eudaimonia to *consist in* exercising rational agency.

---

32 Nagel 1972, 252–259 (reprinted in Rorty 1980) calls this "the condition of autonomy." (See *EN* 1099b18–25; and *Pol.* 1323b24–29.) The importance of autonomy stems not so much from the practical benefits of self-sufficiency as from Aristotle's conception of eudaimonia as an *activity* of the agent's soul. [It follows from this that an agent must, *logically speaking*, achieve eudaimonia *for herself.* For more on this point, see section 4 of "Self-Love and Authoritative Virtue" (Chapter 4, this volume).]

33 If these desires or goals are personal (as opposed to impersonal) then it may be conceptually true that the *only* way for them to be satisfied or attained is *by me.* [On the distinction between personal and impersonal desires, see sections V–VI and X of "Friends and Future Selves" (I.1). For the idea that one must achieve virtue for oneself, see again section 4 of "Self-Love and Authoritative Virtue" (Chapter 4, this volume).]

34 This does not mean that someone cannot be deprived of eudaimonia by luck or by chance. Even if someone must be responsible for his eudaimonia, he may not be responsible for his failure to achieve eudaimonia. This asymmetry of responsibility is not necessarily objectionable; we often attribute responsibility to people for acquired skills, which, however, can be lost through accidents, as in the case of the young pianist who was recently pushed in front of an oncoming subway train. But this leaves Aristotle with a problem of explaining why someone should cultivate his powers of rational agency even if, as a result of misfortune, his own eudaimonia should fail to result. [Note that there is theoretical support for the existence of such asymmetries in Aristotle's teleology, which allows formal explanations to dominate when things go as they ought (teleologically speaking) to go, while material-efficient explanations take over when things go wrong. For more on this point, see "Hylomorphic Virtue" (III.6) and "*Nicomachean Ethics* VII.3 on Akratic Ignorance" (co-authored with Martin Pickavé), (III.7).]

35 See note 1 above.

7

So far our objector, if she adopts Aristotle's naturalistic framework, may agree. But she is likely to complain that this still tells us very little about what eudaimonia or human welfare is. Surely it consists in the rational pursuit of one's own goals, but which goals are these? Could my eudaimonia consist in the deliberate pursuit of evil ends (e.g., in torturing children)? Or could it consist in the rational and calculating pursuit of sensual pleasure?

Aristotle does not think so. He thinks that a full account of human nature can show us not only that eudaimonia consists in the rational pursuit of our own conceived ends, but also something about what these ends are or ought to be. This is clear from Aristotle's discussion of friendship and self-love.[36]

Aristotle thinks that only virtuous friends wish one another well for the other's sake. They do so because they wish one another well for the sake of what each is essentially and not (as in friendships for advantage and pleasure) for the sake of what each is accidentally [*EN* 1156a10–19, b7–24]. What does Aristotle mean by this?

Business associations are typical cases of friendship for advantage. Suppose that my friend and I are stockbrokers who wish well to one another in that respect in which we are friends. We each hope that the other will be successful in her pursuit of profit. But this does not show that each wishes well to the other *for her own sake*. For that depends not only on why each of us pursues profit, but also on each of us understanding where profit fits into the *other's* aims. Suppose that my friend values the money only instrumentally and as means to things that she values for their own sakes—e.g., as tuition for a philosophy course so that she can achieve contemplation. It is only if I wish her well in pursuing these ultimate ends and not simply as a profiteer that I wish her well for her own sake.

But there is a problem here. What if I, unlike my friend, make profit my ultimate end? Does this mean that any true friend who wishes me well for my own sake must wish me well in my pursuit of profit? Aristotle does not think so, for he thinks that when I pursue profit as an ultimate end, I do not even wish *myself* well for my own sake. This is clear from Aristotle's distinction between two kinds of self-love.

Aristotle says that the person who loves and gratifies the dominant part of himself—that is, his intellect or rational part—is most truly a lover of self. But someone who places too high a value on money, honor, or pleasure, and so gratifies his affections and the non-rational part of himself, is less truly a lover of self. For he assigns goods to the non-rational part, which is less truly what he is than the rational part, which is most of all (and perhaps even exclusively) who or what he is [*EN* 1168b25–1169a6]. Aristotle thinks that like the intemperate man and the present-aim theorist, this person makes a mistake about who he is, and so, about what is good for him.

---

[36] [For more on these issues, see "Self-Love and Authoritative Virtue" (Chapter 4, this volume) and "The Nicomachean Account of *Philia*" (Chapter 6, this volume).]

In sum, Aristotle thinks that we are essentially creatures who intentionally pursue our own good (or our own conceived good). So he thinks that there is a sense in which we must be pursuing what is really or objectively good for us, even when we deliberately pursue specific ends that are not in fact good for us. In such cases, we desire the good and are simply mistaken about what it is.

Suppose, e.g., that I believe that sensual pleasure is good (for me) and, on the basis of this belief, make pleasure my ultimate end. Because I pursue pleasure *as good* (or on the basis of that belief), Aristotle thinks that *if* pleasure is not really good for me, then there is a sense in which I do not get what I am after, no matter how much pleasure I achieve in the process. It is as though I had captured Oswald in the belief that he is the killer of JFK. If someone else killed JFK, then whether or not I know it, I have *not* got what I *want*. And this, Aristotle says, is like getting nothing at all [*EN* 1164a13–16]. Aristotle thinks it is like this with pleasure and the good.

In this sense, Aristotle may allow that a person can sincerely believe that he is eudaimôn and still be mistaken in that belief—something *we* would not be very likely to say about what we call "happiness." Aristotle believes that someone whose desires rest on mistaken beliefs about what is good for him will be better off if his beliefs (and desires) are corrected so that he has *true* beliefs about what is good for him, and so desires what is *really* good for him [*EN* 1129b4–6]. And Aristotle thinks that this is true, no matter how subjectively satisfied he is with his present lot.

Now the things that are objectively good for a person, whatever his actual beliefs and desires, are the categorical goods that Aristotle thinks will benefit him simply insofar as he is essentially human. What these things are will depend on what the human essence is. If, as some commentators think, Aristotle identifies us exclusively with our theoretical intellects, then contemplation alone will be categorically good for us. And this is true even if virtues such as temperance and prudence are instrumentally valuable in our pursuit of contemplation. But if (as I think Aristotle believes) practical intellect is also part of our essence, then moral virtue will also be categorically good for us. Similarly, if the non-rational desires are part of the human essence, then even certain sensual pleasures may be categorically good for us. And these things will be categorically good for us and components of our eudaimonia in the same way in which photosynthesis is categorically good for plants. The fundamental difference between us and plants is that we *intentionally* pursue our categorical good and they do not.

8

Before concluding, I want to point out just how ambitious Aristotle's project really is. He initially appeals to the human function in order to give content to our uncontroversial but uninformative account of eudaimonia as the ultimate end of human action. But much of his success depends on how much he is willing or able to build into his account of human nature in the first place. For as we saw, the specification of man simply as a rational agent does not get him very far. It may (given Aristotle's naturalistic framework) show that eudaimonia consists in the rational pursuit of one's own goals. But it does not show much about what these goals ought to be.

If Aristotle wants to show more about these goals, he needs a fuller account of human nature. For example, if (as Aristotle says) man is by nature a social or political animal, then this may show that friendship and political activity are components of eudaimonia [*EN* 1097b8–11, 1169b18–19; *Pol.* 1253a8–9]. Similarly, if theoretical intellect is part of human nature, then contemplation will also be a component of eudaimonia. But Aristotle needs to be careful here—especially if he wants to argue against Thrasymachus, Callicles, and Co. that all the traditional virtues benefit a human being. For Aristotle then needs some independent means of deciding which things are, and which are not, parts of human nature—in other words, means that are not entirely dependent on views about what the traditional virtues or the components of eudaimonia are. This is crucial, if Aristotle's appeal to human nature is supposed to provide a way of determining what eudaimonia is.

This is why it is important that in *Nicomachean Ethics* I, Aristotle appeals to his general teleology and to the independently plausible psychological theory of the *De Anima* in order to establish that man is essentially a rational animal. But the further Aristotle strays from these independently plausible teleological and psychological theories, and the more he tries to restrict the contents of eudaimonia by filling in the account of human nature, the more suspect his conclusions become. We may not agree that reading Aristotle's *Metaphysics* is good for me if I prefer to spend my time playing basketball—or that an occasional cocktail party or political appointment is good for me if I prefer to devote all of my time to Aristotle's *Metaphysics*. But whatever we think of these more specific conclusions, Aristotle's general identification of what it is to be human with rational agency is not altogether implausible—at least not to those of us who would prefer to trust our hearts to pacemakers than our deliberations and the pursuit of our ends to another, no matter how benevolent and wise she happens to be.[37]

POSTSCRIPT [2021]

I should like to respond briefly to a question raised by Sara Magrin at the Author-Meets-Critics session held at the Central Division APA in February 2020: how do I reconcile the argument of this chapter with the McDowellian views expressed in my later work, starting with Chapter 5 below and continuing in "Hylomorphic Virtue" (III.6)?

The aim of Chapter 1 was largely to provide an account of Aristotle's naturalism and the theoretical resources to which he could appeal in answering common objections to

[37] I am grateful to audiences at Rice University, UCLA, and the University of Pennsylvania—and to Richard Boyd, David Brink, Leon Galis, Phil Mitsis, Steve Strange, Gisela Striker, and the referees of this journal [*Ancient Philosophy*]—for their comments on previous versions of this essay. I should especially like to thank Terry Irwin for repeated criticism and encouragement.

it. But I hint toward the end at questions broached in Chapter 5 below, questions about the extent to which the function argument can secure any place for *determinate* forms of virtue in Aristotle's conception of eudaimonia. And though I was tacitly assuming when I wrote Chapter 1 that the function argument was intended to secure fairly determinate forms of virtue, I explicitly left the door open to less ambitious readings of that argument—readings, for example, according to which the argument might secure the need for *some* conception of courage or other, but not precisely this or that specific conception of it; for *some* conception of justice or other, but not precisely this or that specific conception of it; and so on. And there is room here for local practices to play *some* role in determining the contents of the specific conceptions of justice that bind the members of particular communities, a role that Aristotle himself recognizes when he acknowledges the importance of the *nomimon*, or "lawful," form of justice. But that is a topic for future work.

The crucial point here is this. My reading of the function argument is not as deflationary as McDowell's. McDowell sees this argument as ruling out only (a) "a life of unreflective gratification of appetite" ["The Role of Eudaimonia in Aristotle's Ethics," McDowell 1980, sec. 10] and (b) a solitary life ["Some Issues in Aristotle's Moral Psychology," McDowell 1998a, sec. 9]. He takes (a) to be excluded by Aristotle's identification of eudaimonia with *rational* activity; and he takes (b) to be ruled out by Aristotle's repeated appeals to our nature as *political* animals. But I take the emphasis Aristotle places on our nature as political animals, together with his recognition of the *nomimon* form of justice, to open the door to the idea that readers of the function argument may derive from their appreciation of that argument the sort of "reflective reassurance" of which McDowell speaks in "Two Sorts of Naturalism" (1996) (discussed in Chapter 5 below): if the determination of justice that prevails in a reader's polis really is a form of justice, then her appreciation of that argument may serve to reinforce her commitment, especially in moments of crisis, to justice so conceived. The fact that a fully virtuous agent will (as I argue in Chapter 5) have no need for such reassurance is beside the point. For Aristotle's ethical/political works are not concerned primarily with ideal agents.

It is worth pausing here to note that Aristotle is pretty clearly engaged in his *Politics* in what is now known as "non-ideal theory" and that this is connected to his hylomorphism: what constitution (or "form") is best for a particular state is a function of the distribution of capacities in the population (or the "matter") with which it must work. So even if the specific determination of justice that prevails in a state cannot be *deduced* from the function argument, the reader's grasp of that argument can play a role in supporting her commitment to the specific determination of justice that prevails in the state in which she lives, provided of course that it really *is* a determination of justice. And reading the function argument this way is compatible with the emphasis McDowell places on Aristotle's claim that students of his ethics-cum-politics must come equipped with a proper upbringing if they are to benefit from the arguments he presents: even given the abstractness of the function argument, Aristotle may regard the sort of reflection in which he is engaged as reflection on an "inherited scheme of values . . . from *inside* the ethical way of thinking [he] finds [himself] with, not [a matter of] contemplating it from an external standpoint of a theory about motivation built into human beings as such" ["Eudaimonism and Realism in Aristotle's Ethics," in Heinaman 1995, 201–18].

The plausibility of some such reading should be clear from the way in which the contents of Aristotle's preferred conceptions of the virtues are due largely to manifestly *ethical* endoxa—i.e., to *ethical* views that are taken by Aristotle to be especially worthy of investigation, either because they are widespread (and so constitute a kind of "common sense") or because they are accepted by those with reputations for wisdom. This is an explicit feature of Aristotle's method, described at *Eudemian Ethics* 1216b26–32 and quoted at the start of Chapter 5 below. Aristotle opens each of his investigations into a canonical virtue—for example, courage or justice—by surveying the beliefs about it held by the many and the wise; he then presents various puzzles to which these beliefs, taken together, give rise; and he seeks in the end to resolve the puzzles in ways that allow him to preserve all—or at least the most important—of these beliefs, many of which are clearly *ethical*. And he sees no incompatibility between this and the way he employs the function argument. Neither, I submit, should we.

BIBLIOGRAPHY

Aristotle. *De Anima*. W. D. Ross (ed.) 1956. Oxford Classical Texts. Oxford: Clarendon Press.

Aristotle. *The Eudemian Ethics*. H. Rackham (ed. and trans.) 1935. Loeb Classical Library XX. London: William Heinemann.

Aristotle. *Ethica Nicomachea*. I. Bywater (ed.) 1894. Oxford Classical Texts. Oxford: Clarendon Press.

Aristotle. *Metaphysica*. W. Jaeger (ed.) 1957. Oxford Classical Texts. Oxford: Clarendon Press.

Aristotle. *Meterologica*. H. D. P. Lee (ed. and trans.) 1952. Loeb Classical Library VII. London: William Heinemann.

Aristotle. *Nicomachean Ethics Book VI*. L. H. G. Greenwood (ed.) 1909. Cambridge: Cambridge University Press.

Aristotle. *Parts of Animals*. A. L. Peck (ed. and trans.) 1937. Loeb Classical Library XII. London: William Heinemann.

Aristotle. *Physica*. W. D. Ross (ed.) 1950. Oxford Classical Texts. Oxford: Clarendon Press.

Aristotle. *Politica*. W. D. Ross (ed.) 1957. Oxford Classical Texts. Oxford: Clarendon Press.

Aristotle. *Topica*. F. S. Forster (ed. and trans.) 1960. Loeb Classical Library II. London: William Heinemann.

Clark, S. 1972. "The Use of 'Man's Function' in Aristotle." *Ethics* 82: 269–83.

Clark, S. 1975. *Aristotle's Man*. Oxford: Clarendon Press.

Cooper, J. 1975. *Reason and Human Good in Aristotle*. Cambridge, MA: Harvard University Press.

Cooper, J. 1980. "Aristotle on Friendship." In Rorty 1980, 301–40.

Glassen, P. 1957. "A Fallacy in Aristotle's Argument about the Good." *Philosophical Quarterly* 66: 319–22.

Hardie, W. F. R. 1980. *Aristotle's Ethical Theory*. Oxford: Clarendon Press.

Heinaman, R. (ed.) 1995. *Aristotle and Moral Realism*. London: UCL Press, 1995.

Irwin, T. H. 1980. "The Metaphysical and Psychological Basis of Aristotle's Ethics." In Rorty 1980, 35–53.

Irwin, T. H. 1981. "Aristotle's Methods of Ethics." In D. J. O'Meara (ed.), *Studies on Aristotle*. Washington, DC: Catholic University Press, 193–223.

Irwin, T. H. 1985. "Permanent Happiness: Aristotle and Solon." *Oxford Studies in Ancient Philosophy* 3: 89–124.

Keyt, D. 1978. "Intellectualism in Aristotle." George C. Simmons (ed.), Special Aristotle Issue, *Paideia*: 138–57.

Kraut, R. 1979a. "The Peculiar Function of Human Beings." *Canadian Journal of Philosophy* 9: 467–78.

Kraut, R. 1979b. "Two Conceptions of Happiness." *Philosophical Review* 88: 167–97.

Nagel, T. 1972. "Aristotle on *Eudaimonia*." *Phronesis* 17: 252–59. Reprinted in Rorty 1980, 7–14.

Nozick, R. 1971. "On the Randian Argument." *Personalist* 52: 282–304.

McDowell, J. 1980. "The Role of Eudaimonia in Aristotle's Ethics." In Rorty 1980, 359–76.

McDowell, J. 1996. "Two Sorts of Naturalism." In R. Hursthouse, G. Lawrence, and W. Quinn (eds.), *Virtues and Reasons: Philippa Foot and Moral Theory*. Oxford: Clarendon Press, 149–79; reprinted in McDowell 1998b, 167–97.

McDowell, J. 1998a. "*Some Issues in Aristotle's Moral Psychology*." In S. Everson (ed.), *Ethics*. Cambridge: Cambridge University Press, 107–28; reprinted in McDowell 1998b, 23–49.

McDowell, J. 1998b. *Mind, Value, and Reality*. Cambridge, MA: Harvard University Press.

Pickavé, M. and Whiting, J. 2008. "*Nicomachean Ethics* VII.3 on Akratic Ignorance." *Oxford Studies in Ancient Philosophy* 34: 323–72. [III.7]

Rorty, A. (ed.) 1980. *Essays on Aristotle's Ethics*. Berkeley: University of California Press.

Siegler, F. 1967. "Reason, Happiness and Goodness." In J. J. Walsh and H. L. Shapiro (eds.), *Aristotle's Ethics: Issues and Interpretations*. Belmont, MA: Wadsworth Publishing, 30–47.

Sorabji, R. 1964. "Function." *Philosophical Quarterly* 14: 289–302.

Suits, B. 1974. "Aristotle on the Function of Man: Fallacies, Heresies and Other Entertainments." *Canadian Journal of Philosophy* 4: 23–40.

Thompson, M. 1995. "The Representation of Life." In Hursthouse, Lawrence, and Quinn 1996, 247–296.

Thompson, M. 2008. *Life and Action: Elementary Structures of Practice and Practical Thought*. Cambridge, MA: Harvard University Press.

Whiting, J. 1986. Human Nature and Intellectualism in Aristotle." *Archiv für Geschichte der Philosophie* 68: 70–95. [Chapter 2, this volume]

Whiting, J. 1986. "Friends and Future Selves." *Philosophical Review* 95: 547–80. [I.1]

Whiting, J. 1990. "*Aristotle on Form and Generation.*" *Proceedings of the Boston Area Colloquium of Ancient Philosophy* 6: 35–64. [III.2]

Whiting, J. 1992. "Living Bodies." In M. Nussbaum and A. Rorty (eds.). *Essays on Aristotle's "De Anima."* Oxford: Clarendon Press, 75–91. [III.3]

Whiting, J. 1996. "Self-Love and Authoritative Virtue: Prolegomenon to a Kantian Reading of Eudemian Ethics VIII.3." In S. Engstrom and J. Whiting (eds.), *Aristotle, Kant, and the Stoics: Rethinking Happiness and Duty.* Cambridge: Cambridge University Press, 162–99. [Chapter 4, this volume]

Whiting, J. 2002 "Eudaimonia, External Results, and Choosing Virtuous Actions for Themselves." *Philosophy and Phenomenological Research* LXV: 270–90. [Chapter 3, this volume]

Whiting, J. 2002. "Strong Dialectic, Neurathian Reflection, and the Ascent of Desire: Irwin and McDowell on Aristotle's Method of Ethics." *Proceedings of the Boston Area Colloquium of Ancient Philosophy* 17, no. 1: 61–122. [Chapter 5, this volume]

Whiting, J. 2006. "The Nicomachean Account of Philia." In R. Kraut (ed.), *The Blackwell Guide to the Nicomachean Ethics*. Oxford: Wiley-Blackwell, 276–304. [Chapter 6, this volume.]

Whiting, J. 2012 "The Pleasure of Thinking Together: Prolegomenon to a Complete Reading of EE VII.12." In F. Leigh (ed.), *The Eudemian Ethics on the Voluntary, Friendship, and Luck: The Sixth S. V. Keeling Colloquium in Ancient Philosophy*. The Hague: Brill: 77–154. [Chapter 7, this volume.]

Whiting, J. 2014. "False Pleasures in Plato's *Philebus*." In M. Lee (ed.), *Strategies of Argument: Essays in Ancient Ethics, Epistemology, and Logic*. Oxford: Oxford University Press, 21–59.

Whiting, J. 2019. "Hylomorphic Virtue: Cosmology, Embryology, and Moral Development in Aristotle." *Philosophical Explorations* 22: 222–42. [III.6]

Wilkes, K. V. 1978. "The Good Man and the Good for Man in Aristotle's Ethics." *Mind* 87: 553–71. Reprinted in Rorty 1980, 341–57.

2

Human Nature and Intellectualism in Aristotle

1

I imagine that many commentators wish Aristotle had never written the tenth book of the *Nicomachean Ethics* (*EN*). For in that book, Aristotle is apparently committed to Strict Intellectualism—that is, the view that contemplation is the sole component of εὐδαιμονία (or happiness).[1] And while most of us are likely to object that there is more to εὐδαιμονία than contemplation, the real problem is that throughout the middle books of the *EN* Aristotle himself seems to agree.[2] In these books, he argues that moral virtue is among the components of εὐδαιμονία. But in Book X, Aristotle distinguishes the life according to νοῦς (i.e., a life devoted primarily and perhaps exclusively to contemplation) from the life according to the other virtue (i.e., a life devoted primarily and perhaps exclusively to moral virtue).[3] He describes the former as something divine

[1] This formulation of Strict Intellectualism is from David Keyt, "Intellectualism in Aristotle," George C. Simmons (ed.), Special Aristotle Issue, *Paideia* (1978): 138–57. The components or parts of εὐδαιμονία are here distinguished from the instrumental means to or necessary conditions of it. See *Eudemian Ethics* (*EE*) 1214b6–28; *Politics* (*Pol.*) 1328a21–b4, 1239a34–39; and L. H. G. Greenwood (ed.), *Aristotle: Nicomachean Ethics Book VI* (Cambridge: Cambridge University Press, 1909), 46–47.

[2] I shall hereafter refer to *EN* II–IX as the "middle books." It is important that Aristotle's view that moral virtue is a component of εὐδαιμονία be supported by books other than *EN* V–VII, which are common to the *Eudemian Ethics* (*EE*). Otherwise we might hypothesize that this is a Eudemian view and explain the conflict as due simply to someone's inserting books originally written for the *EE* into the *EN*. For this reason I shall appeal primarily to evidence from the non-common middle books *EN* II–IV and VIII–IX.

[3] It is difficult to determine exactly which two lives Aristotle intends to compare in *EN* X. He may be comparing (a) a purely contemplative life (i.e., one that attaches no independent value to moral virtue) with a purely

Living Together. Jennifer Whiting, Oxford University Press. © Oxford University Press 2023.
DOI: 10.1093/oso/9780199969678.003.0003

and the latter as specifically human, and then claims that we must not listen to those who tell humans to think human thoughts and mortals, mortal thoughts, but must try as far as possible to imitate[4] the immortals and to live according to intellect [*EN* 1177b31–1178a1]. This apparent injunction to maximize contemplation makes it difficult to deny that *EN* X rejects the middle books' view that moral virtue is among the components of εὐδαιμονία and thus adopts Strict Intellectualism. The *Nicomachean Ethics*' views about εὐδαιμονία seem internally inconsistent.

John Cooper thinks that the *Nicomachean Ethics* is inconsistent. He attempts to account for the inconsistency with the following developmental hypothesis: Aristotle thinks that the components of εὐδαιμονία are determined by human nature. In the middle books of the *Nicomachean Ethics*, Aristotle continues to hold his early Eudemian account of human nature. On this account, a person is a complex creature, essentially composed of both practical and theoretical intellect. Because practical intellect is part of the human essence, moral virtue is (along with contemplation) a component of εὐδαιμονία. But in the mature psychology of the *De Anima* (*DA*), Aristotle sharply separates theoretical from practical intellect. This leads to a new account of personal identity in *EN* X, where Aristotle identifies a person exclusively with his theoretical intellect. Given this new identification, contemplation is the sole component of εὐδαιμονία.[5]

---

moral or political life that does not include contemplation; (b) two mixed lives, each of which involves both contemplation and moral virtue (mixed, however, in different proportions); (c) a mixed life that includes moral virtue but has also attained contemplation with a narrowly virtuous life that is inferior insofar as it has not attained contemplation; or (d) a purely contemplative life not subject to the constraints of moral virtue with a mixed life that includes contemplation but less than that of the purely contemplative life. Aristotle does not say enough to allow us to decide this issue, but I agree with John Cooper that (a) is unlikely on the grounds that it would be strange for Aristotle to rank the purely contemplative and purely political lives as best and second best without even mentioning the *EE's* mixed ideal. See *Reason and Human Good in Aristotle* (Cambridge: Cambridge University Press, 1975), 166; unless otherwise noted, all subsequent references to Cooper will be to this work. Concerning Cooper's preference for (d), I am willing to allow it, provided that we interpret Aristotle as saying that the purely contemplative life is most εὐδαίμων for one kind of creature—e.g., for a god or a purely theoretical intellect—while the mixed life is most εὐδαίμων for human creatures not identified exclusively with their theoretical intellects. (This involves taking εὐδαιμονέστατος from *EN* 1178a8 with δεύτερος in a9 and allowing that different types of lives may be *most* εὐδαίμων for different types of creatures, and that some of these lives may in some sense be better than others even if not better or best for certain creatures.) But I am not willing to allow that Aristotle is ranking for human beings the purely contemplative life ahead of a life that contains both moral virtue and contemplation for human creature. For I think his inclusive conception of εὐδαιμονία (discussed in section 2 below) rules this out. And although I can see nothing to rule out (b), I think that (c) makes good sense, given this inclusive conception of εὐδαιμονία. Finally, (c) takes Aristotle as claiming that the purely political life is less εὐδαίμων than a mixed life that also includes contemplation (here called the life according to νοῦς, not because it lacks moral virtue but because Aristotle follows his customary practice of referring to things by their last differentiae). For the purely political life would be made even more choiceworthy by the addition of contemplation. [For an argument that the purely contemplative life would be made more choiceworthy by the addition of friendship and other forms of political activity, see "The Pleasures of Thinking Together" (Chapter 7, this volume).]

[4] Irwin suggests that we translate 'ἀθανατίζειν' following the use of 'λακονίζειν' to refer to imitating the Lacedaemonians. See H. W. Smyth, *Greek Grammar* (Cambridge: Cambridge University Press, 1920), 888.6 on verbs in -ιζω derived from proper names to express the adoption of language or manners.

[5] Cooper 1975, 169–80.

Cooper's intellectualist interpretation of *EN* X thus rests directly on the identification of a person exclusively with his theoretical νοῦς. The main project of this essay is to argue against Cooper that *EN* X does not defend Strict Intellectualism by appeal to this identification, nor, more generally, by appeal to the *De Anima*. I discuss Cooper's interpretation because I think that his approach to the problem of εὐδαιμονία by way of personal identity is fundamentally correct. It points toward an alternative interpretation that agrees with Cooper in arguing that Aristotle thinks that the case for Strict Intellectualism depends upon the identification of a person with theoretical νοῦς, but disagrees with him by denying that Aristotle ever accepts this identification. On this alternative account, *EN* X argues only that Strict Intellectualism would follow *if* a person *were* identified exclusively with theoretical νοῦς. If this alternative succeeds, then there may be no need to pronounce the *Nicomachean Ethics* internally inconsistent on this point.[6]

2

Someone might object that another way to resolve the apparent inconsistency is to show that the middle books do not argue that moral virtue is a component of εὐδαιμονία. But this strategy is ruled out when Aristotle's conception of the formal criteria for an ultimate end in *EN* I is combined with the explicit testimony of the middle books themselves; given the correct (i.e., inclusive) account of these criteria, the significant independent value that the middle books attach to moral virtue shows that these books are committed to the view that moral virtue is a component of εὐδαιμονία.

The middle books argue that the φρόνιμος (who knows and deliberates about the ultimate end, or εὐδαιμονία) must choose moral virtue [*EN* 1140a25–28, 1140b7, 1144a36–37]. And since moral virtue is essentially the sort of thing that cannot be chosen simply as a means to some further end, she must choose it at least partly for its own sake [*EN* 1105a28–34, 1127a27–30.][7] Moreover, in his discussion of "good" self-lovers, who attempt to outdo one another in the performance of, e.g., just and temperate acts, Aristotle says that the virtuous agent chooses τὸ καλόν (or the noble, which is common to all the virtues, *EN* 1122b6–7) in preference to all things, and that virtue—which in this context refers at least (if not exclusively) to *moral* virtue—is among the greatest of goods [*EN* 1169a8–31]. Aristotle goes on to argue, on the grounds that friends are the greatest of external goods, that it would be strange to call a friendless

[6] I shall sketch this alternative below but an adequate defense of it lies beyond the scope of this essay.

[7] Since Aristotle distinguishes what is necessary (presumably what is hypothetically necessary or necessary *if* a certain end is to be achieved) both from what is noble or καλόν [*EN* 1120a34–b1, 1155a28–29] and from what is chosen for its own sake [*EN* 1147b23–31, 1176b1–9], I take the following passages in which Aristotle says that virtuous actions are chosen for the sake of τὸ καλόν also to support this claim: *EN* 1115b10–13, b22–24, 1122b6–7. [For discussion of the requirement that the virtuous agent choose virtuous actions "for themselves," see "*Eudaimonia*, External Results, and Choosing Virtuous Actions for Themselves" (Chapter 3, this volume).]

person εὐδαίμων [*EN* 1169b8–10]. But given that internal or psychic goods are better than external ones, it would be even stranger to call someone εὐδαίμων if she lacked moral virtue, which is certainly a great psychic good. And Aristotle confirms this when he claims that, "by however much more someone has all virtue, he is more εὐδαίμων" [*EN* 1117b6–9]. These passages, primarily from non-common middle books, strongly suggest that those books treat moral virtue as a component of εὐδαιμονία.

Nevertheless, someone might attempt to reconcile the significant independent value that these books attach to moral virtue with the claim that contemplation is the sole component of εὐδαιμονία by adopting an exclusive interpretation of *EN* I. On this interpretation, εὐδαιμονία is to be identified with the single most perfect psychic activity—i.e., with contemplation. So as long as contemplation is more perfect than moral virtue or friendship, it will not matter how much independent value Aristotle attaches to these other goods. But Aristotle's account of the formal criteria for an ultimate end tells against this exclusive interpretation.[8]

The first requirement—that an ultimate end be final [τέλειον] or, if there are several final goods, that it be the most final [τελειοτάτην] of these—does not decisively favor either the inclusive or the exclusive interpretation. On the inclusive account, there might be a number of goods (e.g., contemplation and moral virtue) each of which is τέλειον in the sense that it is chosen for its own sake. But if each of these is regarded as a component of εὐδαιμονία, then we might say that none is "most final," because each is also chosen for the sake of εὐδαιμονία. Only εὐδαιμονία is chosen *only* for its own sake and not for the sake of anything else. So it is the most τέλειον good we seek.[9]

On the exclusive account, contemplation might be the τελειοτάτην good we seek because it is the only first-order good that is chosen only for its own sake, while moral virtue is chosen both for its own sake and for the sake of contemplation. On this account, moral virtue might be chosen at least partly for its own sake without thereby being a component of εὐδαιμονία. But as we shall now see, Aristotle's second formal requirement for being an ultimate end—i.e., the self-sufficiency requirement—rules this out.

The self-sufficiency requirement demands that εὐδαιμονία "taken alone makes life choiceworthy and lacking nothing" [*EN* 1097b14–16]. Aristotle explains this by saying that εὐδαιμονία is the most choiceworthy of all goods "not being counted as one among others" [*EN* 1097b17–19]. Although this might be taken exclusively as saying

[8] On these formal requirements I generally follow J. L. Ackrill, "Aristotle on Eudaimonia," *Proceedings of the British Academy* 60 (1974): 339–59; reprinted in A. Rorty (ed.), *Essays on Aristotle's Ethics* (Berkeley: University of California Press, 1980), 15–33.

[9] *See EN* 1097a25–b6 where Aristotle seems to regard being chosen for its own sake as necessary and sufficient for an end's being τέλειον; and being chosen *only* for its own sake as necessary and sufficient for an end's being τελειότατον. This passage allows that there are several τέλειον goods (e.g., honor, pleasure, νοῦς, and every virtue) each of which is τέλειον in the sense that it is chosen for its own sake, but none of which is τελειότατον, because each is also chosen for the sake of εὐδαιμονία (which alone is chosen only for its own sake). So this passage allows that εὐδαιμονία is an inclusive second-order end for the sake of which all the others are chosen.

that, taken apart from the other goods, εὐδαιμονία is the most choiceworthy of all, the next sentence appears to say that if εὐδαιμονία *were* simply one good among others, then the most choiceworthy good *would be* εὐδαιμονία taken together with these other goods.[10] This supports the inclusive interpretation according to which εὐδαιμονία is the most choiceworthy of all goods in the sense that it *includes* all the others.[11]

Aristotle's reference to self-sufficiency [*EN* 1169b5–6] in his account of friendship shows that this requirement (along with the inclusive conception of εὐδαιμονία it supports) lies behind his claim that we would not call a life without friends εὐδαίμων. For that life, no matter how choiceworthy, would be made even more so by the addition of friends. And the same goes for a life without moral virtue. So friendship and moral virtue are basic goods[12] without which a life would *not* be lacking *nothing*, and so would *not* be εὐδαίμων. In this way, *EN* I's account of the formal criteria for an ultimate end supports the middle books' view that moral virtue is a component of εὐδαιμονία.

Cooper accepts this conclusion and argues that Aristotle can avoid it only by rejecting the *Eudemian Ethics*' bipartite conception of human nature. If we are identified exclusively with theoretical intellect, then we shall not choose moral virtue for its own sake or treat it as a basic good. So it will not be a component of εὐδαιμονία.

Cooper's interpretation is important because it differs from most Strict Intellectualist interpretations in not relying on the less plausible exclusive reading of *EN* I.[13] It shows instead how the correct inclusive reading, which is generally taken to oppose Strict

---

[10] It is also possible to read this sentence indicatively and thus as consistent with the exclusive interpretation. See Anthony Kenny, "Happiness," *Proceedings of the Aristotelian Society* 66 (1965–1966): 93–102; and *The Aristotelian Ethics* (Oxford: Clarendon, 1978), 204–5; and S. R. L. Clark, *Aristotle's Man* (Oxford: Oxford University Press, 1975), 153–54. But I agree with Cooper that this passage, along with *Magna Moralia* 1184a34–38, shows that Aristotle takes εὐδαιμονία to be an inclusive second-order end. See Cooper 1975, 122 and his review of Kenny in *Nous* XV, no. 3 (1981): 384–85.

[11] Someone may object that this account of the inclusive view is too expansive on the grounds that it requires us to treat any good that is chosen for its own sake, no matter how trivial, as a component of εὐδαιμονία, and that adopting a more restrictive variant of the inclusive view attributes a more reasonable position to Aristotle. Such a variant would presumably exclude trivial pursuits from the class of components of εὐδαιμονία by restricting the extension of this class in some principled way—e.g., by adding a further requirement (beyond that of being chosen for its own sake) that the components of εὐδαιμονία must satisfy. Some likely candidates for this further requirement are that the components of εὐδαιμονία be καλόν or that they be the actualizations of essentially human psychic capacities. Furthermore, goods satisfying both of these requirements will presumably be "basic goods" without which life would *not* be lacking nothing. So satisfying these requirements will presumably be jointly sufficient for being a component of εὐδαιμονία, which is an inclusive second-order end in the sense that it includes all of these *basic* goods, even if not *all* goods chosen for their own sakes. I cannot now discuss these requirements, but it seems clear to me (for the reasons cited in the second paragraph of this section) that they are satisfied by moral virtue and friendship. So any plausible restriction of the inclusive view must allow that moral virtue is a component of εὐδαιμονία. On this issue, see A. W. Price, "Aristotle's Ethical Holism," *Mind* 89 (1980): 338–52.

[12] See note 11 above.

[13] See W. F. R. Hardie, "The Final Good in Aristotle's Ethics," *Philosophy* 40 (1965): 277–95 and *Aristotle's Ethical Theory* (Oxford: Clarendon, 1968), chap. 2. [I am less confident now, than when I wrote this article, that an exclusive reading of *EN* I should be rejected. For discussion of my current views, see the Introduction to this volume.]

Intellectualism and other monolithic conceptions of εὐδαιμονία, is compatible with such views. Very roughly, εὐδαιμονία can include all intrinsic or basic goods and still be identified exclusively with contemplation, if contemplation is the only intrinsic or basic good Aristotle recognizes. And this will be the only such good he recognizes if Aristotle identifies a person *exclusively* with theoretical νοῦς. In order to see this, we must turn to the function argument. There Aristotle attempts to tie these formal criteria to a substantive conception of εὐδαιμονία by appeal to the human ἔργον.

3

The function argument shows that Cooper's approach is fundamentally correct; Aristotle does take personal identity to determine the components of εὐδαιμονία. But this argument too can be interpreted either inclusively or exclusively.[14] Taken exclusively, Aristotle's conclusion is that εὐδαιμονία is an activity in accordance with the single most perfect psychic virtue. This is generally taken to be theoretical and so to point toward *EN* X where Aristotle says that contemplation is τέλεια εὐδαιμονία [*EN* 1177b24–25]. Taken inclusively, Aristotle's conclusion is that εὐδαιμονία is complete virtue in the sense that it includes *all* of the soul's virtues, moral as well as intellectual.[15] This is generally taken to support the middle books' view that both moral and intellectual virtues are components of εὐδαιμονία.

But here again the inclusive interpretation is compatible with Strict Intellectualism and with other monolithic conceptions of εὐδαιμονία. If a person's soul is simple and has only one capacity or virtue (e.g., theoretical intellect), then even an inclusive interpretation of the function argument will yield Strict Intellectualism.[16]

This reveals a curious feature of Cooper's argument. Although he generally takes the formal requirements for an ultimate end to support an inclusive conception of εὐδαιμονία, Cooper interprets the function argument exclusively and so takes "the best and most final virtue" as a reference to theoretical wisdom that points toward the

---

14 This is a consequence of Aristotle's use of 'τελειοτάτην' (which may mean either "most perfect" or "most complete") in that argument's conclusion that εὐδαιμονία is "an activity of soul in accordance with virtue, and if there are several virtues, in accordance with the best and τελειοτάτην of these" [*EN* 1098a16–18]. On this passage, see note 19 below. [For more on the function argument, see "Aristotle's Function Argument" (Chapter 1, this volume).]

15 This is certainly how Aristotle intends the function argument in *EE* II.1, where he introduces whole-part language and says that the virtue of the soul is composed of the virtues of its parts. He then explicitly refers to both moral and intellectual parts [*EE* 1219a12–1220a6].

16 This is a point about the logic of the argument. But even if an inclusive interpretation of the function argument is formally compatible with Strict Intellectualism, that argument may contain substantive claims that are not compatible with Strict Intellectualism—e.g., it may claim that practical intellect does in fact belong to human nature. See *EN* 1098a3–4. [See also, *EN* 1154b20–31, where Aristotle explicitly says that there is no one thing that is always pleasant for a human being because our nature is not simple. This is an important passage I had not attended to when writing this piece. I quote it in the Introduction to this volume.]

apparent Strict Intellectualism of *EN* X.[17] He thus finds a tension between the inclusive and exclusive conceptions of εὐδαιμονία within Book I itself. But Cooper does not need this exclusive interpretation of the function argument in order to defend his Strict Intellectualist interpretation of *EN* X. For we have just seen that the inclusive interpretation is compatible with Strict Intellectualism if a person is identified exclusively with theoretical νοῦς.

Furthermore, *EN* X's alleged restriction of personal identity to theoretical νοῦς is unnecessary on the exclusive interpretation of the function argument. On that interpretation, it does not matter how many psychic capacities are constitutive of our identity. The important point is that among the activities associated with various capacities, contemplation is the single most perfect activity. In order to explain why Aristotle should regard the identification of a person exclusively with theoretical νοῦς as necessary and relevant to the argument for Strict Intellectualism, we must suppose that he interprets the function argument inclusively.[18] On the inclusive interpretation, the number of capacities constitutive of our identity is directly relevant to the number of activities constitutive of our εὐδαιμονία. So if Aristotle wants to identify εὐδαιμονία with the exercise of a single capacity, he must identify us with a single capacity.[19]

---

[17] Cooper 1975, 100, n. 10.

[18] I take Aristotle's claim that the contemplator qua man chooses to act according to moral virtue to show that qua identified at least partly with practical (and not exclusively with theoretical) νοῦς, the contemplator attaches some independent value to moral virtue and so (on the inclusive account) regards moral virtue as a component of εὐδαιμονία. (See sections 9–10, this chapter.) And I take this to suggest that Aristotle thinks that Strict Intellectualism follows *only if* a person is identified exclusively with theoretical intellect. If this is correct, then Aristotle regards that identification as necessary (and not simply sufficient) for Strict Intellectualism.

[19] Cooper allows that his Strict Intellectualist interpretation of *EN* X does not *require* the exclusive reading of the function argument. But he thinks that this exclusive reading is required by the text; so he thinks that the fact that combining the exclusive reading with the identification of a person exclusively with theoretical νους renders one of these premises idle or redundant is *not* a reason for adopting an inclusive reading of the function argument. I disagree. First, I do not agree that the exclusive reading of that argument is required by Aristotle's use of 'τελειοτάτην' in its conclusion. So given the availability (and on my view the greater plausibility) of the inclusive reading, the fact that this reading allows us to explain why Aristotle seems to think that the identification of a person exclusively with theoretical νοῦς is necessary for Strict Intellectualism *does* provide some reason for preferring the inclusive reading of the function argument. Cooper's arguments for the exclusive reading are far from conclusive. On p. 100, n. 10 he claims (1) that "the contrast between πλείους αἱ ἀρεταί and τὴν ἀρίστην καὶ τελειοτάτην surely does *strongly invite one* to take the 'best and most final excellence' as one among the several particular excellences" (my italics); (2) that "the superlative, by its very nature exclusionary" could refer only to excellence as a whole "in a very special context"; and (3) that "it seems likely that the sense of τελειοτάτη here is in any case a special one introduced earlier in the chapter [*EN* 1097a25–b6] where τελειότατον is explained [a34–b1] as meaning something like 'most having the character of an end.'" I agree with (3) that, if possible, we ought to interpret the superlative of 'τέλειον' similarly in both of its occurrences in *EN* I.7 and that the context of its first occurrence establishes that there at least, 'τελειοτάτην' means "most final" in a sense that requires that something be chosen *only* for its own sake and not for the sake of anything else. But, as Cooper agrees, Aristotle allows even there that εὐδαιμονία taken as an inclusive second-order end is τελειοτάτη in the sense that it is always chosen for its own sake and never for the sake of any of its constituent activities (which are chosen both for their own sakes *and* for the sake of *it*). So this passage, which also contrasts several goods with the most final good [*EN* 1097a30–31], shows that this contrast (although it may "strongly invite us") certainly does not *require* us to take the

4

Cooper defends his claim that *EN* X *does* identify a person exclusively with theoretical νοῦς by appeal to chaps. 7–8 where Aristotle

(1) says that each person seems to be (most of all) his νοῦς [*EN* 1178a2, a9],
(2) distinguishes νοῦς from the (psychophysical) compound [*EN* 1178a14–23],
(3) associates practical wisdom and moral virtue with the compound [*EN* 1178a14–23], and
(4) claims that the virtue of νοῦς is separate [*EN* 1178a22].

Cooper then takes this reference to separability as pointing toward the *De Anima* where Aristotle says that νοῦς and the theoretical faculty seem to be a different kind of soul, which is capable of being separated [*DA* 413b25–27].[20]

This reference to actual separability or the capacity for independent existence is crucial to Cooper's argument.[21] He uses it to argue that the *De Anima* account of human nature differs from the early Eudemian one in recognizing two distinct souls associated with each person. The *De Anima* is thus supposed to raise a new question for Aristotle—namely, with which of his two souls is a person to be identified?[22] Cooper's argument runs roughly as follows:

(5) Aristotle's primary account of the soul in the *De Anima* is hylomorphic; the soul is the form of a certain sort of body and is not actually separable from such a body.
(6) νοῦς and the theoretical faculty belong to or constitute a different kind of soul, which is actually separable from body.
(7) Therefore (by Leibniz' Law), theoretical νοῦς does not belong to the hylomorphic soul.

superlative as referring to "one among the several particular excellences." In other words, this earlier passage creates the "very special context" required if we are to take the superlative in the function argument as referring to excellence as a whole.

20 Cooper 1975, 175–76.

21 Although Aristotle speaks of separability in two ways (sometimes to refer to separability in thought or definition, and sometimes to refer to actual separability or the capacity for independent existence), he is clearly referring to actual separability in this passage. This is plain from his distinction between the way in which νοῦς is separable and the way in which the other psychophysical functions are. The latter are different (or separable) in account—τῷ λογῷ—while νοῦς seems to be separable as the eternal is from the perishable. [I discuss these issues of separability in "Locomotive Soul" (III.5).]

22 Cooper 1975, 176. But Cooper's argument for the non-identity of theoretical νοῦς and the hylomorphic soul does not show that they cannot both be parts of some further compound. In other words, it does not clearly force Aristotle to answer Cooper's question by identifying a person with one or the other of his two souls. Aristotle could instead identify a person with both and so regard him as essentially a compound creature. So although I do not myself think Aristotle associates each person with two souls, I argue in section 9 that his use of the "qua" locution shows that something like the compound view is his answer.

Cooper concludes that each person has two distinct souls—one hylomorphic, the other theoretical. Cooper assigns all of the psychophysical functions (including practical thought) to the hylomorphic soul. He relies on *EN* X's association of φρόνησις (or practical wisdom) with the compound in order to justify assigning it to the hylomorphic rather than the theoretical soul. Cooper then appeals to *EN* X's distinction between νοῦς and the compound in order to justify his claim that when Aristotle identifies a person with νοῦς in *EN* X he identifies him exclusively with theoretical νοῦς. This in turn is supposed to support Strict Intellectualism.

5

In asking whether the *De Anima* supports Cooper, there are two important questions. First, does the *De Anima* argue that any intellectual faculty is actually separable from the psychophysical compound? Second, if the *De Anima* does actually separate any form of intellect, is this theoretical intellect?

There are two passages in which the *De Anima* says that νοῦς is separable.[23] But it is not clear that both passages refer to actual separability or even to the same intellectual faculty. So I shall discuss each in turn.

At *De Anima* 429b4–5 Aristotle says that "the perceptive faculty is not without body, while this (i.e. νοῦς) is separable." But if this passage claims that νοῦς and its activities are actually separable (i.e., capable of *existing* apart) from a body, then it contradicts what Aristotle says elsewhere in the *De Anima*. For at *De Anima* 403a8–10, Aristotle claims that if thought is not without imagination, then it is not possible without a body. And Aristotle subsequently affirms that images (and so imagination) are necessary for thought [*DA* 431a14–17, 432a8–9]. So thought is not possible without a body. How can we reconcile this with Aristotle's claim that νοῦς is separable?[24]

---

[23] *DA* 413b25–27, the passage to which Cooper explicitly refers, says only that νοῦς seems [ἔοικε] to be a different kind of soul that is capable of being separated. The presence of a textual variant makes it unclear whether the scope of 'ἔοικε' covers only the suggestion that νοῦς is a different kind of soul or whether it extends also to the suggestion that νοῦς is separable. But since Aristotle subsequently says that νοῦς *is* separable, there is not much to be gained by pushing for the wider scope. And although Aristotle often uses 'ἔοικε' (and 'δοκεῖ') to state his own convictions, I think the initial clause here (i.e., that it is *not yet clear* concerning the theoretical faculty) confirms my general point that this passage is tentative and cannot be taken as an assertion of Aristotle's considered view. And as I argue in the text, the subsequent passage to which this refers discusses only active intellect.

[24] Someone might try to reconcile these passages by arguing that *De Anima* 429b4–5 refers to the faculty (rather than to the activity) of thought, while *De Anima* 431a14–17 and 432a8–9 refer to the activity of thought. She could then claim that Aristotle believes that the faculty of νοῦς can *exist*, but cannot *function* or think, apart from a body. But I do not think this interpretation is plausible, given Aristotle's commitment to the homonymy principle (i.e., the principle that for any *F* that is functionally defined, an *F* that cannot perform the characteristic function or activity of an *F* thing is not a genuine *F* but is only homonymously *F*). See, e.g., *Metaphysics* (*Met.*) 1035b23–25; *DA* 412b14–15, 21–23; *Parts of Animals* 640b34–641a8; *Politics* 1253a21–24. For if νοῦς is functionally defined (i.e., defined by its capacity for thought), then the homonymy principle suggests that νοῦς can exist (as νοῦς) apart from a body *only if*

One possibility is to argue that *De Anima* 429b4–5 refers not to actual separability, but rather to separability in account or definition.[25] On this view, *De Anima* 429b4–5 claims that νοῦς is separable λογῷ from body, while the perceptive faculty is not. And since definitions are of essences [*Topics* 101b37–102a2] and those things which must be mentioned in the definition of a thing are parts of its essence, this amounts to saying that the perceptive faculty is *essentially* embodied, while νοῦς is not. But this leaves open the possibility that being embodied is a necessary condition for the existence of νοῦς; so it allows us to honor Aristotle's claim that thought, being dependent upon imagination, is not possible without a body.[26]

Aristotle confirms this interpretation in *De Anima* I.1 where he discusses affections such as anger, desire, and perceiving in general. He says that these πάθη are enmattered forms [λόγοι ἐνύλοι] and must be defined as such; anger, e.g., is "a certain movement of a certain kind of body or of some part or capacity <of such a body> by this <cause> for the sake of this" [*DA* 403a24–27]. These πάθη cannot be defined without reference to bodily processes and so are *essentially* embodied. Similarly, the perceptual (and most other psychic) capacities are the actualities of various bodily organs and must be defined as such; sight, e.g., is the actuality of an eye.[27] But νοῦς is not the actuality of any bodily organ; there is no organ of thought [*DA* 429a25–27]. Nevertheless, because thought depends on imagination, it is not possible without a body. So thought and νοῦς are only necessarily and not essentially embodied. Although they can be defined without reference to bodies, they cannot exist apart from a body.

Cooper, however, needs an intellectual faculty that is actually separable from body. For he wants to argue from the actual separability of νοῦς to the conclusion that νοῦς cannot belong to the hylomorphic soul. But this does not require Cooper to deny the foregoing dependence of thought on body. And he appears to acknowledge that dependence while taking it to apply only to passive and not to active intellect. This suggests that Cooper relies on the second passage in which the *De Anima* says that νοῦς is separable—that is, on the account of active intellect in *De Anima* III.5.[28]

---

it can function or think apart from a body. So this principle justifies my moves from claims about the inseparability of *thought* to claims about the inseparability of *intellect*.

[25] See note 22 above.

[26] Aristotle distinguishes the essential properties of a thing (which must be mentioned in its definition) from necessary properties—i.e., properties that a thing must have if it is to exist but that need not be mentioned in its definition. See his account of καθ' αὑτά συμβεβήκοτα at *Met.* 1025a30–34.

[27] See *Met.* 1036b21–32 where Aristotle argues that men, unlike mathematical objects, cannot be defined without reference to (perceptible) matter. See also *Met.* 1025b34–1026a6 and *DA* 403a25–b9 where he argues that the study of the soul (either of all of it or of most parts of it) is the business of the physicist whose definitions refer both to form and to matter. [I discuss these issues in "Metasubstance" (III.4]).]

[28] Cooper does not explicitly identify theoretical with active intellect. But his explicit appeal to *De Anima* 413b25–27 (which is similar in language and thought, especially in its contrast between the eternal and the perishable, to the account of active intellect in *De Anima* III.5) suggests that he implicitly relies on this identification. Moreover, his claim (1975, 176) that passive νοῦς "seems to connect even some intuitive thinking with the body" suggests that he takes the theoretical faculty to be separable from body in a way in which passive intellect is not. So the only plausible candidate seems to be active intellect.

This brief account of active intellect is one of the most controversial passages in all of Aristotle, but most commentators agree that Aristotle takes active intellect to be actually separable from body. Fortunately, there is no need to decide this issue here. Once we turn to the second question (i.e., whether the *De Anima* separates theoretical intellect), the actual separability of active νοῦς becomes irrelevant. For Aristotle does not identify theoretical with active νοῦς.

6

Cooper's primary motivation for taking the distinction between theoretical and practical intellect to be coextensive with that between active and passive intellect is to support his conclusion that theoretical intellect is separable from psychophysical activity in a way in which practical intellect is not. The *De Anima* presents two general arguments against this conclusion—one according to which theoretical and practical thought are similarly separable from the psychophysical compound and one according to which they are similarly dependent upon that compound.

The first argument rests on Aristotle's claim that there is no organ of thought [*DA* 429a25–27]. This does not show that theoretical thought is separable from psychophysical activity in a way in which practical thought is not.[29] For Aristotle's claim that there is no organ of thought does not distinguish theoretical from practical thought and so presumably covers both. Nor does it distinguish active from passive intellect. As argued above, Aristotle's point here is that thought in general is separable from the body in the sense that bodily activity is not a component or part of the essence of intellectual activity. This leaves open the possibility that bodily activity is a necessary condition of at least some kinds of thought. So perhaps Cooper can distinguish theoretical from practical thought by arguing that bodily activity is a necessary condition only of practical and not also of theoretical thought.

The second argument, however, provides general reasons for thinking that bodily activity is a necessary condition even for theoretical thought. Aristotle suggests two ways in which thought is dependent upon psychophysical activity, each of which seems to apply equally to practical and to theoretical thought. First, Aristotle suggests that concept acquisition is dependent on perception [*Posterior Analytics* I.18]; and perception is a psychophysical activity. Since it is reasonable to suppose that both theoretical and practical thought involve the use of concepts, we may conclude that they are similarly dependent upon the perceptual activities of the psychophysical compound.[30]

[29] Pace Cooper 1975, 175, n. 29, *DA* 429a25–27 is cited as evidence for the separability of *theoretical* intellect in particular.

[30] Here someone might object that although practical thought requires the use of concepts that must be acquired through perception, theoretical thought does not. But the mathematical example in *Posterior Analytics* I.18's argument that concept acquisition is dependent on perception suggests that Aristotle would not agree. Someone might also object that the fact that the gods can engage in θεωρία shows that perception is not necessary for theoretical thought. (A similar objection might be raised to my next point that images are necessary for theoretical thought.) But this shows only that perception and

Second, Aristotle claims that images are necessary for thought [*DA* 431a14–17, 432a8–9]. Since there is no evidence that he intends to restrict this claim to practical thought, we must assume that it covers theoretical thought as well.[31] Given Aristotle's claim that if thought is not without imagination then it is not possible without a body, we must conclude that neither theoretical nor practical thought is possible without a body. If active intellect is actually separable from body, then theoretical cannot be identified with active intellect.

7

So far the *De Anima* does not seem to support Cooper by separating theoretical intellect from the activities of the psychophysical compound in a way in which it does not also separate practical intellect. This suggests that psychophysical activity is a necessary condition, but not part of the essence, of thought in general. However, the *De Anima* and *EN* X do recognize a distinction between theoretical and practical thought that shows how practical, but not theoretical, thought might be essentially related to the psychophysical compound.

The *De Anima* argues that theoretical and practical thought are distinguished primarily by their ends and secondarily by their objects. The *Nicomachean Ethics* agrees. Theoretical intellect contemplates invariable things [*EN* 1139a6–8] and is concerned with no end beyond itself [*EN* 1177bl9–21]. But practical intellect is concerned with variable things [*EN* 1139a6–8] and is essentially a deliberative or calculative faculty [*EN* 1139a11–15]. Furthermore, Aristotle appeals to the distinction between their objects to argue that the parts of soul associated with theoretical and practical thought must themselves differ in kind [*EN* 1139a8–11]. This suggests that we can interpret the *Nicomachean Ethics* internally—i.e., without appeal to the *De Anima*.

Aristotle's views about the objects of practical intellect explain why *EN* X associates practical wisdom and moral virtue with the psychophysical compound. They show how practical thought may be related to this compound in a way in which theoretical thought is not. For Aristotle believes that practical thought is specifically concerned with human goods [*EN* 1140b20–21]—i.e., with things that are just and noble and good for human beings [*EN* 1143b19–23]. And the objects of practical thought (e.g., what is the courageous or temperate thing to do) require reference to the affections of a psychophysical compound in a way in which the objects of theoretical thought (e.g., god and the celestial bodies) do not. For example, courage is a mean with respect to fear

imagination are *not essential* to theoretical thought. It does *not* show that they are *not necessary* for the theoretical thought *of some creatures*. For the fact that the gods do not need nourishment in order to contemplate does not show that nourishment is not a necessary condition for *our* theoretical activity.

[31] This assumption is confirmed at *DA* 432a8–9 where Aristotle claims that whenever someone contemplates [θεωρῇ], he contemplates some image. And the mathematical example of *De Memoria* 449b30 supports this.

and confidence [*EN* 1107a33] and these (i.e., fear and confidence) are (according to *DA* 403a16–24) psychophysical affections. Similarly, temperance is a mean with respect to (bodily) pleasures [*EN* 1117b24–25, 1118a1–3]. And virtue in general is concerned with the actions and affections (and especially with the pleasures and pains) of a psychophysical compound [*EN* 1104b13–16]. So practical intellect, insofar as it is concerned with moral virtues and human goods, is concerned with such actions and affections.

Furthermore, practical intellect is not just concerned with moral virtue or the human good in general; practical intellect is essentially deliberative; and since no one deliberates about things that it is not possible for him to do [*EN* 1140a30–33], practical intellect is essentially concerned with what is just and noble for itself to do [*EN* 1140a25–28]. In other words, practical intellect is essentially concerned with the actions and affections of the psychophysical compound to which it belongs.[32] And in order for practical intellect to deliberate about what it is to do, it must have a body capable of acting on its decisions. Aristotle evidently recognizes this when he says that if practical intellect (which is a reasoning faculty concerned with desires and affections) belongs essentially to a human being, then he must also possess these parts (i.e., desires and affections) [*EE* 1219b40–1220a2].

This suggests that even if practical thought is not the actuality of any bodily organ, the activities of the psychophysical compound are not simply necessary conditions of practical thought, but rather essential to it. By contrast, psychophysical activity is only a necessary condition for human theoretical thought. This account of the distinction between theoretical and practical thought does not (as the *Nicomachean Ethics* does not) require the actual separability of theoretical intellect. Hence it need not be defended by appeal to the *De Anima*, since it finds support in the middle books of the *Nicomachean Ethics*. This is important, for the *De Anima* would not obviously support the actual separability of theoretical intellect.

Furthermore, *EN* X itself seems to deny that human theoretical thought is actually separable from psychophysical activity. The contemplator, like everyone else, will need the things necessary for life [*EN* 1177a28–29, 1178a25–26]. Human nature is not self-sufficient for contemplation, but needs bodily health, nourishment, and other aids

[32] This appeal to indexicality is important and shows why gods do not have practical thought. However, if theoretical and practical νοῦς are simply two aspects of a single faculty (i.e., the same faculty contemplating different objects) then it looks as though gods would have practical νοῦς if only they had bodies. This in turn may seem to suggest that my νοῦς is only accidentally practical and could, qua theoretical, exist apart from my compound. In this case it would not follow that my νοῦς is essentially concerned with what is beneficial for that compound, for it is only accidentally something that is essentially concerned with the affections of a psychophysical compound. But Aristotle can reply that even if the νοῦς that happens to be yours is only accidentally practical, *your* νοῦς is not. For human νοῦς is essentially something bipartite—i.e., both theoretical and practical. See *EN* 1159a5–12 where Aristotle says that the reason we do not wish a friend to become a god is that we wish a friend good for his own sake, and a necessary condition of his receiving any good is that he remains *what* he essentially is—i.e., a man. Aristotle is evidently saying that we cannot wish for Socrates' sake that he should become a god (i.e., a pure theoretical intellect); for he, Socrates, would not survive that change.

[*EN* 1178b33–35]. Aristotle clearly thinks that bodily and external goods are necessary conditions for exercising both theoretical and moral virtues.

But he also thinks that there is an important difference between these two types of virtue with respect to bodily and external goods. Contemplation is separable in thought or account. This means that unlike the activities of moral virtue, contemplation does not essentially involve bodily or external goods such as strength and wealth. The liberal or just person will need wealth not simply because wealth is a necessary condition for exercising liberality or justice, but rather because these virtues are essentially concerned with wealth. Liberality, e.g., is a mean concerning the giving and taking *of wealth* [*EN* 1120b27–28]. The contemplator, however, will have no need of such things *for his activity* [*EN* 1178b3–4]. This restriction to things needed for his activity is significant.[33] It confirms the claim that theoretical thought is not actually separable from psychophysical activity. But contemplation is separable in thought or account because it (unlike temperance or liberality) can be defined without reference to bodily or external goods.

8

Here it is important to note that Strict Intellectualism does not generally require the actual separability of any intellectual function. Cooper's argument for Strict Intellectualism requires actual separability only because of the way in which he attempts to derive the existence of two distinct souls by appeal to Leibniz' Law. But this is peculiar to Cooper's argument and we must not conclude that Strict Intellectualism itself requires actual separability. There are other arguments for identifying a person with νοῦς and other ways of defending Strict Intellectualism—e.g., the teleological argument of the *Protrepticus*.[34]

Aristotle himself is reluctant to allow the case for or against Strict Intellectualism to rest on the actual separability of any intellectual function. He says that it makes no difference to the present inquiry whether the rational and nonrational parts of the soul are distinct as parts of the body are, or whether they are two in thought but inseparable by nature, just as the convex and the concave [*EN* 1102a28–32].[35]

---

[33] See section 10 below.

[34] The *Protrepticus* contains a teleological argument for Strict Intellectualism that does not rest on a sharp distinction between theoretical and practical intellect or on the actual separability of either function. This is not the only evidence of Intellectualism in Aristotle's earlier works. See especially *EE* 1249a21–b23 (and the similar passage at *EN* 1145a7–14), whose apparent Intellectualism Cooper 1975 (135–43) tries to explain away. These passages, along with the *Protrepticus*, suggest that Cooper's genetic account is mistaken. Intellectualism is not a late development in Aristotle's thought. If the argument of *Nicomachean Ethics* X does rest on the mature psychology of the *De Anima*, this psychology is not the source of Aristotle's Intellectualism but simply provides a new argument for it.

[35] [I make much of this "no difference" claim in other places: see sec. 5 of "Locomotive Soul" (III.5) and sec. 3 of "Hylomorphic Virtue" (III.6).]

What matters is which parts of the soul belong to the essence of a person and which are simply necessary conditions of her existence. Even if actual separability fails, Aristotle can still defend Strict Intellectualism by identifying a person exclusively with her theoretical νοῦς and arguing that the other psychophysical functions are simply necessary conditions of her existence.

Aristotle evidently recognizes this connection between Intellectualism and the identification of a person with theoretical νοῦς in *EN* X when he says that, if (theoretical) νοῦς is μάλιστα [most of all or exclusively][36] what each person is, then the contemplative life will be most εὐδαίμων [*EN* 1178a6–8]. So far, Aristotle's conclusion is only conditional: if theoretical νοῦς is exclusively (or most of all) what a human being is, then contemplation will be the sole (or the dominant) component of εὐδαιμονία.[37]

But Aristotle subsequently claims that the contemplator will choose to act according to moral virtue insofar as he is human—i.e., in so far as he is identified at least partly with practical and not exclusively with theoretical νοῦς [*EN* 1178b5–8]. Here Aristotle suggests that Strict Intellectualism follows only if a person is identified exclusively with theoretical and not also with practical νοῦς.[38] This, in conjunction with *EN* 1178a9, suggests that Aristotle is committed to the following biconditional: contemplation is the sole component of εὐδαιμονία if and only if a person is identified exclusively with theoretical νοῦς. So the important question is, does *EN* X identify a person exclusively with theoretical νοῦς?[39]

---

36 'μάλιστα' need not be taken exclusively here, for Aristotle sometimes distinguishes being μάλιστα *F* (i.e., primarily *F*) from being μόνον *F* (i.e., only or exclusively *F*). See *Met.* 1039a19–20 and *Protrepticus* 62. See also *EN* 1168b3–4 where Aristotle says that the virtuous man and the best sort of friend is μάλιστα a lover of himself. [I discuss this passage in section 4 of "Self-Love and Authoritative Virtue" (Chapter 4, this volume).] Because Aristotle seeks here to derive the virtuous person's friendly attitudes toward others from such attitudes toward herself, he *cannot* be using 'μάλιστα' here in its exclusive sense. And the very possibility of taking it nonexclusively here shows that even if Aristotle does affirm the antecedent of this conditional, he may not be identifying a person *exclusively* with theoretical νοῦς. In that case, then instead of advocating *Strict* Intellectualism (i.e., the view that contemplation is the *sole* component of εὐδαιμονία), he may be advocating some version of *Moderate* Intellectualism (i.e., the view that contemplation is the *dominant* component of εὐδαιμονία). But I cannot discuss all of these possibilities here. I mention them only to alert the reader that things are not as simple as Cooper and I sometimes make them seem.

37 Ross translates 'εἴπερ' here as 'since' rather than as 'if,' but I believe that there are reasons for preferring 'if.' First, as I argue in section 9 below, Aristotle seems to deny in the very next chapter that we are identified exclusively with theoretical intellect. And while this denial may be compatible with reading 'since' here *if* we take 'μάλιστα' nonexclusively, it is certainly incompatible with reading 'since' if we take 'μάλιστα' exclusively. Furthermore, reading 'if' rather than 'since' and then arguing that Aristotle denies the antecedent of this conditional allows us to reconcile *EN* X with the middle books, and so to provide a consistent interpretation of the *Nicomachean Ethics* as a whole. That itself is a reason for preferring 'if.'

38 It is important that Aristotle accepts this additional claim that the identification of a person with theoretical νοῦς is *necessary* for Strict Intellectualism. Otherwise, showing that Aristotle rejects this identification would not be sufficient to show that he rejects Strict Intellectualism in *EN* X. See note 18 above and section 10 below.

39 There are many passages outside of *EN* X that suggest that practical intellect is part of the human essence and so that Aristotle does not identify a person exclusively with theoretical νοῦς—e. g., the function argument's suggestion that practical reason is the distinctive (or ἴδιον) capacity of man. (See

9

Aristotle's claim that the contemplator qua man will choose to act according to virtue is significant. Given the contrast between νοῦς and ἄνθρωπος, it suggests that Aristotle does not identify the contemplator exclusively with theoretical νοῦς but thinks that she is also a human being and so partially identified with practical νοῦς and its associated compound. Here, as elsewhere, Aristotle uses the "qua" locution to indicate that he is not talking about two separate things, but about two aspects of a single subject—the contemplator qua νοῦς and the contemplator qua human being.[40]

But someone might object that Aristotle's reference to the contemplator qua human does not show that Aristotle identifies a person at least partially with practical νοῦς and its associated compound and not exclusively with theoretical νοῦς. For although Aristotle generally uses the "qua" locution to pick out two aspects of a single subject, these aspects need not be constitutive of that subject's identity. The "qua" locution may also pick out an accidental feature, as in the claim that Callias qua musician needs to develop a sense of rhythm. This does not show that Callias is essentially a musician. Nor does a reference to the contemplator qua human show that the contemplator is essentially human or that practical intellect is part of her essence and not simply a necessary condition of her existence. For the contemplator qua having a body needs nourishment, but the nutritive faculty is not part of her essence. Nor, in turn, is nutrition a component of her εὐδαιμονία. Similarly, Cooper argues that Aristotle's claim that the contemplator qua human needs to act according to virtue does not show that the contemplator is being identified with a human being, or that moral virtue is a component of her εὐδαιμονία.[41]

Here we must distinguish two ways in which Aristotle might intend the contrast between the contemplator qua νοῦς and the contemplator qua human. First, he may be contrasting being human with something distinct from and not included in the human essence. (Let's call this the "transcendental" account.) Second, he may be contrasting a whole (i.e., being human) with some part of it (i.e., having theoretical νοῦς). (Let's call this the "holistic" account.) On the holistic account, but not on the transcendental one, having divine theoretical νοῦς is part of the human essence.

Coherence favors the holistic account. For the transcendental account requires us to say that *EN* X abandons the central project of *EN* I, which is to investigate the highest human good. That account not only undermines the Strict Intellectualist's attempt to connect the "best and most τέλειον" virtue of the function argument with the contemplative virtue of *EN* X, but also threatens the unity of the *Nicomachean Ethics* as a whole. But *EN* X itself refers back to the function argument [at *EN* 1176a3–4] and

---

EN 1098a3–4 and *EE* 1219b26–31.) But since Cooper thinks that *EN* X represents a departure from this view, I cannot appeal to these passages; so I focus in what follows on evidence from *EN* X itself.

[40] See *Met.* 1078a23–26 and *EN* 1161b5–6.

[41] Cooper 1975, 165.

EN X.6 clearly resumes Book I's discussion of εὐδαιμονία. Aristotle is still seeking the "end of human things" [*EN* 1176a30–32] and he says explicitly that the life according to moral virtue is εὐδαίμων because the activities according to moral virtue are human [*EN* 1178a9–10]. Given the availability of the holistic account, it is difficult to justify adopting the transcendental one.

Nevertheless, some commentators believe that the transcendental account is required by Aristotle's claim that it is not qua human, but rather qua having something divine in him that a man will live the contemplative life [*EN* 1177b27–28].[42] These commentators also think that the transcendental account is required by Aristotle's injunction that we ignore those who tell us to think human thoughts and that we strive as far as possible to imitate the immortals. On their account, we must conclude that for some reason or other—perhaps owing to the mature psychology of the *De Anima*—*EN* X abandons the naturalistic project of *EN* I and argues that it is not our *human* nature that determines the components of εὐδαιμονία.

But the foregoing passages do not require the transcendental account. For Aristotle may be using 'human' in either of two ways and the transcendental account is required only if he is using 'human' in the broad sense in which it refers to anything that belongs to the human essence whether or not that thing also belongs to the divine (or to any other) essence.[43] But 'human' can also be used in a narrow sense to refer to what belongs exclusively to the human essence and not to anything else. This narrow sense allows us to interpret Aristotle as claiming that it is not insofar as we have *merely* human capacities (i.e., capacities belonging *only* to humans) that we shall achieve the contemplative life, but only insofar as divine theoretical intellect is part of our (broad) human essence. Similarly, Aristotle's apparent injunction to maximize contemplation need not be interpreted as claiming that we ought not think any human thoughts or that we should not attach any independent value to moral virtue. He may be saying only that we should not restrict ourselves to merely human thoughts and activities, but should remember that theoretical intellect is also part of our (broad) human essence and so that contemplation is also a component of εὐδαιμονία.[44] And this would not be pointless, given that Aristotle has just devoted nine books primarily to the distinctively human moral virtues.

Because these passages do not require the transcendental account, we ought to prefer the holistic one. For it preserves *EN* X's connection with the function argument and also offers some hope of reconciling *EN* X with the middle books' commitment to moral virtue.[45] The holistic account identifies a human being at least partly with

[42] H. H. Joachim, *Aristotle: The Nicomachean Ethics* (Oxford: Clarendon, 1951), 50.

[43] See Richard Kraut, "The Peculiar Function of Human Beings," *Canadian Journal of Philosophy* IX, no. 3 (1979): 469–71. Fred Miller has pointed out to me a similar inconsistency in Cooper's use of "human being" to refer on p. 165 to "the human being" with which the theorizer "refuses to identify himself" and in his claim (on p. 174) that "Aristotle here means to identify a human being with his mind."

[44] This account would support the possibility that Aristotle is comparing the mixed contemplative life with the purely political or moral life and recommending the former over the latter. See possibility (c) in note 3 above.

[45] See sections 10–11 below.

her practical intellect and so rejects the exclusive identification with theoretical νοῦς required by Strict Intellectualism.[46] The contemplator qua human—i.e., qua identified at least partly with practical intellect—will choose to act according to moral virtue. This concludes my main argument that *EN* X does not defend Strict Intellectualism by identifying a person exclusively with her theoretical νοῦς.

10

At this point, someone might concede that *EN* X does not identify a person exclusively with theoretical νοῦς, but still think that *EN* X is committed to Strict Intellectualism. She may object that Aristotle's claim that the contemplator qua human chooses to act according to moral virtue does not show that the contemplator qua human is supposed to attach any independent value to moral virtue or to regard moral virtue as a component of εὐδαιμονία. In other words, someone might reject my claim that this passage shows that Strict Intellectualism follows only if we are identified exclusively with theoretical intellect. For one might, like Cooper, argue that the contemplator qua human chooses to act according to moral virtue for entirely instrumental reasons.

Cooper recognizes that this is incompatible with actually being morally virtuous, for that requires choosing such actions for their own sakes. So Cooper appeals to Aristotle's distinction between doing acts such as the virtuous person would do and actually being morally virtuous [*EN* 1105b5–9]. Cooper then says that although Aristotle allows that his contemplator may perform virtuous actions, "Aristotle conspicuously avoids saying that his theorizer will be a virtuous person."[47] On this account, the contemplator qua human will choose to do acts such as the virtuous person would do. But she will do so only for instrumental reasons and so will not regard moral virtue as a component of her εὐδαιμονία.

This view assumes an analogy between the contemplator's choice of the bodily and external goods necessary for life and her choice of the goods associated with moral virtue; the contemplator must choose both simply because they are necessary for her successful pursuit of contemplation. So she must choose both as instrumental means to her ultimate end, which is to maximize contemplation.

But immediately before saying that contemplator qua human chooses to act according to moral virtue, Aristotle distinguishes the external goods required for exercising moral virtue from those which are necessary for life and describes the former as "impediments" to contemplation [*EN* 1178b3–5]. Aristotle nevertheless goes on to say that the contemplator qua human and living with others will choose to act according to moral virtue and so will need such goods for being human (πρὸς τὸ ἀνθρωπεύεσθαι)

---

[46] This allows Aristotle's identification of a person with his νοῦς in *EN* X to agree with the similar identifications in *EN* IX [at 1166a10–23 and at 1168b28–1169a3], where Aristotle seems to include practical νοῦς in the νοῦς with which a person is being identified.

[47] Cooper 1975, 164.

[*EN* 1178b5–7]. In other words, although the contemplator does not need such goods for her activity [*EN* 1178b3–4], and although such goods are actually impediments to her activity, she will nevertheless need such goods in order to act according to moral virtue. But this raises an awkward question for Cooper: if the external goods required for moral virtue (or for Cooper's pseudo-virtue) are not necessary for contemplation and are in fact impediments to it, why does the contemplator qua human choose to do actions (whether virtuous or only pseudo-virtuous) that require her to have such goods?

Two possible replies suggest themselves at once. First, the contemplator qua human may choose to do these actions because these actions themselves promote her contemplation. Given that she lives in society, she finds that occasionally performing actions such as the virtuous person would do contributes to the maximization of her contemplation; people will leave her alone and some may even fund her research. But if this is Aristotle's answer, then it becomes more difficult to see why Aristotle should describe having the external goods required for performing such actions as impediments to contemplation. On this account, these goods should rather be assimilated to the goods necessary for life. Though not essentially related to contemplation itself, both types of good ultimately contribute to contemplation by providing the necessary (or optimal) conditions for it. But in that case it is hard to see how Aristotle could describe such goods as *impediments* to contemplation.

This suggests that we turn instead to the second possible reply—namely, that the contemplator qua human chooses to perform actions according to moral virtue for some independent reason (i.e., for some reason apart from their promoting her contemplation). She may choose to perform them for their own sakes or—less probably—for the sake of something else (besides contemplation) that she values for *its* own sake. So she will need these goods (which are admittedly impediments to contemplation) because they enable her to achieve something else that she values for its own sake. This something else is presumably moral virtue itself (perhaps including friendship). For Aristotle certainly regards moral virtue as worth choosing for its own sake and as more so than any of the available candidates besides contemplation (e.g., pleasure, honor, wealth). In this case then, the contemplator qua human thinks that what she gains from acting according to virtue compensates for the impediments to contemplation incurred by having the goods required by such action. This more plausible reply suggests that qua human, the contemplator attaches some independent value to moral virtue.

Now the conclusion that the contemplator qua human attaches some independent value to moral virtue is compatible with Strict Intellectualism on the exclusive account. On this account, the contemplator can pursue moral virtue both for its own sake and for the sake of contemplation. So contemplation is the ultimate end because it is the only thing pursued only for its own sake and never as a means.[48] But this account is unavailable to us. For we have seen that the inclusive account is required by

[48] This exclusive account may help to make sense of Cooper's claim that the contemplator will perform morally virtuous actions without actually being morally virtuous. On this account, the contemplator

Aristotle's conception of the formal requirements for an ultimate end, especially the self-sufficiency requirement. And on the inclusive account, anything that is pursued for its own sake (or any basic good)[49] must be a component of εὐδαιμονία.

Since Aristotle thinks both that the external goods required for moral virtue are impediments to contemplation and that the contemplator qua man nevertheless chooses to act according to moral virtue, he must think that the contemplator qua human at least sometimes chooses moral virtue for its own sake and in spite of its incumbent impediments to contemplation. In other words, the contemplator qua identified at least partly with practical (and not exclusively with theoretical) νοῦς will attach some independent value to moral virtue. So given the inclusive account of εὐδαιμονία, she will regard moral virtue as a component of εὐδαιμονία.

11

Much remains to be said about how Aristotle thinks it is possible to combine the pursuit of moral and intellectual virtues within a single life.[50] I shall conclude for the time being with a few brief and programmatic remarks.

---

will sometimes pursue moral virtue for the sake of contemplation (e.g., she will restrict her appetites so that they do not interfere with contemplation), while there will be other occasions when she pursues moral virtue for its own sake. Because contemplation is her ultimate end, these will only be occasions on which the requirements of moral virtue do not compete with the maximization of contemplation. She may, e.g., value doing something for a friend for its own sake whenever the library is closed. Because such a person will ordinarily be unreliable in her pursuit of moral virtue, she will fail to satisfy the requirement that the morally virtuous person act from a fixed and unalterable character.

Here someone may object that someone who pursues moral virtue for its own sake whenever the library is closed, every Monday and Friday, or according to any other fixed principle, will satisfy the fixed and unalterability requirement. But Aristotle's discussion of the stability [βεβαιότης] of virtue—especially the conclusion that the virtuous person will *never* do hateful and base things [at *EN* 1100b34–35]—suggests that Aristotle would not agree with this objection. If this is correct, then the exclusive account allows us to make sense of Cooper's claim that the contemplator will perform virtuous actions without actually being morally virtuous. But the exclusive account is unavailable to us for the reasons discussed in my main text.

[49] See note 11 above.

[50] Some commentators question whether Aristotle thinks it *is* possible to combine the pursuit of moral and intellectual virtue within a single life. The pursuit of each may seem so demanding that neither leaves time or energy for the other. So *EN* X may simply express Aristotle's frustration at attempting to find a satisfactory combination. He may be claiming that because we are essentially bipartite, and because meeting the demands of each part of our nature is incompatible with meeting those of the other, we must choose between two lives—one devoted primarily (or perhaps exclusively) to contemplation, and the other devoted primarily (or perhaps exclusively) to moral virtue. And although there is little evidence that Aristotle believed the requirements of moral virtue to be so consuming, there are other reasons for rejecting this view. It is important to notice that, given the inclusive account, the choice between these two lives will be painful in the sense that either way we choose, we must sacrifice something which, given our nature, we value for its own sake and so regard as a component of εὐδαιμονία. This shows that neither choice would leave us with something that fully satisfies the completeness and self-sufficiency requirements. So neither choice would allow us to achieve genuine εὐδαιμονία. If this interpretation is correct, then Aristotle's point will be that εὐδαιμονία is beyond our reach—but not, as usually supposed, because our physical and emotional natures prevent us from contemplating continuously. If Aristotle thinks we cannot achieve εὐδαιμονία it is only because we are

Aristotle's apparent injunction to maximize contemplation [*EN* 1177b31–1178a1] might seem to indicate that he thinks that intellectual virtue is dominant and may sometimes be justifiably pursued at the expense of moral virtue. This, however, seems to be no less objectionable than Strict Intellectualism, and worse yet it seems equally difficult to reconcile with the middle books' commitment to moral virtue, according to which the virtuous man will act from a fixed and unalterable character and will never do base and hateful things [*EN* 1100b34–35]. But this is not the only available interpretation.

There is an alternative interpretation that appeals directly to Aristotle's use of the "qua" locution in order to qualify the worrisome injunction to maximize contemplation.[51] On this account, the contemplator qua having theoretical νοῦς will do as much as possible to maximize contemplation, while the contemplator qua human and having practical νοῦς will choose moral virtue. Because the goods required for exercising moral virtue are impediments to contemplation, she must be choosing moral virtue for its own sake and thus (on the inclusive account) as a component of her εὐδαιμονία. But since she is essentially human and does not stop being human when she is maximizing contemplation, the contemplator qua human will consistently act according to moral virtue. In other words, she will satisfy the criteria for actually being morally virtuous.

In this way the "as far as possible" restriction on Aristotle's injunction to maximize contemplation may be taken to include moral as well as physical, mental, and external restrictions. Aristotle may thus be recommending that we maximize contemplation to whatever extent is consistent not only with our physical natures, but also with the life of practical reason and moral virtue. But this is just the view that Cooper finds both in the *Eudemian Ethics* and in the middle books of the *Nicomachean Ethics*. There Cooper attributes to Aristotle the view that "once moral virtue is securely entrenched, then intellectual goods are allowed to predominate."[52] If this alternative account succeeds, then there will be no need to find the *Nicomachean Ethics* internally inconsistent on this point.

This interpretation raises one further question. In arguing that we ought to maximize contemplation only once the requirements of moral virtue have been satisfied, is Aristotle conceding that moral virtue is dominant? The answer will depend on how Aristotle thinks of moral virtue and what would satisfy its requirements. If Aristotle were a consequentialist and thought that moral virtue required the maximization of some moral value, then he would evidently be giving moral virtue absolute priority over intellectual virtue. But if Aristotle views morality as a set of minimal side

limited in ways that prevent us from fully realizing both our moral and our intellectual capacities. But since Aristotle seems to think that εὐδαιμονία can be achieved [*EN* 1095a16–17; *Pol.* 1328a38–40], we ought to reject this interpretation.

[51] Here I follow Keyt 1978.

[52] Cooper 1975, 143. This is the view that Keyt calls "the superstructure view."

constraints within which we must maximize contemplation, then intellectual value may still be dominant. But these alternatives are not exhaustive and I cannot resolve this issue here. The important point is that whether or not moral virtue is dominant, it is nevertheless a component of εὐδαιμονία. Aristotle evidently agrees with our initial objection that there is more to εὐδαιμονία than contemplation.[53]

[53] I have learned much in discussing these issues with J. L. Ackrill, Richard Boyd, Myles Burnyeat, and Phil Mitsis, and from the written comments of Fred Miller Jr., John Cooper, Jay Tate, and an anonymous referee. I am especially grateful to Leon Galis and Terry Irwin for their sustained criticism and encouragement.

3

Eudaimonia, External Results, and Choosing Virtuous Actions for Themselves

ARISTOTLE IS COMMITTED to several familiar claims the conjunction of which threatens—at least on standard interpretations—to cast Aristotle's virtuous agents in a morally unattractive light. These claims, and their standard interpretations, run roughly as follows.

First, there is the "eudaimonist axiom" according to which all things are chosen (or ought to be chosen) for the sake of eudaimonia.[1] Most commentators take this axiom to refer primarily, if not exclusively, to the agent's *own* eudaimonia; the eudaimonia of others is typically included, if at all, only as *part* of the agent's own.[2] So the eudaimonist axiom is standardly interpreted as claiming that an agent chooses (or ought to choose) all things for the sake of her *own* eudaimonia, where this may in some sense

[1] I borrow the label "eudaimonist axiom" from Gregory Vlastos, *Socrates: Ironist and Moral Philosopher* (Ithaca, NY: Cornell University Press, 1991), 203. For evidence that Aristotle accepts it, see *Nicomachean Ethics* (*EN*) I.1–2 in conjunction with I.4, and *Eudemian Ethics* (*EE*) I.1. The standard translation of '*eudaimonia*' is 'happiness.' But, as Richard Kraut has argued, contemporary conceptions of happiness tend to be subjectivist in ways that Aristotle's conception of *eudaimonia* is not. So 'welfare'—or, as John Cooper suggests, 'human flourishing'—might be more appropriate. It seems to me preferable, however, simply to use the Greek term. See R. Kraut, "Two Conceptions of Happiness," *Philosophical Review* 88 (1979): 167–97; and J. Cooper, *Reason and Human Good in Aristotle* (Cambridge, MA: Harvard University Press, 1975), 89. For further discussion of this issue, see the Introduction to this volume.

[2] See, for example, Terence Irwin, *Aristotle's First Principles* (Oxford: Oxford University Press, 1998), chaps. 16–18, especially sec. 212. For some criticism of egocentric interpretations of Aristotle's eudaimonism, see my "Impersonal Friends," *The Monist* 74 (1991): 3–29 [I.2] and Richard Kraut, *Aristotle on the Human Good* (Princeton, NJ: Princeton University Press, 1989), chap. 2. I shall reserve for another occasion extended discussion of this relatively standard interpretation of the eudaimonist axiom.

Living Together. Jennifer Whiting, Oxford University Press. © Oxford University Press 2023.
DOI: 10.1093/oso/9780199969678.003.0004

include the eudaimonia of those—like friends, loved ones, and perhaps even fellow citizens—to whom she stands in certain special relations.

Second, there is the function argument's identification of eudaimonia with "activity of soul in accordance with virtue [*psuchês energeia kat' aretên*] or, if there are several virtues, in accordance with the best and most complete [*kata tên aristên kai teleiotatên*]" [*EN* 1098a16–18].[3] There is of course much dispute about whether Aristotle's reference to activity in accordance with the best and most complete virtue is a reference to contemplation alone or whether it is a reference to something that combines the quasi-divine activity of contemplation with the distinctively human activity of moral virtue. So it is difficult in this case to talk of *the* standard interpretation. There is, however, *a* standard interpretation according to which Aristotle means here to include the activity of moral virtue.[4] On this interpretation, the function argument identifies eudaimonia at least in part—and perhaps primarily—with virtuous activity. If this is right, then (given the eudaimonist axiom) all things are or ought to be chosen at least in part—and perhaps primarily—for the sake of virtuous activity.

Third, there is the requirement that genuinely virtuous activity involves choosing virtuous actions "for themselves" [*di' auta*, *EN* 1105a32]—or, as many commentators put it, "for their own sakes." This requirement in fact constitutes one of the primary arguments for taking the activity of soul in accordance with the best and most complete virtue to include, as a dominant component, morally virtuous activity. For taking the relevant activity to consist exclusively (or even largely) in contemplation seems (given the eudaimonist axiom) to require agents to choose virtuous actions exclusively (or largely) for the sake of contemplation. So taking the relevant activity to consist largely in morally virtuous activity makes it easier to understand how agents can choose virtuous actions for their own sakes. For choosing to perform virtuous actions for the sake of engaging in virtuous activity, where such activity *consists in* performing virtuous actions, is arguably a way of choosing virtuous actions for their own sakes. But this idea—that the virtuous agent chooses to perform virtuous actions for the sake of engaging in virtuous activity—encourages a morally unattractive picture of Aristotle's virtuous agent. It encourages the idea that the virtuous agent chooses to perform virtuous actions not primarily because of the way in which such actions benefit *others* but primarily because of the way in which performing such actions allows her to engage in the sort of activity in which her *own* eudaimonia consists.

This picture is no doubt encouraged by Aristotle's account of the distinction between action [*praxis*] and production [*poiêsis*], which Aristotle says [at *EN* 1140b3–4] belong to different genera.

---

[3] I discuss this argument in "Aristotle's Function Argument," *Ancient Philosophy* 8 (1988): 33–48 [Chapter 1, this volume].

[4] I defend this interpretation in "Human Nature and Intellectualism in Aristotle," *Archiv für Geschichte der Philosophie* 68 (1986): 70–95 [Chapter 2, this volume]. [For subtle (and alas inconclusive) changes in my thought, see the Introduction to this volume, especially sections 3–4 and 6.]

> For the end of production [*tês poiêseôs*] is different <from the production itself>, while <the end> of action [*tês praxeôs*] is not <different from the action itself>; for acting well itself is <the> end <of action> [*esti gar autê hê eupraxia telos*]. [*EN* 1140b6–7][5]

The apparent sharpness of Aristotle's distinction between *praxis* and *poiêsis* has in fact led one recent commentator *first* to analyze a generous action, such as building a house with Habitat for Humanity, into two numerically distinct but concomitant acts—(1) the generous action, which is chosen for its own sake, and (2) the act of producing a house, which is chosen for the sake of providing shelter to the homeless—and *then* to treat the productive act as a means to the end of performing a generous action.[6] But this, if we are to have any faith in the *endoxa*, gets things exactly the wrong way round. The virtuous agent performs generous actions for the sake of benefiting others; she does not benefit others for the sake of performing generous actions or even for the sake of exercising her generosity. It is of course true that *in* seeking to benefit others, she exercises her generosity and thus promotes her own eudaimonia. But these cannot be the primary ends for the sake of which she seeks to benefit others—not unless we are willing to attribute to Aristotle's virtuous agents an objectionable form of moral self-indulgence.

I doubt, however, that we need to foist any such moral self-indulgence on Aristotle's virtuous agents. For there is another way to interpret his requirement that virtuous agents choose virtuous actions for themselves. Moreover, this alternative interpretation offers to solve several problems that arise—given the eudaimonist axiom—in connection with the requirement that virtuous agents choose virtuous actions for themselves.

First, there is the problem of how to reconcile this requirement with the fact that virtuous actions typically aim at ends beyond themselves: generous actions typically aim at ends like providing shelter to the homeless or scholarships to needy students, and courageous actions typically aim at ends like securing the safety of one's polis or

[5] I use square brackets to indicate the Greek for what precedes them; and angular brackets, as here, to indicate what I understand in spite of its not being explicitly stated. In some cases what I understand is implicit in the text, but this is not always the case. I tend to make liberal use of angular brackets so as to make it clear exactly how *I* fill in various gaps that one must *somehow or other* fill in. I am *not* thereby claiming that my way is the *only* way to fill them. My aim is twofold: to make it clear how as a matter of fact I understand what is to be filled in and to flag my interpretive decisions for the reader to make of what she will.

[6] See David Charles, "Aristotle: Ontology and Moral Reasoning," *Oxford Studies in Ancient Philosophy* 4 (1986): 119–44. See also Irwin 1998, secs. 195–98, where talk of actualizing capacities is prominent. Aristotle's conception of the relationship between *praxis* and *poiêsis* is complicated, and I cannot adequately address it here. I think, however, that the sorts of problems that lead to the view that I oppose here can be solved (as Irwin suggests we solve them) by allowing (1) that an action can be chosen both for its own sake and for the sake of something else and (2) that one and the same event can be both a *praxis* (in virtue of some of its properties) and a *poiêsis* (in virtue of other of its properties). See Irwin's review of Charles: T. Irwin, "Aristotelian Actions," *Phronesis* 31 (1986): 68–89 (especially 73–74).

fellow citizens. So we need to ask how virtuous actions can be chosen for themselves when they are typically chosen for the sake of ends beyond themselves. This raises a general problem about where the value of virtuous activity comes from, if *not* from the value of its external aims.

Second, there is the problem of how to reconcile the requirement that virtuous actions be chosen for themselves with the requirement that virtuous actions be chosen for the sake of eudaimonia. This problem is especially acute if the eudaimonist axiom refers primarily to the agent's own eudaimonia. For although there may appear to be structurally similar problems in both cases, it is intuitively more plausible to say that I choose to perform a generous action for its own sake if I choose to perform it for the sake of *your* eudaimonia than if I choose to perform it for the sake of *my own*. For generosity typically consists in seeking to promote the eudaimonia of others, and my choosing to perform a generous action for its own sake seems to require at least some willingness on my part to perform that action apart from the contribution that doing so makes to my own eudaimonia.

Third, there is the problem of explaining the relationship between eudaimonia and the external aims of virtuous activity. Once again, this problem is especially acute if the eudaimonist axiom refers primarily to the agent's own eudaimonia. For if *all* things—including virtuous activity and its external goals—are or ought to be chosen ultimately for the sake of the agent's *own* eudaimonia, then it looks as though both the activity itself and its external goals ought to contribute somehow to the agent's *own* eudaimonia. If, for example, I pay your tuition not only for the sake of your eudaimonia but also for the sake of my own, then it looks as though *your* education (as well as my generous activity) should contribute to *my* eudaimonia (as well as of course to yours).

I shall consider each of these problems in turn. I want eventually to argue that Aristotle may—even if we assume that the eudaimonist axiom refers primarily to the agent's own eudaimonia—believe that the external results of my virtuous activity contribute, and contribute non-instrumentally, to *my* eudaimonia. I say "*may* believe" because the relevant assumption is one that I am inclined, in spite of its plausibility and prevalence, to question. But that is a task for another occasion. My argument here is simply that *if* the eudaimonist axiom must be taken to refer primarily to the agent's own eudaimonia, then there is nonetheless a plausible interpretation of Aristotle according to which the external results of an agent's virtuous activity contribute, and contribute non-instrumentally, to the agent's *own* eudaimonia.

1. THE FIRST PROBLEM: CHOOSING VIRTUOUS ACTIONS FOR THEMSELVES *AND* FOR THE SAKE OF THEIR EXTERNAL RESULTS

The crux of my view is an unorthodox interpretation of Aristotle's requirement that the virtuous agent choose virtuous actions for themselves [*di' auta, EN* 1105a32]. Many commentators, encouraged no doubt by Aristotle's distinction between *praxis* and *poiêsis*, tend to interpret this requirement in a Kantian vein: like Kant, Aristotle is read as claiming that what gives an action moral value is something intrinsic to the action itself and independent of its consequences—its "intrinsic rightness" (to borrow a phrase from Christine Korsgaard).[7] Just as on Kant's view, "an action done from duty has its moral worth, *not in the purpose attained by it*, but in the maxim in accordance with which it is decided upon," so too on Aristotle's view, the moral value of an action is supposed to depend not on the results achieved by it but on something internal to the action itself.[8] Part of the point is no doubt to allow that an agent's virtue need not be compromised by the failure of her actions, through no fault of her own, to achieve their intended effects. But we can, I think, allow this without having to deny the fundamental importance of the external results at which virtuous actions typically aim. For there is a plausible—and more explicitly teleological—interpretation of choosing virtuous action for itself, one that incorporates the important role played by these external results (even in the agent's eudaimonia) without however requiring unmitigated success in achieving such results on the part of a genuinely virtuous agent.

The basic idea is to model choosing a virtuous action for itself on Aristotle's account of loving a virtuous person for herself.[9] For Aristotle claims that virtuous agents—and only virtuous agents—love one another for themselves [*di' hautous, EN* 1156b10]. And he explains this in terms of their loving one another simply for being persons of a certain sort [*tô(i) poious tinas einai*] and insofar as each is just who he is [*hê(i) estin hoper estin*], and not—as in friendships for utility and pleasure—insofar as the beloved happens to provide either pleasure or utility to the lover.[10] Those who love their friends on

---

[7] See Christine Korsgaard, "From Duty and For the Sake of the Noble," in S. Engstrom and J. Whiting (eds.), *Aristotle, Kant, and the Stoics: Rethinking Happiness and Duty* (Cambridge: Cambridge University Press, 1996), 205.

[8] See sec. 399 of Immanuel Kant, *Groundwork of the Metaphysic of Morals*, 3rd edn., H. J. Paton (trans.) (New York: Harper and Row, 1956).

[9] On this point, I follow Richard Kraut, "Aristotle on Choosing Virtue for Itself," *Archiv für Geschichte der Philosophie* 58 (1976): 223–39. Kraut, however, does not address the issue of the relationship between choosing a virtuous action for itself and choosing it for the sake of a certain sort of external result. And his account stresses—in a way I want to resist—the priority of choosing a virtuous action for the sake of *eudaimonia* over choosing it for itself. So my account differs substantially from his. [For further discussion of Aristotle's account of loving another *for herself*, see "The Nicomachean Account of *Philia*" (Chapter 6, this volume) and "The Pleasures of Thinking Together" (Chapter 7, this volume).]

[10] I am inclined to think that Aristotle's talk of the friend's being a person of a certain sort and of the friend's being just who he is [*hoper estin*] is meant to refer to what the friend is *essentially* (as opposed to coincidentally), and that Aristotle takes this essentialist restriction to play an important role in his argument that virtuous agents, who love one another for their respective virtues, love one another for *themselves*: the idea is that a virtuous agent loves her friend for what he most truly, or essentially, is. See, for example, *EN* 1166a14–23:

> <The decent [*epieikês*] person> wishes goods and apparent <goods> to himself and acts <accordingly> and for his own sake [*heautou heneka*]. For <he acts> for the sake of his thinking faculty [*tou gar dianoêtikou charin*], which is just what each <person> seems to be [*hoper hekastos einai dokei*]. And he wishes himself to live and to be preserved, especially that part with which he reasons [*kai malista touto hô(i) phronei*]. For being is good to the excellent person, and each wishes goods to himself. But no one would wish to have all <goods> while coming to be someone else [*genomenos allos*]—for God in fact has the good—but <only> being exactly who he is [*all' ôn ho ti*

account of the utility or pleasure they derive from their friends love their friends not in themselves [*ou kath' hautous*] but only coincidentally [*kata sumbebêkos*]. To the extent that they love their friends for being the sorts of persons they are it is only because their friends' being persons of the relevant sorts *coincides* with what is useful or pleasant for *them*: they do not love their friends *simply* for being persons of the relevant sorts [*EN* 1156a10–19].

So we might take choosing virtuous actions for themselves similarly to involve choosing virtuous actions *simply* for being actions of a certain sort and insofar as each is just the sort of action it is, and not insofar as it happens to provide either pleasure or utility to the agent.[11] On this account, someone who chooses to perform an apparently virtuous action on account of the utility or pleasure such an action provides for her either fails to perform a genuinely virtuous action or performs such an action only coincidentally.[12] So the fact that Aristotle describes the person who chooses to act virtuously in order to secure external goods as doing fine things only coincidentally [*EE* 1249a15–16] suggests that this account is on the right track.[13]

---

pot' estin] and each would seem to be his thinking faculty [*to nooun*] or <this> most of all. (See also EN 1168b34–1169a3 and 1156b7–11.)

The idea here seems to be that wishing good to *x* for *x*'s *own* sake involves wishing goods to *x* insofar as *x* is whatever *x* is *essentially*. Note that there seems to be a disanalogy with the action case, such that talk of the essential (as opposed to coincidental) properties of an *action* may be irrelevant to explaining what is involved in choosing an action for *itself* in a way in which talk of the essential (as opposed to the coincidental) properties of a *friend* is not irrelevant to what is involved in loving a friend for *himself*. For we do not choose an action for *its* sake in the way in which we love a friend for *his* sake: the friend is a potential beneficiary in a way in which an action is not. I am nevertheless inclined to think that Aristotle may make essentialist assumptions in the action case as well, and that he may be assuming here something like the "natural kind theory of processes" that David Charles attributes to him in chap. 1 of *Aristotle's Philosophy of Action* (London: Duckworth, 1984). I cannot adequately defend this view here, but the idea is roughly that the properties of an action that are explained teleologically by the goals of the psychic capacity of which it is the actualization will be its essential properties, while those properties of an action *not* explained in this way will be mere coincidents of it. This would allow Aristotle to distinguish choosing a virtuous action for itself from choosing a virtuous action only coincidentally by appeal to the distinction between those properties of a virtuous action that are essential to it—where these are the properties that *make* it virtuous—and those properties of a virtuous action that are only coincidental to it. I hope to develop this idea in future work.

[11] A virtuous action will of course provide some pleasure to the virtuous agent and may also provide utility for her. Whether or not she chooses such an action for itself will thus depend on the truth of certain counterfactuals. Would she have performed the action even if it had not provided any such utility to her? Would she have performed it even if (perhaps per impossible) it had not provided any such pleasure for her? The issue of the extent to which virtuous actions must be pleasant to the virtuous agent is complicated and I return to it briefly in section 3 below.

[12] I think that Aristotle is torn between two ways of describing such cases: between describing them as cases in which the agent performs a genuinely virtuous action but does so only coincidentally and describing them as cases in which she fails to perform a genuinely virtuous action. But I do not think it matters much for present purposes which way he goes here. [See, however, note 15 below.]

[13] This fact may also support the suggestion made in note 10 above that Aristotle is relying on a distinction between the essential and the merely coincidental properties of a virtuous action. See also *EN* V.8, for more (admittedly non-decisive) evidence of this distinction.

Of course this account seems to require that we be able to classify virtuous actions as the sorts of actions they are independently of their agents' motives for choosing them, so that an agent might choose to perform a virtuous action either for itself or from some other motive (such as the desire for utility or pleasure). And there are in fact good reasons for wanting the account to satisfy this requirement. For as Hume says,

> . . . the first virtuous motive, which bestows merit on any action, can never be a regard to the virtue of that action, but must be some other natural motive or principle. To suppose, that the mere regard to the virtue of the action, may be the first motive, which produc'd the action, and render'd it virtuous, is to reason in a circle. Before we can have such a regard, the action must be really virtuous; And consequently the virtuous motive must be different from the regard to the virtue of the action.[14]

Moreover, Aristotle has reasons of his own for agreeing with Hume on this point. For he wants to say that we *become* virtuous by performing virtuous actions. And in the course of replying to the objection that this is not possible, since we must already *be* virtuous in order to perform virtuous actions, Aristotle explicitly distinguishes (a) performing a virtuous action from (b) performing a virtuous action in the way that a virtuous agent performs it. This distinction seems to turn on the presence in (b) and the absence in (a) of what Hume calls "regard for the virtue of the action." For Aristotle includes among the requirements for doing a virtuous action in the way that a virtuous person would do it the requirement that the agent choose to perform the action for itself [*EN* 1105a26–b10]. It is thus clear that what makes an *action* virtuous cannot be (on Aristotle's view) the fact that it is chosen for itself. For this is a condition not for an action's being virtuous but for an action's being done in the way that a virtuous agent would do it.[15] What makes an *action* virtuous is the fact that it is the sort of action that a virtuous person of the relevant sort would do: a just action is the sort of action that a just agent would do, a generous action the sort of action a generous agent would do, a courageous action the sort of action a courageous agent would do, and so on.[16]

[14] *A Treatise of Human Nature*, Book III, Part II, sec. I, edited by P. Nidditch (Oxford: Clarendon Press, 1978 [1739]).

[15] [I am in the process of re-thinking this point in light of arguments made by Marta Jimenez in *Aristotle on Shame and Learning to Be Good* (Oxford: Oxford University Press, 2021); a revised version of her Ph.D. thesis, Toronto, 2011.) Jimenez argues persuasively that Aristotle needs to treat those who are learning to be virtuous, and so not yet reliably performing the relevant sort of actions simply for themselves, as not simply engaging in the sort of external behavior characteristic of the virtuous person but as at least occasionally performing *genuinely* virtuous actions. For it is only thus, says Jimenez, that Aristotle can explain how the learners can bridge what Jimenez calls "the moral learning gap": it is only thus that he can explain how a learner moves from performing the sort of actions characteristic of a virtuous person to *being* a virtuous person. Her point—an excellent one—is that unless the actions have something of the sort of motivation required of genuinely virtuous agents, it is hard to see how repeatedly performing such actions will bring it about that the *agent* is genuinely virtuous.]

[16] Aristotle is of course committed to the unity of these virtues, so that one cannot have one without having all the others. I mention them separately in order to bring out the way in which the sorts of

And what makes an *agent* virtuous is, among other things, the fact that she *routinely* chooses to perform such actions *for themselves*.[17]

This way of putting the point brings out a potentially problematic circularity in Aristotle's account: he seems to want both to define virtuous actions in terms of the virtuous agent (i.e., as the sorts of actions a virtuous *agent* would perform) and to define the virtuous agent in turn in terms of virtuous actions (i.e., as the sort of person who routinely performs virtuous *actions* for themselves). But the circularity need not trouble Aristotle if he can provide some independent content to the virtuous agent's conception of virtuous actions—that is, some content independent of these actions being the sorts of actions the virtuous agent would perform.[18] Moreover, it seems to me that Aristotle can—and perhaps does—seek to provide such content partly by appeal to the external ends at which virtuous actions of various sorts typically aim. For in the case of at least some virtues, he seems to identify virtuous actions of the relevant sort at least partly by appeal to the sorts of ends at which such actions typically aim.

Consider, for example, stereotypically generous actions, as described in *EN* IV.1. Aristotle claims that the generous person is one who gives, and enjoys giving, the right amount to the right people at the right times. He also says that the generous person does not acquire wealth in the wrong ways or from the wrong sources; she does not, for example, rob or gamble. But Aristotle associates generosity primarily with the giving rather than the taking of wealth. This is presumably because the generous person takes in order to give and because giving (and not mere possession) is the proper use of wealth [*EN* 1120a8–12]. In giving, the generous person aims to benefit others [*EN* 1120a21–23]. And Aristotle's account of why the generous person does not give to the wrong people, at the wrong times, and so on, suggests that the generous person gives with the aim of securing the most important benefits she can, given her resources; if she gives to wasteful or vicious people who will use her gift to harm themselves or others, or if she devotes too much to small causes and has nothing left for more important causes, she will fail to secure the most significant benefits her money can buy [*EN* 1120b20–24]. So stereotypically generous actions seem to involve giving so as to provide to others the most significant benefits one can in the long run provide.[19]

---

characteristics that make an action just may be different from the sorts of characteristics that make an action generous or courageous. For this is an important feature of my account.

[17] [On the view of Jimenez, described in note 15, it is primarily the "routinely"—and not the "for themselves"—that habituation serves to secure.]

[18] See Bernard Williams, "Acting as the Virtuous Person Acts," in R. Heinaman (ed.), *Aristotle and Moral Realism* (London: UCL Press, 1995), 13–23. My account resembles Williams' in suggesting that we associate with each virtue a specific kind of reason on account of which virtuous persons of the relevant sort act. But he sees more difficulty than I see in attempting to come up with specific sorts of reasons for the sake of which courageous and temperate agents act. More importantly, my account stresses the nature of the external goal in a way in which his account does not.

[19] [I should have said this before: I borrow the relevant notion of *stereotype* from Hilary Putnam, "The Meaning of 'Meaning,'" in K. Gunderson (ed.), *Language, Mind and Knowledge* (Minneapolis: University of Minnesota Press, 1975); reprinted in Putnam, *Mind, Language and Reality, Philosophical Papers, Volume 2* (Cambridge: Cambridge University Press, 1975).]

The important point here is that stereotypically generous actions typically aim at the external result of benefiting others. It is of course true that one can aim at such a result either for itself (as, for example, when one acts simply in order to benefit others) or from some ulterior motive (as, for example, when one aims to benefit others primarily in order to display one's wealth). And someone who aims at such results from some ulterior motive will perform generous actions not for themselves but only coincidentally. Only someone who aims at such a *result* for *itself* will succeed in performing a virtuous *action* for *itself*.

Consider also stereotypically just actions. These aim at the sort of proportionate distribution of benefits and harms by which the stability of the polis is maintained [*EN* 1132b31–33a2]. The unjust person is one who aims to have (or to assign to another) more than her fair share of beneficial things and less than her fair share of harmful things, and who aims to do so under that description (i.e., under the description "more than her fair share of . . ."). This distinguishes the unjust person, who aims to secure more than her fair share, as such, of various goods, from the person who happens to secure more than his fair share of various goods through acting from other motives—from the coward, for example, who happens to secure more than his fair share of safety when he flees the battle in terror. The just person, then, is someone who aims at each person (including himself) having his or her fair share, as such, of beneficial and harmful things, whatever his or her fair share happens to be, and who aims at this under that description (i.e., under the description "each person having his or her fair share as such . . ."). Once again, we see that stereotypically just actions typically aim at a certain sort of external result—namely, the state of affairs in which each person has his or her fair share of beneficial and harmful things. And this, once again, is something one can aim at either for itself (as, for example, when one acts simply in order to bring about this state of affairs) or from some ulterior motive (as, for example, when someone aims at this state of affairs primarily in order to get elected to office so that he and his friends might ultimately acquire *more* than their fair share of goods). And someone who aims at this state of affairs from some ulterior motive will perform just actions not for themselves but only coincidentally. Only someone who aims at this state of affairs for *itself* will succeed in performing a just action for *itself*.

Now although this is sometimes disputed, similar accounts can, I believe, be given for stereotypically courageous and stereotypically temperate actions.[20] These virtues, however, render salient the way in which the external goal is only part of the story about what makes a virtuous action the *kind* of action—and in particular the kind of *virtuous* action—it is. In the case of courage, there are also—in addition to the external goal of securing the safety of one's friends and fellow citizens—what David Pears has usefully dubbed the "countergoals": the death and wounds one seeks to avoid in the course of securing the safety of one's friends and fellow citizens.[21] For seeking to

[20] Williams 1995 disputes this.

[21] See D. Pears, "Courage as a Mean," in A. Rorty (ed.), *Essays on Aristotle's Ethics* (Berkeley: University of California Press, 1980), 171–87.

secure the safety of one's friends and fellow citizens *without* running the risk of death and wounds is not courageous. Moreover, in the case of both courage and temperance, certain affections—fear and confidence in the case of courage, and certain sensual pleasures and pains in the case of temperance—play prominent roles in the classification of the relevant virtues: the affections of the virtuous agent must lie in the relevant mean.[22] But here, as elsewhere, the requirement of medial affections is presumably motivated by the role of such affections in helping to bring about the external results at which temperate and courageous actions arguably aim: health and good disposition in the case of temperance [*EN* 1119a16] and the safety of one's family and fellow citizens in the case of courage. Similarly, in the case of courage, the role played by the countergoals is subordinate to that played by the external goal: someone who risks death and wounds for the wrong end is not courageous but foolish. So even in the cases of courage and temperance, the external goal plays an important (even if not exclusive) role in determining whether or not an action (or indeed agent) exhibits the relevant virtue. And here too the external goals are ones that can be sought either for themselves (as when someone runs the risk of death and wounds in order to secure the safety of his friends and fellow citizens simply for the sake of their safety) or from some ulterior motive (as when someone does this primarily in order to win honor or to avoid punishment).[23] Only someone who aims at the external goals for themselves will succeed in performing genuinely virtuous actions.

In sum, each of the canonical virtues is associated with a certain sort of external result at which stereotypically virtuous actions of the relevant sort typically aim: stereotypically generous actions typically aim at the welfare of others, stereotypically just actions at the sort of distribution in accordance with merit by which the stability of the polis is maintained, stereotypically temperate actions at health and good disposition, and stereotypically courageous actions at the security of one's friends and fellow citizens. In each case, aiming at a certain sort of external result is part—though not the whole—of what makes a virtuous action the kind of virtuous action it is. And in each case, one can aim at the relevant external result either for itself or from some ulterior motive. The virtuous person is one who aims at these results simply as such, and not insofar as aiming at such results coincides with or is instrumental to other ends she happens to have. The person who aims at these ends not as such, but insofar as doing so coincides with or is instrumental to other ends she happens to have, is not a virtuous person, even though she may perform virtuous actions. For she performs such actions at best only coincidentally. Only someone who aims at the relevant sort of *result* for *itself* succeeds in performing a virtuous *action* for *itself*.

This account builds aiming at a certain sort of external result *into* the notion of choosing a virtuous action for itself, but it does so in a way different from that in

[22] This is not to deny that a similar requirement applies to the other virtues. The point is only that the relevant affections seem to play more prominent roles in the classification of courage and temperance.

[23] See *EN* 1116a15–b3. [See also the general discussion of *EN* III.8 in Jimenez 2021.]

which Stoic accounts seek to do so. On Stoic accounts, what is chosen for itself is ultimately *the aiming* and *not the external result* at which one aims: what the Stoic sage chooses for itself is *aiming*-at-a-certain-sort-of-external-result.[24] But on the teleological (and I submit Aristotelian) account proposed here, choosing a virtuous action for itself *just is* choosing that action simply insofar as it aims at a certain sort of external result. So what is chosen for itself is ultimately the external result at which one aims. Talk of choosing a virtuous *action* for itself is thus elliptical for talk of aiming at a certain sort of *result* for itself—elliptical, that is, for talk of aiming at a certain sort of result simply for the sake of that *result*. So talk of choosing virtuous action for itself is potentially misleading, but only partly so. For I want eventually to argue that Aristotle's notion of virtuous action is expansive, and so takes in, as it were, the external results at which it aims. If, as I argue in section 3 above, my act of generosity is completed in its effects on my intended beneficiary, then its effects on my intended beneficiary, which are my ultimate object of choice, are included within my virtuous action itself. So what ends up being misleading is talk of an *external* result. The deed done is on this view no less internal to virtuous action than a dance danced is internal to dancing; and *eupraxia* (or acting well) is like a dance well danced. A virtuous action that fails (through no fault of the agent's own) to bring about its intended effect is no less a virtuous action than a dance poorly danced is a dance; it is, however, *less complete* than one that succeeds in bringing about its intended effect.

Aristotle's general teleology renders it natural to attribute the teleological (as opposed to the Stoic) view to him. Moreover, the teleological account seems to be supported by Aristotle's claim that "courage is *kalon* to a courageous man and so also is its end, for each thing is defined by its end" [*EN* 1115b21–22]. For his point here seems to be that courage is *kalon* because its end is and not vice versa. This is striking, given Aristotle's requirement that virtuous actions be chosen for themselves. For it suggests that he does not take this requirement to be based on the claim that the value of virtuous activity is independent of the value of the results at which it aims. So it lends support to my teleological account of choosing virtuous action for itself.

Nevertheless, the argument for attributing the teleological view to Aristotle is far from complete. There appear, in fact, to be some obstacles to this attribution. The most serious of these stems from Aristotle's commitment to the eudaimonist axiom. For suppose, as traditionally supposed, that this axiom requires an agent to choose virtuous actions primarily for the sake of her own eudaimonia, and suppose also that choosing virtuous actions for themselves involves choosing them primarily for the sake of their external results. In this case, it is hard to see how we can reconcile the requirement that virtuous actions be chosen for themselves with the eudaimonist axiom. Let us turn then to this problem.

---

[24] See Cicero, *De Finibus*, 3.22.

2. THE SECOND PROBLEM: CHOOSING VIRTUOUS ACTIONS FOR THEMSELVES AND FOR THE SAKE OF *EUDAIMONIA*

There would be little problem here if the eudaimonist axiom were interpreted non-egocentrically—if, that is, the eudaimonist axiom required only that all actions be chosen for the sake of *someone's* eudaimonia or for the sake of eudaimonia *in general*. For each of the external results for the sake of which virtuous actions must be chosen, if they are to be chosen for themselves, arguably involves the eudaimonia of someone or other. Even if temperance contributes primarily (though no doubt not exclusively) to the agent's own health and good disposition, generosity aims straightforwardly at the eudaimonia of others. And promoting the safety of one's friends and fellow citizens is surely a way of promoting *their* eudaimonia. So is promoting the sort of distribution by which the stability of the *polis* is secured. So there would be little problem reconciling the teleological account of choosing virtuous actions for themselves with the eudaimonist axiom if that axiom were to be interpreted non-egocentrically. The problem arises when we interpret that axiom—as many commentators interpret it—as requiring that each agent do all things primarily for the sake of her *own* eudaimonia. How then, if at all, can we reconcile the teleological reading of the requirement that virtuous actions be chosen for themselves with the egocentric reading of the eudaimonist axiom?

The place to begin is with the function argument's account of eudaimonia as an "activity of soul in accordance with virtue" [*psuchês energeia kat' aretên*, *EN* 1098a16–18]. The idea here is that eudaimonia consists in the actualization (or exercise) of those capacities—or some subset of those capacities—that constitute the human soul or essence. At this point, I shall ignore the difficulties posed by the apparent intellectualism of *Nicomachean Ethics* X and assume—as I have argued elsewhere—that Aristotle takes the potentialities for moral virtue and friendship to be essentially human and so takes our eudaimonia to consist at least partly in their actualization.[25] The problems that arise if Aristotle identifies eudaimonia exclusively with contemplation are familiar—especially the problem of explaining how virtuous actions can be chosen for themselves if *all* things are to be chosen ultimately for the sake of the agent's eudaimonia (i.e., for the sake of her *contemplation*). What I want to do here is to raise some structurally similar but less widely discussed problems that arise if Aristotle allows that moral virtue is a component (and not simply a necessary condition) of eudaimonia.[26]

---

[25] See "Human Nature and Intellectualism in Aristotle" [Chapter 2, this volume].

[26] By a "component" I mean something that contributes non-instrumentally to eudaimonia in the sense that its value is not exhausted by its contribution to other ends—the sort of thing that is at least sometimes chosen for its own sake and apart from its contribution to other ends. On this point, see *EN* 1097b1–5. [Note: there is some variation in what follows between talk of an agent aiming *ultimately* at some end and talk of an agent aiming *simply* at some end. And in some places where I wrote "simply" I now think I should have written "primarily"; for an agent can aim at an end for more than one reason. The crucial issue, which I seek to get at in my original note, is whether the agent would aim at *x even if x* did *not also* conduce to the other end, in which case we can say that they are aiming at *x primarily* for itself—though not perhaps (as things actually stand) *simply* for itself.]

If eudaimonia consists in the actualization (or exercise) of our essential capacities, then the eudaimonist axiom might seem to require that we choose all things ultimately for the sake of actualizing (or exercising) these capacities.[27] And this might seem to require that we choose to perform virtuous and friendly actions ultimately for the sake of actualizing our capacities for friendship and virtue.[28] But this seems to conflict with Aristotle's requirements (a) that we choose to perform virtuous actions for themselves (especially on the teleological interpretation of that requirement) and (b) that we love our friends for themselves and not insofar as doing so coincides with or is instrumental to other ends we happen to have. These requirements suggest that the capacities for virtue and friendship are such that they *cannot* be actualized by someone aiming ultimately at their actualization. For their actualization requires the agent to aim ultimately at something *other* than their actualization. In the case of virtue, the agent must choose virtuous action for itself, which (as I have argued) involves aiming at certain sorts of external results for themselves and not insofar as doing so coincides with or is instrumental to *further* ends she happens to have (such as the end of actualizing her capacity for moral virtue). And in the case of friendship, the agent must similarly aim at a certain sort of external result—namely, the welfare of her friend—and she must aim at this simply for itself and not insofar as it coincides with or is instrumental to *further* ends she happens to have (such as the end of actualizing her capacity for friendship).

But if eudaimonia consists in the actualization of capacities such that they *cannot* be actualized by someone aiming ultimately at their actualization, then it is most uncharitable to take the eudaimonist axiom to require that an agent aim ultimately at her own eudaimonia—or even at the actualizations in which it consists—on particular occasions of choice. We should, if possible, interpret the axiom so as to allow that an agent making the sort of choices in which eudaimonia consists can be said to choose, for the sake of eudaimonia, whatever it is she thus chooses. So if eudaimonia consists in choosing to perform virtuous actions for themselves (where this involves aiming at certain sorts of external results for *themselves*), and in choosing to benefit our friends for *their* sakes, we ought, if possible, to say that an agent who chooses these things and chooses them for themselves chooses them *ipso facto* for the sake of eudaimonia.

The idea here is to reconcile the requirement that virtuous actions be chosen for themselves with the eudaimonist axiom that all things be chosen ultimately for the sake of (the agent's) eudaimonia, *first*, by taking her eudaimonia to consist at least partly in the actualization of her capacities for moral virtue, and *second*, by taking these capacities to be essentially capacities whose actualization consists in aiming at exactly the sorts of results for the sake of which virtuous actions must be chosen if

[27] I add "exercise" here to call attention to the fact that it is second (and not first) actuality to which "actualization" here (and throughout) refers. I shall henceforth use "actualization" alone to refer to *second* actualization. See *De Anima* 412a22–26.

[28] This seems to me to be the view to which David Charles is committed in his "Ontology and Moral Reasoning" (Charles 1984). It is the view that I am primarily concerned to attack.

they are to be chosen for themselves. In other words, her eudaimonia will consist at least partly in her actualizing her capacity for generosity, which is essentially a capacity aimed at benefiting others for *their* sakes. So in order to actualize her capacity for generosity, she must perform generous actions primarily in order to benefit others and not for some other reason. But this is just to perform generous actions for themselves, if the foregoing account of choosing virtuous action for itself is correct. The idea here is that eudaimonia consists (at least partly) in choosing virtuous actions because they aim at the very sort of results for the sake of which virtuous actions must be chosen if they are to be chosen for themselves. So choosing virtuous actions because they aim at certain external results will be compatible with choosing virtuous actions for the sake of eudaimonia, if we allow that someone making the sort of choices in which eudaimonia consists can be said to be choosing for the sake of eudaimonia whatever it is she thus chooses. On this account, the agent can be said to be choosing things for the sake of (her own) eudaimonia even though she does not self-consciously aim in choosing these things at her own eudaimonia. And this is plausible given Aristotle's general teleology, which admits many cases where things happen for the sake of ends without anyone or anything ever aiming self-consciously at those ends—for example, cases where nutritive processes occur for the sake of growth.[29]

It is worth noting that this account employs a strategy that is often employed by commentators who want to reconcile choosing virtuous action for itself with choosing it for the sake of (one's own) eudaimonia. Such commentators typically distinguish choosing *x* as an instrumental means *to y* from *choosing x* as a component of *y*. They then claim that where *y* is not separable from *x* in the sense that *y consists in x* (perhaps along with other things), choosing *x* for itself is compatible with choosing *x* for the sake of *y*. For in this case, choosing *x* for itself is a *way* of choosing *y* (which consists at least partly in *x*) and not simply an instrumental means to choosing *y*. This strategy is typically applied to the case of virtuous action and eudaimonia. Assuming that virtuous action is a component of eudaimonia, and not simply an instrumental means to it, so that eudaimonia *consists* at least partly in virtuous action, one can say that choosing virtuous action for itself is a way of choosing virtuous action for the sake of that (namely, eudaimonia) which consists at least partly in virtuous action. For that for the sake of which one chooses virtuous action—namely, eudaimonia—is not something separable from virtuous action: to choose virtuous action *just is* to choose *it* (i.e., eudaimonia).

My proposal is that we should apply this strategy more generally, so that the external results at which virtuous actions must aim if virtuous actions are to be chosen for themselves are treated as *components* of virtuous action, which is in turn to be treated as a component of eudaimonia.[30] On this account, to aim at a certain sort of external

[29] [I have substituted "self-consciously" here for "intentionally."]

[30] As noted at the end of section 1 above, it is somewhat misleading given my account to speak of these results as *external*. But I shall continue for the sake of simplicity to use this intuitive and pre-theoretical terminology.

result for itself is to aim at it as a component of (and not simply as an instrumental means to) virtuous action: aiming at that external result for itself *just is* a way of choosing virtuous action for itself. Moreover, aiming at such a result for itself is in turn a way of aiming at eudaimonia, for eudaimonia consists in virtuous action, which *just is* a matter of aiming at such results for themselves.

Here, however, we should pause to ask what role, if any, the agent's *belief* that eudaimonia consists in the actualization of her capacities for virtue and friendship is supposed to play in her deliberation and in the creation and sustenance of her motivational attitudes. Suppose, for example, that this belief is at least partly responsible for her deciding initially to acquire the disposition to choose virtuous actions for themselves. We might think this makes it more plausible to say that when she chooses to perform these actions for themselves she *also* chooses them for the sake of eudaimonia. For if she lacks the belief that her eudaimonia consists in the actualization of these capacities—or if she has the belief but it plays no role in her coming to choose virtuous actions for themselves—then it is hard to see why we should say that she chooses these things for the sake of eudaimonia. If, on the other hand, her belief that eudaimonia consists in the actualization of these capacities is partly responsible for her initial decision to acquire the disposition to choose virtuous actions for themselves, then we might wonder whether it is really appropriate to say when she makes such choices that she chooses virtuous actions for themselves.

Here, however, it is important to remember that Aristotle thinks that habituation plays an important role in the acquisition of virtue. Virtuous agents acquire their dispositions to choose virtuous actions *for themselves* by repeatedly performing stereotypically virtuous actions and coming increasingly to perform them for the *right sorts of reasons:* it is only thus that they come to see eudaimonia as consisting at least partly in choosing such actions *for themselves*. In other words, the belief that eudaimonia consists in choosing virtuous actions for themselves is typically a *consequence* and *not a cause* of the acquisition of virtue: one might even say that acquiring this belief is part of *what it is* to acquire virtue. The idea here is that we come to *regard* something as a component of eudaimonia because we come to think it good for its own sake. But this does not mean that our thinking something good for its own sake *makes* it a component of eudaimonia. It means only that our coming to think something good for its own sake is part of what it is to *regard* it as a component of eudaimonia. Whether or not it *is* a component of eudaimonia will depend to a great extent on other factors, such as what our essential capacities are.[31]

I am not sure what Aristotle would say about a case in which someone believes that eudaimonia consists in the actualization of her capacities for virtue and so sets out to acquire and then to actualize these capacities. If, as seems plausible, Aristotle thinks that she will not succeed in actualizing these capacities unless she acquires a settled

---

[31] [I have made minor changes in this paragraph, to accommodate points due to Jimenez 2021. See note 15 above.]

disposition to choose virtuous actions for *themselves*, he might argue that her initial motivation is irrelevant once she has acquired this disposition, and that what is relevant at that point is what *sustains* her choice of virtuous actions. This is reasonable, since this is more or less the way it happens with everyone. We *all* start off performing virtuous actions only coincidentally, for the sake of rewards (for example) or to avoid punishment. But this ceases to matter once we have acquired the disposition to choose virtuous actions for *themselves*.

There remains a question here about whether the belief that eudaimonia consists in the actualization of our capacities for virtue can play any role in our deliberative or motivational economies once we have acquired the disposition to choose virtuous actions for themselves. I am inclined to think that it cannot—that this would involve, as Bernard Williams might say, "one thought too many."[32] But the question here is complicated by the difficulty of asserting the counterfactuals we should need to assert in order to make sense of this possibility. For to the extent that the virtuous agent's beliefs about her eudaimonia track her beliefs about what is worth choosing for itself, one cannot easily resolve the question by asking whether she would continue to regard choosing virtuous actions for themselves as worthwhile if she did not regard doing so as a component of her eudaimonia. For part of what it *is* for her to think this worthwhile in the relevant sense is for her to regard it as a component of her eudaimonia. So while she can certainly *recognize* that having and actualizing the capacity for virtue is a component of her eudaimonia, it seems unlikely that this recognition can play any role in her deliberative or motivational economy. This, however, is a controversial issue that cannot be satisfactorily resolved at this point.[33] For we need to turn to the third of our original problems, the problem of explaining the relationship between the agent's eudaimonia and the external results for the sake of which virtuous actions must be chosen if they are to be chosen for themselves.

3. THE THIRD PROBLEM: THE RELATIONSHIP BETWEEN THE EXTERNAL RESULTS OF VIRTUOUS ACTIVITY AND THE AGENT'S *EUDAIMONIA*

Taking eudaimonia to consist in the actualization of capacities that are essentially aimed at achieving certain sorts of external results raises a question about the relationship between these results and the agent's eudaimonia. Is her eudaimonia supposed

[32] See Bernard Williams, "Persons, Character and Morality," in *Moral Luck* (Cambridge: Cambridge University Press, 1981), 18.

[33] A crucial passage here is *EN* 1097b1ff. My account requires me to read this passage as saying that we choose virtue for the sake of eudaimonia simply in the sense that we *recognize* that virtue will contribute to our eudaimonia (which is how I take *dia toutôn hupolambanontes eudaimonêsein*) even though this is *not* our ultimate reason for choosing it: we would choose virtue even if nothing (including *eudaimonia*) resulted from it—nothing, that is, apart from the results that I have been suggesting are *internal* to virtuous action *itself*. [For more on these issues, see section 4 of "Strong Dialectic, Neurathian Reflection, and the Ascent of Desire" (Chapter 5, this volume).]

to consist simply (as on the Stoic view) in *aiming* at such results? Or is some degree of success in *achieving* these results also necessary for—perhaps even partly constitutive of—her eudaimonia?

Since most people who aim at things aim at them for the sake of achieving them, it is difficult to see why anyone not under the influence of a theory would take eudaimonia to consist simply in the aiming itself. One theoretical rationale for such a choice would be the identification of eudaimonia with the actualization of capacities whose actualization consists in *aiming* at certain things, for this would entail the identification of eudaimonia with the aiming itself. But if someone identifies eudaimonia with such aiming qua actualization of one of her essential capacities, then it seems more appropriate to say that she aims at certain external results for the sake of actualizing her essential capacities than that she aims at these results for themselves. And this is incompatible with the actualization of those capacities whose actualization requires the agent to aim ultimately at something other than their actualization. So insofar as the capacities in whose actualization our eudaimonia consists require us to aim ultimately at something other than their actualization, we ought to allow a sense in which agents aiming ultimately at something other than their actualization can be said to be aiming at these *other* things for the sake of eudaimonia. And this suggests that some degree of success in achieving these things should contribute to the agent's eudaimonia.

Aristotle's discussion of courage supports this view. Aristotle believes that the virtuous person will generally enjoy virtuous activity, but the example of courage suggests that this is not always the case. The courageous person finds death and wounds painful; and the more virtuous and the more eudaimôn she is, the more she stands to lose, and so, the more pain she feels at the prospect of death [*EN* 1117b9–11]. But she still chooses courageous action over all these goods. Aristotle concludes from this that "it is not true that the active exercise of every virtue is pleasant; it is pleasant only insofar as we attain the end" [*EN* 1117b15–16, Irwin's translation]. Aristotle's point here seems to be that when we make sacrifices or endure pain for the sake of achieving valuable results, our activity is more pleasant to the extent that we achieve these results.[34]

This point is important, given Aristotle's general views about the relationships among pleasure, activity, and eudaimonia. Aristotle believes that *eudaimonia* consists in the unimpeded activity of our essential capacities. He also believes that such activity is pleasant and that pleasure completes (or perfects) such activity [*EN* 1153b9–25, 1174b14–33]. So to the extent that failure to achieve the results at which virtuous activities aim decreases the pleasure taken in such activities, such failure renders the activities themselves less complete (or perfect) than they might otherwise be. So if eudaimonia consists in *complete* activity of soul in accordance with virtue, an agent will be more eudaimôn the more successful she is in achieving the external results

---

[34] It seems to me significant that Aristotle does *not* say that this point applies *only* to courageous action. For Irwin's translation, see T. Irwin, *Aristotle: Nicomachean Ethics* (Indianapolis: Hackett Publishing, 1985).

at which her virtuous activities aim. Aristotle may view this as a consequence of two things—first, his view that the value of virtue derives at least in part from the value of the results at which it aims, and second, his view that eudaimonia is the most desirable of all goods in the sense that it cannot be increased by the addition of other goods [*EN* 1097b16–20]. Taken together, these views suggest that successful virtuous activity is better (or more complete) than unsuccessful virtuous activity, and so, that a life of virtuous activity which is on the whole successful is more desirable and more complete than a life of virtuous activity that is on the whole unsuccessful.

Aristotle can endorse this conclusion without giving up his view that eudaimonia is an activity of soul, for Aristotle allows that the *energeia* (or actualization) of some capacities need not occur in the *agent's* soul. He says, for example, that teaching, which is an energeia of the teacher, can take place in the learner [*Physics* 202b5–22]. The idea seems to be that the completion of the activity of teaching lies in certain processes occurring in the learner. Something similar might be said about many of the activities of virtue. For just as the beneficial activities of the generous or magnificent agent may be completed in their beneficiaries, so too the just and courageous activities of just and courageous agents may be completed in the polis at large (that is, in the correct distribution of benefits and harms and in the safety of their friends and fellow citizens).

Aristotle supports this account when he compares the relationship between benefactors and their beneficiaries to that between producers and their products. He says that the beneficiary [*to peponthos*] is the benefactor's product and that the product [*to ergon*] is the producer in actualization [*energeia(i)*] [*EN* 1168a3–8]. Similarly, children are the products of their parents and so (in some sense) the actualizations of their parents. Furthermore, Aristotle allows that the things we enable our friends to do are, in a way, done by us [*EN* 1112b27–28]. This suggests that some of *my* activity or actualization may occur in my friends and *their* activities. This is yet another way in which activities of soul may extend beyond the souls of their original agents.

The view that not all of the activities or actualizations of my psychic capacities must occur in my soul suggests that my eudaimonia, even if it is an activity of soul, may be a relatively global rather than a local affair. This would help to explain why Aristotle takes the fortunes of our families and friends to affect our own eudaimonia—even, in some cases, after we have died [*EN* 1100a14–30]. The idea is this: insofar as my eudaimonia consists in activities that aim at the welfare of my friends and family for *their* sakes, and not simply for the sake of something like actualizing my capacity to *aim* at such things, the completion of these activities will depend on what happens to my loved ones as a result of what I have done for their sakes. If *good* things happen to them as a result of my activities, then my activities will be more complete and my life more eudaimôn. If *bad* things happen to them—either as a result of what I have done or as a result of what I have failed to do—then my activities will be less complete and my life less eudaimôn. In general, then, insofar as my eudaimonia consists in aiming at certain sorts of external results—and in aiming at such results *for themselves*—the achievement of such results as a consequence of my actions will complete or perfect the aiming activities in which my eudaimonia consists, and so will complete or perfect my eudaimonia.[35]

4. CONCLUSION: A VIRTUOUS CIRCLE?

So far, I have focused on the relationships among the *agent's* eudaimonia, *her* virtuous activity, and the results at which she aims. At this point, I should like to turn briefly to the relationship between the external results at which she aims and the eudaimonia of *others*.

First, given Aristotle's view that eudaimonia is the highest human good, it should be obvious that benefiting others consists largely if not exclusively in promoting their eudaimonia. And since the virtues that are aimed at benefiting others are primarily concerned with the distribution of external goods, there seems to be an important connection between promoting others' eudaimonia and supplying them with external goods. One reason for this is that having a reasonable supply of external goods is typically necessary for exercising the virtues: generosity requires wealth; temperance requires access to food, drink, and sexual partners; and courage seems to require some degree of health and bodily strength.[36] But Aristotle may think that the value of my

---

[35] [The conception of eudaimonia that I ascribe to Aristotle is entirely compatible with the ideas (a) that the virtuous agent can be pained by the pain and suffering of others and can wish either that the pain of others had not occurred or would soon end; and (b) that the virtuous agent can be pleased when the pain and suffering of others cease as a result of actions performed by someone *other than*—indeed *unrelated to*—*herself*. The point is simply that when the relevant actions are performed by someone else, neither those actions nor any of their consequences count as activities of *her soul* in either the local or the global sense identified here; so none of them contributes to her eudaimonia, even globally construed. But there is no reason to think that the agent's own eudaimonia is the only eudaimonia (besides that of her loved ones) whose vicissitudes cause her pain and pleasure. It is thus highly misleading for Thomas Hurka to cite the present section of this chapter (in the note signaled by "FN" below) in support of ascribing to Aristotle the following view:

> Aristotle's benefactor cares first about her own virtuous action and only derivatively about its effects on others, as something she brought about. *She may be pleased that another is free from pain as making her own act of seeking that outcome more successful and therefore a greater contributor to her own eudaimonia.*[FN] But she's pleased by it only or mainly because it was produced by her. ["*Aristotle on Virtue: Wrong, Wrong and Wrong*, p. 20, in Julia Peters (ed.), *Aristotelian Ethics in Contemporary Perspective* (New York: Routledge, 2013), 9–26.]

It should be clear to an intelligent reader with a modicum of sympathy that it is no part of the view I ascribe to Aristotle that a virtuous agent who aims successfully to reduce or eliminate the pain of another is pleased only—or even primarily—because any consequent pain reduction is due to her own activity. Moreover, pleasure plays a minimal role in the view I ascribe to Aristotle. The focus of this view is on the value of the results at which the virtuous agent's activity, as such, is aimed. And, as I point out here, Aristotle himself recognizes that these results may come about (and thus make the agent's activity more complete than it would otherwise be) *after her death*. As honored as I am that Hurka appeals to my authority as a reader of Aristotle, I hope that reading the essays collected here, which deal in detail with many of the issues skated over in "Wrong, Wrong and Wrong," will make it clear that Hurka misrepresents my view. But my essays can of course be dispensed with. There is no substitute for reading Aristotle *himself* and deciding on the basis of *his* work what views to attribute to him.]

[36] See John Cooper, "Aristotle on the Goods of Fortune," *Philosophical Review* 94 (1985): 173–96.

external goods is *not* exhausted by their contribution to my *virtuous* activity. In other words, he may think that my external goods contribute something to my eudaimonia apart from what they contribute to my virtuous activity. They may, for example, make possible other activities in accordance with other sorts of excellence, which activities also contribute non-instrumentally to my eudaimonia. Wealth, for example, may provide me with more leisure to contemplate; bodily strength may give me the endurance to play more squash; and good looks may enable me to succeed as an actor.

This possibility—that the value of my external goods is not exhausted by their contribution to my virtuous activity—is important for the following reason. Suppose instead that the value of my external goods were exhausted by their contribution to my virtuous activity, and similarly that the value of the external goods that my virtue secures for others were exhausted by their contribution to others' virtue. In that case, the value of my virtuous activity would be exhausted by its contribution to the virtuous activity of others and the same would be true of the value of anyone else's virtuous activity. In that case, Aristotle's view would involve a "virtuous circle" in which the virtuous activity of A promotes the virtuous activity of B and C; the virtuous activity of B promotes the virtuous activity of C and A; and so on. And in that case, virtuous activity would ultimately be valued *only* for its own sake. But this would involve taking away with one hand the emphasis on external results that Aristotle seems to have given with the other.[37]

Of course, a "virtuous circle" in which the virtuous activity of A promotes the virtuous activity of B and C, the virtuous activity of B promotes that of C and A, and so on, is not necessarily vicious. But its acceptability seems to depend on there being other eudaimonic values (besides virtue) that virtue promotes. Part of the point here is that virtue is neither difficult nor sublime if there are no other eudaimonic values—like, for example, the value of contemplation—with which virtue might conflict. Here, though, it is important to distinguish between my valuing my own virtuous activity because of the other eudaimonic values it enables *me* to achieve, and my valuing my own virtuous activity because of the eudaimonic values it enables *others* to achieve. The former (valuing my own virtuous activity for the sake of *my* eudaimonia) sounds objectionably egoistic, while the latter (valuing my own virtuous activity for the sake of *others'* eudaimonia) is the *essence* of virtue.[38]

---

[37] It is worth noting here that the emphasis on external results distinguishes virtuous activity from contemplation, which is chosen *only* for its own sake and not for the sake of any such external results. This does not, of course, mean that contemplation is not also (or ipso facto) chosen for the sake of eudaimonia. For we can give the same sort of account of the relationship between choosing contemplation for itself and choosing it for the sake of eudaimonia that we gave of the relationship between choosing virtuous action for itself and choosing it for the sake of *eudaimonia*: to choose it for itself *just is* to choose it for the sake of eudaimonia.

[38] I should like to thank audiences at the University of Pittsburgh, Johns Hopkins, MIT, the University of Kentucky, and SUNY Buffalo, for discussion of this essay. I should also like to thank David Charles, Terry Irwin, Paul Matthewson, and John McDowell for written comments on early drafts; and Karen Jones and Michael Thompson for helpful discussion in the final stages of revision.

4

Self-Love and Authoritative Virtue

PROLEGOMENON TO A KANTIAN READING OF *EUDEMIAN ETHICS* VIII.3

MY PRIMARY TEXT is the last chapter of the *Eudemian Ethics* (*EE*), where Aristotle introduces the distinction between the merely *agathos* (or good) human and the *kalos-kagathos* (or fine-and-good) one.[1] Since the concerns of this text may seem somewhat far removed from the topic of self-love and self-worth, I should explain how I came to focus on it.

Allen Wood and I were originally paired (at the conference where this essay was first presented) because he had been relying in his interpretation of Kant on a view I had

[1] I follow Franz Susemihl, *Aristotelis Ethica Eudemia* (Leipzig: Teubner, 1884), in referring to this chapter as *EE* VIII.3, taking it together with the two preceding chapters to constitute (part of) a book distinct from *EE* VII. So does Michael Woods, *Aristotle: Eudemian Ethics Books I, II and VIII* (Oxford: Oxford University Press, 1982). Others take these chapters as belonging to *EE* VII, referring to them as *EE* VII.13–15, as in the Revised Oxford Translation, edited by Jonathan Barnes (Princeton, NJ: Princeton University Press, 1984), and the new Oxford Text, prepared by R. R. Walzer and J. M. Mingay (Oxford: Oxford University Press, 1991). There is controversy about the proper location of these chapters, which are fragmentary and seem to pick up in the midst of a discussion that does not follow naturally on the discussion of friendship in *EE* VII. See note 43 below.

I use the following abbreviations to refer to other works by Aristotle (all in the Revised Oxford Translation): *EN* for *Nicomachean Ethics*; *MM* for *Magna Moralia*; and *Pol.* for *Politics*. Except where indicated, translations are my own. I use square brackets to supply the Greek for what precedes them; and angular brackets to indicate what I understand in spite of its not being explicitly stated. In some cases what I understand is implicit in the text, but this is not always the case. I tend to make liberal use of angular brackets so as to make it clear exactly how *I* fill in various gaps that one must *somehow or other* fill in. I am *not* thereby claiming that my way is the *only* way to fill them. My aim is twofold: to make it clear how as a matter of fact I understand what is to be filled in and to flag my interpretive decisions for the reader to make of what she will.

Living Together. Jennifer Whiting, Oxford University Press. © Oxford University Press 2023.
DOI: 10.1093/oso/9780199969678.003.0005

attributed to Aristotle: i.e., the view that there is an important sense in which self-love is, or should be, based on self-worth.[2] Kant's idea, according to Wood, is that the capacity to set ends is what gives rational nature an absolute or unconditional worth, making it an end in itself. Moreover, the exercise of this capacity is the condition for the goodness of all other ends. On this view, "the goodness of any [other] end consists in the fact that it is an object of rational choice." Rational choice thus becomes what Korsgaard calls a "value-conferring property," and practical reasoning is grounded in the self-worth of rational beings in the following way: it makes sense for an agent to value the ends she sets, only to the extent that she esteems herself as a being who sets ends according to reason.[3]

Since Wood was suggesting similarities between Kant's view and the view I had attributed to Aristotle, I set about contemplating the extent to which my Aristotle could agree with Wood's Kant. What troubled me most was the idea of attributing to Aristotle the view that rationality is (in the relevant sense) a value-*conferring* property. What stuck in my head was Aristotle's claim—in a passage where he is explicitly concerned with *rational* desire—that we do not think things *kalon* (or fine) because we desire them; rather, we desire them because we think them fine [*Metaphysics* (*Met.*) 1072a28–29]. And though we might take this simply as a psychological claim that has no bearing on the issue of what *makes* things fine, I have always taken it to suggest that Aristotle takes the independent value of the objects of choice to be what justifies the choice of these objects. If this is right, then Aristotle—insofar as he takes the value of the *object* to determine the value of the *choice*—*seems* to deny that rational choice is what confers value on its objects.

There is, however, one text where Aristotle seems to suggest that a certain sort of rational choice confers a certain sort of value on an object. So I turned to that text, thinking that there, if anywhere in the Aristotelian corpus, I could find something at least *structurally* similar to taking rational choice as a value-conferring property. What I found was a text whose Kantian themes far surpassed my expectations. Not only does Aristotle allow something structurally similar to taking rational choice as a value-conferring property. He seems also to share Kant's concern with the problem of constitutive luck; expresses doubts about the extent to which someone like Kant's man of sympathetic temperament deserves to be praised for acting from his sympathetic inclinations; and introduces something like Kant's distinction between acting in *conformity* with duty and acting from the *motive* of duty. Moreover, he concludes with the recommendation that rational agents choose among natural or external goods (such as

---

[2] Allen Wood, "The Dignity of Rational Nature" (unpublished), relying on my "Impersonal Friends," *Monist* 74 (1991): 3–29 [I.2]. [The papers presented at the conference to which the parenthetical remark refers are collected in *Aristotle, Kant and the Stoics: Rethinking Happiness and Duty*, S. Engstrom and J. Whiting (eds.) (Cambridge: Cambridge University Press, 1996).]

[3] See Christine Korsgaard, "Kant's Formula of Humanity," *Kant-Studien* 77 (1986): 181–202 (esp. 196–97); reprinted in C. Korsgaard, *Creating the Kingdom of Ends* (Cambridge: Cambridge University Press, 1996), 106–32.

wealth, honor, and power) with the least possible interference from the non-rational part of the soul—that is, with the least possible interference from their inclinations.[4]

The text is *EE* VIII.3, where Aristotle suggests that the *kaloskagathos*—in choosing natural goods for the sake of something fine—confers a certain sort of value on those goods: *because* he chooses them for the sake of something *fine*, they *become* fine for him.[5] In this respect, the *kaloskagathos* differs from the merely *agathos*, for whom the natural goods, not being chosen for the sake of something fine, are good but not also fine. The merely *agathos* in turn differs from the non-*agathos* for whom these things are not even good.

Aristotle's account of the distinction between the *agathos* (whether *kalos* or not) and the non-*agathos* appears to rest on the Socratic view (expressed in Plato's *Euthydemus*) that the so-called natural goods are in themselves neither good nor bad for an agent, because these things, when misused (as they tend to be) by an ignorant or vicious agent, are more harmful to the agent than their opposites. For Aristotle says, in introducing this distinction,

> A good man, then, is one for whom the natural goods [*ta phusei agatha*] are goods. For the goods that are contested [*ta perimachêta*] and seem greatest—honor, wealth, bodily excellence, good fortune and power—are natural goods, but may be harmful to some <men> on account of their dispositions [*dia tas hexeis*]. For neither the foolish nor the unjust nor the intemperate would gain any benefit from using them, just as one who is sick does not <benefit from> using the food of the healthy man and one who is weak and maimed does not <benefit from using> the accessories of one who is healthy and whole. [*EE* 1248b26–30]

On Socrates' view, wisdom—which he elsewhere identifies with virtue—is the only thing that is good in itself or, as Kant might say, the only thing that is unconditionally good: the goodness of all other things is conditional on their being used correctly by wisdom or virtue.[6]

This Socratic "conditionality thesis" should call to mind the opening of the *Grundlegung* (*Gr.*), where Kant claims that a good will is the only thing that is good without qualification, and then argues that qualities of temperament as well as goods of fortune and even happiness itself, though obviously good and desirable in many

---

[4] On natural or external goods, also known as goods of fortune, see John Cooper, "Aristotle and the Goods of Fortune," *Philosophical Review* 94 (1985): 173–96; reprinted (with postscript) in J. Cooper, *Reason and Emotion* (Princeton, NJ: Princeton University Press, 1999), 292–311.

[5] This need not conflict with the *Metaphysics*' claim that we desire things because we think them fine, which may refer only to what is fine in itself and not to things that become fine (or fine for the agent) as a result of being chosen for the sake of what is fine in itself.

[6] See Plato's *Euthydemus* 279–81, and compare *Meno* 87–88. On these texts, see Gregory Vlastos, *Socrates: Ironist and Moral Philosopher* (Ithaca, NY: Cornell University Press, 1991), 200–232; T. H. Irwin, "Socrates the Epicurean?," *Illinois Classical Studies* (1986): 85–112; and Christopher Bobonich, "Plato's Theory of Goods in the Laws and *Philebus*," *Proceedings of the Boston Area Colloquium of Ancient Philosophy* (1995): 101–39.

respects, can also be extremely bad and harmful when the will that uses them is not good.[7] It is worth noting that Kant includes among the things whose goodness is conditional on their use by a good will even things like "moderation in the affections and passions, self-control, and sober reflection" [*Gr.* 393–94]. For Aristotle too suggests something like this when he says that the natural virtues, which do not involve practical wisdom [*phronêsis*], are harmful to those who possess them in the absence of understanding [*nous*] [*EN* 1144b4–14].[8] It thus appears that Aristotle and Kant agree not only in accepting something like the conditionality thesis, but also in applying this thesis even to qualities of temperament or to what Aristotle calls "natural" virtues: these things—in the absence of phronêsis or a good will—may harm their possessors.

Before laying the ground for my "Kantian" reading of *EE* VIII.3, I should note that it is important to me that there be Socratic sources for the "Kantian" views I ascribe to Aristotle. This is important lest the alleged Kantianism of Aristotle be attributed to an anachronistic tendency on my part to read Aristotle through Stoic lenses. If, as I suspect, my "Socratic" Aristotle was an important influence on the Stoics, it may also have been (via the Stoics) an important influence on Kant.[9]

1. *EUDEMIAN ETHICS* VIII.3: TWO PUZZLES

We can better interpret our text, and appreciate its Socratic background, if we examine it in context. For Aristotle clearly has Socrates in mind throughout *EE* VIII, even if it is not always clear whether (and to what extent) he agrees or disagrees with Socrates. *EE* VIII (or what remains of it) proceeds roughly as follows. Chap. 1 explicitly rejects Socrates' identification of virtue with knowledge [*epistêmê*] as Socrates conceives it, but hints at the possibility of identifying virtue with Aristotelian phronêsis, which,

[7] See Immanuel Kant, *Groundwork of the Metaphysic of Morals*, H. J. Paton (trans.) (London: Hutchinson and Co., 1956; third edition). Compare with *Euthydemus* 280b–281b, where Socrates emphasizes the importance of use (*hê chrêsis*)—and ultimately of *right* use—as distinct from mere acquisition or possession (*hê ktêsis*).

[8] Socrates may agree. He introduces temperance, justice, and bravery (at *Euthydemus* 279b5) separately from wisdom [*sophia*]. And he explicitly considers (at *Euthydemus* 281c) the possibility of misusing (to one's own detriment) bravery and temperance. For a comparison of Kant's views with those expressed by Socrates in the *Euthydemus* and *Meno*, see Stephen Engstrom, "Kant's Conception of Practical Wisdom," *Kant-Studien* (1997): 16–43.

[9] There is, however, debate about the Stoics' familiarity with Aristotle. See F. H. Sandbach, *Aristotle and the Stoics* (= *Proceedings of the Cambridge Philological Society* 10 [1985]). Moreover, one might object that I read Socrates as well through Stoic lenses, but that is a matter that I cannot discuss here. On Kant's acquaintance with the ancients, see Klaus Reich, "Kant and Greek Ethics," *Mind* 48 (1939): 339–54, 446–63. See also Julia Annas, "The Hellenistic Version of Aristotle's Ethics," *Monist* 73 (1990): 80–96; and "Aristotle and Kant on Morality and Practical Reasoning," in Engstrom and Whiting, *Rethinking Happiness and Duty*, 237–58. The latter fails (in my view) to do justice to the Socratic antecedents of the Stoic views that Annas contrasts with those of Aristotle. And I find it odd that she turns to the Stoics (rather than to Socrates) for evidence that a sharp distinction between moral and non-moral reasoning was conceptually available to Aristotle.

unlike epistêmê, cannot be misused. Chap. 2 then rejects the Socratic attempt (in Plato's *Euthydemus*) to assimilate (or reduce) good fortune to wisdom [*sophia*], which might easily be identified with Aristotelian phronêsis. In Chap. 3, then, Aristotle proceeds to clarify the relationship of phronêsis, first to the goods of fortune, and then to theoretical wisdom (references to which are conspicuously absent from statements of the Socratic view). It is thus possible—pace Woods and other commentators—to read *EE* VIII as a coherent (if fragmentary) whole in which Aristotle aims to clarify his somewhat complicated relationship to Socrates.[10]

Let us turn, then, to *EE* VIII.3, which falls reasonably neatly into two parts. In the first part, Aristotle explains the distinction between the merely *agathos* and the *kaloskagathos*. Since the difference between them lies primarily in their mode of choosing among natural goods, Aristotle goes on in the second part to specify the *horos*, or standard, with reference to which one ought to choose among natural goods. The idea is presumably that the *kaloskagathos* chooses with reference to this standard in a way in which the merely *agathos* does not. The standard is as explicit—and as explicitly contemplative—as anything we find in the entire corpus.[11] After claiming that phronêsis rules by issuing commands for the sake of the theoretical faculty—just as medical science issues commands for the sake of health—Aristotle concludes by saying,

> Then whatever choice and acquisition of natural goods will produce above all the contemplation of the divine—whether of bodily <goods> or money or friends or the other goods—this <choice> is best, and this standard [*horos*] is most fine [*kallistos*]. And whatever <choice> either on account of deficiency or on account of excess hinders serving and contemplating the divine, this is base [*phaulos*]. Thus it is with the soul, and this is the best standard for the soul—whenever it perceives as little as possible the non-rational [*alogou*] part of the soul, insofar as it is such [*hê(i) toiouton*]. [*EE* 1249b16–23]

Let's focus now on the first part of the chapter. The announced topic is *kalokagathia*, or fine-and-goodness, which Aristotle describes as a whole composed of each of the particular virtues. Aristotle then introduces a distinction among ends, or things such-as-to-be-chosen for their own sakes.[12] Some are such-as-to-be-praised [*epaineta*], and

---

[10] This raises the possibility of reading Aristotle's conception of *phronêsis* as the result of reflection on the sort of knowledge required if we are to accept the Socratic identification of virtue with knowledge. For discussion of this possibility, see John McDowell, "Virtue and Reason," *Monist* 62 (1979): 331–50.

[11] I discuss intellectualist interpretations of *EN* X in "Human Nature and Intellectualism in Aristotle," *Archiv für Geschichte der Philosophie* 68 (1986): 70–95 [Chapter 2, this volume].

[12] Since the '*-etos*' suffix in adjectives like '*hairetos*' and '*epainetos*' may indicate either (a) that something is *in fact* the sort of thing that is chosen (or praised) or (b) that something is the sort of thing that *ought* to be chosen (or praised), I render these adjectives "such-as-to-be-chosen" and "such-as-to-be-praised," with a view to capturing this ambiguity. This formulation (unlike "choiceworthy" and "praiseworthy") seems to me to allow sense (b) without requiring it: an action may be such-as-to-be-praised in the sense (a) that members of a given society typically praise such actions, even though it is not such-as-to-be-praised in the sense (b) that it is praiseworthy.

these are fine [*kala*]. They include the various virtues, like justice and temperance, and actions stemming from these virtues. Others are not such-as-to-be-praised, and these are good but not also fine. They include things like health and strength, and their effects. Aristotle's explanation of this distinction as one between ends that are and ends that are not suitable objects of praise suggests that he has in mind a distinction between ends that are somehow "up to the agent" and ends that are not "up to the agent," but rather mere "goods of fortune." And his examples bear this out.

Aristotle relies on this distinction among ends in explaining the distinction between the merely *agathos* and the *kaloskagathos*. While natural goods are good but not fine for the merely *agathos*, such goods are both good and fine for the *kaloskagathos* because he—unlike the merely *agathos*—*chooses* them for the sake of something fine. As Aristotle puts it,

> Things are fine whenever that for the sake of which men do and choose them is fine. Wherefore the natural goods are fine for the *kaloskagathos*. [*EE* 1249a5–7]

Now this may give us pause. It is easy enough to understand how the virtues and virtuous actions, being up to the agent, are suitable objects of praise (where this is a condition of their being fine). But what should we make of Aristotle's claim that the natural goods are fine for the *kaloskagathos*, if this is supposed to involve their being suitable objects of praise? For Aristotle generally views the natural goods as goods of fortune, goods the possession of which is not within the agent's control. So how can these goods—or even their possession—be suitable objects of praise? This is the first of two puzzles that I aim eventually to resolve.

The second puzzle arises from the fact that Aristotle illustrates the character of the merely *agathos* by appeal to the "civic disposition" [*hexis politikê*] characteristic of the Spartans. These men believe correctly that they ought to possess virtue, but they believe incorrectly that they ought to possess it *for the sake of natural goods*. Because of this mistaken belief, the Spartans do fine things only coincidentally [*kata sumbebêkos*]. Kant might say that they act only in *conformity* with duty and not *from* duty. Aristotle thus claims that the Spartans are merely *agathoi*. For *kalokagathia* requires choosing fine things for their own sakes, and not for the sake of natural or external goods.

But Aristotle's distinction between performing virtuous actions and being virtuous raises a puzzle about the sense in which he takes the Spartans to be good. For on his view, it is not sufficient for being virtuous that one reliably performs virtuous actions. There are three further conditions: first, one must know what one is doing; second, one must decide on doing these things and decide on them "for themselves"; and third, one must act being firmly and unalterably disposed to do so [*EN* 1105a30–34]. And it seems clear that the Spartans fail the second condition: they do not decide on virtuous actions "for themselves." That is why Aristotle says that they do fine things only coincidentally. Aristotle says nevertheless that they are good, and applies some version of the conditionality thesis to them, distinguishing them from the non-*agathoi* who—on account of ignorance and vice—misuse the natural goods so that these things are not even good for them. In what sense, then, are the Spartans supposed to be good, given their failure to choose virtuous actions "for themselves"?

Sarah Broadie proposes to resolve this puzzle by distinguishing the first-order attitudes of agents engaged in practice from the second-order attitudes of agents reflecting on their first-order practices. On her view, we cannot explain Aristotle's claim that the Spartan is good unless we allow that the Spartan's first-order practice (like that of the *kaloskagathos*) involves choosing virtuous actions "for themselves."[13] The difference lies in what the merely *agathos* will *say* when he reflects on the ultimate rationale for his first-order practices (including their concomitant attitudes). As Broadie puts it,

> The merely good man certainly cares about virtue: he seeks to inculcate it in his children; he deplores its absence in others; in each situation he wants to know what it is right to do so as to act upon it; and he may put even his life on the line in doing what he sees himself called upon to do. He behaves as if good conduct matters most, and his behavior is itself a judgement to this effect. But when asked why virtue matters most, the answer he gives, *if he makes anything at all of the question*, is that it is for the sake of the natural goods. We should note that for a person to count as good and as living a life of virtue, it is not necessary that he have a general view about why virtue is important. Nor is it necessary that he think about his own virtues or about his actions as exercises of virtue. He may simply make and stand by good decisions, each as it comes along.[14]

Broadie thus represents the merely *agathos* as a nonreflective but nevertheless genuinely virtuous agent. Though she allows that false reflection can undermine good practice, she denies that true reflection is necessary for good practice. So the *kaloskagathos*, though superior in reflective understanding, is not necessarily superior in practice. Broadie takes Aristotle to be making the anti-Socratic point that virtuous practice does not require articulate knowledge of the good.

I myself am less confident than Broadie in the practical congruence of the *kaloskagathos* and the merely *agathos*. It is clear from *Politics* (*Pol.*) II.9 and elsewhere that Aristotle thinks that the reflective view that virtue is to be pursued for the sake of natural goods renders the Spartans practically deficient in a variety of ways.[15] They emphasize one part of virtue (namely, bravery) at the expense of others (particularly justice and temperance). And though the demands of war provide temporary incentives to just and temperate behavior, these incentives do not survive in times of peace.

[13] Think here of Kant's men of sympathetic temperament, who "without any further motive of vanity or self-interest find an inner pleasure in spreading happiness around them" [*Gr.* 398]. For more on these men, see C. M. Korsgaard, "From Duty and for the Sake of the Noble: Kant and Aristotle on Morally Good Action," in Engstrom and Whiting, *Rethinking Happiness and Duty*, 203–36.

[14] Sarah Broadie, *Ethics with Aristotle* (Oxford: Oxford University Press, 1991), 379, emphasis added. Cf. Anthony Kenny, *Aristotle on the Perfect Life* (Oxford: Oxford University Press, 1992).

[15] For useful general discussion of the Spartans, see Stephen White, *Sovereign Virtue* (Stanford, CA: Stanford University Press, 1992), 219–46.

Moreover, the Spartans, though knowing how to *acquire* natural goods, do not know how to *use* these goods correctly: they know nothing about how to spend or enjoy the leisure for the sake of which war is waged. This last point reinforces the second puzzle. For insofar as the Spartans fail to use natural goods correctly, they seem to resemble the non-*agathoi*. In what sense, then, does Aristotle think them good?

The last point serves also to indicate the connection between the first and second parts of *EE* VIII.3. Aristotle's point seems to be that knowing the contemplative standard with reference to which natural goods are to be chosen is what distinguishes the *kaloskagathos* from the merely *agathos*, and saves him from the fate of the Spartans. We need not take this to require that the *kaloskagathos* himself live the contemplative life. He may be a legislator who arranges the state so that those who are capable of contemplation are able (unlike their Spartan counterparts) to achieve it, at least during times of peace. I want to leave that question open for now. I also want to suspend judgment on the extent to which Aristotle is making an anti-Socratic point.

But my dissatisfaction with Broadie's account of the distinction between the merely *agathos* and the *kaloskagathos* leads me to seek an alternative—one that explains, moreover, how natural goods can be fine (and so objects of praise) for the *kaloskagathos*, thus resolving the first as well as the second puzzle.

2. *MEGALOPSUCHIA* AS *KALOKAGATHIA*?

Let us begin by turning to the *Nicomachean Ethics*, to see whether it sheds any light on the Eudemian distinction between the merely *agathos* and the *kaloskagathos*. Though it is often claimed that this distinction is without parallel in the *Nicomachean Ethics*, this is not obviously so. For the *Nicomachean Ethics* introduces two distinctions, each similar in important ways to the distinction between mere goodness and *kalokagathia*. One is the distinction (discussed in section 7 below) between "natural" and "authoritative" virtue. The other is the distinction (discussed here) between *megalopsuchia* and its unnamed (but modest) counterpart.

Megalopsuchia (magnanimity) resembles *kalokagathia* in two ways. First, each consists in having all the particular virtues. Second, each involves having the right attitude to natural (or external) goods. This raises the possibility of taking the distinction between *megalopsuchia* and its modest counterpart as a Nicomachean version of the distinction between *kalokagathia* and mere goodness. This may seem implausible, given that *EE* III.5 also contains an explicit discussion of *megalopsuchia* that is parallel to the discussion in *EN* IV.3. But I think this possibility worth exploring briefly, if only on account of what we learn in rejecting it.

The *megalopsuchos* (or magnanimous man) is one who rightly thinks himself worthy of great things. Aristotle presents him as lying in a mean between the conceited man, who wrongly thinks himself worthy of great things, and the pusillanimous man, who is worthy of great things but thinks falsely that he is not. Aristotle also recognizes another character who resembles the *megalopsuchos* in having a true conception of his own worth but who differs from the *megalopsuchos* insofar as he is worthy only of modest (and not of great) things. His virtue is unnamed, but he lies in a mean between the honor lover [*ho philotimos*] and his contrary [*ho aphilotimos*], who is indifferent to honor.

Aristotle says that this unnamed virtue stands to *megalopsuchia* as ordinary generosity stands to magnificence, thus suggesting that the difference between *megalopsuchia* and its unnamed counterpart is primarily one of scale, where this may involve some distinction between public and private deeds. This suggestion is confirmed by the fact that the Eudemian account says explicitly that the man with the unnamed virtue is "the same in nature as the *megalopsuchos*," and the sort of man who might become *megalopsuchos* [*EE* 1233a22–25]. This suggests that their common nature lies in the sort of self-knowledge we might call "appreciating one's own virtue," however grand or modest it may be. So we might treat *megalopsuchia* and its unnamed counterpart as two forms of *appreciating one's own virtue*.

Talk of appreciation is especially apt insofar as it connotes valuing and so has practical implications. Agents who correctly appreciate their own virtue will not make the Spartan mistake of choosing virtue for the sake of what are in fact lesser goods. Nor will they be tempted to sacrifice their virtue in exchange for lesser goods. In this respect, agents who appreciate their own virtue seem to resemble the *kaloskagathos*. But there is no obvious difference in this respect between the *megalopsuchos* and his unnamed counterpart. Each has the right attitude toward honor, valuing it correctly in relation both to virtue and to other goods. So neither seems likely to make the Spartan mistake of choosing virtue for the sake of what are in fact lesser goods. The difference between them seems to lie in the magnitude and not in the nature of their respective virtues.

The distinction between the *megalopsuchos* and his unnamed counterpart thus seems to be quantitative in a way in which that between the *kaloskagathos* and the merely *agathos* is not. For the latter distinction turns on a difference in motive: the *kaloskagathos* chooses virtuous actions for themselves, while the merely *agathos* chooses virtuous actions for the sake of external goods. It seems, then, that we must reject the suggestion that *kalokagathia* is to be identified with *megalopsuchia*. This conclusion seems required, moreover, by Aristotle's claim (at *EN* 1124a3–4) that *megalopsuchia* is "not possible without *kalokagathia*." But this claim, in suggesting that *kalokagathia* is a necessary condition for *megalopsuchia*, suggests another possibility—namely, that *megalopsuchia* is something like large-scale (or heroic) *kalokagathia*. On this account, *megalopsuchia* would stand to *kalokagathia* as magnificence stands to generosity.

Some might object to this hypothesis on the grounds that the *megalopsuchos*, in choosing virtue for the sake of honor, makes the Spartan mistake, and so cannot be *kaloskagathos*. This objection, if correct, would of course conflict with Aristotle's claim that *kalokagathia* is necessary for *megalopsuchia*. But the objection rests on the misguided view that the *megalopsuchos* is excessively concerned with honor and indeed motivated by consideration of it. It will prove worthwhile to consider precisely what is wrong with this objection.

3. THE *MEGALOPSUCHOS* AS *PHILOTIMOS*?

Commentators who represent the *megalopsuchos* as thus concerned with honor may be misled by the fact that Aristotle describes these virtues, along with their respective vices, as being "about honors and dishonors" [*peri timas kai atimias, EN* 1123b21–22]. But this does not mean that winning honor (or avoiding dishonor) is the primary object of concern or end for the sake of which the *megalopsuchos* and his unnamed counterpart act. The point is simply that these men have the right attitude toward honor, valuing it neither too much nor too little in relation to other goods. This should be clear from a quick look at what Aristotle says some of the other virtues are "about."

Bravery is "about fear and confidence" [*peri phobous kai tharrê, EN* 1115a5–6]. It is, roughly, a state lying in a mean between excessive or inappropriate fear and excessive or inappropriate confidence. But having appropriate fear and confidence is not itself the object of the brave man's concern or the end for the sake of which he acts: his object or end is to secure the safety of his *polis* or of his friends and loved ones. Appropriate fear and confidence are part of what enable him to secure these objects.

Generosity is "about wealth" [*peri chrêmata, EN* 1119b23]. More specifically, it is about the correct *use* of wealth. So it is concerned more with giving and spending than with taking and keeping, which are forms of possession [*ktêsis*] rather than use [*chrêsis, EN* 1120a8–9]. Because the generous man does not honor wealth and regards acquisition "not as fine but as necessary in order that he be able to give," he does not take from the wrong sources [*EN* 1120a31–b2]. Giving, however, he regards as fine, and does for the sake of the fine [*EN* 1120a23–24]. It is, in fact, characteristic of the generous man to exceed in giving, so as to leave less for himself. This makes it clear that Aristotle's claim that generosity is "about wealth" is not meant to suggest that wealth is the object of the generous man's concern or the end for the sake of which he acts. The generous man does not honor wealth for itself. He values it primarily for the sake of the generous actions it enables him to perform. These actions (along with their intended results) are the proper objects of his concern, and the ends for the sake of which he acts. Wealth, Aristotle might say, is something he values "coincidentally."[16]

Here, however, someone might object that the practical necessity of wealth for the exercise of generosity makes it easy to explain the sense in which generosity is "about wealth" in a way that it is not so easy to explain the sense in which *megalopsuchia* and its counterpart are "about honor." The instrumental status of wealth allows us to take wealth as a coincidental object of the generous man's concern, the proper object being that to which wealth contributes (where this includes not only generous action but also, and more importantly, its intended effects). But there is nothing so obvious for which honor is practically necessary or to which honor contributes in quite the same way: although the desire for honor may serve as an inducement to virtue, neither

---

[16] [For more on this, see "*Eudaimonia*, External Results, and Choosing Virtuous Actions for Themselves" (Chapter 3, this volume).]

honor nor the desire for it is necessary for virtuous action in the way that wealth is necessary for generous action. This helps to explain the temptation to assume that honor is the proper and not the coincidental concern of the *megalopsuchos* and his counterpart.

But even if honor is not necessary for virtuous action in quite the way that wealth is necessary for generous action, it might be necessary in some other way. It may, for example, be part of the concept of virtue that it is the sort of thing for which one *deserves* to be honored. The institution of virtue might be such that it could not exist apart from its agents' tendencies to honor and dishonor one another. In this case, honor and dishonor would be necessary for virtue, not in the sense that one could not perform a virtuous action without being honored (or without aiming to be honored) for it, but in the sense that we could not attribute virtue to someone without thereby thinking of him as deserving honor. In this case, the pursuit of virtue would coincide with the "pursuit" of worthiness-to-be-honored, even where the agent himself is relatively indifferent to considerations of honor. So the *megalopsuchos* can value honor coincidentally, though in a way somewhat different from that in which the generous person values wealth coincidentally. And the same goes for his unnamed counterpart. Each can value honor insofar as he values virtue and views honor as the proper reward (though not the object) of virtue.

The common emphasis on honor is unfortunate because it obscures a point that comes out most clearly in Aristotle's discussion of the *pusillanimous* man—the man who is worthy of great things but fails to claim them because he thinks, falsely, that he does not deserve them. Aristotle says that such men "hold back from fine actions and practices, and similarly also from external goods, on the grounds that they are unworthy" [*EN* 1125a25–27]. The point here seems to be that having a proper sense of one's own worth plays an important role in the production of virtuous action: the agent who underestimates his own worth will attempt (and therefore accomplish) less in the way of fine action than he would if he had a proper appreciation of his own worth. He may, for example, decline political office (which can constitute a kind of honor) because he thinks falsely that others are more capable (and hence more deserving) than he is. This shows how honor can play an important role in the production of virtuous action without itself serving as an incentive or motive to such action: the practice of honoring agents in proportion to their virtue contributes to the sort of self-knowledge necessary for virtuous action by teaching agents what exactly they are and are not capable of achieving. So honor may after all play an instrumental role in the production of virtuous action much like that played by wealth in the production of generous action. This of course assumes proper practices of honor: honor bestowed by those who know and appreciate one another's virtues for what they are.

The foregoing examples should suffice to show that Aristotle's claim that *megalopsuchia* and its unnamed counterpart are "about honors and dishonors" should not be taken to imply that honor is the *object* of the *megalopsuchos'* concern or the end for the sake of which he and his counterpart act. It is no more reasonable to represent the *megalopsuchos* or his counterpart as preoccupied with honor than to represent the generous man as preoccupied with wealth. The point is not that the *megalopsuchos* cares very much about honor, but only that he cares more about honor than about any other external good, though less about honor than he cares about internal goods (like virtue and contemplation). In this respect, the *megalopsuchos* differs from the Spartans, about whom Aristotle says in the *Politics*, "They are right in thinking that the contested goods are acquired by virtue rather than vice, but wrong in thinking these things superior to virtue" [*Politics* 1271b7–10]. So the *megalopsuchos*' attitude toward honor is no obstacle to identifying *megalopsuchia* with large-scale *kalokagathia*.

This account of the *megalopsuchos*' attitude to honor receives further support from the unequivocal location of honor among contested goods in Aristotle's account in *EN* IX.8 of the distinction between proper and improper self-love. For Aristotle draws a clear distinction there between the proper self-lover's pursuit of the *kalon* and the improper self-lover's pursuit of honor and other contested goods. And he firmly locates the *megalopsuchos* among proper self-lovers—that is, among those who pursue the *kalon* and not among those who pursue honor and other contested goods. Let us turn then to this chapter, which has often been interpreted as recommending a kind of "moral competition" in which virtuous agents—especially the *megalopsuchoi—seek* to outdo one another in performing virtuous action.

4. COMPETITIVE SELF-LOVE?

The announced topic of *EN* IX.8 is whether one ought to love oneself or someone else most of all. Aristotle goes on to distinguish two ways in which we speak of self-love, one "loose and popular," the other "strict and philosophical."[17] He then argues that the self-lover in the "loose and popular sense" should not love himself in that sense at all (let alone above all others), while the self-lover in the "strict and philosophical sense" should love himself in this sense (apparently above all others).[18]

The first sort of self-lover identifies his "self" with his appetites and the non-rational part of his soul. His self-love consists in lavishing upon *that* self contested goods like money, honors, and bodily pleasures. This is the sort of self-love that Aristotle regards as improper. It is crucial to note that Aristotle locates honor—the object of the naturally competitive spirit or *thumos—here* among contested goods.

[17] I borrow these labels from Bishop Butler's discussion of personal identity in the first appendix to *The Analogy of Religion* (1736).

[18] I add the parenthetical 'apparently' here because I want to suspend judgment for now on Aristotle's commitment to the comparative claim, which is the focus of my discussion. Although Aristotle begins with an explicitly comparative (actually superlative) question—namely, whether one ought to love oneself or someone else *most of all*—it does not follow that his answer will ultimately be comparative. For in prefacing his question by saying "it is puzzled [*aporeitai*]," Aristotle indicates that he seeks here to resolve an *aporia*. And it is characteristic of him to resolve such *aporiai* by rejecting the initial terms in which they are stated.

The second sort of self-lover identifies his "self" with his *nous*—that is, with his reason or understanding, which Aristotle says is his best and most authoritative [*kuriōtatō(i)*] element.[19] His self-love consists in gratifying and obeying *that* in everything he does, and Aristotle makes it clear in the remainder of the chapter that this sort of self-love may even require one to give up one's life for the sake of one's friends and polis. There is little doubt that Aristotle intends to refer here to the *megalopsuchos*, whom he described at *EN* 1124b8–9 as "unsparing of his life since he does not think life at all costs worthwhile" (Irwin's translation).

In order to reconcile what appears to be such extreme sacrifice with what Aristotle explicitly describes as the best sort of self-love, commentators often read the remainder of the chapter as touting what they call "moral competition" or "moral rivalry," as if Aristotle identified proper self-love with aiming to outdo all others (except perhaps one's other selves) in virtuous action.[20] Some even introduce the notion of competition explicitly in their translations, as Irwin did in early printings of his translation at *EN* 1169a8–11:

> And when everyone competes [*hamillômenôn*] to achieve what is fine and strains to do the finest actions, everything that is right will be done for the common good, and each person individually will receive the greatest of goods, since that is the character of virtue.[21]

Such "competitive" readings help to explain Wood's view that Aristotle's proper self-love corresponds to that essentially comparative satisfaction with oneself that Kant condemns—that is, "self-conceit" [*arrogantia*, or *Eigendünkel*].[22] But *EN* IX.8 need not be read competitively, and there is a strong case for saying it should not be read this way. Proper self-love may yet prove more Kantian than it appears at first glance.

---

[19] I say 'element' here rather than 'part of soul' in order to allow for the possibility that *nous* is (as Menn has argued) the *virtue* of the rational part of soul. See Stephen Menn, "Aristotle and Plato on God as Nous and as the Good," *Review of Metaphysics* 45 (1992): 543–73. [I discuss the appropriateness of talk about "parts of soul" in "Psychic Contingency in the *Republic*" (I.7); "Locomotive Soul" (III.5); and "Hylomorphic Virtue" (III.6).]

[20] See Richard Kraut, *Aristotle and the Human Good* (Princeton, NJ: Princeton University Press, 1989), esp. 115–28; and Julia Annas (with comments by Kraut), "Self-Love in Aristotle," *Southern Journal of Philosophy* 27, supplementary volume (1988): 1–23.

[21] Irwin has changed this in recent printings, which now read "when everyone *contends* to achieve what is fine and strains to do the finest actions" (emphasis added). But Irwin still speaks of competition in his commentary, ad *EN* 1168b26. The change in translation is no doubt motivated by his desire to discourage the tendency to read Aristotle as committed to an objectionable sort of moral competition. But Irwin still wants to say that Aristotle is committed to an unobjectionable sort of moral competition, like that attributed to him by Kraut. See Irwin, "Prudence and Morality in Greek Ethics," *Ethics* 105 (1995): 284–95, commenting on Nicholas White, "Conflicting Parts of Happiness in Aristotle's Ethics," *Ethics* 105 (1995): 258–83. See also note 27, this chapter.

[22] See Allen Wood, "Self-Love, Self-Benevolence, and Self-Conceit," in Engstrom and Whiting, *Rethinking Happiness and Duty*, 141–61.

Let me begin by explaining how I propose to use the "competitive" label. I propose to take the absence of any need for interpersonal comparison as sufficient for a reading's being "noncompetitive." I recognize of course that we often speak of "competing against oneself" or "against the clock," and that one might thus interpret self-contained striving to achieve an absolute standard as involving a kind of competition. But this metaphorical extension threatens to obscure the important difference between these cases and those in which interpersonal comparisons are required. The need for interpersonal comparison is thus a minimal condition for a reading's being "competitive." But something further seems required as well—something like a process that aims to yield a winner (even if we sometimes end up with a tie) or a zero-sum condition (in which one person's gain is another's loss).[23] We need not, however, worry too much for present purposes about how exactly to formulate this further condition. I have said enough, I think, to allow for reasonably clear and uncontroversial classification of the relevant interpretations. Let us turn then to my argument that there is a strong case for adopting a "noncompetitive" (or "noncomparative") reading of *EN* IX.8.

First, consider the passage quoted earlier. Although the verb '*hamillaomai*' is most often used in a competitive sense, where interpersonal comparisons are essentially involved in an attempt to identify winners, it can also be used in a noncompetitive sense, where no interpersonal comparisons need be involved. See, for example, *Republic* 490a, where Plato speaks of the philosopher "striving after" being or truth. In this case, no interpersonal comparison seems to be involved: the philosopher strives after truth, and may attain truth, regardless of how and what others do. This may be the sort of striving Aristotle has in mind when he suggests that *everyone* can achieve the greatest good if everyone strives to do what is fine, the idea being that each can seek and attain the good *regardless* of how and what others do.

This noncomparative or noncompetitive reading is plausible, given the role played in Aristotle's argument by the distinction between contested goods [*ta perimachêta*], like honor and power, and goods that are not so contested, like virtue and contemplation. The point is presumably that it is at least logically possible for everyone equally to achieve virtue or contemplation in a way in which it is not logically possible for everyone equally to achieve essentially comparative goods like honor and power.[24]

---

[23] Strictly speaking, a zero-sum condition (in which one person's loss is another's gain because the sum of benefits to be distributed is fixed) is too strong. For competition may increase the sum of benefits to be distributed, and this seems especially likely in the sort of competition Aristotle seems to have in mind. But insofar as competition is essentially comparative in that one person wins (regardless of his absolute "score") only if he has more than his competitors, so that one person's gain (even if only relative) is typically another person's loss (even if only relative), we might represent the competitive dimension itself as having a kind of zero-sum character.

[24] A point apparently missed by Kraut, who speaks as if competitions never ended—and indeed could not end—in ties. See also Annas ("Self-Love in Aristotle") for a reading similar to mine, though she finds it so difficult to admit that Aristotle is not talking about competition that she ends up claiming that he "reinterprets the notion of competition" so that "true competition is not really competition at all." It seems to me less oxymoronic to claim that he is talking about competition (if at all) only in the metaphorical sense mentioned above.

Moreover, and more importantly, it is in principle possible for each to achieve his goal, and to know that he has achieved it, without knowing how he stands in relation to the achievements of others.

Next, consider the following passage, which is often taken to support the competitive interpretation:

> The decent person does the things he ought to do. For every *nous* chooses the best for itself, and the decent person obeys *nous*. And it is true of the excellent person that he does many things for the sake of his friends and fatherland, and will even die for them if he must. He will yield[25] money, honors, and contested goods generally, in achieving the *kalon* for himself. For he would choose to be intensely pleased for a short time rather than moderately pleased for a long time, to live finely [*kalôs*] for one year rather than in any old way for many years, and <to perform> one fine and great action rather than many small ones. This is presumably true of those who die for others. For they choose something great and *kalon* for themselves. They will yield money, if their friends gain more. The friend gets money, while he gets the *kalon*. So he awards himself the greater good. It is the same way, with honors and offices; he will yield all these to his friend, for this is *kalon* for him and such-as-to-be-praised. So he is reasonably thought to be excellent, choosing the *kalon* above all things. And it is even possible that he will yield <virtuous> actions to his friend, it being finer to be the cause of his friend's doing them than to do them himself. [*EN* 1169a16–34]

This passage, which clearly refers to the *megalopsuchos*, sharply distinguishes the pursuit of the *kalon* from the pursuit of honor: the agent, in pursuing the *kalon*, yields honors (along with wealth and power) to his friends. This fits the picture of the *megalopsuchos* sketched earlier: he may care more about honor than about any other external goods, but this does not mean that he cares very much about honor.

Now giving up things that one does not value much to begin with isn't all so heroic, and one might even object that such "sacrifice" is ultimately selfish insofar as the agent thereby secures for himself the *kalon*, which is explicitly said to be a greater good than these other things. And this, according to some commentators, is exactly the point if such "sacrifice" is to be viewed as a form of *self*-love. But there are two things to notice here.

First, it is important, though rarely remarked, that the *kalon*—insofar as it consists in virtue and virtuous action—is not generally the sort of thing one *can* secure for one's friends. Aristotle notes, as if to forestall the foregoing objection, that one may provide one's friends with *opportunities* to secure the *kalon* by providing them with *opportunities* for virtuous action: but virtuous action is—and this is a logical point—something

[25] I prefer the more neutral 'yield' to Irwin's 'sacrifice' for '*proêsetai*,' which is often used in the sense of "to abandon freely," as in the case where someone gives something up without asking anything in exchange.

one can secure only for oneself.[26] The *kalon* is not like money or political office: it is not the sort of thing you can choose either to give to another or to keep for yourself. You can provide others with opportunities to achieve it, but the achievement itself is largely up to them. That helps to explain why the *kalon* is not among the goods of fortune.

Second, commentators tend to speak as if Aristotle's claim that the agent awards himself the greater good must be read as involving a choice between awarding the greater of two goods to *himself* and awarding the greater of two goods to *someone else*. But we have just seen reasons for doubting that this *could* be the relevant choice. Moreover, assuming that the relevant goods here are the *kalon* (which is the greater good) and some external good (which is the lesser good), and assuming that one can achieve the *kalon* only for oneself, it is perfectly reasonable to view the agent's choice as one between awarding himself the greater good and awarding himself the lesser good. Aristotle may be claiming only that the agent, in choosing the *kalon*, awards himself the greater of two goods than he would have awarded himself had he chosen the external good instead. In this case, the relevant comparison is not with what the agent *actually* awards to *someone else*, but rather with the goods he might *hypothetically* have awarded *himself* instead of the greater good.[27]

The main obstacle to this reading is at *EN* 1169a8–10, where the contrast, signaled by the '*men* . . .*de* . . .' construction, is clearly between what the friend gets (i.e., external goods) and what the agent gets (i.e., the *kalon*). But even in this situation, the agent gets a greater good than he would have got had he acted differently. So this passage does not show that Aristotle does not also have in mind the contrast I suggest. Moreover, I think my reading is supported by the fact that Aristotle goes on almost immediately to speak of situations in which the agent may secure something more *kalon* for himself by yielding actions (or opportunities to secure the *kalon*) to his friend. For it is not at all obvious in this case, where both may secure the *kalon*, that the agent secures a greater good than his friend secures. It is clear here that the comparative need not be taken as claiming that the agent secures for himself something more *kalon* than what his friend secures: the point may be simply that he secures for himself something more *kalon* than he would have secured had he not provided his friend an

[26] Kant makes a similar point in the *Metaphysics of Morals*, where he claims (at 386) that "it is a contradiction for me to make another's *perfection* my end" (translation from M. Gregor ed., *Kant: Metaphysics of Morals* (Cambridge: Cambridge University Press, 1996).

[27] This suggests that one might also reject Irwin's rendering of *EN* 1168b25–29, which (like the Revised Oxford Translation) represents Aristotle as saying that the proper self-lover aims to do virtuous actions above all other *agents*. It is possible, however, to read Aristotle as claiming that the proper self-lover aims to do virtuous actions above all other *things*, taking '*pantôn*' as neuter. But even if one insists on taking '*pantôn*' as referring to persons, one needn't take it as part of the *content* of the virtuous person's aim. We can take Aristotle as claiming (a) that the virtuous person, above all others, aims to do virtuous actions; rather than (b) that the virtuous person aims at outdoing all others in virtuous action. Irwin, however, wants (in his comments on White, "Conflicting Parts of Happiness") to attribute a version of (b) to Aristotle. But as I argue in note 29 below, it is not obvious that Aristotle views the virtuous agent as seeking to outdo his friends in the pursuit of virtuous action.

opportunity to secure the *kalon* too. The fact that Aristotle chooses to end on this note renders it plausible to read the chapter as "deconstructing" or rejecting the terms of the comparative question with which it began. For it seems to me significant that he concludes by saying not that one ought in the "strict and philosophical sense" to love oneself "most of all," but *only* that one ought to love oneself in this sense *period*.[28]

But even if one declines to read Aristotle as deconstructing his initial *aporia* in this way, one can still make sense of his claim, that the good person ought to love himself most of all, without introducing moral competition. Since loving someone (whether oneself or another) consists at least partly in awarding goods to the beloved, and since the best sort of goods—internal goods like virtue and contemplation—are the sorts of things that one can strictly award only to oneself, there is an important sense in which the good person cannot help but love himself most of all: if he is going to award the greatest goods to anyone at all, he must award them to himself. This may sometimes involve asking whether it would be more *kalon* to provide someone else an opportunity for virtuous action than to do the action oneself. But even in this case, the agent cannot (logically) award the *kalon* directly to someone else. Moreover, in providing someone else with an opportunity to achieve the *kalon*, the agent does not then award the *kalon* to someone else instead of himself. For in providing another with the opportunity to achieve the *kalon*, the agent thereby achieves the *kalon* for himself. That is why the *kalon* is not among the contested goods.

One might of course object that taking the "self-sacrifice" passage as referring to the *megalopsuchos* undermines my attempt to read it noncompetitively, given the competitive terms in which Aristotle describes the *megalopsuchos* elsewhere. I am thinking primarily of the passage in *EN* IV.3, where he says that the *megalopsuchos* prefers benefiting others to receiving benefits from others, because benefiting others is a sign of superiority and receiving benefits from others a sign of inferiority. Aristotle goes on to say that the *megalopsuchos* seeks to display his greatness only in the company of those who are worthy, where it is difficult and impressive to achieve superiority, and not in the company of average men, where superiority is easy to achieve but vulgar to pursue.

There is of course no denying the presence of competition here. But it is worth noting an important limitation in its scope: the *megalopsuchos* no more bothers competing with average men than world-class athletes bother competing with local amateurs. This may suggest that it is not superiority per se that he seeks, but rather the sort of accomplishment to which competition with formidable opponents is often—though not always—the best means. I say "not always" because truly exceptional individuals who are not sufficiently challenged by the available competition often do better to aim at an absolute or impersonal standard instead. Such cases suggest that interpersonal comparison is not essential—and so that competition is not essential—to the life of the *megalopsuchos*.[29]

---

[28] See note 18 above.

[29] It seems plausible that the competition to which Aristotle refers in *EN* IV.3 is *not* competition between the *megalopsuchos* and his character friends, but rather competition between the *megalopsuchos* and less intimate but nevertheless worthy characters. This would be fully compatible with the *megalopsuchos*

This clears the way for a noncompetitive reading of *EN* IX.8, which suggests the possibility of reading Aristotle in something like the way in which Wood reads Kant—that is, as recommending that our assessments of self-worth be based not on any comparison of ourselves with others, but rather on a comparison of ourselves with something like Kant's moral law. This is suggested by one moral that Aristotle draws (in a somewhat different context) from the identification of a man with his *nous*—namely, that he ought to strive as far as possible to live the life of a god. For there is no suggestion in Aristotle's text that the agent will be satisfied with outdoing actual competitors, who may or may not be worthy competitors: the agent is supposed to do the best of which he is capable, whatever others do. Moreover, this is perfectly compatible with his seeking to help his friends—especially his character friends but perhaps also citizen friends—to do the best of which they are capable, even in cases where they threaten to outstrip him. The point is simply that the virtuous person will aim at this standard whatever others, however much better or worse than he is, happen to do.

There are thus grounds for a Kantian reading of Aristotle's identification of a man with his *nous*. But before developing this reading, we must pause briefly (after summarizing the argument thus far) to examine the connection Aristotle sees between justice and proper self-love. For Aristotle's meritocratic conception of justice seems far removed from the radical egalitarianism that Wood ascribes to Kant.

5. SELF-LOVE, JUSTICE, AND *KALOKAGATHIA*

We began searching in section 2 above for Nicomachean parallels to the Eudemian distinction between *kalokagathia* and mere goodness. And while rejecting the hypothesis that *megalopsuchia* is to be identified with *kalokagathia*, we retained the hypothesis that *megalopsuchia* is large-scale *kalokagathia* (the idea being that the unnamed counterpart of the *megalopsuchos* also possesses *kalokagathia*, but on a smaller scale). But this hypothesis is tenable only given the plausibility (demonstrated in section 3

doing all he can to bring it about that his character friends achieve the best of which they are capable, even in cases where they are likely to outstrip him. That superiority per se is probably not the issue can be seen by asking oneself whether the *megalopsuchos* would be more likely to choose as his character friend (a) someone slightly superior to him in virtue or (b) someone slightly inferior to him in virtue. My hunch is that the true *megalopsuchos*, appreciating the value of virtue as he does, will choose the superior friend. This hunch receives some support from *Laws* 731d–2b, where Plato says (in a passage that anticipates Aristotle's association of *megalopsuchia* with proper, as distinct from improper, self-love) that the man who strives to be "great" (*megan*) will not love himself excessively (i.e., improperly) but will pursue one who is better than himself. Plato's use of *diôkein* with the accusative of person suggests a lover's "pursuit" of his beloved, thus suggesting that the *megalopsuchos* will pursue someone better than himself, not only in order to associate with his superior (presumably for the sake of self-improvement), but also (as suggested here) with a view to awarding goods (like political office) to those (if any) more deserving than himself (cf. *MM* 1212b15–20, quoted in section 5, this chapter). Plato also says here that improper self-love is the cause of all wrongdoing, thus anticipating the view I attribute to Aristotle (in section 5) that proper self-love is in a sense the whole of virtue. For more on Plato's anticipation of the views I attribute to Aristotle, see note 39 below.

above) of rejecting the common picture of the *megalopsuchos* as concerned primarily with honor. For Aristotle clearly distinguishes the *kaloskagathos*, who chooses virtuous actions for themselves, from the merely *agathos*, like the Spartan, who chooses virtuous actions for the sake of external goods (including honor).

Section 4 above was meant to reinforce the argument for rejecting the common picture of the *megalopsuchos* by appealing to *EN* IX.8, where Aristotle assigns the *megalopsuchos* to the class of proper self-lovers (who pursue the *kalon*), as opposed to the class of improper self-lovers (who pursue contested goods like honor), thus preserving the tenability of the hypothesis that *megalopsuchia* is large-scale *kalokagathia*. Given Aristotle's claim that the *megalopsuchos* and his unnamed counterpart share the same nature, it seems plausible to view both as proper self-lovers, and to draw some distinction within proper self-love (parallel to that drawn within *kalokagathia*) between larger- and smaller-scale instantiations. This allows us to hypothesize that *kalokagathia* is to be identified with proper self-love, without abandoning our hypothesis that *megalopsuchia* is large-scale *kalokagathia*. For we can easily take *megalopsuchia* as proper self-love writ large, while taking its unnamed counterpart as proper self-love writ small. And this distinction makes good intuitive sense: an agent of modest ability does himself no good—and may actually harm himself—by laying claim to goods (like political office) that he is not equipped to handle.

Here, however, there might seem to be a problem, given Aristotle's claim that *kalokagathia* is complete virtue in the sense that it is a whole composed of each of the particular virtues [*EE* 1248b8–16]. For Aristotle says in his account of justice that justice is "complete virtue" [*teleia aretê*, *EN* 1129b30] and "not a part but the whole of virtue" [*ou meros aretês all' holê aretê*, *EN* 1130a9]. And this might seem to suggest that *kalokagathia* is more plausibly identified with justice than with self-love, which seems at most only a part of virtue.

Before I address this problem, it is necessary to say a few words about Aristotle's conception of justice. The first thing to note is that Aristotle regards a distribution as just if it involves what he calls "proportional" as distinct from "numerical" equality, where this means that external goods (like wealth, honor, and political office) are to be distributed to agents according (or in proportion) to their merit or worth [*kat' axian*].[30] Since Aristotle identifies an agent's worth largely if not exclusively with the extent to which he succeeds in actualizing virtue, Aristotelian justice consists roughly in distributing external goods in proportion to actualized virtue. This has both a retrospective (or meritocratic) and a prospective (or quasi-utilitarian) rationale. The virtuous person makes the best (or most beneficial) use of the external goods he receives because he benefits others not equally but in proportion to their virtue. Speaking roughly, then, he benefits others in proportion to *their* tendency to benefit others. Note, however, that the just man must also distribute external goods to himself according to the same principle. This helps to explain the claim (at *MM* 1212a37–40) that the virtuous agent

[30] See *EN* 1131a24ff. and *Pol.* 1301b30ff.

will yield goods like wealth and political office to those who are able to make better use of these goods than he will. For this is required not only by justice, but also (as we have just seen) by proper self-love: a man may harm himself by laying claim to goods that others can put to more beneficial use.

The next thing to note is that Aristotle seems to think that (at least in well-ordered societies) actions in accordance with each of the particular virtues tend to promote just distributions, while actions that violate any of the particular virtues tend to upset just distributions. (Intemperance, for example, leads men to help themselves to other men's women, while temperance restrains them from doing so.)[31] Aristotle is thus inclined to regard all genuinely virtuous actions as just (insofar as they promote just distributions) and all vicious actions as unjust (insofar as they upset just distributions), with the result that he views each of the particular virtues as parts of what he calls "general justice," which he identifies roughly with obeying the laws enjoining virtuous actions and prohibiting vicious ones.

But Aristotle recognizes an important distinction between agents who commit acts of general injustice out of greed or the desire to have more than their fair share, as such, of various goods, and agents who commit acts of general injustice from other motives, like the desire for pleasure (which might on its own lead a man to seduce his neighbor's wife) or fear (which might on its own lead a man to shirk his military duty). Agents motivated by greed—or a desire for *more than their fair share as such*—commit what Aristotle calls "special" injustice. Agents who commit only general injustice perform actions that tend as a matter of fact to promote unjust distributions, though this is not the end for the sake of which they act. But unjust distributions are precisely the ends for the sake of which those who commit special injustice act. These men aim at more than their fair share of contested goods like money, honor, and political power.[32]

Note, however, that in both cases—the special and the general—it follows from the conditionality thesis that any so-called goods that an agent secures for himself in excess of his fair share will *not* be good for him, and may actually harm him. So injustice, both general and special, is incompatible with self-love conceived as a form of what Kant calls "self-benevolence."[33] This suggests that general justice (including special justice) coincides with proper self-love, which might explain why Aristotle qualifies his claim that justice is complete virtue by saying that it is complete virtue "not absolutely but in relation to another" [*EN* 1129b25–27]. For the qualification may be intended to reflect the fact that proper self-love is the flip side of justice, something

[31] Distribution of women *kat' axian* may sound silly to some of us—though not, I fear, to enough of us. But one need think only of the quarrel between Achilles and Agamemnon to see how seriously Aristotle might have taken it.

[32] For a discussion of this distinction, see Bernard Williams, "Justice as a Virtue," in Amélie Rorty (ed.), *Essays on Aristotle's Ethics* (Berkeley: University of California Press, 1980), 189–99; and David K. O'Connor, "Aristotelian Justice as a Personal Virtue," *Midwest Studies in Philosophy* 13 (1988): 417–27.

[33] See Wood, "Self-Love, Self-Benevolence, and Self-Conceit," on Kant's distinction between "self-benevolence" [*Eigenliebe*, or *philautia*] and "self-conceit" [*Eigendünkel*, or *arrogantia*].

Aristotle might call "complete virtue in relation to *oneself*."[34] If so, then justice and proper self-love are plausibly viewed as *two aspects of a single virtue* that consists in distributing external goods—to oneself and to others—in proportion to virtue.

The coincidence of justice with proper self-love thus solves the foregoing problem. For given this coincidence, Aristotle's reference to general justice as "complete virtue" does not require us to identify *kalokagathia* with justice rather than proper self-love. We can instead view *kalokagathia* as a single virtue that can be viewed either under the aspect of justice or under the aspect of self-love.

It is important to the coincidence of justice with proper self-love that the principle of distribution in proportion to virtue be *impartial* in the following sense: the agent is to distribute goods—to himself and to others—in proportion to their virtue and without regard to any relationships (including that of identity) in which they stand to himself. That this is a matter not simply of justice but of proper self-love is suggested by a passage from the *Magna Moralia* parallel to the account in *EN* IX.8 of proper self-love:

> In one sense, <the good man> loves his friend more than himself; in another sense, he loves himself most of all. For <he loves> his friend more in matters of profit [*kata to sumpheron*], but <he loves> himself most of all in matters of the fine and good [*kata to kalon kai agathon*]. For he gains these things, which are most fine, for himself. He is, then, a lover-of-good [*philagathos*], not a lover-of-self [*philautos*]. For he loves himself only, if at all, because he is good. [*MM* 1212b15–20][35]

This suggests that the proper self-lover values his virtue primarily qua virtue and not qua his. And it follows from this that he values virtue impartially: he will value it, and want to reward it, whenever and wherever it appears. So he is no more (and no less) inclined to value virtue in himself than to value virtue in others.[36]

---

[34] The fact that *EN* IX contrasts proper self-love with friendship rather than justice is not a problem for this view. For it is clear in *EN* VIII.9 (and elsewhere) that Aristotle takes friendship and justice to be closely related. See, for example, his claim (at *EN* 1155a28) that "the justice that is most just seems to belong to friendship" (Irwin's translation). Consider also the importance he attaches to "civic friendship," discussed by John Cooper in "Political Animals and Civic Friendship," in G. Patzig (ed.), *Aristoteles' "Politik"* (Gottingen: Vandenhoeck & Ruprecht, 1990), 220–41; reprinted in J. Cooper, *Reason and Emotion* (Princeton, NJ: Princeton University Press, 1999), 356–77.

[35] For some defense of the authenticity of the *Magna Moralia*, see Franz Dirlmeier, *Aristoteles, Magna Moralia* (Berlin: Academie Verlag, 1963); and John Cooper, "The *Magna Moralia* and Aristotle's Moral Philosophy," *American Journal of Philology* 94 (1973): 327–49; reprinted in J. Cooper, *Reason and Emotion* (Princeton, NJ: Princeton University Press, 1999), 195–211. Even if the *Magna Moralia* was not itself written by Aristotle, I take it to provide genuine evidence of his views. [For an interesting take on the project of the *Magna Moralia* and its author, see Brad Inwood, *Ethics After Aristotle* (Cambridge, MA: Harvard University Press, 2014). Inwood—who follows an anonymous colleague in referring to the author as "Magnus"—suggests that "Magnus," while drawing on both the *Nicomachean* and the *Eudemian Ethics*, is an innovator, someone who aims to present his own, broadly Aristotelian views, which differ in various ways from Aristotle's own (most notably perhaps in being more open than Aristotle to Platonic views and more critical than Aristotle of Socratic intellectualism).]

[36] [The ideas expressed here derive from those expressed in "Impersonal Friends" (I.2)].

This talk of "valuing virtue" should call to mind section 3's account of *megalopsuchia* and its unnamed counterpart as sharing a common nature insofar as each consists in a sort of self-knowledge that is aptly described as "appreciating one's own virtue" (however grand or modest it proves to be). But it is now tempting (in light of the *Magna Moralia* passage) to drop the reference to self, and to speak simply of "appreciating virtue" (whether one's own or another's). And such appreciation is plausibly identified with *kalokagathia*. For this identification serves to explain why the *kaloskagathos* makes neither the Spartan mistake (of choosing virtue for the sake of lesser goods) nor the vulgar mistake (of sacrificing virtue in exchange for lesser goods).[37] Moreover, this identification is consistent with our hypothesis that *megalopsuchia* is large-scale *kalokagathia*. For *megalopsuchia*, like its unnamed counterpart, is a form of appreciating virtue.

6. *NOUS* AND THE MORAL LAW

There are no doubt important differences between the Kantian view (according to Wood) that all rational beings have absolute (and therefore equal) worth and Aristotle's conception of justice as a kind of proportional (as opposed to numerical) equality. But the commitment to impartiality implicit in Aristotle's conception of justice is arguably a step in the Kantian direction. For even if Aristotle's demand that external goods be distributed to agents in proportion to their merits requires Aristotelian citizens to make the sort of comparative judgments that Kant eschews, this need not be taken to involve any *intrinsically* inegalitarian motives on their part or even on Aristotle's. Moreover, Aristotle seems to allow that it is in principle possible—and perhaps ideally the case—that all men (anyhow) should be equally virtuous, in which case they should take turns ruling and being ruled.[38]

Aristotle discusses this point in *Politics* III.16, where his commitment to some sort of impartiality is evident. After saying that equals should take turns ruling and being ruled, he suggests that the rule of law [*nomos*] is in principle preferable to the rule of men, and that men should rule primarily as servants and guardians of the law. He seems to think that rule by men is a matter of practical necessity because the law cannot determine and legislate in advance what should be done in all possible or even actual circumstances. For this reason, men who administer the law are explicitly allowed to correct the law in cases where experience proves something superior to the

[37] We need not worry here that identifying virtue with appreciating virtue is circular or regressive. For we are talking about the whole of virtue, whose content is provided by the various particular virtues (just as the content of general justice is provided by the particular virtues of which it is said to be the whole). But it is instructive to think here of the problems raised in Plato's *Charmides* concerning the proposed identification of temperance with self-knowledge. [For more on the independent content of the virtues, see "*Eudaimonia*, External Results, and Choosing Virtuous Actions for Themselves" (Chapter 3, this volume).]

[38] See *Pol.* VI.14 and the use Kraut makes of it in chap. 2 of *Aristotle on the Human Good*.

established law. But Aristotle contrasts such rule by men, even as servants and guardians of the law, with rule by law alone:

> The one, then, who commands that the law should rule seems to command that the God and intelligence alone [*ton theon kai ton noun monous*] should rule, while the one who commands that man <should rule> adds also a beast. For appetite [*epithumia*] is such, and *thumos* corrupts even the best of men who rule. Wherefore, the law is *nous* without desire [*aneu orexeôs nous*] [*Pol*. 1287a28–32; cf. 1296a16–20 and *EN* 1134a35–b8][39]

It is clear from what follows that Aristotle prefers rule by law to rule by men because he takes rule by law to be impartial in a way in which rule by men is not. For he proceeds to contrast human administration of law with human administration of medicine by saying that doctors do nothing contrary to principle [*para ton logon*, presumably medical principle] from motives of friendship, but simply cure for a fee, while those who administer the law are accustomed to do many things with a view to profit or favor [*pros epêreian kai charin*]. The idea is apparently that desire (for goods like pleasure) and *thumos* (for goods like honor) leads men who administer the law to act against principle (including the principle of distribution according to worth) for the sake of personal or filial gain.

Such behavior is no doubt an expression of improper self-love, and incompatible with proper self-love. For given the conditionality thesis, any so-called goods that a ruler secures by violating the principle of distribution according to worth will not in fact be good for him and may actually harm him. This explains why the identification with one's *nous*, associated in *EN* IX.8 with proper self-love, is so valuable a trait in a ruler. For one who identifies with his *nous* will not be led by desire or *thumos* to administer the law in ways that are contrary to the principle of distribution according to worth. Moreover, it follows from Aristotle's identification of (anorectic) *nous* with law that the agent who identifies with his *nous* identifies ipso facto with this law. He will thus serve himself by serving this law.

Furthermore, Aristotle's association of *nous* with the divine provides some license for taking the identification of self with *nous* as positing an absolute standard, within

[39] The idea of *nous* as divine and as providing a kind of law within the self did not originate with Aristotle, and is familiar from Platonic texts. See, e.g., *Laws* 714a, where Plato says that we should obey what is immortal in us, assigning the name "law" to the distribution (presumably of goods and offices) commanded by *nous* [*tên tou nou dianomên*], and *Republic* 591d, where Plato says that it is better for everyone to be governed by what is divine and intelligent [*hupo theiou kai phronimou archesthai*], the best situation being one in which this principle is proper [*oikeion*] and internal to the subject rather than imposed from without. Other sources invoke the idea of a law within the soul, an idea whose time for historical study has come. See, e.g., Democritus B 264, which says that one should have a sense of shame (or awe) most of all in relation to oneself [*heôuton malista aideisthai*], letting this be established as *law in one's soul* [*touton nomon têi psuchêi kathestanai*]. For discussion of this and other texts relevant to many of my present concerns, see Douglas L. Cairns, *Aidôs: The Psychology and Ethics of Honor and Shame in Ancient Greek Literature* (Oxford: Oxford University Press, 1993).

the self, analogous to Kant's moral law. And this renders my noncompetitive reading more plausible. For this makes it easier to read Aristotle as recommending that our assessments of self-worth be based on a comparison of ourselves not with other human agents, but with an absolute standard analogous to Kant's moral law—that is, with the God.

7. *NOUS* IDENTIFICATION AND CONSTITUTIVE LUCK

My Kantian reading derives further support from the plausibility of taking Aristotle to share something like Kant's concern with autonomy. This is best seen if we read *EE* VIII.3 in the context provided by VIII.2, where Aristotle is concerned with something like the problem known among contemporary Kantians as that of constitutive luck.[40] It is clear from VIII.2 that Aristotle takes some men to be consistently fortunate in the sense that they "do the right thing" in spite of the fact that they lack the sort of knowledge or understanding that ordinarily explains such success (including, most importantly, "ethical" success). Aristotle is tempted to attribute such success to the fact that nature has endowed such men with good impulses in much the same way that nature endows some men with the musical talent that enables them to sing in spite of the fact that they lack musical knowledge.

But there is a disanalogy here, insofar as Aristotle's teleology requires the relevant impulses to be relatively widespread in a way in which natural operatic talent is not: these are the impulses from which virtue develops, and the capacity for virtue (though occasionally lacking) belongs by nature to those to whom it belongs (i.e., to most men). Assuming, then, that the majority of men are neither wise nor consistently fortunate, there will be many men who have good impulses but consistently fail (on account of their ignorance) to do the right thing. So good natural impulses cannot be the whole story.

Aristotle suggests, not surprisingly, that something divine makes the difference, though he has just expressed worries about this on the grounds that it would be

[40] On this problem, concerning the role played by factors beyond our control (like upbringing and natural endowment) in determining what sorts of characters we have, see Thomas Nagel, "Moral Luck," in *Mortal Questions* (Cambridge: Cambridge University Press, 1979), 24–38; and Michele Moody-Adams, "On the Old Saw That Character Is Destiny," in O. Flanagan and A. Rorty (eds.), *Identity, Character and Morality* (Cambridge, MA: MIT Press, 1990), 111–31. I do not mean to suggest that Aristotle's concerns are precisely the same as those of contemporary Kantians. I think, for example, that my view is compatible with Meyer's view that Aristotle's concern with responsibility for character does not stem from the "modern" assumption that responsibility for character is a necessary condition for holding agents morally responsible (and so praise- and blameworthy). See Susan Sauvé Meyer, *Aristotle on Moral Responsibility* (Oxford: Blackwell, 1993), esp. chap. 5. For I assimilate Aristotle's concern with responsibility for character to his view that we should strive as far as possible to achieve the sort of self-sufficiency characteristic of the gods, whom Aristotle takes to be beyond praise and blame. So even though I disagree with many of the details of Meyer's account, I do not think her basic picture incompatible with mine. But a full discussion of Aristotle's views on responsibility for character and their relation to my basic picture calls for a separate discussion.

strange for a god or a *daimôn* to favor the ignorant (and thus undeserving) rather than the wise (and thus deserving). But the issue here is the agent's initial endowment, not what he deserves or merits as a result of what he does with this endowment. And though Aristotle is ultimately ambivalent about whether to describe the source of initial endowment as natural or divine, he remains confident that there is such a thing. And he thinks that there is an important difference between what nature or divine causes make of one, and what one makes of oneself.

This is clear from *EN* X.9, where Aristotle—in discussing whether men come to be good by nature, habit, or instruction—says,

> It is plain that the <contribution> of nature is not up to us [*ouk eph' hêmin*], but belongs on account of some divine causes [*dia tinas theias aitias*] to those who are truly fortunate [*tois hôs alêthôs eutuchesin*]. [*EN* 1179b20–23]

Aristotle makes essentially the same point in *Eudemian Ethics* I.3, though the divine appears there in a slightly different role:

> If, on the one hand, living finely [*kalôs*] lies in the things that come to be as a result of fortune or in the <things that come to be> as a result of nature, then it would be a hopeless prospect for the many. (For the possession <of it> is not <in this case> the result of practice, nor up to them or their conduct.) But if, on the other hand, <living finely> lies in one's self as well as one's actions being of a certain character [*tô(i) auton poion tina einai kai tas kat' auton praxeis*], then the good would be both more common and more divine—more common because it is possible for more to partake of it, and more divine because *eudaimonia* belongs to those who make themselves and their actions to be of a certain sort [*tois autous paraskeuazousi poious tinas kai tas praxeis*]. [*EE* 1215a13–19]

The shifting role of the divine can be explained in the following way.

What we are like depends initially on external sources, whether natural or divine. (Habituation, for which our elders are typically responsible, eventually comes to play a similar role.) But with the development of *nous*, which Aristotle describes as "the divine in us," the role played by external sources in determining what we are like diminishes, and that played by internal sources, particularly *nous*, increases—presumably because *nous* allows us to reflect critically on what nature and habit have made of us, and to change ourselves if *nous* disapproves of what it sees. So to the extent that we come to *identify* with *nous*, and *nous* is responsible for what we are like, we ourselves become responsible for what we are like.[41] In coming to determine our characters, we come to

---

[41] Here I accept Meyer's account of habituation as proceeding in two stages, an early stage in which parents and educators are responsible for a child's development, and a later stage (in play at *EN* 1179b34–1180a4, 1103b4–21, and 1114a3–13) in which a young adult, who now knows that one becomes virtuous (or vicious) as a result of repeatedly performing what he has been taught are virtuous (or vicious) actions,

do for ourselves what we initially relied on nature or the divine to do for us, as a result of which we gradually become more self-determined and more like God.[42]

Note that God serves here as the standard against which we compare ourselves. Here, however, God serves as our standard, not qua contemplator, but qua self-determined. That Aristotle takes God to serve as a standard in this sense is clear from *Politics* VI.1, where he explicitly connects the issue of responsibility for character with the relationship between virtue and natural goods. This passage provides the clearest evidence for my interpretation of *EE* VIII.3 as concerned with autonomy. After saying that no one will dispute that there are three kinds of goods or that the *eudaimôn* agent must have all three, Aristotle says—as in *EE* VIII.3—that men do differ about the relative superiority of these goods. The passage concludes as follows:

> The external <goods> have a limit, like any instrument, and all are useful for something; and an excess of these must either harm or be of no benefit to those who possess it. But with goods of the soul, each is, by however much it exceeds, that much more useful (if it is even appropriate to apply not only <the term> '*kalon*' but also <the term> '*chrêsimon*' to them) . . .
>
> Further, it is for the sake of the soul that these [viz., external and bodily goods] are naturally such as to-be-chosen, and that all those who are wise ought to choose, them, and not the soul for the sake of them. Let us agree then that each person has as much *eudaimonia* as he has virtue and *phronêsis*, and acting in accordance with these, taking the God as our witness. He is *eudaimôn* and blessed, not on account of any external goods, but on account of himself [*di' hauton*], and being of a certain sort with respect to his nature [*tôi poios tis einai tên phusin*], since good fortune [*eutuchia*] must differ from *eudaimonia* on account of these

thus comes to be responsible, in performing such actions, for the sort of person he is. Meyer argues that this responsibility is only "qualified" and not "full," since the young adult may fail (through no fault of his own) to be properly equipped to embark on the final stage of habituation: he may, for example, have been poorly habituated at the first stage, so that he now has the wrong beliefs about what sorts of action are and are not virtuous. Here, however, I should like to suggest that Aristotle's attitudes toward responsibility for *character* may be asymmetrical in a way in which his attitudes toward responsibility for *actions* are not. Even if he rejects the Socratic view that agents are responsible for virtuous actions in a way in which they are not responsible for vicious actions, Aristotle may still believe that agents are responsible for having virtuous characters in a way in which they are not responsible for having vicious characters. For he may think that those who are fortunate enough to have a good upbringing develop the *nous* that enables them to "ratify" their characters, thus achieving fuller responsibility for their characters than their poorly habituated counterparts can achieve. I take it that Aristotle's teleological approach to explanation renders him receptive to asymmetrical accounts of this sort. [For further discussion of the way in which Aristotle's teleology affords different kinds of explanation when things go as they ought (teleological speaking) go and when things go wrong, see "Locomotive Soul" (III.5); "Hylomorphic Virtue" (III.6); and "*Nicomachean Ethics* VII.3 on Akratic Ignorance" (with Martin Pickavé) (III.7).]

[42] There is need here for an account of what *nous* is, and of how exactly this process of identification with one's *nous* is supposed to work. These are tasks for another essay, which *must* take as its point of departure the work of Stephen Menn (see note 19 above).

things: of goods external to the soul, the cause is the automatic [*t'automaton*] and fortune [*hê tuchê*], but no one is just or temperate as a result of fortune or on account of it. [*Pol.* 1323b7–29]

The context provided by *EE* VIII.2—in conjunction with this passage from the *Politics* and the foregoing passage from *EE* I.3—supports taking *EE* VIII.3 to suggest that the *kaloskagathos* is self-determined in a way in which the merely *agathos* is not.

This raises the possibility of taking the distinction between mere goodness and *kalokagathia* to coincide with the other possible Nicomachean parallel mentioned at the outset—that is, the distinction between natural virtue and what Aristotle calls "*kuria*" (or "authoritative") virtue. For he takes the authoritatively virtuous agent to be the *author* of his actions—and presumably also of his self—in a way in which the naturally virtuous agent is not.

8. *KALOKAGATHIA* AS AUTHORITATIVE VIRTUE?

The plausibility of taking the distinction between mere goodness and *kalokagathia* to coincide with that between natural and authoritative virtue receives support not only from the fact that *kalokagathia* and authoritative virtue resemble each other (and differ from mere goodness and natural virtue) in being identified with the whole of virtue, but also from the similarities between the passages in which each of these distinctions is introduced. Aristotle introduces the distinction between natural and authoritative virtue in *EN* VI.13, where he is concerned, as in *EE* VIII generally, with the Socratic identification of virtue and knowledge. Both passages speak of men becoming simultaneously wise and good. And both refer to *deinotês* (cleverness), which is rarely mentioned by Aristotle. Moreover, there is the striking similarity between the end of *EN* VI.13 and the end of *EE* VIII.3, each of which invokes the analogy between phronêsis and medical science in the service of what appears to be the same point.[43]

Aristotle introduces the distinction between natural and authoritative virtue by comparing it to that between mere cleverness [*deinotês*] and genuine *phronêsis*. One

[43] Such similarities together with the order of topics in the *MM*—which tends to follow the order of the *EE*—support Dirlmeier's hypothesis (to which I am sympathetic) that *EE* VIII was meant to precede the discussion of friendship in *EE* VII. If this is right, then it is plausible to view *EE* VIII as an early version of material later replaced by the common books on the intellectual virtues and incontinence. This has the advantage that it allows us to remain agnostic about the original home of the common books, though it fails as a result to provide an unambiguously Nicomachean parallel to *EE* VIII.3. But I am less concerned with the original home of the distinction between natural and authoritative virtue than with its correspondence to (and ability to shed light on) the distinction between mere goodness and *kalokagathia*. [I no longer think it desirable to remain agnostic about the origin of the common books: it seems to me clear that they were originally Eudemian. So I think that we should be speaking here of *EE* V.12–13. Perhaps Hendrik Lorenz (personal communication) is right that the common books were so thoroughly revised before the versions we have that we can treat them as largely, if not originally, Nicomachean. But I hesitate to go quite that far.]

point of this comparison is to suggest that authoritative virtue develops from natural virtue in much the same way that *phronêsis* develops from cleverness. The developmental picture is clear from *EN* 1144b2–14:

> As phronêsis is to cleverness—not the same but similar—so natural virtue is related to authoritative [*kuria*] <virtue>. For each type of character [*hekasta tôn êthôn*] seems to belong to all <those who possess it> somehow by nature. For we are just and temperate and brave and have the other <characters> immediately from birth. Nevertheless, we seek something different, the authoritatively good [*to kuriôs agathon*] and <suppose that> such <characters> belong in a different way. For the natural states belong even to children and beasts, but without intelligence [*aneu nou*] they are evidently harmful . . . just as it happens to a strong body moving about without sight to take a strong fall, so too it happens here. But if one gets hold of *nous*, he excels in action. His state [*hexis*], being similar [to natural virtue], will then be virtue in the authoritative way [*kuriôs aretê*].

The plausibility of viewing the process of acquiring *nous* as one in which we shed the effects of constitutive luck is suggested by a memorable slogan, taken from a passage in the *Magna Moralia* that bears a striking resemblance to *EE* VIII.2: "Where there is most *nous* and *logos*, there is least fortune [*tuchê*]; and where there is most fortune, there is least *nous*" [*MM* 1207a4–6]. The most obvious way to take this is as making the point made in the *Euthydemus*, that you are better off being caught in a storm with a knowledgeable than with an ignorant pilot. But the context here suggests another way to take it, compatible with the first: we can take it as saying that in identifying your "self" with *nous*, you insulate your "self" as far as possible from the effects of fortune in the sense that you become responsible for who you are and what you do. The significance of this will be clear when we return to VIII.3.

First, we must examine the case for taking the distinction between natural and authoritative virtue to coincide with that between mere goodness and *kalokagathia*. One superficially plausible argument for accepting this coincidence runs as follows. Aristotle says explicitly (in *EE* VIII.3) that *kalokagathia* is a whole composed of each of the particular virtues, thus associating *kalokagathia* with the sort of unity (or reciprocity) of virtue that he takes to characterize authoritative (as distinct from natural) virtue. And Aristotle says explicitly (in *Pol.*) that the Spartans cultivate one part of virtue at the expense of others: he thus associates the mere goodness of the Spartans with the lack of unity characteristic of natural as distinct from authoritative virtue. So it is tempting to conclude that Aristotle takes the distinction between natural and authoritative virtue to coincide with that between mere goodness and *kalokagathia*.

Note, however, that *EE* VIII.3 does not mention the lopsidedness of Spartan virtue: it focuses instead on the fact that the Spartans rank virtue behind natural goods. So we should not rashly assume that it is the lopsidedness of their virtue that leads Aristotle to take the Spartans as exemplars of the merely *agathoi*. But even so, it does not follow that we are on the wrong track in taking *kalokagathia* to coincide with authoritative virtue. For the *Politics* passage quoted at the end of section 7 shows that Aristotle links the Spartans' other flaw—that of ranking virtue behind natural goods—with a failure of self-determination. So even if Aristotle does not *identify* mere goodness with natural virtue, he may still object to mere goodness on the grounds that it (like natural virtue) lacks the self-determination characteristic of authoritative virtue, thus confirming my suggestion that we identify *kalokagathia* with authoritative virtue. The point is simply that we need to recognize other states, besides natural virtue, that fall short of authoritative virtue.

This strategy receives support from *EN* III.8, where Aristotle describes five states that resemble authoritative bravery, and are often called by the same name. One is the so-called bravery of those who endure dangers on account of spirit, or *thumos*. Aristotle says that this sort of bravery is "most natural" and becomes genuine bravery once the agent acquires decision [*prohairesis*] and the right goal, clearly referring to the transition from natural to authoritative virtue [*EN* 1116b24–1117a6]. Another such state, especially relevant for our purposes, is what Aristotle calls "civic" [*politikê*] bravery, as a result of which citizens endure dangers both to avoid penalties and disgrace, and to win honors. Aristotle says that this state is most like genuine bravery because it stems from a kind of virtue, being associated with a sense of shame and a desire for what is fine. The fact that Aristotle refers to this state, like that of the Spartans, as "civic" suggests that this may be the sort of state he has in mind when he speaks of mere goodness in *EE* VIII.3.

The connection between *thumos* and both shame and the desire for honor is clear from some of Plato's more graphic images: the image (at *Republic* 439e) of Leontius, whose *thumos* renders him ashamed of his necrophilia; and the image (at *Phaedrus* 253d) of the good horse, said to be a lover of honor with temperance and a sense of shame. Aristotle's account of *thumos* preserves the central features of Plato's account, particularly the idea that *thumos* is capable of hearing and obeying reason, though it sometimes—especially when corrupted or poorly trained—mishears or disobeys. When Aristotle says in *EN* X.9 that the soul of one who is to become virtuous must be habituated to feel affection for the fine and distaste for the shameful, so that it can appreciate reason and argument, his point surely concerns the proper training of the *thumos*.[44]

Moreover, there are important similarities between Plato's account (in *Republic* VIII) of the timocratic constitution and man, and Aristotle's criticisms (in *Pol.* II.9) of the Spartan constitution: both mention the bad influence of greedy women, as well as the predominant emphasis on military and competitive virtues. There is an important connection between these points: since property, wealth, and political office can all be forms of honor, competition for honor often takes the form of competition for such material goods. Plato connects these points when he claims that the timocratic son grows up hearing his mother complain that her husband is not among the rulers and

---

[44] [For more on this passage, see "Psychic Contingency in the *Republic*" (I.8)].

does not care much about wealth, the idea being that she acquires fewer of the material rewards of honor than she would like. Plato explicitly blames the competitive aspects of the timocratic constitution on the predominance of the *thumoeidês*, and it is hard to imagine that Aristotle would disagree.

These passages return our attention to the problem of constitutive luck, hinting at how Aristotle's concern with this problem might lead him to classify civic virtue together with natural virtue, and to contrast both states with authoritative virtue.[45] For just as it is bad constitutive luck to be born too sanguine or too hot blooded, or to grow up with a timocratic father, so too it is bad constitutive luck to grow up in a place like Sparta, especially since critical reflection—one's only hope for the sort of self-determination required for authoritative virtue—is not encouraged in such places.

The fact that constitutive luck seems to be involved not only in the case of natural virtue, but also in the case of civic virtue, supports taking civic virtue (like natural virtue) to be contrasted with authoritative virtue. The fact that the Spartans possess civic virtue can then be taken to suggest that the contrast in *EE* VIII.3 between mere goodness and *kalokagathia* is ultimately one between civic and authoritative virtue. This allows us to identify *kalokagathia* with authoritative virtue without having to identify the distinction between mere goodness and *kalokagathia* with the distinction between natural and authoritative virtue: the contrast in *EE* VIII.3 is between authoritative and civic virtue.

Moreover, it seems plausible—given Aristotle's claim that civic bravery is most like genuine bravery—to suppose that civic virtue is (among the five semblances of virtue) the most like authoritative virtue. The fact that the Spartans possess civic virtue will then help to explain Aristotle's willingness to call the Spartans "good" even though they fall short of *kalokagathia*, thus helping to resolve our second puzzle, about the sense in which the Spartans are good, given that they mistakenly value virtue for the sake of external goods. Here it is important to recall Aristotle's claim (in his discussion of *megalopsuchia*) that honor is the "greatest of external goods" [*EN* 1123b20–21]. For honor is clearly the external good most valued by the Spartans, who presumably value virtue primarily for the sake of honor. Aristotle clearly thinks that the Spartans, though wrong in valuing virtue for the sake of honor, are on the right track in valuing honor above all other *external* goods.

This is the key to solving our second puzzle. For those who value honor above the other external goods will be least tempted to sacrifice virtuous action for the sake of the other goods, and best situated to develop a proper appreciation of virtue. Focused as they are on honor, with other goods out of their deliberative way, they are best situated to grasp the true connection between honor and virtue. If they reflect, they may come to see that the phenomena—namely, that men are honored because they are virtuous and not virtuous because they are honored—betray the primacy of virtue

[45] We might also ask whether the other states falling short of authoritative bravery can be construed as products of something like constitutive luck. This certainly seems plausible in the case of those who appear brave because they tend to be hopeful [*euelpides*] as a result of past victories.

over honor, thus suggesting that virtue is to be chosen for itself, and perhaps also (in times of peace) for the sake of contemplation. There is of course no guarantee that the Spartans will come to see this. But they are as close to authoritative virtue as they can get without already being there. What they need now is reflection.

I shall return to this puzzle about the sense in which the Spartans are good after suggesting a solution to the first puzzle. But before tackling that, I should note that identifying *kalokagathia* with authoritative virtue does not require us to abandon any of our preceding claims. We can still take *kalokagathia* as a single virtue that can be viewed equally under the aspect of justice and under the aspect of self-love. And we can still allow within *kalokagathia* a distinction between the large- and small-scale versions, thus preserving our hypothesis that *megalopsuchia* is large-scale *kalokagathia*. We shall simply have to allow a similar distinction within authoritative virtue, and to allow that authoritative virtue can be viewed equally under the aspect of justice and under the aspect of self-love. Whatever goes for *kalokagathia* will also go for authoritative virtue.

9. SOLUTION TO THE FIRST PUZZLE: DISTRIBUTION *KAT' AXIAN*

Let us return, then, to our first puzzle. It is clear in *EE* VIII.3 and elsewhere that Aristotle thinks that what is fine is such-as-to-be-praised in a way in which what is merely good is not. This leads to our first puzzle, which is concerned with the question of how natural goods, being goods of fortune, can be fine, where this involves their being suitable objects of praise.

The puzzle arises because there is a tension between something's being a suitable object of praise (and so up to the agent) and its being a good of fortune (and so not up to the agent). We can resolve this puzzle by taking Aristotle's claim that the natural goods are *kala* for the *kaloskagathos* as claiming that the *kaloskagathos' possession* of these goods is *kalon*, where this involves taking his *possession* of these goods to be a suitable object of praise. We can take his possession of these goods as a suitable object of praise not only insofar as he deserves such goods on account of his virtue, but also—and more importantly—insofar as he has whatever such goods he happens to have on account of his deserts and not simply as a result of fortune.[46]

Aristotle's commitment to the conditionality thesis renders this claim true, even if only trivially so: insofar as the goodness of natural goods for an agent is conditional on his virtue, his virtue will in fact be what *makes* whatever natural goods he happens to have *good for him*. However many friends and possessions the non-virtuous

[46] This does not require us to take praise to play any role in motivating the *kaloskagathos*, though it may play a role in motivating others to distribute goods to him according to his worth. Nor does this require us to say that Aristotle regards virtue as an infallible means to securing the natural goods that one deserves on account of one's virtue. It requires only that he take virtue to be the *cause* of an agent's having whatever such goods he happens to have.

agent has, these things will not be good for him, and they may actually (especially if he is vicious) harm him. This yields a sense in which genuine (as distinct from merely apparent) good fortune is unavailable to the non-virtuous agent: however many undeserved "externals" he has, these things will not be goods for him, so his having them cannot count as genuine good fortune. Moreover, if an agent is vicious, these things may actually harm him. In his case, what appears to be good fortune is really ill fortune.

There is another sense, less trivial and more vulnerable to external circumstances, in which the virtuous agent may have the goods he has *because* he deserves them. In a well-ordered Aristotelian society, where external goods are distributed according to worth [*kat' axian*], the virtuous agent will to some extent have the external goods he has on account of his virtue. In this case, however, it will not be appropriate to say that his possession of them is due to fortune. Here again, fortune—at least good fortune—seems to recede. The apparent good fortune of the virtuous agent is not fortune but desert, while the apparent good fortune of the non-virtuous agent is not good.

This suggests that Socrates' assimilation—or better, reduction—of good fortune to wisdom contains a deeper insight than appears at first glance. In a well-ordered society, where justice prevails, there will be an important sense in which it is no longer appropriate to speak of the external goods as "goods of fortune": if such goods are distributed to agents in proportion to their virtue, each agent will have the external goods he has not as a result of fortune, but because he deserves them. If I am right in suggesting that Aristotle adopts this Socratic view, then Aristotle may anticipate Kant's conception of the summum bonum as happiness in proportion to virtue (wherein happiness is not Aristotelian eudaimonia, but rather the sort of happiness Kant associates with fortune—namely, *Glückseligkeit*).[47]

10. SOLUTION TO THE SECOND PUZZLE: PRAISE VERSUS ESTEEM

The connection between praise and the *kalon* leaves us with a variant of the second puzzle, concerning the sense in which the Spartans are good. For this connection may seem to imply that the merely *agathos* differs from the *kaloskagathos* in not being subject to praise and blame. But this seems implausible, given that Aristotle views the Spartans as exemplars of the merely *agathoi*, for he clearly regards the Spartans as subjects of praise and blame. It seems more likely that Aristotle views the *kaloskagathos* as subject to a different (and higher) sort of praise than that to which the merely *agathos* is subject.

[47] See Stephen Engstrom, "Happiness and the Highest Good in Aristotle and Kant," in Engstrom and Whiting, *Rethinking Happiness and Duty* (Cambridge: Cambridge University Press, 1996), 102–38; and "The Concept of the Highest Good in Kant's Moral Theory," *Philosophy and Phenomenological Research* 52 (1992): 747–80.

There are thus two ways in which we might interpret *EE* VIII.3. First, we might appeal to the ambiguity in '*epainetos*,' and take Aristotle to be suggesting that the *kaloskagathos* is praiseworthy, while the merely *agathos*, though not praiseworthy, is *such-as-to-be-praised* (presumably for instrumental or pragmatic reasons).[48] Alternatively, we might take Aristotle to be suggesting that the merely *agathos*, though genuinely praiseworthy, merits a different (and lesser) sort of praise than the *kaloskagathos*. The second alternative is reminiscent of Kant's claim (at *Gr.* 398) that a beneficent action done from inclination rather than duty

> stands on the same footing as other inclinations—for example, the inclination for honour, which if fortunate enough [*glücklicherweise*] to hit on something beneficial and right and consequently honourable, deserves praise and encouragement [*Lob und Aufmunterung*], but not esteem [*Hochschätzung*].[49]

Aristotle may be making a similar point: that the merely *agathos* deserves praise and encouragement, but not esteem. And this seems plausible, if praise and encouragement play a role in establishing and maintaining the natural or habitual virtues that might, given the right sort of reflection, become authoritative.

Such a reading receives some support from the *Magna Moralia*, which draws a distinction between *timia* (goods that are honored, including *nous* and virtue), and *epaineta* (goods that are praised, including the virtues):

> Of goods, some are to-be-honored [*timia*], and others are such-as-to-be-praised [*epaineta*], while others are potential.
>
> By to-be-honored I mean this sort of thing: the divine, the better (for example, soul and *nous*), the more ancient, the [first] principle, and such things. For to-be-honored are all the things to which honor applies, and honor attends all such things. Virtue [*aretê*], then, is to-be-honored, at least in cases where someone has come to be excellent as a result of it. For then he has *already attained* the character of virtue.
>
> Such-as-to-be-praised are, for example, virtues [*aretai*], for praise stems from actions according to these.
>
> Potential are, for example, office, wealth, strength and beauty. For the excellent man is able to use these well, the base man badly.[50]

---

[48] On this ambiguity, see note 12 above.

[49] Note also that Kant sometimes appears to subscribe to something like the first view: beneficent actions done from inclination are such-as-to-be-praised (by our legislators and fellow citizens who take an external and legal point of view) even if such actions are not praiseworthy (the determination of which requires us to take an internal and moral point of view). Kant would say that our legislators and fellow citizens are no more able than we ourselves are to know exactly how praiseworthy our actions really are.

[50] *MM* 1183b20–30, emphasis added. See *EN* I.12, where Aristotle asks whether *eudaimonia*, which is clearly not a potential good, is among the *epaineta* or rather (as he affirms) among the *timia*. Both passages should be compared with *EE* 1219b8–16.

The shift from the singular '*aretê*' to the plural '*aretai*'—where the singular '*aretê*' is to-be-honored and the plural '*aretai*' are such-as-to-be-praised—may indicate implicit reliance on the distinction between *kalokagathia* (complete and authoritative virtue) and the various particular natural or civic virtues. If so, then it is plausible to read *EE* VIII.3 as allowing that the natural or civic virtues of the merely *agathos* are such-as-to-be-praised but not to-be-honored, thus recalling Kant's claim.[51]

Since Aristotle explicitly places the divine among things to-be-honored, the fact that *EE* VIII.3 goes on to say that the divine—qua object of contemplation—provides a standard with reference to which the *kaloskagathos* is to select among natural goods strengthens this suggestion and appears to add a decidedly non-Kantian but characteristically Aristotelian intellectualist twist. It suggests that Aristotle may take the *kaloskagathos* to deserve honor (and not simply praise) because he—unlike the merely *agathos*—*is* virtuous for the sake of contemplation (and not for the sake of honor and other external goods).

There is, however, another more Kantian way to read this passage, not necessarily incompatible with the first. For we have seen that the divine—qua final cause and object of imitation—may serve as our model in either, and indeed both, of two ways. The god is not only a subject (and object) of contemplation. The god is also maximally—indeed entirely—self-determined both in the sense that she is governed by an internal standard and in the sense that fortune plays no role in determining her being. Fortune does not endow her with natural impulses that might tempt her to depart from her own internal standard. So praise will not in her case serve its normal practical role. It will not, for example, motivate her to resist temptations posed by unfortunate desires. In this sense, the god is beyond praise: she is to-be-honored.

Eudemian Ethics VIII.3 can thus be read as suggesting that the *kaloskagathos* deserves honor (and not simply praise) because he (unlike the merely *agathos*) is maximally self-determined. For his *nous*, with which he identifies, serves as an internal standard—a "law within"—regulating his conduct. *Nous* enables him to determine the relative values of various goods *for himself* and without reference to externally imposed standards. He sees that contemplation and virtue are to be chosen for themselves and not for the sake of contingent rewards like wealth and honor. So he is internally and not externally motivated.

In this respect, the *kaloskagathos* differs from those (like the merely *agathoi*) who choose virtue for the sake of external goods (like wealth and honor). For their behavior is (as Aristotle clearly recognizes) vulnerable to public opinion about what is and is not to be honored in their society in a way in which the behavior of the *kaloskagathos* is not.[52] In this sense, the behavior of the merely *agathos* is "heteronomous." But the

---

[51] It is important to note that the two puzzles concern different objects of praise. Praising the *virtues or virtuous actions* of the merely *agathos* (as required by our solution to the second puzzle) is not incompatible with refusing (as required by our solution to the first puzzle) to praise his *possession of external goods*.

[52] See *EN* 1095b24–26, where Aristotle says, "[Honor] seems to depend more on those honoring than on the one being honored, while we divine that the good is something proper [*oikeion ti*] [to the agent] and not easily taken away."

kaloskagathos, in identifying with his *nous*, is maximally self-determined. He has shed as far as possible the effects of constitutive luck and has made the transition from civic virtue, a product of (external) habituation, to authoritative virtue, a product of (internal) reflection. In his case, praise no longer plays its normal practical role, which we can now see is primarily developmental. For praise serves to motivate those—like the merely *agathos*—who have not yet come to appreciate virtue for itself. But the *kaloskagathos*, who *has* come to appreciate virtue for itself, no longer needs praise and encouragement: and he now deserves honor or esteem.[53]

[53] I should like to thank the Andrew W. Mellon Foundation for supporting my fellowship at the Center for Advanced Study in the Behavioral Sciences, during which I completed this essay. I should also like to thank Allen Wood, David Gauthier, Brad Inwood, Phillip Mitsis, and Gisela Striker—as well as those attending the Aristotle-Kant seminar I gave with Steve Engstrom—for helpful comments at various points along the way. I am especially indebted to Steve for much profitable discussion and many helpful comments on the penultimate draft. But my greatest debt is to Terry Irwin, for all that I have learned from him about Aristotle's ethics.

5

Strong Dialectic, Neurathian Reflection, and the Ascent of Desire

IRWIN AND MCDOWELL ON ARISTOTLE'S METHODS OF ETHICS

> We ought, as in other matters, having set out the appearances and having first worked through the puzzles in this way, to prove if possible all the reputable views . . . and if not then most and the most authoritative ones. For whenever the puzzles are solved and the reputable views remain in place, a thing is adequately proved.
>
> —*NICOMACHEAN ETHICS* 1145B2–7[1]

> We must try, concerning all these matters, to get conviction through reasoning . . . For it is best if all men clearly agree with the claims to be made; if not, all <should agree> at least in some respect, which being brought around [μεταβιβαζόμενοι] they will do. For each possesses something akin to the truth [οἰχεῖόν τι πρὸς τὴν ἀλήθειαν] from which it is necessary to prove how <things stand> concerning these matters.
>
> —*EUDEMIAN ETHICS* 1216B26–32

MY AIM HERE is to effect a kind of reconciliation between Terence Irwin's "rationalist" reading of Aristotle's ethics and what (for lack of a better term) I shall call the "non-rationalist" reading recommended by John McDowell. Irwin's reading is "rationalist" in (at least) two senses that are relevant here, and McDowell's reading is "non-rationalist" in two correlative senses.

---

[1] Unless otherwise noted, all translations are my own. For the *Nicomachean Ethics*, I have translated the text of Bywater 1894; for the *Eudemian Ethics*, the text of Walzer and Mingay 1991. For 'reputable views' as a rendering of 'τὰ ἔνδοξα,' see Barnes 1981, 490–511.

Living Together. Jennifer Whiting, Oxford University Press. © Oxford University Press 2023.
DOI: 10.1093/oso/9780199969678.003.0006

First, Irwin's reading is "rationalist" in the sense that it represents Aristotle's ethical works as seeking to defend the rationality of virtue by means of arguments that are capable of persuading any *rational* interlocutor, whether or not she has any prior commitment to Aristotelian virtue, that she *ought* to pursue such virtue, arguments capable of persuading even a radical critic like Plato's Callicles. McDowell's reading is "non-rationalist" in the corresponding sense: he represents Aristotle as "modestly" rejecting the possibility of giving any such arguments, and so as foregoing any attempt to persuade radical critics—or even moral skeptics—that *they* ought to pursue Aristotelian virtue. That is why, according to McDowell, Aristotle requires that those who would attend his lectures on ethics come already equipped with a proper upbringing [*Nicomachean Ethics* (*EN*) 1095a2–11, b4–8], which consists at least partly in being habituated not simply to *recognize* what is fine and what is base, but also to *love* what is fine and to *hate* what is base [*EN* 1179b24–1180a18]. For McDowell's Aristotle takes ethical argument to be ineffective in the absence of some such motivational tendencies, which he thinks required in order for the student even to *understand*—and so to be moved by—the sort of reasoning offered in his ethical works.

Irwin's reading is "rationalist" and McDowell's "non-rationalist" in a second sense as well. Irwin represents the operations of virtue itself in what might be called "rationalist" terms: his account of the virtuous person's actions emphasizes the role played in their production by "decision" [προαίρεσις], which he takes to be connected not simply with deliberation or reasoning about how (for example) to achieve a given end but also with rational (as distinct from non-rational) desires. Deliberation about how to achieve an end set by non-rational desires is not enough for "decision": the deliberation must start from a rational desire, which must itself result (at least in part) from the agent's deliberation about the *components* of her ultimate end (as distinct from merely instrumental means to it). Irwin explicitly represents this end (i.e., eudaimonia) in "inclusivist" terms: eudaimonia is supposed to include all the significant ends or goods worth pursuing for themselves, and an agent's conception of eudaimonia is supposed both to involve and to yield relative rankings of these various ends or goods.[2] The *virtuous* agent's conception of eudaimonia assigns to virtue a dominant role, one such that no sacrifice of virtue could ever be outweighed by a corresponding gain in other goods. The reason for this is (according to Irwin's Aristotle) that any sacrifice of virtue involves a sacrifice of rational agency and thus—given that we are *essentially* rational agents—a sacrifice of *oneself*. This emphasis on our rational agency is a further aspect of Irwin's "rationalism."

McDowell's reading agrees with Irwin's in taking Aristotle to be committed to the dominance of virtue. But McDowell's account of the nature of Aristotelian virtue is less "rationalist" than Irwin's account. For example, McDowell downplays the role of deliberation in the etiology of the virtuous person's action and stresses instead Aristotle's apparent identification of virtue with a kind of *perception*—i.e., the virtuous agent's

[2] See especially Irwin 1986b. [I discuss "inclusivist" readings at length in the Introduction to this volume.]

perception of what is required by the circumstances in which she finds herself. And McDowell views the relevant sort of perception as motivationally pregnant: the agent's perception of the requirement as such—i.e., as a *requirement*—is supposed to be what moves the agent to act in accordance with it. But in being so moved, the virtuous agent does *not* typically *deliberate:* she does *not weigh* the advantages and disadvantages of the virtuous course against the advantages and disadvantages of alternative possible courses of action. If here and now her pursuit of ends that ordinarily provide reasons for action conflicts with the virtuous course, her desire to pursue such ends is here and now "silenced": opportunities that would in *other* circumstances count as reasons for action—for example, opportunities to secure physical safety or sensual pleasure—are *not seen* by her as providing *any* reasons for action *here and now.*

McDowell takes his "silencing" account to do a better job than "weighing" accounts of explaining Aristotle's distinction between the genuinely virtuous agent and a merely continent one. Both agents do the right thing for the right reason, but the merely continent agent experiences internal conflict and regret of a sort that the genuinely virtuous agent does not. That is presumably because the merely continent agent—unlike the genuinely virtuous agent—continues to see things that would in *other* circumstances constitute reasons for action *as* constituting reasons for action *then and there.* On the sort of "inclusive" or "all-things-considered" interpretation of the ultimate end proposed by Irwin, these things *do* constitute reasons then and there, reasons that are, however, *outweighed* by the reasons in favor of the virtuous course. But McDowell's "silencing" interpretation is associated with a different sort of account of eudaimonia—one in which eudaimonia is the ultimate end *not* in the sense that *includes* all the others but *rather* in the sense that there is no *higher* end for the sake of which one might sacrifice it. On McDowell's view, Aristotle's conception of eudaimonia—which is coextensive with an ethically loaded conception of "doing-well" [εὖ πράττειν]—is supposed to capture a distinctive sort of reason for action, one that cannot be grasped by someone who lacks the distinctive modes of valuation and conceptualization in terms of "the noble" [τὸ καλόν] and "the base" [τὸ αἰσχρόν] that are inculcated in a proper upbringing, modes of valuation and conceptualization that *cannot* be induced simply by means of rational argument.

Why attempt anything so apparently quixotic as a "reconciliation" of these two views, which seem so fundamentally opposed *in spirit* to one another? There are (at least) two related reasons. First, it is difficult to decide between these readings on textual grounds. Each can appeal to passages that seem, when read in what is arguably the most "natural" way, to favor it. And each can offer *possible* readings of those passages that seem to favor the other view, readings intended to show that the relevant passages do not *decisively* support the other view.

For example, where McDowell thinks the passages requiring students of ethics to have a proper upbringing are most naturally read as showing that Aristotle takes a proper upbringing (with its motivational trappings) to be required in order for someone even to *understand* the sorts of arguments offered in Aristotle's ethical works, Irwin offers a deflationary and more instrumental reading of these passages:

(I1)[3] If Aristotle believes that dialectical reasoning justifies his conception of the virtues, and not only to those who already *accept* common beliefs about them, why does he require his students to have been well brought up? His requirements are not quite clear, and he does not defend them clearly. Twice he demands a good upbringing, so that the student will already want to do recognized virtuous actions [1095b4–6, 1179b23–30].* But elsewhere he demands only the capacity to control affections [1095a2–11]; self-controlled people might not have been trained in virtuous actions. Aristotle might have various reasons for these demands.

(1) The student must be aware of those common beliefs about the virtues which are the material of Aristotle's argument—though for this purpose he need not *accept* them.
(2) He must have some self-control; otherwise he may be persuaded by rational argument against his non-rational desires and affections [*Politics* 1332b6–8], but be unable to act on his new convictions.
(3) If he is too attached to his non-virtuous ways, he may not be able to change his ingrained non-rational desires even though he is self-controlled. If he is persuaded by Aristotle's arguments, he may become continent, but not virtuous.
(4) If he is too attached to vice, he may be unwilling to listen to reason, and may not be persuaded by an argument that it would be rational for him to accept.

These reasons show why someone who is to benefit and become virtuous from ethical theory should have been well brought up. *Aristotle does not imply that rational dialectic cannot rationally justify the Aristotelian virtues to a vicious person.* He can quite fairly promise to prove that a vicious man has good reason to change his way of life without promising that the vicious man will *accept* the proof; vice causes prejudice as well as weak will. [Irwin 1978, 261–62, my italics]

Irwin inserts an important footnote where I have inserted the asterisk (*): the note says, (with my italics) "Aristotle seems to want [a proper upbringing] as a prerequisite . . . *only because it produces self-control;* and some bad upbringings might surely produce that." The remainder of the passage suggests that self-control is required for various reasons. For example, in order to be persuaded by Aristotle's argument, the student must be willing and able to sit still and pay attention (4). And if she *is* persuaded, she may need still self-control in order to *act* on her new convictions, which are likely to be opposed by her non-rational desires and affections (2). Even so, self-control may lead her only to

[3] I have labeled all quotations from Irwin 'I' and all those from McDowell 'M.'

continence (3). But that is not (according to Irwin's Aristotle) because the argument has failed to *persuade* her. All she needs in order to be persuaded by the argument—all, that is, besides familiarity with the language of instruction and some of the common beliefs expressed in it (1)—is to think of herself as essentially a rational agent. And the motivational trappings of a proper upbringing are not (in Irwin's view) required for *that*.

On this account, being persuaded by an argument is one thing (a function of reason) and being moved to act on one's reasoned acceptance of the conclusion is another (a function of desire), and there is a sharp distinction between reasoning and desire, each being (as *EN* 1144b14–17 seems to suggest) the function of a distinct part of soul. *EN* 1144b14–17 is in fact one of the passages that seem to favor Irwin's reading over McDowell's reading (according to which *phronêsis* is simply the proper shaping of one's desires and thus belongs to the desiring part of soul).[4]

Another passage that seems to favor Irwin's view is Aristotle's infamous *ergon* (or function) argument. Irwin claims that this is most naturally read as an argument intended to persuade anyone who thinks of herself as human, and so as essentially rational, that she has reason to pursue Aristotelian virtue. But McDowell offers a deflationary reading of it.

> (M1) The thesis that man's *ergon* consists in rational activity obviously excludes what might otherwise have been a conceivable view of *eudaimonia*, namely, a life of unreflective gratification of appetite . . . But no other likely candidate is clearly excluded by the eliminative argument for that thesis [1097b33–1098a7]. Aside from its exclusion of the brutish life, then, the *ergon* argument can be understood *neutrally*. [McDowell 1980, sec. 10][5]

These examples suggest not simply that it is difficult to decide on textual grounds between Irwin's "rationalist" view and McDowell's "non-rationalist" one, but also that an alternative view—one that accommodates the central insights of each—may in the end do greater justice to the full complement of texts. For it seems a priori that an account that reconciles fundamental aspects of each view is likely to have both an easier time than a "rationalist" reading handling texts that appear to favor a "non-rationalist" one and an easier time than a "non-rationalist" reading handling texts that appear to favor a "rationalist" one. I shall not, however, undertake here to argue that my proposed reconciliation in fact does greater justice than either to the full complement of texts, which would require something on the order of a book. My aim here is largely to motivate such a project.

---

[4] See Whiting 2002b ["Locomotive Soul" (III.5)]; 2019 ["Hylomorphic Virtue" (III.6)] and 2021 ["See the Right Thing"].

[5] McDowell 1998b, sec. 9, makes a somewhat more concessive statement of this point. Please note that I cite McDowell's works by section (rather than page number) so that passages can easily be found in his collected papers (1998a).

This brings me to my second and primary reason for seeking some sort of reconciliation—namely, that it has always seemed to me that Irwin and McDowell each possess something "akin to the truth," not just about Aristotle's views but also about the substantive issues involved: Irwin seems to me to possess something "akin to the truth" both about the possibility of a certain kind of argument and about Aristotle's belief in that possibility, and McDowell seems to me to possess something "akin to the truth" both about the nature of virtue and about Aristotle's conception of it. I have thus been troubled by the following puzzle: why couldn't Aristotle—and ultimately we ourselves—accept Irwin's account of the methods of ethical argument and McDowell's account of the nature of virtue?

My puzzlement has been exacerbated by an additional puzzle concerning the difference between Irwin's account of Aristotle's methods and McDowell's account of these methods. For both accounts are explicitly coherentist and anti-foundationalist in ways that make it difficult to see exactly how they are supposed to differ. And to the extent that McDowell's account of the method resembles Irwin's, it becomes more difficult to see why, if McDowell's basic view is coherent, Aristotle—and we ourselves—could not adopt Irwin's account of the method and McDowell's substantive account of virtue.

I shall thus adopt Aristotle's own method, as described in the passages quoted at the outset. I shall first show how these two puzzles arise out of the *endoxa* (in this case the "reputable views" of Irwin and McDowell). I shall then seek to resolve these puzzles while preserving as many of the *endoxa* as possible. The idea is to bring Irwin and McDowell around to a reading of Aristotle on which they can—and I think *should*—agree. But I shall not seek to do so by defending specific interpretations of particular passages, which must typically be read in the light of one's sense of what is going on in other passages the understanding of which is itself typically mediated by considerations of charity. For insofar as Irwin and McDowell are each disposed by their own sense of where the truth lies to view as "charitable" different readings, both of particular passages and of the whole, this strategy is unlikely to succeed either in moving McDowell and Irwin or in moving those sympathetic to their respective views. My preferred strategy is to seek first to narrow the "spiritual gap" between their views by showing how each can afford, without sacrificing his most fundamental claims, to accept many of the other's claims (or at least qualified versions of those claims). My hope is that this will increase their (and their sympathizers') respective senses of what counts as a plausible view, and so of what counts as a suitably "charitable" reading of Aristotle. Perhaps they (and their sympathizers) can then approach the texts from new (and more overlapping) points of view.

Talk of their "sympathizers" raises the question why I choose to focus on the particular readings offered by Irwin and McDowell rather than on "rationalist" and "non-rationalist" views in general. I have adopted this focus for the following reasons (aside from the obvious autobiographical ones). First, I have too often seen philosophers work with "generic" positions that do not quite fit the views of any particular philosopher or commentator, thus allowing those whose views are supposed to be in question simply to dismiss the relevant arguments as not applying to their particular versions of the positions in question. Perhaps this is why Aristotle himself typically chose to discuss the views of particular predecessors, like (for example) Parmenides and Democritus, rather than generic positions, like (for example) Eleatic and Atomist ones. It is in any case my reason for wanting to work with the concrete positions of particular commentators.

Second, I think it important to ask what the most subtle and well-developed versions of each kind of position can say in response to the other, and I take Irwin's and McDowell's readings to be among the most subtle and well-developed versions on offer of the "rationalist" and "non-rationalist" readings. So I have elected to focus on them. I believe, however, that my arguments should be of interest and relevance to those sympathetic to the spirit (even if not faithful to the letter) of their respective readings, and that these arguments promise to shed general light not only on the broader dispute between "rationalist" and "non-rationalist" readings of Aristotle's ethics but also on the substantive issues that divide those of our contemporaries (like Irwin) with fundamentally "rationalist" sympathies from those (like McDowell) with fundamentally "non-rationalist" ones.[6]

1. THE PUZZLE ABOUT METHOD: WHAT IS THE DIFFERENCE BETWEEN THE "DIALECTICAL" METHOD THAT IRWIN ATTRIBUTES TO ARISTOTLE AND THE NEURATHIAN METHOD THAT MCDOWELL ATTRIBUTES TO HIM?

My primary puzzle—about why Aristotle could not adopt Irwin's account of the method and McDowell's account of the nature of virtue—is exacerbated by the secondary puzzle about the differences between the methods that each ascribes to Aristotle. I shall thus start with the secondary puzzle, so as to best convey the full force of the primary puzzle.

The secondary puzzle arises because Irwin and McDowell each ascribe to Aristotle a method that both begins from common beliefs and is explicitly coherentist and anti-foundationalist. On Irwin's account, Aristotle's method of ethical reflection is *dialectical:* it begins from common beliefs and proceeds—after raising and solving puzzles—to test its results by appeal to their coherence with *other* common beliefs. This makes it difficult to distinguish the method that Irwin ascribes to Aristotle from the sort of Neurathian reflection that McDowell ascribes to him.[7] For on McDowell's account, too, Aristotle begins from common beliefs—the planks, so to speak, of our ethical outlook—and he tests these beliefs piecemeal by appeal to their coherence with

[6] [Please note that I think it important to distinguish "non-rationalist" views from "anti-rationalist" ones. For some comparison of Irwin's "rationalist" view of love with Harry Frankfurt's view of it, which I take to be "anti-rationalist," see "Love: Self-Propagation, Self-Actualization, or Ekstasis?" (I.7). For Frankfurt's views, see Frankfurt 1999 and 2004.]

[7] [I perhaps say 'quasi-Neurathian'. For McDowell sees the Neurathian image as having resonance only in the (according to him) distinctively "modern" framework in which confidence in "internal reflection" *has been lost*: he says that "the point of the Neurathian image is to express a philosophically knowing stance that is as close as we, with our irrevocably lost innocence, can come to Aristotle's outlook" [McDowell 1998b: sec. 10]. But with this reminder in place, I shall continue to speak simply in terms of the Neurathian method.]

other common beliefs. This makes it puzzling that McDowell should object so strenuously to Irwin's ascription of the dialectical method to Aristotle.

The first step towards resolving this puzzle is to see that McDowell takes the salient feature of Neurathian reflection to be *not* its coherentism, but rather the way in which it restricts the resources for ethical reflection to materials *internal* to the object of reflection (internal, that is, to the scheme of values on which one is supposed to reflect). On McDowell's view, one begins (as Aristotle says at *EN* 1095b2–8) with "the that" [τὸ ὅτι], which McDowell takes to involve *evaluative attitudes* toward particular actions—"*that* x is *just*" and "*that* y is *cowardly*" or "*that* z is *noble*" and "*that* w is *base*"—attitudes that are acquired through the sort of habituation involved in a proper upbringing. Ethical reflection—or what Aristotle calls the move to "the because" [τὸ διότι]—then proceeds not by showing how the "thats" are supported by a metaphysical theory about, for example, the human end or function, but rather by showing how most if not all of the various "thats" cohere *with one another*.

(M2) On [my] reading, a comprehending acceptance of a scheme of values [i.e., having the *because*] would not differ from an uncomprehending acceptance of it [i.e., having only the *that*] . . . [by] setting the accepted values on a foundation, so that the *because* would not only explain the *that* but also validate it from the outside. Rather, in acquiring the *because* one would not be adding new material to what one acquired when one took possession of the *that*, but coming to comprehend the *that*, by appreciating how one's hitherto separate perceptions of what situations call for hang together, so that acting on them can be seen as putting into practice a coherent scheme for a life.

We can picture the intellectual activity that would be involved in moving to the *because*, on this view, in terms of a version of Neurath's image of a sailor who has to keep his boat in good order while at sea. In this version of the image, the fact that the boat cannot be put ashore for overhaul stands for the fact that when one reflectively moves from mere possession of the *that* to possession of the *because* as well, one has no new material to exploit except the initially unreflective perceptions of the *that* from which one starts. One reflects on one's inherited scheme of values, or the perceptions of choiceworthiness in action in which that scheme of values expresses itself, from *inside* the ethical way of thinking that one finds oneself with, not by contemplating it from an external standpoint of a theory about motivations built into human beings as such. [McDowell 1995a, sec. 5][8]

[8] McDowell has conceded in conversation that "no new materials" is too strong; that one might, through being initiated into alternative schemes or through conversing with those whose schemes are close enough to one's own that one can achieve a partial grasp of them, come to modify one's own scheme in light of new materials. More importantly, however, McDowell has said that he regards Callicles as an *internal* critic; that Callicles's critique poses the sort of threat it does precisely because he rings such familiar bells (about, for example, manliness and honor).

This suggests that McDowell's objection is focused on the distinctive features of what Irwin calls "strong dialectic" (as opposed to "pure" or "ordinary" dialectic), and *not* on the coherentist methods that strong dialectic shares not only with pure dialectic but also with the sort of Neurathian reflection that McDowell himself recommends.[9]

Two distinctive features of Irwin's strong dialectic are relevant here: first, its appeal to *broad coherence*—that is, to the coherence of a set of *ethical* beliefs with *non-ethical* beliefs (such as metaphysical and psychological beliefs); and second, its highly *selective* appeal only to such beliefs as one cannot easily give up without radically altering one's basic conceptual framework, and so to beliefs that are supposed to be relatively constant across a variety of interlocutors whose specifically ethical views may, however, be very different. The premises' wide appeal is supposed (by Irwin) to contribute to securing *widespread* agreement; the difficulty of giving them up is supposed to make the conclusions agreed upon especially *compelling*.

Irwin's paradigm example of strong dialectic is the "dialectical refutation" (in *Metaphysics* III) of someone who purports to deny the Principle of Non-Contradiction (PNC). The idea here is roughly that someone cannot deny PNC without ceasing to refer to determinate subjects and to say anything at all about them; or, in other words, without ceasing to participate in rational discourse altogether.[10] But this is an extreme example: there are very few beliefs that one *must* adopt on pain of ceasing to participate in rational discourse. And the minimal beliefs required here no doubt cohere with a wide range of competing ethical views, probably with all plausible contenders. So the more important examples of strong dialectic for our purposes are Aristotle's attempts (according to Irwin) to support ethical conclusions by appeal to the psychological views of the *De Anima*, and to the metaphysical views about substance on which these psychological views in turn rest.

Irwin takes Aristotle's infamous "function argument" as a prime example of strong dialectic in the ethical sphere.[11] The conclusion of this argument—namely, that the human good is an activity of soul in accordance with virtue—is supposed (according to Irwin) to rest ultimately on the theory of substance defended in Aristotle's *Metaphysics*. Irwin's general account of how Aristotle defends the rationality of virtue by appeal to his metaphysical and psychological theories can be summarized in the following way.

> The *Metaphysics*' defense of the PNC is supposed to show that it is a presupposition of rational discourse about how things are that there are determinate objects

---

[9] Irwin introduces the labels "strong dialectic" and "pure dialectic" in chap. 1 of his 1988 work. For some anticipation of this distinction, see Irwin 1977–1978. McDowell 1996b (n. 42) objects that Aristotle practices only one sort of dialectic—namely, "ordinary dialectic." For more on this, see note 11 below.

[10] See Irwin 1988, secs. 186–87.

[11] Perhaps Irwin should speak not of two different *kinds* of dialectic, but rather of a continuum with the maximally "strong" dialectical defense of PNC at one end and the maximally "weak" forms of dialectic (which involve beliefs that are easily abandoned) at the other, and with arguments like the "function argument" somewhere in between. [For more on this argument, see "Aristotle's Function Argument" (Chapter 1, this volume).]

of reference, with essences that constitute them as the objects they are both at and across times. But this argument does not tell us *which* objects, with what *sorts* of essences, we *must* recognize—whether, for example, these basic objects are things like atoms, or rather individual teleologically defined organisms. That is a matter for the sort of a posteriori investigation we find in the *Physics,* where Aristotle argues that the *best explanation* of the relevant phenomena is one that takes the basic objects to be teleologically defined organisms whose essences are roughly the sets of capacities that enable them to do what it is the *end* of organisms of their respective kinds to do. But this argument does not tell us what it is the end of any given sort of organism to do. That is the task of (among other works) the *De Anima,* where Aristotle distinguishes (in a generic way) the different sorts of activities that characterize plant, animal, and human souls. The account of the human good that we find in Aristotle's *Ethics* is thus supposed to depend on the *De Anima's* account of the human soul as *essentially rational.* Since this account of soul depends in turn on the teleological conception of substance that Aristotle defends in the *Physics,* which rests in turn on the theory of substance that Aristotle defends in the *Metaphysics,* we must take Aristotle to establish his account of the human good by means of a strong dialectical appeal to *non-ethical* metaphysical and psychological views: views whose plausibility to any given interlocutor will *not* depend on the *ethical* views she happens to hold, and so views that are likely to be common to a variety of interlocutors of different ethical stripes. The point of such strong dialectic is to show that anyone who holds these independently plausible metaphysical and psychological views *ought* in the end to prefer Aristotle's ethical views to rival ones (such as those endorsed by Callicles).

It is worth noting here that Irwin's actual language does not generally *require* us to read him (as McDowell sometimes seems to do) as taking Aristotle's ethical conclusions to be *deducible* from his metaphysical and psychological theories: his actual language typically requires us to read him as claiming only that, *given* the relevant metaphysical and psychological theories, Aristotle's ethical views are *more plausible* than their rivals. See, for example, the italicized bits of the following two passages:

(I2) Coherence between ethical principles and common ethical beliefs seems to be a rather fragile justification, allowing very little defense against a radical critic or skeptic. But if Aristotle shows that the principles of ethics *rest on* a view of human nature that can be defended by appeal to psychological and metaphysical principles, the area of coherence is wider. These non-ethical principles *rely on* common beliefs, but on selected common beliefs, those that are especially hard to reject and are not open to the sort of skeptical challenge that might affect ethical common beliefs; they are hard to resist because they are necessary for significant speech or for the correct understanding of nature. Aristotle's ethics, then, is *not wholly autonomous*; it *relies on* principles that are *justified by* non-ethical beliefs. [Irwin 1981: 222, my italics][12]

(I3) I suggest that Aristotle does appeal to *broad coherence* in his ethical theory and that this is why his theory is dialectical throughout. His ethical principles are *supported by* his psychological theory, more particularly by his conception of the human soul and the human essence. His psychological theory *rests* in turn on his metaphysics, the general account of substance, essence, form, and matter. The ethical argument is not merely dialectical, since it does *not rely only* on the interlocutor's acceptance of the ethical common beliefs; it seeks some further defense from Aristotle's non-ethical theories, which themselves *rely on* common beliefs, but not just on ethical common beliefs. The argument is not merely dialectical, but it is still dialectical insofar as it *relies on* beliefs that the interlocutor will accept. [Irwin 1981: 208, my italics]

It is of course possible that Irwin in fact takes the italicized phrases to refer to deducibility, and we shall encounter other passages suggesting that he may at least sometimes do so. But the reading I am suggesting expresses the line I think Irwin *should* take: broad coherence should *not* be confused with deducibility.[13] This distinction is important because McDowell's objections to strong dialectic sometimes seem to turn on the idea that the appeal to strong dialectic involves an attempt to *deduce* ethical conclusions from metaphysical and psychological premises. So it is not clear that McDowell's objections succeed either against what Irwin *actually* says or against what Irwin *should* in any case say.

McDowell raises two sorts of objection to strong dialectic, one more general and one specific to ethics. The more general objection is that strong dialectic encourages us to attempt the impossible—i.e., to step outside an inherited conceptual scheme (or an inherited "form of life") in order to evaluate that scheme (or "form of life") from some external point of view. McDowell (1979) claims that this is impossible because

---

[12] For similar passages in Irwin 1988, see (I11) and (I12) below.

[13] McDowell might defend the claim that Irwin 1988 does in fact have deducibility in mind by appealing to p. 23, where Irwin says,

> Both the *Ethics* and the *Politics* begin with general claims about human nature and seek to *derive* specific normative conclusions from these claims. If Aristotle's account of the soul itself is *derived* from first philosophy, then his moral and political theory rests on metaphysical foundations.

Here, however, Irwin may be using 'derive' loosely to refer not to deducibility but rather to some weaker form of dependence, as suggested by his claim that his account of the soul is itself "derived" from first philosophy. For it seems unlikely that Irwin takes Aristotle's account of soul to be simply *deducible* from his first philosophy. And it seems pretty clear from (I12) below that Irwin does have something weaker than deducibility in mind. Still, however, Irwin's desire for a kind of rational compulsion (to be discussed below) tends in the other direction: it may lead him to insist on deducibility rather than some weaker form of dependence. This seems to me an issue on which Irwin could usefully clarify his view for readers.

occupying an inherited conceptual scheme (or an inherited "form of life") is a *presupposition* of reflection on that scheme (or "form of life"), which scheme (or "form of life") provides the very context in virtue of which reflection on such a scheme (or "form of life") is possible.

Now this general objection might succeed against any would-be strong dialectical attempt to defend one's *global* conceptual scheme (or *global* "form of life") by appeal to something outside of *it*. But it is not clear that Irwin wants—or anyhow *needs*—to attribute so radical a strong dialectical project to Aristotle. If someone who purports to deny PNC is *really* outside a conceptual scheme (or "form of life") that recognizes both determinate objects of reference at a time and stable objects of reference across time, there is—as Irwin and Aristotle surely recognize—little if anything that even the strongest of strong dialectic can do to draw her into such a conceptual scheme (or "form of life"). In fact, Irwin's recognition of the way in which the dialectical defense of PNC begs the question against its opponent suggests that he is aware that Aristotle's dialectical defense of this principle proceeds by way of material that is in some sense *internal* to the conceptual scheme (or "form of life") in question, even if it is not *proper to* that specific scheme (or "form of life"). Moreover, even if it turns out that Irwin cannot claim that choices like that between a substance ontology and a process ontology are matters of merely local dispute, he can still allow that there is little that strong dialectic can do to resolve such radical disagreements among conceptual schemes (or "forms of life"). So whatever we think about McDowell's general objection, it seems unlikely to succeed against strong dialectical attempts to defend local aspects of one's global conceptual scheme (or "form of life"). It is unlikely to succeed, for example, against strong dialectical attempts to defend an *ethical* outlook by appeal to features of the broader conceptual scheme (or "form of life") *within* which that ethical outlook resides.

This brings us to McDowell's *specific* objection to taking Aristotle to deploy strong dialectic in support of *ethical* conclusions. The objection here is to strong dialectic's attempt to provide an *extra-ethical* foundation, or *extra-ethical* support, for *ethical* conclusions.[14]

> (M3) It is often thought that this Aristotelian realism points to an extra-ethical basis for reflection about what eudaimonia consists in. The idea is that it is possible to show that a virtuous agent's conception of eudaimonia is genuinely correct . . . by showing that a life organized in the light of that conception would be recognizably worth living anyway; that is, worth living by standards that are prior to the distinctive values acquired in what

[14] We should distinguish two possibilities: (a) foundational support (whose credentials are not themselves open to challenge) and (b) non-foundational support of the sort favored by coherence theories of justification. Although Irwin seems at times to appeal to (a), he often appeals (more plausibly) only to (b). And as we shall see in section 4 below, McDowell's appeal to what he calls "reflective reassurance" raises questions about the extent to which he can afford to object to (b).

> Aristotle conceives as a proper upbringing. These prior standards would be standards for worthwhileness or choiceworthiness that *any human being, just as such, could accept independently of any acquired values and the motivational dispositions that are associated with them* . . .
>
> For the purposes of readings of this sort, the goodness of the component goods has to be established without presupposing the distinctive conception of worthwhileness in action that is supposed to be validated, the conception of worthwhileness in action that is inculcated when someone is brought up into the virtues. Only so could an external validation be forthcoming. In readings of this sort . . . the goodness of the component goods is [supposed to be] revealed by the fact that they appeal to motivational forces—needs or aspirations—that are *built into the human organism as such.* [McDowell 1995a: secs. 1 and 2, my italics]

McDowell clearly has Irwin in mind here, though Irwin tends to speak not in terms of *human beings* or *human organisms* as such, but rather in terms of *rational agents* as such.[15] According to McDowell, Irwin represents Aristotle as seeking to provide the relevant sort of foundation or support by seeking to show that virtuous action is worthwhile according to standards that are prior to and independent of "the distinctive values acquired in . . . a proper upbringing"—standards, as Irwin suggests, that *any* rational agent *should* accept, whether or not she has as a result of her upbringing acquired the relevant virtues (or even the relevant proto-virtues). But McDowell thinks that this appeal to independent standards violates the sort of autonomy of ethical reasons that Aristotle seeks to acknowledge when he demands that a genuinely virtuous agent choose virtuous actions "for themselves" [δἰ αὐτά, *EN* 1105a31–32]. McDowell takes this demand to show that Aristotle thinks that virtuous agents must take virtuous actions to be justified on their *own* terms, and *not* by appeal to independent standards acceptable to virtuous and non-virtuous agents alike.

This suggests a simple solution to the first puzzle—namely, that what distinguishes the method Irwin ascribes to Aristotle from the method McDowell ascribes to him is the fact that Irwin's "strong dialectic" involves "external" or "extra-ethical" arguments for ethical conclusions in a way that McDowell's Neurathian reflection does not.[16] But

---

[15] See, however, the following passage from page 216 of Irwin 1981, which suggests that he takes Aristotle to view rational agency as belonging to any non-defective member of the human kind simply as such.

> Aristotle believes that an agent has reason to regard himself as a broad rational agent, since broad rational agency expresses *an essential property of a human being, as a natural organism with a rational soul* and the capacity for decision and choice.

Irwin's account of Aristotle's conception of rational agency thus appears to differ from McDowell's account. For (as we shall see in section 3 below) McDowell seems to take Aristotle to view the sort of rational agency in question as the product of a certain sort of *upbringing*.

[16] Please note that "external" and "extra-ethical" are being used here (as McDowell seems to use them) interchangeably: an "external" or "extra-ethical" argument for an "ethical" conclusion is roughly one whose premises do not make use of "ethical" considerations that are part of the "ethical" framework

the puzzle seems to resist this easy solution. For it is an important part of Irwin's general developmental story that Plato and Aristotle *disagree* with Socrates on precisely this point: Irwin's Plato and Aristotle are supposed to criticize *Socrates* for seeking to defend the rationality of virtue by means of an "external" or "extra-ethical" argument. See, for example, the following passage from *Plato's Moral Theory*, the italicized bits of which I find it amusing to read in McDowell's tone of voice:

> (I4) Plato agrees with Socrates that there is objective moral knowledge, that some people's moral judgments can be rationally justified . . . But Socrates looked for some external guarantee of correctness; virtuous action had to contribute to some final good accepted as a determinate end by virtuous and non-virtuous alike. *Plato rejects the external standard; moral beliefs cannot be tested for correctness except by the procedure of the elenchos, which may yield a systematic, coherent account of moral judgments, but may not link them to any external standard. When Plato rejects Socrates' guarantee of objectivity for moral beliefs, and offers no substitute, he rejects the demand* [or "the hankering"] *for such a guarantee as illegitimate.* [Irwin 1977: 159–60][17]

This feature of Irwin's developmental story suggests that the simple solution is too simple. For Irwin seems to agree with McDowell in taking Aristotle (along with Plato) to reject appeal to an "external" or "extra-ethical" standard.

This introduces a variation on our secondary puzzle—a variation that arises because McDowell seems to criticize Irwin's *Plato and Aristotle* for giving exactly the same sort of argument that Irwin's Plato and Aristotle are supposed to criticize *Socrates* for giving. So what is going on here? Does McDowell simply *misrepresent* Irwin's Plato and Aristotle?

Not necessarily. Irwin's Plato and Aristotle may (if McDowell is right) make the very mistake that they seek (if Irwin is right) to avoid. They may, for example, mistake external arguments for internal ones, and present arguments that are in fact external without recognizing them as such. Another possibility is that Irwin and McDowell are working with different conceptions of external argument: Irwin's Plato and Aristotle may succeed in avoiding the sort of external argument they find objectionable in Socrates, even though they themselves give a different sort of external argument, one to which McDowell in turn objects.

---

of which the intended conclusion is itself a part. This is important because I shall introduce in section 2 below a somewhat different sense in which an argument (or premises in an argument) for an ethical conclusion might be said to be "external"—a sense in which the argument (or its premises) need not be entirely outside the ethical framework of which the intended conclusion is itself a part.

[17] Please note that this passage does not quite express McDowell's view, since he thinks that *Socrates too* rejects the demand for an external standard. (Thanks to Lionel Shapiro for suggesting that my attempt to imitate McDowell while reading this passage would be more convincing if I substituted 'hankering' for 'demand.')

2. DIFFERENT CONCEPTIONS OF "EXTERNAL" ARGUMENT: THE *SYMPOSIUM*'S ACCOUNT OF THE ASCENT OF DESIRE

We should perhaps begin by considering the possibility that Irwin and McDowell are in fact working with different conceptions of external argument. For this possibility is clearly suggested by a footnote in which McDowell refers to Irwin's account of the *Symposium* ascent of desire:

> (M4) Irwin . . . attributes the idea of an external standard for the rationality of virtue exclusively to Socrates . . . For Irwin's Plato, the standard by which virtue is revealed to be rational is *not* (as for Irwin's Socrates) external to the distinctive valuations of a virtuous person; being persuaded into acceptance of the standard is the same thing as being persuaded into virtue. And Irwin's account of Aristotle's view on this matter is similar. This is certainly an important distinction; for Irwin's Socrates, the rationality of virtue *is reducible to something extra-ethical,* and for Irwin's Plato and Aristotle this is not so. The fact remains, however, that Irwin conceives persuasion into accepting the standard . . . as proceeding stepwise in such a way that each step is revealed as *rationally required according to standards of rationality already endorsed before the step is taken.* This is precisely a picture of validation from outside; that it is non-reductive makes no difference to that. (McDowell 1998b: n. 2, my italics).[18]

If we accept what McDowell says in this note, we should perhaps conclude that he and Irwin are working with different conceptions of external argument, and that Irwin identifies giving an external argument with attempting to *reduce* the rationality of virtue to something apparently different (like the rationality of hedonism), while McDowell identifies giving an external argument with the weaker project of attempting to show that a certain conclusion is *rationally required* by standards the interlocutor *already* accepts *before* she comes to accept the conclusion. For even if Irwin's Plato and Aristotle reject the attempt by Irwin's Socrates to *reduce* the practice of virtue to the pursuit of pleasure, they might still think it possible to *demonstrate* to a non-virtuous agent—by appeal to standards of rationality she *already* accepts—that it is *irrational* for her *not* to pursue the *non-reducible* practice of virtue. In other words, Irwin's Plato and Aristotle might think it possible to demonstrate to a non-virtuous agent that living a virtuous life, according to its own *internal* standards of rationality, will as a matter of fact best satisfy some independent standard she already accepts (for example,

[18] This passage suggests that McDowell takes an argument to be external to some domain if the argument reveals the move into that domain to be required by standards of rationality capable of being accepted from outside that domain. But as we shall see below, the issue is complicated if (as in Plato's ascent of desire) we are moving from a more to a less partial grasp of some domain.

a hedonist one). To see the plausibility of this one has only to recall the "paradox of hedonism" or the principles behind various forms of indirect consequentialism.

There is evidence that Irwin does in fact represent Plato and Aristotle as attempting to *demonstrate* to non-virtuous agents, by appeal to standards of rationality they *already* accept, that they are rationally *required* to adopt a non-reductive conception of virtue. This suggests that McDowell does not simply misrepresent Irwin's Plato and Aristotle. So at this point, I want to turn briefly to Irwin's account of Plato, particularly his account of the *Symposium's* ascent of desire, which McDowell clearly has in mind in (M4). For Irwin's discussion of the ascent reveals the complexity of distinguishing his general position from McDowell's and suggests a possible path of reconciliation. Moreover, Irwin's account of the ascent is not irrelevant to his account of Aristotle. For Irwin sees this ascent as the Platonic analogue of the sort of deliberation about the components of *eudaimonia* that he finds in Aristotle. And there is strong textual support for this.

First, the ascent passage represents ὁ ἔρως as love of τὸ καλόν or (as in most translations of the *Symposium*) "love of *beauty*." But τὸ καλόν is the term that Aristotle uses when he speaks of the virtuous agent as choosing virtuous action for the sake of τὸ καλόν or (as in most translations of Aristotle's ethics) "for the sake of the *noble*." (Irwin renders it "for the sake of the *fine*.")[19] So there is a clear connection between the motives operative in the ascent and the motives operative in Aristotle's virtuous agent, who is supposed to choose virtuous actions for the sake of τὸ καλόν. (See, for example, *EN* 1115b10–13, 1122b6–7.) Second, the *Symposium* explicitly connects love of τὸ καλόν with the pursuit of *eudaimonia*, which is what the *Symposium* lover is supposed to have when he has secured the various καλά goods. So there is a clear connection between the end of the *Symposium* ascent and the end of Aristotelian deliberation. Moreover, the ascent, like Aristotelian deliberation, seems to involve *reasoning*. Irwin says explicitly that the ascent involves the elenctic revision of the subject's beliefs: at each stage the subject is "led by his own reasoning" and "from principles he already accepts" to see that he has reason to move to the next stage [Irwin 1977: 168–69].

Note, however, that this—although it sounds like the sort of *internal* reflection that McDowell himself recommends—is the focus of McDowell's attack in (M4): he objects to the idea that each step in the ascent must be motivated by appeal to standards of rationality *already* endorsed *before* the step is taken. But McDowell himself suggests that we are stuck on a Neurathian raft, and that we can appeal only to standards we *already* accept. How else *could* we proceed? And Irwin in turn seems to acknowledge this: he says, for example, "Evidently I must deliberate in the light of values I have, since nothing else is available to me" [Irwin 1988: 366]. We are thus back to our secondary puzzle: what exactly is the difference between the method of ethical reflection that *Irwin* ascribes to Plato and Aristotle and the method of ethical reflection that

[19] See, for example, his translation of Aristotle's *Nicomachean Ethics*: Irwin 1985 and (for the second edition) 1999.

McDowell ascribes to them? In order to make progress with this question, we must examine Irwin's account of the ascent and what McDowell might say is wrong with it.

Here then is Irwin's account:

(I5) Plato insists that a pupil beginning the ascent must already be "pregnant in soul.". . . [His] *desires are altered by the development of his conception of the beautiful throughout the ascent.* The account has six stages with corresponding objects: S1 [the object] = a single beautiful body; S2 [the object] = the beauty in all bodies; S3 [the object] = the beauty of souls; S4 [the object] = the beauty of practices and laws; S5 [the object] = the beauty of sciences; S6 [the object] = Beauty Itself).

The first stage. The transition from S1 to S2 makes clearest the kind of process Plato finds in the ascent. The pupil at S1 loves a single body for its beauty . . . *He realizes that the beauty in all beautiful bodies is akin, and becomes a lover of them all, thinking less of this one* (210a8–b6). *He has been induced to move from S1 to S2 by his own reasoning:* if he loves the first body for its beauty, he sees that he has equal reason to love any body of equal beauty; and since beauty is the same in all beautiful bodies, he has reason to love them all. *This conclusion is reached by elenchos,* just as Socrates overturned Laches' initial narrow definition of courage by showing him that courage can be displayed in all kinds of conditions. *The pupil gradually comes to realize his own demands on an adequate object of love when a candidate is found unsatisfactory.*

The later stages. The movements between S2 and S6 are not so fully described . . . but the same account will work for them as for the first movement.

1. To pass from S2 to S3 the pupil must see that the beauty of souls is *more honorable* than the beauty in bodies [210b6–7] . . . he reasonably decides that a beautiful soul is a more suitable object of his attention than a beautiful body.
2. When he reaches S3 he looks for the suitable discourses to improve his beloved . . . Naturally he will think of the admirable practices and norms or rules he wants observed; so he will aim at this kind of beauty, which leads him to S4 [210c1–6] . . .
3. Beautiful practices express knowledge, and someone should aim at this knowledge, rather than solely at the practices; when the pupil realizes this, he moves to S5 . . .
4. When the pupil values knowledge, he will come to value knowledge of what is beautiful; for this will be the best guide for his efforts to create virtue. When his search for knowledge is over, he will have reached S6.

Throughout this sequence the pattern of elenctic argument can be discerned. *Plato does not just mean to describe a curriculum, where the pupil sees no reason*

> *to pass from one stage to the next.* We might suppose that just as we need to learn some mathematics to learn physics, we must see the less abstract kinds of beauty at the lower stages before we see the more abstract at the higher stages. But this alone will not satisfy Plato; for it would still require compulsion to move a pupil from the lower to the higher stages. *In Plato's ascent, a pupil at each stage has to be shown, from principles he already accepts, that he has reason to move to the higher stage.* [Irwin 1977: 167–69, my italics]

Irwin's account begins by noting that Plato insists that the pupil undertaking the ascent must *already* be "pregnant in soul": the pupil must recognize and love at least one instance of beauty as such—i.e., at least one beautiful body as such—if he is to begin the ascent. Now there would be no point to Plato's insisting on this if he did not think that some people lacked this prerequisite, and Plato does indeed distinguish those who are pregnant in *soul* from those who are pregnant only in *body*. At 208e, he says that those pregnant only in *body* turn more to women and seek, in giving birth to merely human offspring, only the *illusion* of immortality; only those who are pregnant in *soul* can be brought to pursue genuine immortality through seeking to produce the genuinely immortal products of wisdom and virtue. Plato clearly thinks that *not everyone* can begin the ascent: one must *already* be *motivated* in certain ways *before* one can begin. And Irwin implicitly recognizes this when he notes at the outset that Plato "insists" that the pupil "*already* be pregnant in soul." So Irwin seems to allow—and *should* in any case allow—that not everyone is prepared to undertake the ascent: not everyone has the *right* sort of *love* for even one beautiful body as such.[20]

Irwin goes on to claim that the pupil who has reached the initial stage will move from this stage to the next when he comes to realize that "the beauty in all beautiful bodies is *akin* [ἀδελφόν]" and so comes to love *all* beautiful bodies. Irwin says explicitly that the pupil is induced to move from (S1) to (S2) "by his own *reasoning*" and that a similar account can be given for each step in the ascent. The move from (S2) to (S3) is effected when the pupil comes to see that the beauty of souls is *more honorable* than the beauty of bodies, and thus comes to love beautiful souls even more than he loves beautiful bodies. The idea is that the reasons he has for loving beautiful bodies somehow *commit him* to loving beautiful souls, whose beauty is superior to that of beautiful bodies.

The crucial point here is that the ascent—as described not only by Plato but also by Irwin—involves attitudes that are in some sense *internal* to the evaluative scheme into which the pupil is being inducted. Consider first the requirement that the pupil already recognize some instances of beauty as such, and Plato's insistence that not everyone satisfies this requirement. Those who fail to satisfy this requirement are too

[20] It is worth comparing this to the various places where Irwin acknowledges that Plato's or Aristotle's arguments will work only on certain sorts of interlocutors—for example, only on those who think of themselves as rational agents or only on those who think of themselves as what Irwin calls "broad rational agents." See, for example, (I8)–(I10).

far outside the relevant scheme for initiation into even the lower reaches of it to commence: they do not, so to speak, have even a foot in the door. So the elenctic methods involved in the ascent will not work on *them*. Consider also the belief that the beauty of souls is *more honorable* than the beauty of bodies. The belief depends on a conception of honor—and of what is more honorable than what—that is arguably part of what McDowell calls an "inherited ethical scheme" and a relatively specific one at that: not all societies will take the beauty of souls to be more honorable than the beauty of bodies, since (among other reasons) some societies may lack the relevant conception of soul.[21]

If McDowell were giving an account of the ascent, he would no doubt make much of the ways in which the attitudes Plato exploits are *evaluative* attitudes, arguably the products of proper habituation and *internal* to the evaluative scheme into which the pupil is being inducted. He might even suggest that the requirement that the pupil already be "pregnant in soul" is analogous to Aristotle's requirement that his students already grasp that the "thats" instilled by a proper upbringing—that is, that his students already grasp "*that* this is fine," "*that* that is just," and so on.[22] But Irwin does not call attention to the ways in which the attitudes explicitly mentioned in his own account might be viewed as internal to the evaluative scheme into which the pupil is being inducted. Why not? Does Irwin think that the attitudes in question are *external*? If so, does he *mistake* internal attitudes for external ones?

Not necessarily. The issue here is complicated by the fact that the attitudes in question are internal in one sense and external in another. The ambiguity arises because Irwin takes the attitudes involved *in* the higher stages in some sense to *include* the attitudes involved in the lower stages.[23] When the pupil comes to love *all* beautiful bodies, he does *not cease* to love the one he loved first (though he comes to care *less* for it in the sense that he now recognizes others on a *par* with it). And when he comes to love beautiful *souls*, he does not cease loving beautiful *bodies* (though he comes to care *less* for them in the sense that he now recognizes objects of *superior* beauty). To the extent that the attitudes of the lower stages *survive* in the higher stages, the ascent seems to rely on attitudes that are in some sense *internal* to the higher stages into which the pupil is being inducted.[24] But the attitudes in question are *not proper* to the higher stages: they are attitudes that someone who has not yet reached the higher stages

[21] See Vasiliou 2002 on the importance to Socrates' argument against Polus of getting Polus to recognize the idea of harm to the soul.

[22] For this account of the "thats," see Burnyeat 1980. Aristotle says at *EN* 1098b3–4 that the principles of different things are acquired in different ways, some by means of perception, some (as perhaps here) by means of habituation, and others in other ways. For more on this issue, see Vasiliou 1996.

[23] See Irwin 1977, 169. His account differs here from the "exclusive" accounts of the ascent offered in Vlastos 1973 and Moravcsik 1971.

[24] I say "to the *extent* that these attitudes survive in the higher stages" in order to allow that the generic attitudes involved may undergo a kind of transformation, one that might be described in terms of their "being shaped" or "being given more specific (or more determinate) form." One could argue that the relevant sort of transformation is more radical than that, but that would seem to require the sort of "exclusive" interpretation of the ascent that Irwin explicitly rejects.

may have. The lower-stage attitudes might thus be viewed as *external* (in a refined sense of 'external') to the higher-stage evaluative scheme. And this is the feature of these lower-stage attitudes that Irwin emphasizes. So we need not interpret Irwin as *mistaking* internal attitudes for external ones: he may simply emphasize their external aspect (in this refined sense) where McDowell would emphasize their internal aspect. For Irwin wants to use the pupil's *prior* commitment to these lower-stage attitudes to *move* the pupil to the higher stages (in which the lower-stage attitudes may of course be transformed). So although Irwin does not explicitly say that the attitudes in question are "external" to the higher-stage scheme, his account seems to depend on the fact that the attitudes in question are external in the refined sense according to which they can be held by someone who has not yet reached the higher-stage scheme.

But this does *not* mean that these attitudes are external in the crude sense that they are *non-ethical* or *non-evaluative*. These attitudes *are* evaluative and even in a sense *ethical*—though to the extent that they are *not distinctive* of the higher-stage ethical scheme into which the pupil is being inducted, or survive in the higher stages only in a *transformed* state, we might prefer to call them "proto-ethical." And this seems to be a point that Irwin can and should allow. In fact, the ability of these attitudes to *move* the agent to the higher stages seems to *depend* on their evaluative force: it is the fact that these attitudes embody judgments about their objects' *worthiness to be loved* that explains how having these attitudes can move someone to love the radically different sorts of objects that she eventually comes to see as even *more* worthy in the relevant respects than the original ones. So Irwin seems to be at least implicitly committed to allowing that these attitudes are evaluative and proto-ethical.

But to the extent that Irwin allows this, it is unfair to represent him as seeking to provide arguments that are external in the crude sense that they do not involve *any* evaluative or proto-ethical premises. This is clearly not his view. We should thus distinguish—as McDowell does not—"extra-ethical" arguments (which do not contain *any* evaluative or proto-ethical premises) from "external" arguments in this *refined* sense (arguments that may contain evaluative or proto-ethical premises so long as these premises are not "proper to" or "distinctive of" the *specific* ethical scheme for which they are supposed to provide arguments). And we should acknowledge that at least in his account of the ascent, Irwin does *not* represent Plato as giving *extra-ethical* arguments, though he does represent Plato as giving arguments that are *external* in the refined sense that they appeal to attitudes or standards of rationality that the interlocutor can accept *without* having accepted the *specific* evaluative scheme for which they are supposed to be arguments. We can then resolve the variation on the secondary puzzle by saying that Irwin's Socrates differs from Irwin's Plato and Aristotle in that Irwin's Socrates defends the rationality of virtue by appeal to an argument that is *extra-ethical* in the sense that it seeks to *reduce* the rationality of virtue to the rationality of something non-ethical, while Irwin's Plato and Aristotle do *not* seek to reduce the rationality of virtue in this way but nevertheless give arguments that are in fact *external* (though Irwin does not call them that) in the refined sense (to which McDowell may still object) that they appeal to attitudes or to standards of rationality that the interlocutor can accept *without* having accepted the *specific* evaluative scheme for which they are supposed to be arguments.

Here, however, it is important to note that the question whether an attitude or standard is external to a given stage in this sense is *independent of the genesis of* that attitude—independent, in particular, of whether the attitude is the product of habituation or upbringing. The pupil's initial appreciation of beautiful bodies as such, or his grasp of the relevant "thats" may be external to some higher-stage evaluative scheme while at the same time being the product of habituation or upbringing—even of the sort of habituation or upbringing that leads, if all goes well, to acceptance of the relevant evaluative scheme. Moreover, this seems to me to be a point that Irwin can afford to accept, as long as he allows (as McDowell too wants to allow) that reason eventually enables the pupil to achieve some degree of critical detachment from these initial attitudes.

One sign that Irwin can afford to accept the claim that the lower-stage attitudes are products of the sort of habituation or upbringing that culminates in acceptance of the higher-stage scheme is the fact that his doing so would be unlikely to pacify McDowell. I assume that McDowell would still object to Irwin's requirement that at each stage the pupil be "shown, from principles he already accepts, that he has reason to move to the higher stage." Here, however, we should distinguish two different ways in which we might interpret this requirement. Irwin might simply be making the *generic* demand that each step be *motivated* by standards of rationality already endorsed by the pupil before the step is taken. Or he might be making the more *specific* demand that each step be *rationally required* by such standards.

To see the distinction, consider the difference between the following two sorts of case. First, a case in which someone views his move from single-minded anti-racist politics to a broader agenda that includes anti-sexist politics as *rationally required* because he comes to see that the very principles that support his anti-racism *also* support anti-sexism, so that it would be *inconsistent of* him to embrace anti-racist politics on the basis of these principles without also embracing anti-sexist politics on the basis of the *same* principles. And second, a case in which someone views her move from working-class politics to teaching in a public university as *rationally motivated* (but *not rationally required)* by these politics: she need not view the move as *rationally required* by these politics, because she can imagine someone with the same politics deciding to teach in a private institution so as to reach not only students who have had no exposure to working-class realities but also upwardly mobile students who would all too easily forget such realities.[25] There are other sorts of examples we might imagine here, such as

[25] In speaking of this move as "rationally *motivated*," I am not introducing any distinction between motivating reasons and justifying ones. The relevant point in *both* of the cases imagined here is one about *justifying* reasons: in one case the subject sees the move (whether or not she actually makes it) as *rationally required* and in the other case the subject sees the move (whether or not she actually makes it) as *rationally motivated* (though not rationally required). I shall turn shortly to the question of motivating reasons—i.e., to the question of the sorts of factors that explain particular subjects' actual moves from (for example) the lower to the higher stages of the ascent.

that of someone who regards her move from an interest in bebop to an interest in free jazz as rationally motivated but not rationally required. Our question is whether the ascent *may* involve such moves, or whether it involves only moves that are rationally *required.*

It seems pretty clear that McDowell would reject the *specific* demand, both in its own right and as an interpretation of the ascent. For it would be natural for McDowell to interpret the ascent as a version of the sort of initiation into the conceptual space of the "noble" and the "base" in which initiation he takes Aristotelian moral development to consist (at least in part).[26] And McDowell would, I think, be most unlikely to say that such initiation is exhausted by moves that are *rationally required* in the sense that refusing to make such a move would involve some sort of *logical* inconsistency. His idea is that the pupil gradually acquires, through proper habituation, a grasp that *this* is *just*, that *that* is *cowardly*, that *this* is *noble* and *that base*, etc. The pupil thus comes, as Burnyeat 1980, 72) puts it, "to internalize from a scattered range of particular cases a general evaluative attitude which is not reducible to rules or precepts." To the extent that this requires the pupil to see, and thus to achieve some *cognitive* grasp of, similarities and differences between various particular situations and actions, the process is *not non-rational*: but it is *not* primarily an *argumentative* process, at least not a *deductivist* one. This is especially clear at the higher stages of the ascent, which seem to involve something like the move from having a relatively full complement of "thats" to a grasp of what Aristotle calls the "because"—a move that McDowell takes to involve Neurathian reflection, which is clearly a form of *reasoning* even if it is *not* purely *deductive.*

There is some question, though, about whether McDowell would object even to the *generic* demand that the moves involved in the ascent be *motivated* by standards the pupil already accepts. For McDowell's paper on external reasons suggests that he wants to make room for the possibility that, at least in some cases, the transition to accepting a correct standard might be effected not by reasoning but by something like conversion. His main point there is that someone's claim to be seeing things aright is not impeached by the fact that she came to see things that way through some sort of conversion experience rather than some process of reasoning. And McDowell cites in support of this point the fact that the sort of habituation involved in a proper upbringing, which he regards as a form of initiation into a conceptual scheme, is "not itself a rational route" to acceptance of that scheme. See, for example, the following passage:

(M5) If we think of ethical upbringing in a roughly Aristotelian way, as a process of habituation into suitable modes of behavior, inextricably bound up with the inculcation of suitably related modes of thought, there is no mystery about how the process can be *the acquisition, simultaneously, of a way of seeing things and of a collection of motivational directions or practical concerns*, focused and activated in particular cases by exercises of the way of seeing

[26] McDowell has in fact accepted this suggestion in conversation.

> things . . . *Here talking of having been properly brought up and talking of considering things aright are two ways of giving expression to the same assessment* . . .
>
> What if someone has not been properly brought up? In order to take seriously the idea that someone who has been properly brought up tends to consider matters aright in the relevant area, we surely do not need to embrace the massively implausible implication that someone who has not been properly brought up . . . can be induced into seeing things straight by directing some piece of reasoning at him. On the contrary, reasoning aimed at generating new motivations will stand a chance of working only if it appeals to something in the audience's existing motivational make-up . . . What it would take to get such a person to consider the relevant matters aright . . . [is] something like conversion . . . The idea of conversion would function here as the idea of an intelligible shift in motivational orientation that is exactly *not* effected by inducing a person to discover, by practical reasoning controlled by existing motivations, some internal reasons that he did not previously realize he had. But if its upshot is a case of considering matters aright, why should such a process not count as someone's being made aware of external reasons, reasons that he had all along, for acting in the relevant ways?
>
> . . . It is plausible, then, that from certain starting points there is *no rational route*—no process of being swayed by reasons . . . that would take someone to being as if he had been properly brought up. *(Being properly brought up is not itself a rational route into being that way.)* But this has no evident tendency to disrupt the natural connection between being that way and considering things aright. [McDowell 1995b: sec. 4][27]

The last bit of this passage, however, strikes me as potentially misleading. For there is an important sense in which McDowell does *not* want—or at least *should not* want—to *deny* that initiation into the conceptual space of the "noble" and "base" is a *rational* process: his point is simply that such initiation is not accomplished primarily by means of *argument*, particularly not by means of *deductive* argument. (This is partly why the label "non-rationalist" is potentially misleading.) So the difference between McDowell and Irwin seems to be partly a matter of Irwin's having a narrower, more procedural conception of "the rational"—what McDowell might call a "deductivist" conception.[28]

[27] See also Nussbaum 1995, to which I am much indebted for my own understanding of the ways in which Plato's and Aristotle's arguments are *internal* and involve *evaluative* premises.

[28] McDowell begins his attack on the "deductivist" conception of rationality in his 1979 article. For further discussion of how the "deductivist prejudice" is supposed to distort our reading of Aristotle, see his 1996a book chapter. McDowell's basic view is roughly as follows. He takes the deductivist conception or "prejudice" both to support and to be supported by the demand for external justification, which he takes to stem ultimately from what he calls the "non-cognitivist assumption" that there is a sharp distinction between cognitive and motivational states. And he claims that this assumption leads commentators to see only two ways to interpret Aristotle: (1) a quasi-Humean way according to which practical reason is subservient to wholly autonomous and extra-intellectual motivational propensities, and (2) a way involving a "rationalist" recoil from the quasi-Humean view, a recoil in which a wholly autonomous

Assuming then that McDowell would be willing to distinguish the ascent (taken as involving the sort of mechanisms normally involved in a proper upbringing) from sheer conversion, McDowell might be willing to interpret the ascent as satisfying the *generic* demand that the moves be *rationally motivated* (as distinct from *rationally required*), provided the relevant account of a move's being *rationally motivated* is sufficiently liberal. So *if* Irwin were to embrace only the *generic* demand and to expand his conception of what counts as *rationally motivated*, there *might* be room here for reconciliation.

It is pretty clear, however, that Irwin has in mind the *specific* demand when he says that the reason the pupil has for choosing the initial object "*really* justifies the choice of something else." For while the reason one has for choosing a certain object might "*also* justify" something else without, however, rationally *requiring* it, the "*really* justifies" suggests that this is not what Irwin has in mind. Moreover, Irwin generally represents Plato and Plato's Socrates as seeking a sort of *rational compulsion.* See especially Irwin 1986a, where he clearly attributes to Plato a form of "strong dialectic" like the one he attributes to Aristotle:

> (I6) From here [*Republic* II on] the argument is no longer an encounter with a particular person. Plato wants to answer the best statement of the case against justice, not merely to answer someone's case . . .
>
> This does not mean that the argument ceases to be dialectical. Plato is still arguing from common beliefs, and arguing with someone who holds them. But he wants to appeal to the subset of common beliefs that characterize a rational agent . . . Plato exploits the Socratic conversational method, and argues from what the interlocutor agrees to. But he relies not on what the particular empirical interlocutor *happens* to agree to, but on what *any rational* interlocutor *must* agree to . . .
>
> Plato looks for a justification that relies not simply on the agreement of individuals, but on general features of a rational agent who raises these questions about his life. We have found no reason to accuse Plato of coercion in these arguments; their *rational compulsion* results not from his intervention, but *from the nature of the agents themselves*. [Irwin 1986a: 73–74, my italics]

Here, though, we need to ask what Irwin means by "rational compulsion." For that term is often associated with the idea of *deductive* reasoning. And I have been suggesting that strong dialectic (even as represented by Irwin) *need not* be taken to involve *deduction:* strong dialectic may show us only that *given* the premises, certain ethical conclusions are *more plausible* than their rivals. In that case, any compulsion would

---

practical intellect fully determines the virtuous person's motivational orientation. The implausibility of the quasi-Humean interpretation thus leads commentators like Irwin to embrace the "rationalist" interpretation, which leads (according to McDowell) to the demand for external justification, a demand that McDowell takes both to fuel and to be fueled by the "deductivist prejudice."

seem to depend on the extent to which the premises themselves are compelling. And it is indeed a large part of Irwin's strategy to appeal to especially compelling premises—that is, to premises that *any* rational interlocutor or *any* rational agent *must* accept simply in virtue of recognizing herself as such. But insofar as Irwin wants to represent the *conclusions* as rationally compelling, it is not clear that he can get by simply with *premises* that are rationally compelling in the sense that we cannot refuse to accept them without ceasing to think of ourselves as rational agents: it would seem that the conclusions must also *follow from* the premises. So it is tempting to suppose that Irwin at least sometimes requires deducibility and not simply broad coherence. For some confirmation of this, see the following passage:

(I7) The [Parmenidean] inquirer frees himself from the force of irrational habit, to subject himself to *rational necessity*; necessity determines both how the world must be and what the rational inquirer *must conclude.*

Plato shares this Parmenidean ideal of rational compulsion. . . . Plato never [in the middle dialogues] represents mathematics as meeting the highest standards of certainty or accuracy. In *Republic* V–VII the highest place belongs not to mathematics, but to dialectic, the familiar Socratic conversation. [Irwin 1986a: 53–54]

But it is not clear that Irwin *should* require deducibility (especially not in his account of Aristotle, where he tends to speak simply of "broad coherence"). So let us suppose for a moment that Irwin were to allow here—in his account of the ascent—the possibility that the moves might, at least in some cases, be rationally *motivated* without being rationally *required.* Could he and McDowell then agree to occupy some common ground?

We should begin by noting that there are (at least) three general ways to interpret the mechanisms by means of which the ascent is effected. If we agree with Irwin in viewing the ascent as effected by means of some sort of *reasoning*, we might view it in either of two ways. We might view it as effected primarily (or even exclusively) by means of *deductive* reasoning. Or we might view it as effected largely (even if not exclusively) by means of *non-deductive* reasoning. The third option is to view it as effected *not by reasoning* but by something like *conversion.*[29]

(1)	(2)	(3)
Deductivist account of the sort of elenctic reasoning involved in the ascent	*Non-deductivist account* of the sort of elenctic reasoning involved in the ascent	*Non-reasoning or "conversion" account* of the ascent

[29] One might think the conversion model especially appropriate in connection with the *Symposium* ascent, which suggests initiation into mysteries. But what is striking about the ascent is the way in which (as Irwin emphasizes) it contains elements of *reasoning* according to which it is supposed to seem *arbitrary* to refuse to take various steps.

The ascent may of course involve more than one of these mechanisms, perhaps even a combination of all three. But I want to focus for the moment on accounts that emphasize one or the other of these mechanisms. The issue here is which mechanisms Irwin and McDowell are, respectively, likely to emphasize, and so in which column we should locate each of their views. Part of the question is whether McDowell's views, particularly in his paper on external reasons, *require* us to locate him in the third column. And part of the question is whether Irwin *must* be located in the first column—that is, whether Irwin *must* be read as assuming a deductivist model of the sort of elenctic reasoning he takes to be involved in the ascent or whether he might allow elenctic reasoning to include at least some non-deductivist moves.

I think in fact that McDowell has always belonged squarely in the middle, and that it is only misinterpretation of him, encouraged no doubt by his misleading talk of initiation into the conceptual space of the "noble" and "base" as "not itself a rational [process]," that would lead someone to place him in column (3).[30] So I shall focus here on the question of whether there is any way to get *Irwin* to move to the middle.

To see what I am recommending, consider Irwin's account of the move from S1 to S2, in which the pupil is supposed to move by means of something like elenctic reasoning from love of one beautiful body to love of all equally (or more) beautiful bodies. We might picture the pupil as actually engaged in a piece of deductive reasoning, with major and minor premises, as follows:

> The beauty in this body is akin to (or not relevantly different from) the beauty in any other beautiful body.
>
> The beauty in this body gives me reason to love it.
>
> ---------------------------
>
> Therefore, the beauty in any other beautiful body gives me similar reason to love it.

And straightaway the pupil acts, running out and "mechanically" (as McDowell might say) seeking beautiful bodies to love.

Alternatively, we might picture the pupil as being moved in the following way. He loves a particular body for its beauty. At some point, he notices what he takes to be an equally or perhaps more beautiful body and begins to struggle with the question why he should not love it as well as (or instead of) the first. (I assume we all know how this works.) This may lead him to reflect on the question whether there might not be other equally or even more beautiful bodies that he should perhaps love as well. Perhaps the hundredth body he comes to see as beautiful is that of a girl or a barbarian, and it had never occurred to

---

[30] McDowell has confirmed this in conversation.

him that girls or barbarians could be beautiful, too, with the result that he has to revise his conception of beauty. All of this may involve lots of attention to particular bodies and reflection on what it is about them that makes them beautiful, the sort of reflection that is likely to lead to an appreciation of the difficulties of giving an account of beauty (even of bodily beauty) in observational terms.[31] This is precisely the sort of reflection that is likely to lead the pupil to recognize other sorts of beauty—the non-bodily beauty of souls, the beauty of norms and practices, and so on. Here again the pupil may have to pay lots of attention to particular souls and to what it is about them that makes them beautiful, each perhaps in its own special way. There is no reason to think that this sort of reflection proceeds by way of deductive argument of the sort described above, argument that would *compel* its subject *on pain of irrationality* to move to the next stage. Nevertheless, the moves in question are in some sense *motivated* by prior attitudes. So why *can't* Irwin understand the sort of reasoning involved in the ascent in this way? Why *can't* Irwin allow that the pupil undergoes—either in the early stages of the ascent or perhaps before—the sort of initiation into the conceptual space of the "noble" and "base" of which McDowell speaks? And why *can't* Irwin allow that the ascent involves the sort of Neurathian reflection that leads on McDowell's account from the "thats" to the "because" (which is clearly analogous, in explanatory pretension, to Platonic Forms)? Isn't that in fact Irwin's point when he claims that the ascent proceeds by way of elenctic reasoning?

One thing to note here is that even if Irwin is inclined in the end to want deductive arguments to *move* the pupil, he can allow that a lot of the sort of situation-specific discernment of particulars involved in the non-deductivist model plays a role in the pupil's coming to grasp the relevant premises, both major and minor. But this raises a question about what is involved in embracing the deductivist model. Does that model require that each move *in fact* be deductively effected? Or does it require only that each move be *capable* of being deductively effected? Suppose, for example, that there are two ways in which someone might make the move from S1 to S2, both of which involve lots of situation-specific discernment of particulars but one of which involves articulation of a universal premise while the other does not: in one case, the pupil explicitly says to himself that the beauty in all beautiful bodies is relevantly similar; in the other case, the pupil simply comes to see each beautiful body he encounters as warranting love similar to (though not perhaps exactly the same as) the love he has for other beautiful bodies. Should it matter—either from Irwin's point of view or from McDowell's—how the move from S1 to S2 is *actually* effected?

McDowell, I think, would say that it does not matter how the move is actually effected, though he might worry that its being deductively effected in *some* cases might lead us to conclude that it *must* be deductively effected in *all* cases.[32] I am less sure what

[31] Irwin 1977 discusses this issue (along with the *Symposium* ascent) in chap. VI. It is worth comparing this with the discussion in chap. 10 of Irwin 1995 (a reworking of Irwin 1977). His 1995 discussion of the *Symposium* ascent is far briefer and less methodological in emphasis than his 1977 discussion. But I do not see any fundamental differences in doctrine that should affect the claims I make here.

[32] See sec. 4 of McDowell 1979.

Irwin would say. But I expect that even if he allowed for some actual non-deductively *effected* moves, he would still insist (as McDowell would not) that such moves be deductively *justified.* For it is pretty clear that Irwin wants the moves to be *rationally required.* Here, as elsewhere in his accounts of Socratic argument, Irwin represents Socrates as wanting to *compel* his opponent—on *pain of inconsistency*—to accept Socrates' conclusions.[33] This may simply reflect what McDowell calls "the deductivist prejudice" about the nature of rationality—i.e., the idea that a move is *rationally* justified only if it is *deductively* justified. Or it may (as I am somewhat inclined to think) reflect an assumption about the kind of rationality associated with *virtue in particular*—i.e., the assumption that the demands of virtue must be rationally *compelling* in a way in which other sorts of rationally legitimate demands (such as those of etiquette) need not.

In either case, the following hypothesis about the fundamental difference between the method that Irwin sees in Plato's account of the ascent and the method that McDowell would see in Plato's account of the ascent seems plausible: the difference lies less in the extent to which the arguments that each ascribes to Plato are external (in either the crude or the refined sense) than in the extent to which the arguments are *deductively justified.* For each seems to recognize (at least implicitly) that the lower-stage attitudes are *both internal* to the evaluative scheme into which the pupil is being inducted (in the sense that they are evaluative attitudes that survive in the higher stages) *and external* to the higher stages into which the pupil is being inducted (in the refined sense that the pupil can have these attitudes without having reached the higher stages). The main difference in their respective accounts seems to be that Irwin requires the moves from the lower to the higher stages to be *deductively justified* (even if they need not always be deductively *effected*), whereas McDowell would eschew this requirement: it is enough for him that the moves involved be capable of being rationally *motivated,* which does not in his view require that they be capable of being deductively *effected,* nor even that they be capable of being deductively *justified.*

3. A NEW HYPOTHESIS ABOUT THE SECONDARY PUZZLE: THAT THE METHODS OF IRWIN'S ARISTOTLE ARE "DEDUCTIVIST" IN A WAY THOSE OF MCDOWELL'S ARISTOTLE ARE NOT

Let us return then with this hypothesis in mind, to Irwin's and McDowell's accounts of Aristotle. It is clear that Irwin attributes to Aristotle arguments for the rationality of virtue that are external in the sense that they appeal to attitudes and/or standards

[33] See Irwin 1986a, where one of Irwin's primary aims is to acquit Socrates of the charge that he "coerces" or "bullies" his interlocutors: Irwin seeks to do this by distinguishing *coercion* from *rational compulsion,* and showing how Socrates can *compel* a rational interlocutor to accept his conclusions without, however, *coercing* her: for it is *her* rationality—not Socrates' influence—that leads her to accept Socrates' conclusions. See, for example, the end of (16). This project—of showing how one can *compel* one's interlocutor without, however, being accused of *coercion*—is one in which McDowell (unlike Irwin) seems to have little interest.

of rationality that the interlocutor can accept without *already* embracing the specific conception of virtue whose rationality is in question. Consider, for example, the initial defense of courage and temperance that Irwin spells out on Aristotle's behalf. This defense seeks to show any rational agent, no matter what particular ends she pursues, that she will be more likely to achieve these ends if she is courageous and temperate than if she is not. See, for example, the following passage:

> (I8) Courage and temperance seem to be the easiest virtues to recommend to a *narrow rational agent* [i.e., a rational agent who considers only his *actual* desires and seeks to maximize their satisfaction].[34] He seems to need them if he is to pursue his longer-term goals without distraction by cowardly fears or by the opportunities for more immediate pleasure that appeal to the intemperate. Perhaps someone who entirely lacked courage and temperance would find it hard to execute any of his rational plans except in very favorable circumstances, free of these distractions; if fear or pleasure distracts him, his life will be a chaos, scarcely displaying rational planning at all but swaying from one distraction to the next. [Irwin 1981: 216–17]

On this account, courage and temperance resemble Rawlsian "primary goods" in the sense that courage and temperance are supposed to be useful for pursuing one's ends, *whatever* particular ends one happens to have. Their value to an agent is thus supposed to be *independent* of the particular conception of the good to which she is committed.

This argument is external, but it is (as Irwin himself recognizes) hardly *deductively compelling*, at least not if one is arguing with what Irwin calls a "narrow rational agent"—that is, an agent who considers only her *actual* desires and seeks to integrate them (perhaps eliminating some in the process) so as to maximize *their* satisfaction. For, as Irwin himself recognizes in (I9), such an interlocutor may simply decide that her desire to avoid fearful situations outweighs those desires whose satisfaction would require her to confront fearful situations and so to cultivate courage, with the result that she chooses to eliminate the relevant desires rather than to cultivate courage.

> (I9) [= continuation of (I8)] But not every narrow rational agent has reason to value courage and temperance as much as Aristotle does. Someone may care more about avoiding fear or frustration on particular occasions even if he must abandon many of his longer-term aims. He will still value some courage and temperance since sometimes they may help him to avoid future pains and frustrations. But often he will not pursue his longer-term goals; he will give them up if they cause fear or deny him more immediate satisfaction . . . *To recommend courage and temperance Aristotle needs to argue*

[34] The contrast here is with the "*broad* rational agent" mentioned in (I9) and (I10)—i.e., an agent who considers not only her actual desires but also what sorts of desires she *ought* to cultivate and what sorts of desires she *ought* to discourage.

> *with a broad rational agent.* He can criticize the outlook of someone who tries to minimize danger and frustration by arguing that such a life prevents the development of many human capacities and restricts the scope and competence of practical reasoning. Someone who drops his projects at the first sign of difficulty will steadily restrict the range of his aims and pursuits; he will leave undeveloped those important aspects of himself that cannot be developed without some effort and difficulty. Someone who persists in trying to be a high-jumper if he is always petrified with fright and cannot think of anything else may be too devoted to this goal for his own good. But someone who refuses to face any difficulty or danger will miss much of what would be good for him. *Aristotle's approval of courage and temperance reflects our own common beliefs, but these beliefs show that we regard ourselves as broad rational agents, and his arguments are cogent only if we regard ourselves this way.* [Irwin 1981: 217, my italics]

Here, however, it should be noted that even if the interlocutor does not choose the "narrow" way out, the argument will at best secure only an *instrumental* commitment to courage. But Aristotle says that virtuous agents must choose virtuous actions *for themselves.*[35] In order to secure the sort of *intrinsic* commitment to virtue that Aristotle requires of a genuinely virtuous agent, Irwin needs to provide Aristotle with a better argument. And Irwin attempts to do that in two stages: *first* by providing an argument capable of showing anyone who thinks of herself as a narrow rational agent that she must (on pain of inconsistency) regard herself as a broad rational agent (i.e., an agent who considers not only her *actual* desires but also what sorts of desires she *ought* to cultivate and what sorts of desires she *ought* to discourage); and *then* by providing an argument capable of showing someone who thinks of herself as a broad rational agent that broad rational agency as such requires an *intrinsic* commitment to virtue.

The argument for viewing oneself as a broad rational agent is supposed to work by getting someone who thinks of herself only as a narrow rational agent to see that there is *no relevant difference* between the restriction of rational agency that she *refuses* to accept when she refuses to consider only her *present* desires and aims, and the restriction of rational agency that she *agrees* to accept in agreeing to consider only her *actual* desires and aims:

> (I10) Now if a rational agent is impartial toward the immediate and more distant desires and their satisfaction, why should he not *also* be impartial towards his actual and his potential desires and their satisfaction? If he refuses to consider his potential desires, he *arbitrarily denies a role to practical reasoning;* he has no better reason for denying it this role than for refusing impartial consideration to his future desires. A rational agent

[35] For more on this issue, see the discussion of "prudent vice" in sec. 205 of Irwin 1988.

> has no reason to identify himself only with his actual desires; he has good reason to consider the claims of his potential desires too and to form a conception of his final good that includes the harmonious satisfaction of actual and potential desires alike. A rational agent who *falsely* regards himself as only a narrow rational agent and not as a broad rational agent is *irrationally limiting the scope of practical reason and deliberation.* The same reasons that are good reasons for regarding himself as a narrow rational agent justify him in regarding himself as a broad rational agent too. [Irwin 1981: 213][36]

The problem with this argument is that it seems to *assume* that the narrow rational agent values exercising her rational agency *as such,* and not simply for instrumental reasons: this is what moves her from rejecting the temporal restriction to rejecting the modal restriction. If she valued rational agency simply as a means to maximizing the satisfaction of her *actual* desires, both present and future, she would *not* be moved by this argument.

It is here that Aristotle's metaphysical and psychological claims about human nature become crucial: the agent who fails explicitly to value the exercise of her rational agency *as such* is supposed to be making a *mistake* about what *sort* of creature she is and so about what is *good* for her. What she needs (according to Irwin's Aristotle) is a better understanding of her own nature; she needs to see (as Irwin puts it) that "broad rational agency expresses an *essential* property of [her] as a *natural organism* with a rational soul and the capacity for rational decision and choice" [Irwin 1981: 216]. And this is supposed to be something that she can in principle be brought to see—presumably by something like a careful reading of Aristotle's *De Anima*—*independently* of the evaluative tendencies she has acquired as a result of her particular upbringing. It may of course be that her upbringing must have established in her the sort of discipline and self-control she needs to make it through the requisite reading (or readings) of the *De Anima*—or perhaps even better of *Aristotle's First Principles.* But the relevant sort of discipline and self-control can be secured by a variety of forms of upbringing, none of which presupposes habituation into Aristotelian virtue strictly so-called. All she needs are whatever capacities it takes to understand—and to attend to—the argument. And Irwin argues that Aristotelian virtue is in no way required for *that.*

Here, it is worth recalling Irwin's deflationary account of Aristotle's requirement that students of his ethics have had a proper upbringing (I1). There (and elsewhere) Irwin acknowledges—in ways not always recognized by McDowell—some of the limitations of argument: "vice," for example, might lead someone to refuse even to listen to Aristotle's arguments. Irwin seems, however, to think that *if* the vicious but

[36] It is important to note the similarity between this objection to "arbitrarily" or "irrationally" limiting practical reason to the consideration of actual desires and the objection in Plato's *Symposium* to arbitrarily limiting love to a particular beautiful body or to the beauty of bodies as distinct from other forms of beauty.

rational agent who thinks of herself as an essentially rational agent attends carefully to Aristotle's arguments, her rationality will lead her to *accept* their conclusions even if her non-rational desires still interfere with her *acting*—or acting *wholeheartedly*—on her acceptance of these conclusions. In other words, Irwin seems to recognize that being rationally persuaded to accept the conclusion of the argument is likely to produce continence at best. His point is largely to deny that an agent must already be at least to some extent virtuous in order even to *understand* (and so to be *persuaded* by) the arguments.

Here, however, we should note that Aristotelian virtue might—if McDowell is right about its nature—make one *impatient* with the argument of *Aristotle's First Principles*. For Aristotle's virtuous agent, as conceived by McDowell, might object that Irwin's argument fails to respect the historical Aristotle's requirement that the virtuous agent value virtuous action *for itself*. Although Irwin claims that the broad rational agent succeeds in valuing rational agency and the associated virtues for themselves insofar as she values them as expressions of her nature and not simply as means to the satisfaction of desires and aims she happens to have, McDowell would presumably object that valuing rational agency and the associated virtues as expressions of one's nature is *not sufficient* for valuing virtuous *action* for itself.[37]

McDowell's objection is best understood in terms of his distinction between "first" and "second" nature. A human being's *first nature* is a matter of features—especially motivational tendencies—that belong to her simply in virtue of being human and apart from the particular form of life in which she has been raised. Her *second nature* is a matter of contingent features—especially motivational tendencies—that she acquires as a result of the particular form of life in which she has been raised. Sheer hunger, thirst, and raw sexual urges—as opposed, for example, to acquired tastes for caviar, scotch, and highly regularized S/M practices—are thus examples of *first* natural tendencies; while moral and aesthetic preferences—for example, one's particular sense of justice or one's appreciation of bebop—are examples of *second* natural tendencies, tendencies that we acquire only as a result of a certain sort of upbringing. According to McDowell, virtuous dispositions belong to *second* nature: although, as Aristotle says, they belong to us neither by nature nor contrary to nature, we are *naturally suited* to receive them and to perfect them through *habit* [*EN* 1103a23–26]. But our reception and perfection of them depends on our receiving the right sort of upbringing.[38] Once we have had this sort of upbringing (and *only* once we have had this sort of upbringing) we shall be able to fully appreciate the values they embody in much the same way that someone who

---

37 [On this issue, see "Eudaimonia, External Results, and Choosing Virtuous Actions for Themselves" (Chapter 3, this volume).]

38 Irwin seems to acknowledge something like this when he says "virtues of character resulting from habituation are needed to fulfil the human function, because human nature does not infallibly complete itself" [1988, 374]. The main difference between Irwin and McDowell on this point seems to be that McDowell seems to take such completion to be a prerequisite for appreciating the *reasons* for virtuous behavior: one's first (or as Irwin might say "incomplete") nature does not fully equip one to appreciate the *reasons* there are for living virtuously.

has had the right sort of musical training (and *only* someone who has had the right sort of musical training) can fully appreciate bebop.

So McDowell's objection to Irwin's Aristotle seems to be not so much that Irwin's Aristotle seeks *deductive* justification as that Irwin's Aristotle seeks to validate the second-natural practices of virtue by appeal to first-natural motives common to virtuous and non-virtuous agents alike—in other words, that Irwin's Aristotle seeks to provide an *external* defense of virtue.[39] And this objection seems more apt, given that the arguments that Irwin ascribes to Aristotle are (as Irwin must surely recognize) hardly deductively compelling. The arguments for the relevant metaphysical and psychological theories are essentially *coherentist* arguments to the effect that these theories *best explain* the phenomena. So even if the relevant ethical conclusions themselves *follow* from the relevant metaphysical and psychological theories (which is doubtful), these ethical conclusions are no more secure than the metaphysical and psychological theories on which they "depend" or "rest," not all of which are as compelling as Aristotle's dialectical defense of PNC. So our hypothesis seems to be defeated, at least when we turn to Irwin's and McDowell's accounts of *Aristotle*.[40]

McDowell's primary objection seems rather to be that Irwin's Aristotle fails to respect the historical Aristotle's requirement that virtuous actions be justified on their *own* terms and not by appeal to independent standards that are acceptable to virtuous and non-virtuous agents alike. It thus begins to seem that there may be a connection—at least in McDowell's case—between the substantive ethical views ascribed to Aristotle and the methods of ethical argument ascribed to Aristotle. So we need to turn to our primary puzzle, concerning what connections (if any) there are between the *substantive ethical views* that Irwin and McDowell ascribe to Aristotle and the *methods* they ascribe to Aristotle. Why, for example, couldn't Aristotle adopt the moral psychology that McDowell ascribes to him while employing—perhaps even *as a result of employing*—the "strong dialectical method" that Irwin ascribes to him? Examining this question will suggest a possible way of reconciling (at least partially) the views of Irwin's Aristotle with those of McDowell's Aristotle.

4. THE PRIMARY PUZZLE: WHAT CONNECTIONS (IF ANY) ARE THERE BETWEEN THE METHODS AND THE SUBSTANTIVE ETHICAL VIEWS?

McDowell believes—and this is perhaps the most important difference between him and Irwin—that practical reason is *not* something that belongs to our *first* nature: although we may as a matter of first nature be equipped to receive it, practical

[39] For evidence that Irwin does indeed appeal to something like first nature here, see the passage quoted in note 13 above.

[40] Note, however, that this hypothesis may still be correct (as I am inclined to think it is) about the difference between Irwin's account of the *Symposium* ascent and the way in which McDowell would read that ascent.

reason is something whose reception depends (like virtue) on our receiving the right sort of upbringing. McDowell in fact *identifies* habituation into genuine virtue with the proper development of practical reason: to be habituated into virtue *just is* to be initiated into the conceptual space in which reasons like "this is just," "that is cowardly," "this is noble, that base" operate *autonomously* of other reasons.[41]

Part of McDowell's point is that particular actions are to be justified *within* the practice of virtue by appeal to such *autonomous* considerations: the virtuous agent chooses this or that particular action qua *just* or *noble*, and *not* qua expression of her nature or actualization of her essence (even if it is *in fact* an expression of her nature or actualization of her essence). But it is not clear that Irwin needs—or should anyhow want—to deny this point. He can allow a distinction between (a) an *external* justification of the *practice itself* and (b) the *internal* sorts of justifications of *particular actions* that are given *within* that practice. This raises a question about whether Irwin's drawing this distinction and claiming to give an external justification only of the practice itself—but *not* of any particular actions *within* that practice—would satisfy McDowell or whether McDowell would object *even* to giving an external justification of the practice itself.[42]

What I am suggesting (by way of a first step towards reconciliation) is that Irwin can allow—consistently with the method he ascribes to Aristotle—that the virtuous agent does *not*, *in* deciding what to do on this or that *particular* occasion of choice, *weigh* the benefits of acting virtuously *against* the attractions of competing goods. In other words, Irwin can (consistently with the method he ascribes to Aristotle) allow something like the moral psychology of McDowell's virtuous agent. Whether or not Irwin *wants* to allow this is a separate question, but there is some evidence that he may. He says, for example, that "Aristotle cannot expect the virtuous person to *consider* whether she should sacrifice her virtue for other goods" [Irwin 1988: 446]. Moreover, Irwin seems to agree with McDowell's general picture of the sort of training that Aristotle takes to be required if one is to acquire the virtues. Irwin clearly recognizes the importance that Aristotle attaches to habituation, particularly in training our non-rational desires. And Irwin agrees with McDowell in rejecting the idea that habituation is a matter of "mindless" training.[43] So Irwin seems in fact to agree with much of what McDowell says

[41] See especially sec. 11 of McDowell 1998b; and Whiting 2002b ["Locomotive Soul" (III.5)] and 2019 ["Hylomorphic Virtue" (III.6)].

[42] For some evidence that Irwin draws the distinctions that would allow him to accept this proposal, see sec. 1 of his 1981 book. But compare this with Irwin 1978, where Irwin says on p. 262, "moral theory is part of what makes a moral agent a virtuous man. It follows that only someone who accepts the correct moral theory is a virtuous man." As I note in what follows, Irwin is reluctant to draw a sharp distinction between the thoughts of the moral theorist and those of the moral agent.

[43] See, for example, the entry under "education" in the glossary of Irwin's translation (1985; 1999). There is, oddly, no separate entry under "habit" or "habituation." But see Irwin's note ad 1103b22, where he says,

> We do not learn simply to repeat the actions until they have become automatic or 'second nature' [cf. 1152a32]. We must also acquire the virtuous person's state and motive, 1105a32. Hence habituation must include more than simply becoming accustomed to a type of action.

about moral training, and it seems that he can in principle agree with much of what McDowell says about the psychology of Aristotle's mature virtuous agent.

Still, however, Irwin seems to differ from McDowell insofar as Irwin seems to think it possible to provide a "narrowly" rational but non-virtuous agent with an *argument* that might persuade her to undertake whatever sort of training is required if she is to *become* genuinely virtuous. But it is *not* clear that McDowell needs to *reject* this idea, at least not if Irwin is willing to allow that the argument in question is only *protreptic*—i.e., an argument the acceptance of which might lead someone to turn [*trepein*] toward [*pro*] the pursuit of virtue but the acceptance of which cannot *by itself* make her virtuous. Think, for example, of the way in which someone's acceptance of an argument might turn her towards the study of philosophy (or towards the practice of yoga): in order to become a philosopher (or a yogini), she would then need to undertake the study of *philosophy as such* (or the practice of *yoga as such*).[44] There are two points here whose conjunction promises to advance my reconciliation project.

The 1152a32 passage cited here is worth noting in connection with McDowell's conception of 'second nature.' It runs (in Irwin's translation) as follows:

> Indeed the reason why habit [τὸ ἔθος] is also difficult to change is that it is like nature, as Euenus says, 'Habit, I say, is longtime training, and in the end training is nature for human beings.'

[44] I have been influenced in putting the point in terms of "protreptic" argument by conversations with Iakovos Vasiliou. It is interesting to note that Aristotle uses the verb '*protrepein*' several times in the passage on moral education in *EN* X 9 (one of the passages most naturally read as supporting McDowell's "non-rationalist" view and discussed at length in Whiting 2021). It is perhaps worth quoting here some relevant bits (in Irwin's translation).

> Now if arguments were sufficient by themselves to make people decent, the rewards they would command would justifiably have been many and large, as Theognis says, and rightly bestowed. In fact, however, arguments seem to have enough influence to stimulate and encourage [προτρέψασθαι μὲν καὶ παρορμῆσαι] the civilized ones among young people, and perhaps to make virtue take possession of a well-born character that truly loves what is fine; but they seem unable to turn the many toward being fine and good [πρὸς καλοκαγαθίαν προτρέψασθαι]. For the many naturally obey fear, not shame; they avoid what is base because of the penalties, not because it is disgraceful. For since they live by their feelings, they pursue their proper pleasures and the sources of them, and avoid the opposed pains, and have not even a notion of what is fine and [hence] truly pleasant, since they have had no taste of it. [1179b5–16]

This suggests that the sorts of arguments that Aristotle has in mind include appeals to what is καλόν (fine or noble) and what is αἰσχρόν (base or shameful), arguments that are clearly *internal* to the ethical scheme in question. Aristotle continues a bit further on (again in Irwin's translation) as follows:

> Arguments and teaching surely do not prevail on everyone, but the soul of the student needs to have been prepared by habits for enjoying and hating finely, like ground that is to nourish seed. For someone who lives in accord with his feelings would not even listen to an argument turning him away [λόγου ἀποτρέποντος] or comprehend it [οὐδ' αὖ συνείη] [if he did listen]; and in that state how could he be persuaded to change? And in general, feelings seem to yield to force, not to argument. Hence we must already in some way have a character suitable for virtue, fond of what is fine and objecting to what is shameful [στέργον τὸ καλὸν καὶ δυσχεραῖνον τὸ αἰσχρόν]. [1179b23–31]

Finally, Aristotle sees a close connection between responsiveness to argument (or reason) and aiming at the fine. He says,

First, Irwin need not suppose that the sort of argument he has in mind will be capable of revealing to the "narrowly" rational but non-virtuous agent the distinctive value of any *particular* virtuous action as such. Irwin can, I think, allow that a proper appreciation of the value of any particular virtuous action is, as McDowell claims, something that is available *only* to the genuinely virtuous agent, *however* one gets to be that way. For it seems to me that all Irwin needs, in order to persuade a rational but non-virtuous agent that she ought to undertake the sort of habituation that is required if she is to become genuinely virtuous, is an argument capable of revealing to the "narrowly" rational agent *some* sort of value attaching to virtue in *general*, where this value need not be (and perhaps cannot be) the *distinctive* sort of value that is supposed to attach either to virtue in general or to any particular virtuous action as such. It need not (and presumably does not) follow from the fact that the non-virtuous person accepts this argument that she must then—simply as a result of accepting this argument—be able either to identify *what* virtue requires of her in any particular situation or to explain *why* virtue requires *that*.[45] To acquire the "thats," she will need remedial habituation and/or conceptual reorientation; to move from the "thats" to the "because," she will need the sort of Neurathian reflection recommended by McDowell. In sum, Irwin allows that the available arguments are at best protreptic.[46]

> The many yield more to compulsion than to argument, and to sanctions more than to the fine. That is why legislators must, in some people's view, urge people toward virtue [παρακαλεῖν ἐπὶ τὴν ἀρετὴν] and exhort them to aim at the fine [προτρέπεσθαι τοῦ καλοῦ χάριν], on the assumption that anyone whose habits have prepared him decently will listen to them—but must impose corrective treatments and penalties on anyone who disobeys or lacks the right nature, and must completely expel an incurable. For the decent person, it is assumed, will attend to reason because his life aims at the fine [τὸν μὲν ἐπιεικῆ πρὸς τὸ καλὸν ζῶντα τῷ λόγῳ πειθαρχήσειν]. [1180a4–11]

It is worth noting here that 'πειθαρχήσειν'—which is often translated 'will obey'—comes from '*πειθεῖν*' meaning 'to persuade'. So the last bit might be rendered thus: "the decent person . . . will obey [or be persuaded by] reason *because* his life aims at the fine." This suggests that Aristotle sees a close connection between the sort of susceptibility to reason he is talking about and having some disposition to aim at what is fine.

[45] Irwin seems to recognize this when he says, for example, that

> [t]he self-confined egoist, concerned with no one for his own sake besides himself, may therefore discover that an altruist, whose concerns are *not* confined to himself, is better at securing his own advantage. It does not follow that the self-confined egoist who sees this can at once make himself altruistic.

But what Irwin proceeds immediately to say suggests that he takes the defect here to be simply a failure of *reason*:

> For while he might like to believe that other people matter for their own sakes, he may still see no good reason to believe this, and awareness of the good consequences of the belief may not be enough to make him hold it. [Irwin 1988: 613]

[46] There are presumably differences between the sort of arguments that might move a non-virtuous but rational interlocutor and the sort of arguments that might move a proto-virtuous rational interlocutor. The sort of argument likely to move the proto-virtuous interlocutor may be more like the ascent argument, appealing to—and then extending—her initial sense of what is *kalon*, while the sort of argument likely to move the non-virtuous but rational interlocutor may be more like the function argument, which would be merely instrumental and merely protreptic in a way that the ascent argument is not. For an ascent-type argument provides a kind of initiation into virtue itself in a way in which a function-type argument does not.

Second, it does not follow from the protreptic effectiveness of an argument in persuading someone to undertake the requisite sort of training that the agent will, once she has successfully completed that training, *continue* in deciding what to do to attend to the value that motivated her to undertake the relevant sort of training in the first place: once she has succeeded in acquiring the dispositions of a genuinely virtuous agent, she may be moved only by the *particular* considerations, *internal* to virtue, that move a virtuous agent—that is, by the *particular* reasons that a virtuous agent sees for doing *this* here and now or abstaining from *that* then and there. Even if (as Irwin would no doubt insist) the value that first attracted her to virtue still *attaches* to virtuous action, it need not follow that her commitment to that value is what *sustains* her attachment to virtue: she may now value particular virtuous actions *for themselves* in ways such that she would continue to value them even if she could be shown that they did not in fact promote the value that first moved her to acquire a virtuous disposition. Note, however, that this is a point simply about *motivation*, and *not* about *justification*: we shall return in due course to the question of what *justifies* the virtuous person's attachment to virtue.[47]

If Irwin accepts the first point (that the argument need only be protreptic and need not itself impart to the interlocutor the ability to identify virtuous actions or to appreciate their distinctive value) and McDowell accepts the second point (that what motivates someone *to acquire* virtue may be distinct from what motivates her once she *has acquired* it), then it is not clear why McDowell should object to protreptic uses of argument to motivate "narrowly" rational but non-virtuous agents to do *whatever it takes* to *become* genuinely virtuous (where this may involve some, perhaps largely, non-argumentative means). As long as the agent *ends up* with the motives and conceptual outlook of a genuinely virtuous agent, why should it matter to McDowell that she was *initially* moved in that direction by means of an external (or even extra-ethical) argument? For as McDowell himself insists, *none* of us undergoes the sort of habituation-cum-conceptual initiation that he has in mind because she *already* accepts the *ethical* reasons into which she is being initiated. So why should it matter that the "narrowly" rational but non-virtuous adult does not?

What I am suggesting is essentially that *McDowell* should allow for the possibility of external arguments for virtue, so long as the arguments are only protreptic, and that *Irwin* should recognize the merely protreptic status of such arguments, in which case McDowell should have no objection to Irwin's use of such arguments. In other words, Irwin should recognize *both* that such arguments are *not required* in cases where a proper upbringing occurs *and* that even where such arguments are useful they serve only to motivate someone *initially* to seek out the sort of habituation that is required to *complete* the process of becoming genuinely virtuous: these arguments do not themselves provide what only some sort of not purely cognitive (as distinct from purely

[47] [See section 2 of "Eudaimonia, External Results, and Choosing Virtuous Actions for Themselves" (Chapter 3, this volume).]

non-cognitive) development can provide. This is not to say that Irwin must say that *no* arguments or appeals to reason are required in cases where someone has a proper upbringing. For Irwin can plausibly argue that a proper upbringing itself involves some forms of argument or giving of reasons. But this should be acceptable to McDowell as long as Irwin recognizes that a proper upbringing involves the giving of reasons internal to the relevant ethical outlook in something like the way in which, for example, mathematical education involves the giving of reasons internal to a mathematical outlook: just as teaching mathematics is a matter of teaching pupils what is a *mathematical* reason for what, so too a proper upbringing is a matter of teaching agents what is an *ethical* reason for what. Insofar as an upbringing fails to do that—by appealing, for example, *simply* to threats of punishment or extrinsic rewards—it will fail to produce *genuine* virtue. If Irwin recognizes these things, then McDowell should have no objection to Irwin's use of such arguments.

I suspect, however, that Irwin might object to viewing the relevant sorts of arguments as merely protreptic. For merely protreptic arguments can in principle be unrelated to what *actually* justifies—as distinct from what *pragmatically* justifies—the conclusions whose acceptance they seek to secure. Think, for example, of Pascal's wager as a kind of protreptic argument. What will *actually* justify Pascal's belief in God (if it is justified) will include evidence of God's existence and not simply those benefits he might secure by means of that belief. Similarly here, what will *actually* justify an ethical belief (such as the belief that virtue is a necessary ingredient of *eudaimonia*) will include evidence for the *truth* of that belief and not simply any benefits that might be secured by means of it. If, for example, *eudaimonia* in fact consists exclusively in pleasure, then even if the belief that virtuous action is worth choosing for itself contributes to the maximization of pleasure, that belief (though it may be pragmatically justified) is not justified in the relevant sense. For Irwin needs the agent's commitment to virtue to reflect an *epistemically* justified belief (and not simply a pragmatically justified one): otherwise the agent's commitment to virtuous action may be purely instrumental, thus failing to satisfy the historical Aristotle's requirement that the virtuous agent be committed to virtuous action *for itself.* Irwin's idea is presumably that Aristotle takes an agent to be committed to virtuous action for itself insofar as her commitment to it is based on epistemically justified beliefs about the nature of virtuous action as such. The truth of the matter, according to Irwin's Aristotle, is apparently that the value that attaches to virtuous activity as such resides at least partly in the fact that engaging in virtuous activity is part of the human *ergon* or function—i.e., at least partly in the fact virtuous activity constitutes the actualization of our *essential* capacities.

Here, however, we should note that a protreptic argument *need not* be unrelated to the truth of the conclusion it seeks to secure. Suppose that virtuous activity is in fact valuable at least partly because it constitutes the actualization of our essential capacities, but that the strong dialectical arguments that would persuade someone of this conclusion were *merely* protreptic in the sense that being persuaded by these arguments—and so having a justified true belief in their conclusion—was not sufficient for being able to identify particular virtuous actions as such and so was not sufficient for acquiring virtue. Can Irwin reasonably object to *such* protreptic arguments on the grounds that *not all* protreptic arguments are this good? Surely not.

This leaves us with two questions. First, does Aristotle in fact think that the value of virtue (or virtuous activity) resides at least partly in its constituting the actualization of our essential capacities? Second, and more importantly for our purposes, if Aristotle *does* in fact think this, what would *follow* from this about the motivational economy of Aristotle's virtuous agent? Must she choose virtuous actions qua actualizations of her essential capacities? Or can she—indeed *must* she—choose them qua *just, generous, noble,* and so on? Or qua securing this or that particular benefit (such as shelter for the homeless or the sort of equality that contributes to the stability of the polis)? And if she can or must choose them qua *just, generous, noble,* and so on—or qua securing this or that particular benefit for someone or other—then what role (if any) can be played in her motivational economy by the thought that choosing them as such constitutes the actualization of her essential capacities? Does she *need* to have *that* thought? Or can she be genuinely virtuous without it? Is this perhaps a thought that must be available to her qua moral *theorist* but not necessarily qua moral *agent?*

Irwin has in conversation resisted my suggestion that he distinguish the thoughts that are available from the point of view of the *moral theorist* from those that are available from the point of view of the *moral agent.*[48] It is clear that he wants the thought that virtuous activity contributes to the actualization of her essential capacities to be at least available from—and perhaps also a necessary feature of—the point of view of the virtuous agent. But this raises a question about what that thought is supposed to be doing there. Is it supposed to play a role in *sustaining* the agent's *general* commitment to virtue, even if not in her selection of any particular virtuous action as such? If so, will she fail to satisfy Aristotle's requirement that she choose virtuous action for themselves? Or does Aristotle regard choosing particular virtuous actions for themselves as compatible with having a general commitment to virtue that is sustained (at least in part) by the belief that virtuous activity is a necessary part of the actualization of one's essential capacities?

It seems pretty clear that McDowell would deny that any such belief *must* play a role in the motivational economy of the genuinely virtuous agent. And it seems probable that McDowell would also deny that any such belief *can* play a role—or at least a *direct* role—in the motivational economy of the virtuous agent.[49] But determining

---

[48] There is some general justification for such resistance in the claim (in *EN* I) that the investigation into ethics is *practical*—i.e., something that is supposed to help us to be or become good. But there may be practical advantages to having theory come in the form of what McDowell calls "reflective reassurance" (on which more below), even if the relevant sort of theoretical knowledge is *not strictly necessary* to produce genuinely virtuous behavior: perhaps such knowledge is practically useful primarily for those questioning their inherited ethical outlook or for those who might be persuaded by understanding the theory to undertake whatever sort of habituation or partly affective training is required in order to *become* genuinely virtuous.

[49] It does not follow, though, that McDowell thinks either that the belief must be false or that the belief cannot be available to the genuinely virtuous agent. He may even—as we shall soon see—allow it to play a role in providing what he calls "reflective reassurance" (though his admission of this once again blurs the distinction between him and Irwin, and throws us back to the first puzzle).

McDowell's view on this point is complicated by the fact that he tends to consider the motivational roles that might be played by thoughts about *what members of a species need* rather than the motivational roles that might be played by thoughts about *what actualizes their essential capacities.* I expect, though, that McDowell would run the same sorts of arguments against taking thoughts about *what actualizes our essential capacities* to play a role in the motivational economy of the virtuous agent as he runs against taking thoughts about *what members of our species need* to play some such role.

McDowell's first line of argument against taking thoughts about what members of our species need to play any such role appears in sec. 3 of his "Two Sorts of Naturalism" (1996b). The line here is essentially that thoughts about what members of one's species need are *ineffective.* McDowell asks us to imagine that a wolf acquires reason, where this involves an ability to reflect on—and to consider possible alternatives to—the sort of behavior that comes "first naturally" to wolves (for example, hunting in a pack): the wolf thus asks, "But why should *I* pull my weight in the hunt, when *I* can get away with idling and grabbing my share of the prey?" McDowell then claims that it will be *useless* to respond by appeal to an Aristotelian categorical to the effect that wolves *need* to cooperate if they are to hunt effectively. This response is useless because of what McDowell calls the "deductive impotence" of Aristotelian categoricals. It no more follows from the fact that wolves first-naturally need to cooperate in the pack that our hypothetical rational wolf needs to cooperate in the pack than, for example, it follows from the fact that human beings have thirty-two teeth that any given human being has thirty-two teeth.

McDowell's basic idea here is that the onset of reason unseats the "first" nature of the species from its brute (or "mechanical") authority over the behavior of individual animals. The result, McDowell thinks, is that individual interest can seem to be the only candidate left to play the role previously played by the nature of the species: the rational wolf will all too easily conclude that reason requires him to transcend his species nature in pursuit of his own individual interest. But the transcendence can (according to McDowell) be only partial because the attractions of free-riding "depend [at least partly] on its being a way to secure things that [first] naturally matter to wolves, such as plenty of meat to eat." The importance of this point, about what matters first naturally, will become clearer as we proceed. The point here is that rationality enables a creature to at least partly transcend its first nature. The creature may even—as McDowell suggests by asking us to imagine a Calliclean or Nietzschean wolf—reconceive the project of partly transcending its (first) nature as a project of properly realizing its (rational) nature. But even so, this re-conception need not require it to deny any facts about the first nature of wolves. For the concept of nature can, as McDowell claims, "figure here, without incoherence, in two quite different ways: as 'mere' nature, and as something whose realization requires transcending that." And if one doubts that *Aristotle* would allow any such thought, then let me add that one has only to consult his claim (in *EN* X.7) that we "should not [listen to] those advising us, being human, to think human [thoughts], and being mortal, [to think] mortal [thoughts], but should as far as possible immortalize [ourselves] and do all things with a view to living in accordance with the very best of the [parts] in us" [*EN* 1177b31–34].[50]

It is easy to imagine McDowell running a similar argument against taking thoughts about *what actualizes our essence* to play a role in the motivational economy of the virtuous agent. He need only ask us to imagine how far Irwin's Aristotle would get with Dostoevsky's Underground Man, who would no doubt be *unmoved* by thought—even if he accepted its *truth*—that he is *essentially* a rational animal. But McDowell offers a second argument against taking thoughts about *what creatures like us need* to play a role in the motivational economy of the virtuous agent—an argument that seems to me less easily deployed against taking thoughts about *what actualizes our essence* to play any such role. And this second argument is arguably both more central to McDowell's thought and more pertinent to his disagreement with Irwin. So I want to focus on it.

The second argument against taking thoughts about *what members of one's species need* to play a role in the motivational economy of the virtuous agent is that such thoughts cannot directly engage the will of the genuinely virtuous agent without either compromising her virtue or at least threatening to undermine her commitment to it: what directly engages her will must be the second-natural modes of valuation expressed in claims such as "this is just" and "that is base." Any thoughts about what members of her species need must, as (M6) asserts, "operate at one remove from the subject's rational will." This is so for two reasons: first, because of Aristotle's requirement that the virtuous agent choose virtuous actions *for themselves*: and second, because allowing such thoughts to directly engage the agent's will threatens to undermine the agent's commitment to virtue. If, for example, what directly engages the will of the courageous agent is the Irwinian thought that one needs courage *because* it enables one to stick to one's projects in the face of danger, then it is difficult to see how the agent's commitment to courage will not be undermined in situations where there is any significant probability that courageous action will result in her no longer being around anymore, let alone having any projects to stick to.

It may, however, seem—at least prima facie—more difficult to run this line against taking thoughts about *what actualizes our essence* to play a role in the motivational economy of the virtuous agent. For on Irwin's account, there is a non-contingent connection between any particular virtuous action and what actualizes one's essence in a way in which there is *not* a non-contingent connection between any particular virtuous action and what members of one's species generally need. The courageous action may in some circumstances fail to produce the sort of result whose typical connection with courageous action explains why humans *generally* need courage. But the courageous action will never (on Irwin's account) fail to actualize one's essence: even in cases where one dies as a result of performing the courageous action, performing such an action—and perhaps even dying such a death—will still constitute an actualization

[50] [For discussion of this passage, see "Human Nature and Intellectualism in Aristotle" (Chapter 2, this volume).]

of the human essence.[51] So this line of argument may be more *effective*—at least in dealing with someone who cares about actualizing her essence—than the parallel line about what members of one's species need. It does not seem to suffer in quite the *same* way from the "deductive impotence" of the Aristotelian categorical.

McDowell's *primary* objection, however, is *not* that the relevant thoughts are *ineffective*—though he does, as we have seen, worry about that. It is *rather* that the relevant thoughts are in an important sense *impermissible*. I say "in an *important sense* impermissible" in order to leave open the possibility that McDowell would allow the relevant thoughts—both about what actualizes one's essence and about what members of one's species need—to play a role *somewhere* (perhaps in doing moral *theory*) even if they are *not* allowed to play any role (or at least any *direct* role) in the motivational economy of the genuinely virtuous agent. For McDowell seems to allow something like this when he suggests that thoughts about what members of one's species (first naturally) need belong in the "reflective background" of the second-natural modes of valuation that characterize genuinely virtuous agents (i.e., in the "reflective background" of the autonomous modes of valuation expressed in terms of what is "noble" and what "base," what is "just" and what "unjust," etc.):

> (M6) First nature matters not only . . . in helping to shape the space in which reflection must take place, but also in that first-natural facts can be part of what reflection takes into account. This is where we can register the relevance of what human beings need in order to do well, in a sense of "doing well" that is not just Aristotle's "acting in accordance with the virtues." Consider a rational wolf whose acquisition of practical reason included being initiated into a tradition in which cooperative behavior in the hunt is regarded as admirable, and so as worth going in for in its own right. What wolves need might figure in a bit of reflection that might help to reassure him that when he acquired a second nature with that shape, his eyes were opened to real reasons for acting. The reflection would be Neurathian, so it would not weigh with a wolf who has never acquired such a mode of valuation of conduct, or one who has come unstuck from it. And there would be no irrationality in *thus* failing to be convinced. But this need not undermine the reassurance, if the reflection that yields it is self-consciously Neurathian. The point stands that *what members of one's species need is not guaranteed to appeal to practical reason. But the point is harmless to the genuine rationality of virtue,* which is visible (of course!) only from a standpoint from which it is open to view.
>
> *It is important that when the connections between virtue and doing well*—in a sense that is not Aristotle's "acting in accordance with the virtues," a

[51] [For more on the idea of self-sacrifice as actualizing one's essence, and on Aristotle's views about this, see "Love: Self-Propagation, Self-Preservation, or Ekstasis?" (I.7) and "Self-Love and Authoritative Virtue" (Chapter 4, this volume).]

> sense that is not itself shaped by ethical concerns—*do figure in a reflective reassurance about an ethical outlook, they operate at one remove from the subject's rational will. What directly influences the will is the valuations of actions that have come to be second nature. . . .*
>
> The connection of virtue with doing well, in the relevant sense, is that human beings need courage if they are to stick to their worthwhile projects, in the face of the motivational obstacle posed by danger. Something along those lines belongs in the reflective background for a second nature that values courageous actions. But we should not try to picture such a consideration as what directly engages the will of a courageous person. If we do, we risk losing our hold on how it can be rational to face danger, even in the interest of something we value deeply, if one's own death is a possible upshot. The point of courage was supposed to be that one needs it to ensure that one sticks to one's projects. How can this point *not* be undermined by a probability, even a slight one, that if one acts courageously one will no longer be around to have any projects, let alone stick to them?
>
> . . . [C]ourageousness is primarily a matter of being a certain kind of person. One cannot be that kind of person but stand ready to rethink the rational credentials of the motivations characteristic of being that kind of person, on occasions when acting on those motivations is in some way unattractive; part of what it is to be that kind of person is not to regard those credentials as open to question on particular occasions. [This] is exactly right. But it will work only in the context of my point that the general human need for courage stands at one remove from the rational will of a person engaged in courageous behavior. Without that context, [this] looks like a recommendation to abandon reason—which surely does examine the rational credentials of actions one by one—in favor of blind adherence to a policy. Within that context, the damage that acts of virtue can do to one's interests is unproblematic: the point of particular courageous actions lies not in the fact that human beings in general need courage, focused, as it were, on the circumstances at hand, but in the fact that this action counts as worthwhile in its own right, by the lights of a conceptual scheme that is second nature to a courageous person. [McDowell 1996b: sec. 10, my italics]

McDowell's claim is that thoughts about what members of one's species (first naturally) need, while they are not up to the task of converting those who have never acquired the relevant modes of valuation or of rehabilitating those who have come "unstuck" from them, may nevertheless serve to "reassure" an agent who *has* acquired such modes of valuation that the relevant modes of valuation do in fact track genuine reasons for action: thoughts about what members of our species need may provide what McDowell calls "reflective reassurance" in the sense that these thoughts render it intelligible that we have the sort of second-natural practices of virtue that we do. And I assume that McDowell would be willing to say something similar about thoughts about what serves to actualize our essential capacities. For such thoughts are no doubt intimately related, in Aristotle's scheme, to thoughts about what members of our species need.

McDowell's point here is that the second-natural practices in which virtue consists—although they cannot be *deduced* from first-natural facts—must *make sense* in light of those facts. McDowell is willing to allow—as Irwin insists—that "human beings need courage if they are to stick to their worthwhile projects, in the face of the motivational obstacle imposed by danger". McDowell is even willing to allow that some such thought "belongs in the reflective background for a second nature that values courageous actions," which helps he thinks to explain why the relevant second nature does not regard facing danger *simply* for its own sake, where nothing worthwhile is to be gained by doing so, as "noble" or even "courageous." What *counts* as courageous from the *second* natural point of view of virtue depends partly—though only partly—on what matters *first* naturally to us: it is courageous to face danger in order to provide one's offspring with things (such as food and protection from the elements) that they first-naturally need, but it is also courageous to face danger in order to provide one's offspring with things of cultural (and so of second natural) value.

McDowell is willing to allow all this. But he is *not* willing to allow that thoughts about what members of our species need, or about what actualizes our essence, can *directly* engage the will of Aristotle's virtuous agent. For allowing this not only threatens (as we have just seen) to undermine the agent's commitment to virtue; it is also incompatible with Aristotle's requirement that virtuous agents choose virtuous actions *for themselves* (which seems to me to be McDowell's primary point). So it may be here—in their respective interpretations of this requirement—that we must in the end locate the fundamental difference between Irwin and McDowell: Irwin thinks that an agent who takes the ultimate justification for virtuous action to lie in the fact that virtuous action actualizes her essence *satisfies* this requirement, whereas McDowell does not. If this is right, then the fundamental difference between Irwin and McDowell may be rooted *not* in their different accounts of Aristotle's *method* but rather in their different accounts of the *substance* of Aristotle's ethical views—especially his views about the nature of moral virtue. This raises the question, relevant to our primary puzzle, whether Irwin's and McDowell's different accounts of Aristotle's method—to the extent these accounts are in fact different—are not driven by their different accounts of Aristotle's substantive views rather than the other way round. And I am inclined to give an affirmative answer to this question: it seems to me that each ascribes to Aristotle the method he does largely (even if not exclusively) because of the way he understands Aristotle's substantive ethical views.

Irwin, because he reads Aristotle's claim that we do everything for the sake of eudaimonia as involving a commitment to rational egoism, is driven to understand Aristotelian virtue in a way that renders it compatible with rational egoism: he does this largely by identifying the agent's good primarily with the actualization of her essential capacities, especially her capacity for virtue.[52] And his conception of Aristotle as defending the commitment to virtue in rational egoist terms leads him, I think, to ascribe to Aristotle a method that will enable Aristotle to demonstrate the rationality of virtue to those who question it. I do *not* mean to be suggesting here that *anyone* who views Aristotle as defending virtue in rational egoist terms is *thereby required* to ascribe the strong dialectical method to him. But the appeal of the strong dialectical method to someone who wants to defend virtue in rational egoist terms should be obvious. So even if Irwin's conception of Aristotelian virtue does not strictly *require* him to ascribe the strong dialectical method to Aristotle, we can see how it might nevertheless *motivate* him to do so. It seems plausible then to suppose, as part of our solution to our primary puzzle, that there *is* a connection between the method that Irwin ascribes to Aristotle and the substantive moral views he ascribes to Aristotle, but that the connection runs from substance to method rather than the other way around—to suppose, in sum, that it is partly Irwin's conception of Aristotle as a rational egoist that leads him to view Aristotle's method as involving external argument of a sort that might persuade a rational agent, simply as such, that she ought, as a matter of rational self-interest, to pursue Aristotelian virtue.

This helps to explain the force of our primary puzzle. If one's idea is to *start* with the strong dialectical method, and to *look and see* what sorts of ethical conclusions it yields, one is likely to think that the method is in principle capable of yielding various ethical conclusions, depending on what sorts of premises the method proves to favor, including not only metaphysical premises but also premises about the connection or lack thereof between metaphysical and psychological truths and ethical ones: the content of our ethical conclusions will *depend on* the content of the relevant metaphysical and psychological theories even if it is not straightforwardly *deducible* from these theories. In this case, there will seem a priori to be little (if any) connection between one's commitment to the method and one's substantive ethical views. But this appearance is misleading if one starts with the substantive ethical views and then seeks a method capable of supporting them, or even if one moves back and forth (as seems inevitable) between one's understanding of the substantive ethical views and one's understanding of the method.

Similar claims seem to me to apply to the connection between the method that McDowell ascribes to Aristotle and the substantive moral views he ascribes to Aristotle, though moving from substance to method is perhaps less problematic on his view. McDowell's point of departure is the essentially Kantian conception of the autonomy of ethical reasons that he ascribes to Aristotle on the basis of Aristotle's requirement that virtuous actions be chosen for themselves (or for the sake of τὸ καλόν). This is *not* to say that McDowell's point of departure is *anachronistic*: remember that Kant claimed *not* to have discovered or invented anything new. McDowell's attribution of

[52] Irwin's view (1980, 48) seems to be that Aristotle moves from a kind of psychological egoism (according to which everyone *in fact* pursues her final good in "a rough, implicit way") to a kind of rational (or even ethical) egoism (according to which everyone *should* pursue her final good in "a clear, explicit way").

the autonomy of the ethical to Aristotle leads him to eschew, on Aristotle's behalf, attempts to defend the rationality of virtue except in its own terms. McDowell thus eschews attempts to defend the rationality of virtue either by appeal to facts about what members of our species typically need or by appeal to facts about what is required for the actualization of our essence.

Here, however, we should note that insofar as McDowell is willing to allow the recognition of such facts to play a role in the "reflective background" of the second-natural practices of virtue, and even to *reassure* agents who worry about whether the second-natural practices of virtue really track genuine reasons for action, he does *not* seem to rule out the *possibility* of something like strong dialectic. But this reintroduces our secondary puzzle. For when McDowell claims that it is consistent with his requirement that first-natural considerations operate at one remove from the will of the virtuous agent that first-natural facts might provide the virtuous agent with "reflective reassurance" that her second-natural habits of virtue track genuine reasons for action, he clearly means to allow that the *content* of our ethical views might be different if our first (or non-habituated) nature were different. See, for example, the following:

(M7) [F]acts about what human beings need in order to get on well, on a first-natural conception of what getting on well is for human beings, figure in the reflective background of specific shapings of second nature . . . This should be seen as a case of a relation that Wittgenstein draws to our attention, between our concepts and the facts that underlie them. *The concepts would not be the same if the facts of (first) nature were different, and the facts help to make it intelligible that the concepts are as they are,* but that does not mean that correctness and incorrectness in the application of the concepts can be captured by requirements spelled out at the level of the underlying [first natural] facts. [McDowell 1996b: sec. 11]

McDowell clearly allows a counterfactual dependence such that the facts about our first nature may be taken to play *some* role (even if only indirect) in determining the *content* of our ethical views (about, for example, what temperance requires). But it is not clear that Irwin's appeal to strong dialectic is meant to allow anything more than this, especially not if Irwin abstains from the implausible claim that the content of our ethical views is straightforwardly *deducible* from first-natural facts (or, as Irwin would put it, from the relevant metaphysical and psychological theories). As long as Irwin sticks with broad coherence and says only that the relevant ethical views are—given the relevant metaphysical and psychological views—more *plausible* than rival ethical views, there seems to be no room for McDowell, given his own commitment to the possibility of "reflective reassurance," to object to Irwin's use of strong dialectic. It is thus in one sense not at all surprising—though in another sense quite surprising—that McDowell has conceded in conversation that there may in the end be little difference between his own method of reflective reassurance and Irwin's method of strong dialectic: McDowell has in fact said that it is okay with him if I want to call the method of reflective reassurance a form of strong dialectic—okay, that is, as long as I do *not* represent the search for reflective reassurance as *necessary*.

I assume that McDowell means at least that the genuinely virtuous agent does not feel any psychological need for reflective reassurance and that such reassurance is not practically required in order for her to be motivated to choose virtuous actions for themselves. McDowell may also think that Aristotle would deny that providing reflective reassurance plays an *essential* role in moral *theory*. But this additional step is significantly more controversial, since it makes it difficult to explain why, among other things, Aristotle begins the ethics with a clear reference to his teleology and why he appeals as he does to the human function.[53] Fortunately, however, this additional step seems to me to be *unnecessary* to McDowell's central points about the nature of moral virtue. For it seems to me that McDowell can allow that claims about what members of our species need (or about what actualizes our essence) play a role in moral theory in the sense that they help to explain to the moral theorist—who may be a virtuous agent, though this often fails to be the case—why the second-natural practices of virtue have something like the shape they actually have. For this does *not* require McDowell to say *either* that the contents of the second-natural practices of virtue are straightforwardly deducible from facts about what members of our species need (or about what actualizes our essence) *or* that facts about what members of our species need (or about what actualizes our essence) directly engage the will of the virtuous agent. And these are the points that seem to me to matter most fundamentally to McDowell.

It is in fact interesting that McDowell denies *only* that such facts can *directly* engage the will of the virtuous agent. This suggests that he is willing to allow the recognition of such facts to play an *indirect* role in the motivational economy of the virtuous agent, as his use of the term '*reassurance*,' with its practical connotations, also suggests. For the reassurance in question seems to be intended primarily for the more or less virtuous agent who is questioning the rationality of her commitment to virtue—questioning, that is, whether this or that sort of action *really is* worth choosing for itself, whether an action's being noble (or base) *really is* a reason for choosing (or avoiding) it, and so on. And the idea seems to be that by considering the first-natural facts of human existence—for example, the Humean conditions of justice—the agent can come to see the *point* of the second-natural practices of virtue (such as those involved in justice).[54] This does *not* mean the first-natural facts will determine the content of the second-natural practices of

[53] McDowell does not, I think, do justice to the connection between Aristotle's general teleology and the fact that Aristotle begins the *Ethics* with a reference to the human *telos*. And even if one grants that Aristotle does not expect his "function argument" to yield substantive accounts of particular virtues, one might still think that McDowell's deflationary account of that argument is insufficiently robust.

[54] The following passage from Hume—with its explicit reference to "uncultivated nature" and thus its implicit reference to "cultivated nature"—suggests that Hume too has something like the conception of second nature that McDowell attributes to Aristotle:

> There *are* three different species of goods, which we are possess'd of; the internal satisfaction of our mind, the external advantages of our body, and the enjoyment of such possessions as we have acquir'd by industry or good fortune. We are perfectly secure in the enjoyment of the first.

virtue in the sense that the first-natural facts will yield a *criterion* of virtuous action. And it does *not* mean that the first-natural facts *must* impinge *directly* on the will of the virtuous agent, though they *may* sometimes do so—as, for example, when I build a house with Habitat for Humanity in order to provide a homeless family with warm shelter in the midst of winter. The idea here is simply that the first-natural facts render it *intelligible* that we have the sorts of second-natural practices that we do: the second-natural practices of virtue *make sense* in light of the first-natural facts, even though the specific content of these practices cannot be *deduced* from the first-natural facts. Think, for example, of the way in which our recognition of the Humean conditions of justice can lead us to acknowledge the need for justice without dictating the need for this or that particular *conception* of justice—without, however, resolving the choice among Rawlsian, libertarian, and other possible conceptions. And think of ways in which attempts to resolve disputes among such conceptions typically proceed by means of the method of reflective equilibrium (which is roughly equivalent to Irwin's strong dialectic).[55] The best that we can do is to argue that this or that particular conception of justice (or of virtue in general) is *more plausible* in light of the first-natural facts than its rivals. But such arguments are unlikely to take us all the way to an adequate conception either of any particular virtue such as justice or of virtue in general. Such arguments must thus be supplemented by *ethical* arguments (for example, arguments about *fairness*).

But this seems to be something that Irwin himself recognizes when he says in the following passage that Aristotle's ethics is "not *wholly* autonomous." So it is simply unfair to suggest that Irwin takes the content of virtue to be straightforwardly deducible from a purely first-natural and non-ethical base.

> (I11) Two directions of argument identify the relevant facts: (1) Aristotle constructs a theory of substance from premisses supported by strong dialectic, relying on more than common beliefs. This theory supports an account of souls and animate organisms, including rational agents. In approaching ethical problems, Aristotle is entitled to appeal with some confidence to the conclusions he has reached by these other dialectical arguments that do not depend *wholly* on the ethical common beliefs in dispute. (2) Fairly uncontroversial common beliefs about ethics suggest to Aristotle that his account of substances and souls will be relevant. For it is plausible to assume that answers to the questions "What is the good for F?" and "What is a good F?" both depend on the answer to the question

> The second may be ravish'd from us, but can be of no advantage to him who deprives us of them. The last only are both expos'd to the violence of others, and may be transferr'd without suffering any loss or alteration; while at the same time there is not a sufficient quantity of them to supply every one's desires and necessities . . . In vain shou'd we expect to find, in *uncultivated nature,* a remedy to this inconvenience; or hope for any inartificial principle of the human mind, which might control these partial affections, and make us overcome the temptations arising from our circumstances. [Hume 1978: III.II. ii.]

[55] Irwin 1981 explicitly discusses the method of "reflective equilibrium."

"What is F?." . . . An answer to the first of these questions gives us an account of happiness, and an answer to the second gives us an account of virtue. Aristotle, therefore, has these *two independent and mutually supporting reasons* for believing that his account of the rational soul in the *De Anima* should help him answer questions . . . about methods in ethics by showing him how ethical conclusions can rest on more than pure dialectic. Moreover, it might explain why a rational person with a true conception of his own good has reason to accept and to cultivate the virtues that are commonly recognized. [Irwin 1988: 351–52, my italics]

Irwin continues, a few pages later, as follows:

(I12) This question about the ethical principles [i.e., whether any political demands they imply are plausible] would be inappropriate if they [i.e., the ethical principles] were fundamental principles needing no further justification or were *wholly derived* from such principles. *But Aristotle accepts neither of these foundationalist views about ethical first principles or about their metaphysical and psychological premisses*. [Irwin 1988: 354][56]

This leaves us in the unsatisfactory position of finding that the secondary puzzle is not fully resolved: insofar as the search for reflective reassurance involves (as McDowell concedes) a form of strong dialectic, and insofar as strong dialectic demands only the broad coherence of ethical conclusions with our metaphysical and psychological theories and not the deducibility of ethical conclusions from these theories, there seems

---

[56] See, however, page 346 of Irwin 1988:

> The *DA* argues that the essence of human beings is their capacity for rational thought, desire, and action—that these are the properties that mark them out as a distinct kind, from a teleological point of view, and explain their activities as a whole. The *Ethics* is about what is good for creatures of this kind; from understanding that human beings are essentially rational agents we are supposed to be able to form a theory of their good. This theory will identify virtues and virtuous actions . . .
>
> If Aristotle means this, he commits himself to quite a strong and initially implausible claim. It is essential to a human being that he guides his action by a rational conception of his good referring to his whole life; and Aristotle seems to claim that from this fact we can *derive* an account of his actual good that need not be identical with his good as he conceives it. He seems to claim that someone's acting on a conception of his good implies that *one* conception is the *right* one.
>
> If this is really Aristotle's claim, and if he can justify it, then the psychology of the *De Anima* is still more important than it has appeared so far. For its account of the human essence will *determine* an account of the human good, and hence in Aristotle's view of ethics, the *foundation* of a *complete* ethical theory.

It seems that Irwin must—on pain of inconsistency—be using "foundation" in a looser sense here than that in which he speaks of "foundationalism" in (I12). But the fact that Irwin frequently moves back and forth between passages such as this and passages such as (I12) raises questions about what exactly he means to attribute to Aristotle—the weaker project suggested in (I12) (and elsewhere) or the stronger one suggested here (and elsewhere). McDowell tends to ignore the possibility that Irwin means only to attribute the weaker project, and it is this possibility (for which there is much textual support) that makes it difficult to resolve the first puzzle in a fully satisfactory way.

to be very little difference between the *method* that McDowell ascribes to Aristotle and the *method* that Irwin ascribes to him, especially if Irwin is willing to allow that strong dialectic runs both ways (from metaphysical and psychological views to ethical ones and vice versa). So it is tempting to conclude that the *primary* difference between Irwin's Aristotle and McDowell's Aristotle is a difference in the substantive ethical views: McDowell's Aristotle takes the genuinely virtuous agent to view ethical considerations (about, for example, what is just and what noble) as *autonomous* and as *determining* her conception of eudaimonia in a way in which Irwin's Aristotle does *not*.

According to McDowell, the genuinely virtuous agent regards the chain of explanations about why one should perform this or that particular action (or why one should abstain from it) as coming to an end in the claim that the action is *just* or *noble* (or *unjust* or *base*), and the fact that an action is just or noble is roughly speaking what *makes it the case* that performing that action is what counts as "doing well" [τὸ εὖ πράττειν]—or eudaimonia—here and now. The virtuous agent's conception of what is required for eudaimonia is thus *determined* by the autonomous ethical considerations that she takes as providing her ultimate reasons for action (at least in cases in which such considerations are in play). And this is compatible with her acknowledging when she does moral theory that the autonomous ethical considerations she recognizes would not be what they are were the first nature of human beings radically different (if, for example, we were immortal).

According to Irwin, it is always permissible—and perhaps even required if the *agent* is to be genuinely *rational*—for the virtuous agent to ask the *further* question, "but *why* do the just or noble thing?" And it is permissible—and perhaps even required if *virtue* is to be *rational*—for the answer to be that doing just and noble things contributes to the agent's eudaimonia, where the agent's conception of eudaimonia is to *some* extent independent of her commitment to virtue. The idea here is roughly that she (like everyone else) first-naturally seeks eudaimonia, which she (like everyone else) takes to have certain properties (such as completeness and self-sufficiency) that can be specified without reference to virtue; and that she can then be shown (at least partly by appeal to first-natural facts) that only a life that includes a commitment to just and noble action has the properties that she (and everyone else) takes it for granted eudaimonia (which they all first-naturally want) has. This does *not* require that justice and nobility be *reducible* to anything non-ethical, but it does require there be *some* non-distinctively ethical considerations that speak in favor of just and noble action. For on Irwin's view, the distinctively ethical value of this or that particular virtuous action is *not enough* to guarantee its appeal to a rational agent, who needs to be reassured that engaging in such action is generally speaking a way—perhaps the only way—to reach eudaimonia, her conception of which is at least partly independent of her commitment to virtue.[57]

[57] The demand for a *guarantee* is what makes it difficult for Irwin to restrict himself to mere coherence, as opposed to some sort of deducibility. But we should still distinguish (a) deducing the *content* of the virtues from the relevant metaphysical and psychological theories from (b) deducing the *rationality* of the virtues from the relevant metaphysical and psychological theories. And McDowell need not tar Irwin with (a) in order to run his primary objection to (b).

But given that McDowell too seems to want to allow for the possibility that even a fundamentally (though not perhaps fully) virtuous agent might seek reflective reassurance that the fact that an action is just or noble *really is* a reason for doing it, it may seem that not even the *psychology* of McDowell's virtuous agent is in the end so different from the psychology of Irwin's virtuous agent. Still, however, it seems to me that there *is* an important difference: what distinguishes Irwin's virtuous agent from McDowell's is that Irwin's fully virtuous agent feels the *need* for such reassurance in a way in which McDowell's fully virtuous agent does *not*. Moreover, on Irwin's view it is *legitimate*—indeed *rational*—for the fully virtuous agent to feel this need in a way in which, on McDowell's view, it is not. For even if McDowell were to allow that recognizing the first-natural rationality of having something like the second-natural practices of virtue we do is a necessary part of having an adequate moral *theory* or an adequate *meta*ethics, he need not allow that recognizing this is a *necessary* part of being a virtuous *agent*.

This does *not* mean that McDowell takes *recognizing* the first-natural rationality of virtue to be *incompatible* with being a virtuous agent. It is only *feeling the need* to establish the first-natural rationality of virtue that McDowell takes to be incompatible with being a virtuous agent, and even here feeling the need is incompatible only with being a *fully* virtuous agent. It is after all *re*-assurance that he is talking about. Someone who feels the need for such *re*-assurance is not fully virtuous: she lacks the sort of supreme confidence in the ultimate authority of ethical reasons that is characteristic of a *fully* virtuous agent. She is presumably well on her way to virtue, but she cannot be all the way to recognizing the autonomy of ethical reasons if she seeks to ground ethical reasons directly in first-natural, non-ethical considerations. She may, however, appeal to such considerations for *re*-assurance that the second-natural practices of virtue, which operate according to their own *internal* standards of rationality, make a kind of non-autonomous sense. Here, however, we must acknowledge that her appeal to such considerations is limited in much the same way that we have seen that the use of protreptic arguments is limited: just as an agent's acceptance of an external argument for virtue in general *may* be what induces her to undertake the sort of not purely cognitive training that is required if she is to become virtuous, but *cannot* (if she is to be genuinely virtuous) be what *sustains* her commitment to virtue in general or what justifies her performance of any particular virtuous action, so too the considerations that provide reflective reassurance cannot be what in the end *sustain* an agent's commitment to virtue or what in the end *justify* her choice of this or that particular virtuous action. On McDowell's view, the considerations that provide reflective reassurance are not up to the more demanding tasks of converting those who have not yet acquired the second-natural practices of virtue or of rehabilitating those who have strayed too far from the path; so appeals to such considerations may be even more limited than appeals to the sort of external argument envisaged by Irwin.

Here, however, we should note that Irwin himself is less optimistic about the power of argument than McDowell at times suggests. As we have already seen, Irwin distinguishes the question whether an argument will *in fact* persuade this or that particular interlocutor (warts and all) from the question whether an argument *ought* to persuade any *rational* interlocutor. And Irwin typically claims that his heroes (that is, Socrates, Plato, and Aristotle, as distinct from mere orators and sophists) aim *not* at *actual persuasion* of this or that particular interlocutor (like Callicles) but *rather* at *good arguments*—that is, at arguments that *ought* to persuade any *rational* interlocutor (whether or not they in fact succeed in doing so). Moreover, Irwin explicitly acknowledges—in (I1) as in the following passage referring to Burnyeat (1980)—that vice or corruption can prevent someone from being persuaded by an argument by which she *ought* to be persuaded.

(I13) Burnyeat . . . argues . . . that Aristotle does not intend the *Ethics* to persuade anyone who lacks a good upbringing that the virtuous life is worth while; the function argument, e.g., 'is not an argument that would appeal to anyone who really doubted or denied that he should practice the virtues' [90]. Whether or not this is true . . . , we should *not* infer that Aristotle does *not* intend his argument to prove to any *rational* person's satisfaction that a critic of the virtues is mistaken, and that it is bad for a person to be vicious . . . *If we are too corrupt to be persuaded by a proof that ought to persuade us, that is a fault in us, not in the proof.* [Irwin 1988: 601, my italics]

5. CONCLUSION: THE TERMS OF RECONCILIATION

I have been suggesting that there is a way of reconciling Irwin's Aristotle with McDowell's. The fundamental terms of the reconciliation are as follows:

(1) We distinguish *external* justifications of virtue in *general* from the sort of *internal* justifications of *particular* virtuous actions that are given by genuinely virtuous agents.

(2) We (especially McDowell's Aristotle) allow for the *possibility* of (a qualified form of) strong dialectic that is roughly equivalent to what McDowell calls "reflective reassurance." And we (especially McDowell's Aristotle) allow that a suitably qualified form of strong dialectic *can* provide an *external* justification of the *general* practices of virtue, but only in the *weak* sense that it reveals these practices of virtue to be "more plausible" in light of their broad coherence with the reflective base than rival practices, and *not* in the *strong* sense that the contents of these practices are *deducible* from the reflective base (which includes our preferred metaphysical and psychological theories).

(3) We (especially Irwin's Aristotle) recognize the *limits* of this sort of external argument: we recognize that such argument is *merely protreptic* in the sense that it can induce someone to undertake the sort of not purely cognitive training that is required if she is *to become* genuinely virtuous, but cannot by itself

put someone who accepts its conclusion in a position either to *identify* particular virtuous actions or to explain *why* they are virtuous.

(4) We (especially McDowell's Aristotle) concede the protreptic usefulness of such external arguments, while insisting that the agent's acceptance of such an argument cannot in the end be what *sustains* her general commitment to virtue or what *motivates* her performance of particular virtuous actions. In other words, we require that the genuinely virtuous agent choose virtuous actions on their own autonomous terms—i.e., qua *just, courageous, noble,* etc. and *not* (for example) qua actualizations of her essence (even if performing them does as a matter of fact actualize her essence and she recognizes that this is the case).

(5) We (especially Irwin's Aristotle) allow that the search for reflective reassurance—or for strong dialectical support for ethical conclusions—is *not* something that the genuinely virtuous agent would or should feel any *need* to undertake.

(6) And we (especially McDowell's Aristotle) allow that the sort of arguments that provide such reassurance are a necessary part of an adequate moral *theory* or *meta*-ethics, but we (especially Irwin's Aristotle) allow that having such arguments is not a necessary condition for being a genuinely virtuous agent.

These are the terms of my proposed reconciliation. I cannot at this point undertake the project of arguing that some such "compromise" view is in fact supported by Aristotle's texts, which is a task for another occasion. But to the extent that Irwin and McDowell each possess something akin to the truth in the sense that each grasps genuine features of Aristotle's view, it seems plausible to suppose that some such "compromise" view may do *more* justice to Aristotle's texts taken as a whole than either of their views taken by itself manages to do.

It is perhaps worth noting, in conclusion, that McDowell has shown signs of willingness to accept some such "compromise" interpretation, whereas Irwin has not.[58] Irwin can, I think, easily enough accept (1)–(4); it is (5) and (6) that are the main problem for him, since they involve giving up the kind of rational egoism that he seems to think required by Aristotle's eudaimonism (according to which an agent does everything for the sake of eudaimonia). But if it is Irwin's own sympathy with rational egoism that leads him to think that the most "charitable" reading of Aristotle's eudaimonism is a rational egoist reading according to which an agent does everything for the sake of *her own* eudaimonia (which may, however, include the *eudaimonia* of others), then we may need more than good argument to bring Irwin—or his Aristotle—around to the proposed reconciliation.[59]

[58] McDowell has shown himself surprisingly open to the sort of reconciliation I seek to effect, and has been of great help to me in my attempt to carry out this (according to Burnyeat) "hopeless" project. When I first mentioned it to Myles, he said "it's a hopeless project, but you are just the person to do it."

[59] For some hints of an alternative to the rational egoist reading of Aristotle, see Whiting 1991 ["Impersonal Friends" (I.2)], 1996 ["Self-Love and Authoritative Virtue" (Chapter 4, this volume)] and 2006 ["The Nicomachean Account of *Philia*" (Chapter 6, this volume)].

For as Irwin himself acknowledges in his own diagnosis of *Callicles'* failure to be persuaded by Socrates' arguments, it is not only failures of rationality, but also failures of virtue, that can prevent someone from being persuaded by a good argument (or, I might add, from an adequate interpretation of a philosophical text). And here I am inclined to agree with Rawls (1975, 9) that "rational egoism . . . is not really a moral conception but rather a challenge to all such conceptions." In other words, rational egoism is an example of the sort of failure that can (according to Irwin) prevent someone from accepting an argument he *ought* to accept. Perhaps then the fault is not in my argument, but in Irwin's Aristotle.[60]

BIBLIOGRAPHY

Aristotle. *Ethica Nicomachea*. I. Bywater (ed.) 1894. Oxford: Clarendon Press.

Aristotle. *Nicomachean Ethics*. T. H. Irwin (trans.) 1985. Indianapolis, IN: Hackett.

Barnes, J. 1981. "Aristotle and the Method of Ethics." *Revue Internationale de Philosophie* 34: 490–511.

Burnyeat, M. F. 1980. "Aristotle on Learning to Be Good." In A. O. Rorty (ed.), *Essays on Aristotle's "Ethics."* Berkeley: University of California Press, 69–92.

Frankfurt, H. 1999. *Necessity, Volition, and Love*. New York: Cambridge University Press.

Frankfurt, H. 2004. *The Reasons of Love*. Princeton, NJ: Princeton University Press.

Hume, D. 1978. *A Treatise of Human Nature*. L. A. Selby-Bigge and P. H. Nidditch (eds.) Oxford: Oxford University Press.

Irwin, T. H. 1977. *Plato's Moral Theory: The Early and Middle Dialogues*. Oxford: Oxford University Press.

Irwin, T. H. 1977–1978. "Aristotle's Discovery of Metaphysics." *Review of Metaphysics* 31: 210–29.

Irwin, T. H. 1978. "First Principles in Aristotle's *Ethics*." *Midwest Studies in Philosophy* 3: 252–72.

Irwin, T. H. 1980. "The Metaphysical and Psychological Basis of Aristotle's *Ethics*." In A. O. Rorty (ed.), *Essays on Aristotle's "Ethics."* Berkeley: University of California Press, 35–53.

Irwin, T. H. 1981. "Aristotle's Methods of Ethics." In D. J. O'Meara (ed.), *Studies on Aristotle*. Washington: Catholic University Press, 193–223.

Irwin, T. H. 1985 (second edition 1999). *Aristotle's Nicomachean Ethics*. Indianapolis, IN: Hackett Publishing.

[60] Successive versions of this essay were read at The Ohio State University Conference on Ancient Philosophy (1996), the University of Oslo (1997), New York University (1998), the Pacific Division Meetings of the American Philosophical Association (1999), and the Boston Colloquium of Ancient Philosophy (2000). Discussions with the members of these audiences—as well as with students in my seminars at the University of Pittsburgh and Cornell—have led to improvements in each successive version, for which I thank them: especially Chris Bobonich, Myles Burnyeat, Bridget Clarke, Alan Code, Harold Hodes, Richard Miller, Dominic Scott, Iakovos Vasiliou, Lionel Shapiro, and Pekka Väyrynen. I should also like to thank Michael Pakaluk for his comments (published here [in the *Proceedings of the Boston Area Colloquium of Ancient Philosophy*)] and John Cleary and an anonymous referee for the *Proceedings*. But I am most grateful to Terry Irwin and John McDowell. I first went to Cornell in 1978 to study with Irwin after reading *Plato's Moral Theory*. I then attended a seminar that McDowell gave on that book in 1982. I later had the privilege of being McDowell's colleague for over ten years, before returning to Cornell. So I have been discussing these questions with Irwin and McDowell—from whom I have learned more than I can say—for nearly twenty years.

Irwin, T. H. 1986a. "Coercion and Objectivity in Plato's Dialectic." *Revue Internationale de Philosophie* 15: 49–74.

Irwin, T. H. 1986b. "Stoic and Aristotelian Conceptions of Happiness." In M. Schofield and G. Striker (eds.), *The Norms of Nature*. Cambridge: Cambridge University Press, 205–44.

Irwin, T. H. 1988. *Aristotle's First Principles*. Oxford: Oxford University Press.

Irwin T. H. 1995. *Plato's Ethics*. Oxford: Oxford University Press.

McDowell, J. 1979. "Virtue and Reason." *Monist* 62: 331–50; reprinted in J. McDowell, 1998a, 50–73.

McDowell, J. 1995a. "Eudaimonism and Realism in Aristotle's Ethics." In R. Heinaman (ed.), *Aristotle and Moral Realism*. London: UCLS Press, 201–18.

McDowell, J. 1995b. "Might There Be External Reasons?" in J. E. J. Altham and Ross Harrison (eds.), *World, Mind, and Ethics: Essays on the Ethical Philosophy of Bernard Williams*. Cambridge: Cambridge University Press, 387–98; reprinted in McDowell 1998a, 95–111.

McDowell, J. 1996a. "Deliberation and Moral Development in Aristotle." In S. Engstrom and J. Whiting (eds.), *Aristotle, Kant and the Stoics, Rethinking Happiness and Duty*. Cambridge: Cambridge University Press, 19–35.

McDowell, J. 1996b. "Two Sorts of Naturalism." In R. Hursthouse, G. Lawrence, and W. Quinn (eds.), *Virtues and Reasons: Philippa Foot and Moral Theory*. Oxford: Clarendon Press, 149–79; reprinted in McDowell 1998a, 167–97.

McDowell, J. 1998a. *Mind, Value, and Reality*. Cambridge, MA: Harvard University Press.

McDowell, J. 1998b. "Some Issues in Aristotle's Moral Psychology." In S. Everson (ed.), *Ethics*. Cambridge: Cambridge University Press, 107–28; reprinted in McDowell 1998a, 23–49.

Moravcsik, J. M. E. 1971. "Reason and Eros in the 'Ascent'-Passage of the *Symposium*." In J. P. Anton, G. L. Kustas, and A. Preus (eds.), *Essays in Ancient Greek Philosophy*. Albany: SUNY Press, 285–302.

Nussbaum, M. C. 1995. "Aristotle on Human Nature and the Foundations of Ethics." In J. Altham and R. Harrison (eds.), *World, Mind, and Ethics: Essays on the Ethical Philosophy of Bernard* Williams. Cambridge: Cambridge University Press, 86–131.

Walzer R. R. and Mingay J. M. 1991. *Aristotelis: Ethica Eudemia*. Oxford: Oxford University Press.

Whiting, J. 1986. "Human Nature and Intellectualism in Aristotle." *Archiv für Geschichte der Philosophie* 68: 70–95. [Chapter 2, this volume]

Whiting, J. 1988. "Aristotle's Function Argument: A Defense." *Ancient Philosophy* 8: 33–48. [Chapter 1, this volume]

Whiting, J. 1991. "Impersonal Friends." *The Monist* 74: 3–29. [I.2].

Whiting, J. 1996. "Self-Love and Authoritative Virtue: Prolegomenon to a Kantian Reading of *EE* VIII.3." In S. Engstrom and J. Whiting (eds.), *Aristotle, Kant and the Stoics, Rethinking Happiness and Duty*. Cambridge: Cambridge University Press, 162–99. [Chapter 4, this volume]

Whiting, J. 2002a. "Eudaimonia, External Results, and Choosing Virtuous Actions for Themselves." *Philosophy and Phenomenological Research* LXV (2): 270–90. [Chapter 3, this volume]

Whiting, J. 2002b. "Locomotive Soul: The Parts of Soul in Aristotle's Scientific Works." *Oxford Studies in Ancient Philosophy* 22: 141–200. [III.5]

Whiting, J. 2006. "The Nicomachean Account of Philia." In R. Kraut (ed.), *The Blackwell Guide to Aristotle's "Nicomachean Ethics."* Oxford: Blackwell, 276–304. [Chapter 6, this volume]

Whiting, J. 2013. "Love: Self-Propagation, Self-Actualization, or Ekstasis?" *Canadian Journal of Philosophy* 43, no. 4: 403–29. [I.7]

Whiting, J. 2019. "Hylomorphic Virtue: Cosmology, Embryology, and Moral Development in Aristotle." *Philosophical Explorations* 22, no. 2: 222–42. [III.6]

Whiting, J. (2021). "See the Right Thing: 'Paternal' Reason, Love, and Phronêsis." In M. Boyle and E. Mylonaki (eds.), *Reason and Nature: New Essays on Themes from John McDowell*. Cambridge, MA: Harvard University Press, 2021, 243–84.

Vasiliou, I. 1996. "The Role of Good Upbringing in Aristotle's *Ethics*." *Philosophy and Phenomenological Research* 56, no. 4: 771–97.

Vasiliou, I. 2002. "Disputing Socratic Principles: Character and Argument in the 'Polus Episode' of the Gorgias." *Archiv für Geschichte der Philosophie* 84, no. 3: 245–72.

Vlastos, G. 1973. *Platonic Studies*. Princeton, NJ: Princeton University Press.

6

The Nicomachean Account of *Philia*

1. PRELIMINARY NOTE

Those translating Aristotle into English so readily agree in rendering '*philia*' as 'friendship' and '*philos*' as 'friend' that it is easy to overlook two related difficulties with this. The first is that of preserving the etymological connections present in the original; the second is that of finding terms having roughly the same extensions and connotations as the Greek for which they do duty.

'*Philia*' is an abstract noun derived from the verb '*to philein*,' which means *to love* or *hold dear* in a general sense: one can love or hold dear all sorts of things, from a bottle of wine or a dog through one's family and friends. So we *could* preserve the etymological connection by rendering '*philia*' and its cognates with 'love' and its cognates. But this suggests 'lover' for '*ho philôn*' (from the active participle of '*philein*') and 'beloved' for '*ho philoumenos*' (from the passive participle). And this involves changes in both connotation and extension. For 'lover' and 'beloved' have erotic connotations and tend to refer more narrowly to the subjects and objects of specifically erotic loving.

We might seek to rectify the problem by reserving 'to love' and its cognates for '*to eran*' and its. But we bump immediately into the problem of how to render '*to philein*.' 'To befriend' is awkward. More importantly, it is too weak to capture paradigmatic forms of '*philôn*,' such as the intense love many parents have for their offspring. We need a verb covering both weak and strong forms of attachment. So I propose to

Living Together. Jennifer Whiting, Oxford University Press. © Oxford University Press 2023.
DOI: 10.1093/oso/9780199969678.003.0007

continue using the generic 'to love' for *'to philein*.'[1] We can then use the less erotically charged 'one who loves' and 'one loved' for *'ho philôn'* and *'ho philoumenos*,' while keeping the more erotically charged 'lover' and 'beloved' for the relevant forms of *'to eran*,' which we can render 'to love erotically.' This seems appropriate insofar as Aristotle treats *erôs* as a kind of *philia*.

This would allow us to render *'philia'* simply as 'love,' thus preserving the etymological connections between *'to philein'* and the abstract noun. But *should* we work so hard to preserve this connection? For two reasons, I think we should *not*. First, we must eventually sacrifice the connection in order to render the adjective *'philos'* and the substantive noun *'philia'* that is derived from it: the adjective is best rendered 'dear,' while the noun (which is nondirectional and refers indifferently to those who love and to those who are loved) is best rendered 'friend.' Second, 'friendship' is so well entrenched in translations and the secondary literature that it would be disruptive to depart from it. So I shall retain 'friendship' for *'philia'* and 'friend' for (the noun) *'philos*,' but abandon the etymological connection by using 'to love' (rather than 'to befriend') for *'to philein*.'

2. EUDAIMONISM AND RATIONAL EGOISM

The *Nicomachean Ethics* (*EN*) opens with—and is organized around—what Vlastos 1991 calls "the eudaimonist axiom": eudaimonia is the ultimate end of human action in the sense that (a) it is never chosen for the sake of any further end, and (b) it is that for the sake of which all actions should be (and in some sense are) performed.[2] Many commentators read this as a form of rational egoism according to which each agent should aim primarily at her *own* eudaimonia, construed more or less broadly so as to include the eudaimonia of at least some "significant others." Such commentators sometimes read Aristotle's conception of the friend as an "other self" as explaining how the agent's eudaimonia comes to *include* that of others: because the agent's friend is her other *self*, her friend's eudaimonia is *part* of her *own*, so promoting her friend's eudaimonia is a *way* of promoting her *own*. Some even read Aristotle as making the friend a literal extension of oneself. Irwin 1988, for example, reads Aristotle

---

[1] Pace n. 5 of Cooper 1977a, which is reprinted, along with Cooper's 1977b, in his *Reason and Emotion* (1999), to which I henceforth refer. I am much indebted to these two canonical papers, which are efficiently combined (for less specialist readers) in Cooper 1980. For more on linguistic (and other) issues, see Konstan 1997.

[2] Vlastos defends the traditional rendering of *'eudaimonia'* as 'happiness' (1991, 200–203). This is potentially misleading insofar as modern conceptions of happiness tend to be more subjectivist than Aristotle's conception of *eudaimonia* is. So 'flourishing' (used by Cooper) or 'well-being' is sometimes preferred. I prefer simply to use the Greek. [For discussion of these issues, see the Introduction to this volume. For discussion of the "eudaimonist axiom," see "*Eudaimonia*, External Results, and Choosing Virtuous Actions for Themselves" (Chapter 3, this volume).]

as treating the character and activities of one's friend as an "extension of [one's] own activity": friendship is thus conceived as a mode of "*self*-realization."[3]

But there is some question whether such readings honor Aristotle's repeated insistence that a true friend loves and seeks to benefit her friend for her *friend's* sake. For rational egoism gives normative—and not just explanatory—primacy to the *agent's* eudaimonia: loving and seeking to benefit one's friend for her sake is acceptable *because*, and *only insofar as*, it is a way of loving and seeking to benefit *oneself*. But the *Nicomachean Ethics* does not actually specify the agent's *own* eudaimonia as the ultimate end of all of her actions: it is compatible with what Aristotle says that an agent at least sometimes, perhaps often, takes the eudaimonia of others as the ultimate end for the sake of which she acts in the sense that she aims at their eudaimonia *simply as such* (and *not* as parts of her own).[4]

Aristotle's account of *philia* must of course be interpreted within his eudaimonist framework. But we should not assume straightaway that his eudaimonism is a form of rational egoism. For his account of *philia*, if read *without* this assumption, may tell *against* rational egoist readings of that framework. There is, of course, no escaping the hermeneutic circle. But I propose to reverse the usual order by starting with Aristotle's account of *philia* and then asking what (if anything) it suggests about the nature of his eudaimonism.

3. *NICOMACHEAN ETHICS* VIII.1: NICOMACHEAN CONTEXT AND PLATONIC BACKGROUND

EN I characterizes eudaimonia as "an activity of soul in accordance with virtue, and if there are several virtues, in accordance with the best and *teleiotatên*" [*EN* I.7, 1098a16–18]. Commentators are famously divided over how to take this. Some take '*teleiotatên*' to mean 'highest' and read this as pointing *either* to the purely contemplative activity of theoretical intellect that is apparently championed in *EN* X.7 *or* to the distinctively human activity of practical intellect and the virtues associated with it [*EN* 1177b24–1178a22]. Others take '*teleiotatên*' to mean 'complete' and read this as referring to a compound activity in accordance with the panoply of practical and theoretical virtues covered in the *Nicomachean Ethics*. We cannot resolve this controversy here. But *whichever* way Book X goes, Aristotle seems to model human on divine eudaimonia: he seems to think that human subjects—even those living primarily political lives—are more eudaimôn the more their activities and lives resemble those of the gods. And he takes self-sufficiency to be a prominent feature of divine activities and lives.

3 Irwin 1988, 614 n. 6, 391–97). For criticism of this "colonizing ego" view, see Whiting 1991 ["Impersonal Friends" (I.2)].

4 The issue of egoism in Aristotle is well discussed in Kraut 1989. [For more on the idea of taking the good of another, simply as such, as an ultimate end, see "Love: Self-Propagation, Self-Preservation, or Ekstasis?" (I.7).]

This is the context in which the Nicomachean books on *philia* appear. They precede Book X's problematic return to the topic of *eudaimonia* and open with a reference back to Book I's account of eudaimonia as something self-sufficient in the sense that it "taken by itself makes life choice-worthy[5] and lacking in nothing" [*EN* I.8, 1098b14–15]:

> After these things comes the discussion of *philia*. For it is a kind of virtue or something involving virtue. Further, it is most necessary for life; for without friends, no one would choose to live, even if he had all other goods. [*EN* VIII.1, 1155a3–6]

EN VIII.1 cites various *endoxa*—or common beliefs—in support of this. But the claim itself seems to be in Aristotle's own voice: he seems to think that a life without friends is not simply lacking but not even choiceworthy.

But this generates a puzzle. For the need for friends seems to undermine the self-sufficiency of the would-be eudaimôn. The more she needs friends, the less (it seems) her life can approximate that of the gods. And the more her relationships with her so-called friends are grounded in *her* needs, the less (it seems) her relationships with them qualify as true friendship, which must be based on appreciation of one's friend and not on one's own needs. So the more self-sufficient an agent is, the more capable she will be of true friendship. But the more self-sufficient she is, the harder it is to explain why she will (or should) have friends in the first place.[6]

In seeking to resolve such puzzles, Aristotle follows his standard "endoxic" method: he seeks an account that resolves the puzzles to which common beliefs give rise, while preserving as many of these beliefs as possible. His strategy is to argue that apparently opposed beliefs can be reconciled insofar as each is true in one sense (or one set of cases) but not in another [*Eudemian Ethics* (*EE*) VII.2, 1235b13–18]. *EN* IX.8 provides a classic example: by distinguishing two kinds of self-love, he preserves the claims both of those who commend self-love and of those who condemn it.

EN VIII.1 dismisses the puzzles raised by natural philosophers—such as whether *like* is friend to *like* or whether friendship arises only between contraries—as "not appropriate" to Aristotle's inquiry: they are, as he explains at *EE* VII.1.1235a30, "too universal." But VIII.1 admits specifically human variants, involving human characters and emotions: most notably, whether (as some think) only *good* people can be friends (since friendship requires us to trust our friends in ways we cannot trust those who are bad); or whether (as many think) *any* sort of person can be friends with *any* sort [*EN* VIII.1, 1155b9–13]. These puzzles can be traced to Plato's *Lysis*, which provides immediate and indispensable background for Aristotle's discussion. At 215a–b, Socrates gets Lysis to agree that the good agent is sufficient, and that one who is sufficient will *need*

[5] [Or '*haireton*,' which I often render 'such-as-to-be chosen' for reasons explained in note 12 of "Self-Love and Authoritative Virtue" (Chapter 4, this volume).]

[6] [For more on this, see "The Pleasures of Thinking Together" (Chapter 7, this volume).]

nothing and so will neither cherish [*agapein*] nor love [*philein*] anything. How then, they wonder, can good agents value one another?

Aristotle's conception of the true friend as an "other self" is largely a response to this question—a response at which Socrates himself hints at the end of the *Lysis*, where he distinguishes what is *oikeion* (roughly "appropriate") to a person from what is merely *like* her, and then suggests that the good may be *oikeion* to *everyone* [222b–c]. Socrates gestures here toward a kind of loving that is neither need-based nor a function of what its *subject* is like—a kind of loving motivated not by some deficiency or mere taste in its subject but rather by some positive quality in its *object*. And he has hinted (at 216c) at the relevant quality: *to kalon* (there rendered 'beauty'). Aristotle uses the same term to characterize the end for the sake of which virtuous agents act (in which contexts '*to kalon*' tends to be rendered 'nobility' or 'the fine').[7]

4. *NICOMACHEAN ETHICS* VIII.2: ARISTOTLE'S PRELIMINARY ACCOUNT

Aristotle begins, following Socrates' lead, with a discussion of the object or "what is lovable" [*to philêton*]. This has normative connotations: it refers to what people are apt to love because they deem it *worthy* of love. Aristotle recognizes three such objects: what is good [*agathon*], what is pleasant [*hêdu*], and what is useful [*chrêsimon*] [*EN* VIII.2, 1155b18–19]. These almost certainly correspond to the three objects of choice listed at *EN* II.3 1104b30–31: what is fine [*kalon*], what is advantageous [*sumpheron*], and what is pleasant. For it is, as Broadie suggests, likely that Aristotle avoids using *kalon* in *EN* VIII.2 lest he be misunderstood as referring simply to physical beauty (Broadie and Rowe 2002, 408). But associating the good mentioned here with *to kalon* is especially reasonable, given the three corresponding forms of friendship that Aristotle goes on to discuss: those based on virtue (where *to kalon* is key), those based on pleasure, and those based on utility.

Aristotle adds immediately that things are useful because some good or some pleasure comes to be through them, so that it is ultimately only the good and the pleasant that are lovable "as ends" [*EN* VIII.2, 1155b19–21]. It is worth noting that Aristotle here associates what is pleasant with what is good and opposes *both* to what is useful. For commentators often tend to speak as if he associated pleasure-friendship primarily with utility-friendship and took the two together to be uniformly opposed to character-friendship. But there is evidence here (and elsewhere) that Aristotle associates pleasure-friendships more closely with character-friendships than with those based on utility.[8]

---

[7] [For Aristotle's account of choosing virtuous actions for themselves or on account of *to kalon*, see "*Eudaimonia*, External Results, and Choosing Virtuous Actions for Themselves" (Chapter 3, this volume).]

[8] This is distinct from the familiar point that pleasure-friendships are closer to character-friendships than utility-friendships are. I take the label "character-friendship" from Cooper (1999).

Aristotle next asks whether people love what is good (simply) or what is good *for themselves*; and whether people love what is pleasant (simply) or what is pleasant *to themselves*. For these things do not always agree [*EN* VIII.2, 1155b21–23]. As explained in the *EE*, they agree in the case of properly constituted subjects: what is good simply [*haplôs*] is what is good *for* a healthy body or a well-ordered soul, but some things (such as drugs and surgery) are good *for* a subject only because of peculiarities of her condition. Aristotle draws a similar distinction between what is pleasant *haplôs*, and so pleasant *to* a mature and non-defective body or soul, and what is pleasant *only* to an immature or otherwise defective body or soul [*EE* VII.2, 1235b30–1236a7].

The Eudemian account does not separate the distinction between what is good *haplôs* and what is good *for* someone as clearly as it might from that between what is *really* good and what is *apparently* good. But the Nicomachean account makes it clear that there are two distinctions here. For it explicitly contrasts what is *really* good for oneself with what is *apparently* good for oneself [*EN* VIII.2, 1155b25–26]. Note that the contrast here is not between what is *really* good for oneself and what is *only apparently* good for oneself. For what is *really* good for oneself may also (and should ideally) *appear* to oneself as such; so what is *apparently* good for oneself may or may not be *merely apparently* good for oneself.

Aristotle recognizes that a subject can pursue what *is* good only by pursuing what *appears* to her good, and that this applies equally to what is good *haplôs* and to what is good *for* her. And he thinks (following *Gorgias* 466b–468e) that those who pursue what appears good *because* it appears good are ultimately pursuing what is really good, even if (thanks to defective appearances) they are mistaken about what is *in fact* really good. His view is not just that people *do* tend to pursue what is (really) good for themselves, but also that they *should* do so: he says at *EN* V.1, 1129b5–6 that people should *choose* things that *are* good for themselves, given their actual circumstances, while *praying* that the things that are *haplôs* good *be* good *for* them. This ideal plays an important role in Aristotle's account of *philia*: true friends are good both *haplôs* and *for one another* [*EN* VIII.3, 1156b12–13].

With these distinctions in place, Aristotle produces the following preliminary account: *philia* requires (a) reciprocal loving or affection [*antiphilêsis*]; (b) each party wishing good to the other for the *other's* sake; and (c) mutual awareness of this reciprocal well-wishing [*EN* VIII.2, 1155b27–1156a3]. Conditions (a) and (b) rule out friendship with inanimate objects. Even if a bottle of wine is *philon* (i.e., dear) to me because I have affection for it, it does not return my affection. And even if I wish for its good, I do not wish that for *its* sake; I wish for it to be preserved so that I might enjoy (or perhaps sell) it. But even reciprocal well-wishing for the other's sake is *not sufficient* for *philia*: each party must be *aware* of the other's well-wishing [*EN* VIII.2, 1155b34–1156a5]. The importance of such awareness should become clear in section 11 below.

It is worth noting that when Aristotle explains condition (b), he seems to be reporting how the term '*eunoia*' is *commonly used*: he says that those who wish goods to another for the other's sake are *said* to have goodwill [*eunoia*] toward the other whenever such wishing is not reciprocated by the other; and that *philia* is *said* to be reciprocal *eunoia* [*EN* VIII.2, 1155b31–34]. Aristotle's own account of *eunoia*, in IX.5, is more restricted: he claims that *eunoia* "generally comes about on account of virtue or a certain decency" [*EN* IX.5, 1167a18–20] and he seems to restrict *eunoia* to friendships based on virtue [*EN* IX.5, 1167a14–17].

Some commentators (such as Irwin) take this later restriction to suggest that there is no genuine wishing-goods-to-the-other-for-the-*other's*-sake in friendships based on pleasure or utility.[9] But this does not follow if, as I suggest, Aristotle starts in the endoxic phase of his discussion with the common use (according to which *eunoia* is simply wishing-goods-to-the-other-for-the-other's-sake, *however* such wishing comes about) and then moves in his own positive account to what he regards as the proper use (according to which *eunoia* is such wishing *when it comes to be on account of the parties recognizing some decency or virtue in one another*). For in that case it may be only *eunoia* proper, and not wishing-goods-to-the-other-for-the-other's-sake, that Aristotle takes to be missing in friendships based on pleasure and utility. And if (as I argue in section 6 below) it is *only* wishing-goods-to-the-other-for-the-other's-sake, and not *eunoia* proper, that is necessary for *philia*, then friendships based on pleasure and utility may still (as Cooper insists) make the grade.

5. *NICOMACHEAN ETHICS* VIII.3–4: THREE FORMS OF *PHILIA*?

The next two chapters make it clear that Aristotle counts at least some relationships based on pleasure and utility as genuine friendships. For *EN* VIII.3 describes the three forms of *philia*, and VIII.4 defends the practice of counting the lower two as forms of genuine *philia*. But VIII.4 tends to be misunderstood: because commentators miss a key distinction, they read Aristotle's defense of this practice as more concessive than he means it to be.

To see this, note first how vehemently the *Eudemian Ethics* rejects the restriction of *philia* to character-friendship. After arguing that the various forms of *philia* are so-called in relation to some primary form, Aristotle criticizes those who would restrict *philia* to its primary form:

> *Because they take the universal to be first, they take the first also to be universal. But this is false*. So they are not able to admit all the phenomena. Because one account does not fit <all the forms> they deny that the others are friendships. But they are, only not similarly <in each case>. But these people, whenever the first does not fit <a case> say that the others are not friendships, because they think an account would be universal if it were first.[10] But there are many forms [*eidê*] of

---

[9] See especially the notes to *EN* VIII.2 and IX.5 in Irwin 1999.

[10] Aristotle does not specify his opponents here, but the mistake sounds Academic. Perhaps Plato himself proposed this restriction.

friendship . . . in fact, we have already distinguished three, one *dia* virtue, one *dia* the useful, and one *dia* pleasure. [*EE* VII.2, 1236a23–32][11]

The *Nicomachean Ethics* is at least superficially similar to the *Eudemian Ethics* on this point: it speaks of the lesser forms of *philia* as being so-called on account of their similarity to the primary form. So we need compelling evidence for seeing the alleged restriction in the *Nicomachean Ethics*.

We can best appreciate the Nicomachean defense by starting at *EN* VIII.3, 1156b17–21:

> It is reasonable that such *philia* [viz., character-friendship] should be enduring. For it contains in itself all the things that should belong [*dei huparchein*] to friends.[12] For all *philia* exists *dia* <what is> good or *dia* pleasure, either *haplôs* or for the one who loves, and is <*philia*> in virtue of some similarity <to character-friendship>.

The defense culminates at *EN* VIII.4.1157a20–33:

> [A] And only the *philia* of good people is immune to slander. For it is not easy to trust someone who has not been tested by oneself for a long time. But trusting belongs among these [viz., good people], and so <too> does never doing injustice to one another, and *whatever else people think worthy of true friendship*. [B] And nothing prevents *such things* coming to be in the other [forms of friendship]. For since people apply the term 'friends' both to those who <are friends> *dia* what is useful . . . and to those who are fond of one another *dia* pleasure . . . we should presumably say that such people are friends and that there are several forms of friendship, primarily and in the sense controlling <the other senses>, the friendship of good people insofar as they are good, and the remaining <forms> according to their similarity <to this controlling sense>.

Most English translations take the italicized "such things" as referring to the sort of "distrust" (Irwin), "slander" (Rowe), or "evils" (Ross) that Aristotle has just said arise in the *other* forms of *philia*. So they read the "nothing prevents . . ." sentence as summing up the reasons *against* counting the others as genuine forms of *philia*. They then read the rest of (B) as saying that we should *nevertheless* continue to call the others forms of *philia*.

But it should be clear from (A) that this *cannot* be the correct reading. For "such things" obviously refers back to "trusting . . . and . . . never doing injustice . . . and *whatever else people think worthy of true friendship*." Aristotle's point is that even though such things do not always *in fact* belong to friendships based on pleasure or utility,

[11] On '*dia*' (best rendered 'on account of') see section 7, this chapter.

[12] Or perhaps '*must* belong' (discussed below).

nothing prevents such things *sometimes* belonging (even if only accidentally) to such friendships. And his "nothing prevents . . ." sentence is surely better read as supplying an *argument for* his ostensible conclusion (i.e., that there are several forms of friendship) than as posing an *obstacle to* it.

Moreover, "whatever else people think worthy [*axioutai*] of true friendship" seems to refer back to two previous occurrences of "the things that should belong to friends"—one (quoted above) and one in the opening sentence of *EN* VIII.4. This suggests that "the things that should belong to friends" refers not to the constitutive conditions of *philia* (such as wishing-goods-to-the-other-for-the-other's-sake) but to features that are thought to flow from the constitutive conditions (features like durability, trusting, and not doing injustice to one another). Irwin's 1999 translation obscures this by rendering the '*dei*' (in *dei huparchein*) as 'must' rather than 'should,' thus making it seem as if Aristotle meant to refer to necessary conditions of *philia* and not—as his argument actually *requires*—to features that should ideally belong to friends but do not always in fact do so. And this makes it seem as if Aristotle's argument were more concessive than I take it to be.

In sum, Aristotle is *not* saying (what seems only marginally coherent) that, in spite of the distrust etc. endemic to the relationships based on pleasure and utility, and in spite of their failure to exhibit the features that *must* belong to friends, we should *nevertheless* go on calling such relationships forms of *philia* because that is how people in fact speak. He is rather *defending* the practice of speaking that way by arguing not just that some such relationships exhibit the defining features of *philia* (such as mutually acknowledged and reciprocal well-wishing for the other's sake) but also that nothing prevents relationships that do exhibit the defining features from sometimes also exhibiting (at least to some extent) other features (such as durability) that should ideally belong to friendships but do not always do so. His claim is that these other features belong to character-friendships *in themselves*, while they belong *only accidentally* (if at all) in relationships based on pleasure or utility. But when they *do* belong, even if only accidentally, we are justified in speaking of a kind of friendship.

6. *NICOMACHEAN ETHICS* IX.4–6: *TA PHILIKA* VERSUS THE DEFINING FEATURES OF *PHILIA*

There is evidence in *EN* IX.4–6 that Aristotle distinguishes the defining features of *philia* from other features of it in precisely the way required by my account. IX.4 begins as follows: "*Ta philika* in relation to one's neighbors *and* the features by which friendships [*philiai*] are defined would seem to be derived from the features of one's relation to oneself" [*EN* IX.4, 1166a1–2]. Aristotle then presents a list of various features by which *philia* is said to be defined:

1. Wishing and doing goods or apparent goods for the sake of the other.
2. Wishing the other to exist and to live for his sake (which is what mothers, and friends who have quarreled, experience).

3. Spending time together and choosing the same things.
4. Experiencing pain and pleasure together with one's friend (which happens most of all in the case of mothers).

There is no explicit mention of *eunoia* here, nor anywhere in the remainder of *EN* IX.4's comparison of friendship to (proper) self-love. *Eunoia* reappears as such at the start of IX.5, which is devoted to *eunoia* and begins thus: "*eunoia* seems like [something] *philikon*." And IX.6, which is devoted to like-mindedness [*homonoia*], begins in much the same way: "*homonoia* seems to be *philikon*." So IX.5 and 6 seem to be moving on, after IX.4's discussion of the defining features, to *ta philika*.

EN VIII.6 contains a hint (borne out here) about how Aristotle may distinguish *ta philika* from the defining features. He is speaking there about things like good temper and enjoying one another's company, which he says are "most *philika* and productive [*poêtika*] of *philia*" [*EN* VIII.6, 1158a2–4]. So '*ta philika*' may sometimes refer to things insofar as they are *productive* of *philia*. This does not exclude its sometimes referring to things characteristic of *philia* or even constitutive of it. But it seems that the emphasis, in calling things *philika*, is on their being productive of *philia*. And this is borne out at *EN* IX.5.1167a2–3, where Aristotle says that *eunoia* is a source [*archê*] of *philia*, just as the pleasure occasioned by sight is a source of *erôs*.

If Aristotle regards *eunoia* proper as one of *ta philika* and not as one of the defining features, then it would not follow from any restriction of *eunoia* proper to character-friendship that the lower forms fail to exhibit one of the defining features: they can still count as forms of *philia* if they involve reciprocal wishing-of-goods-to-the-other-for-the-other's-sake (along with whatever other features are required for something to count as *philia*). So we need to ask this: what exactly are the defining features? And to what extent (if at all) are these features present in the lower forms?

We shall see below that (3) and (4) play important roles in Aristotle's account of the character-friend as an "other self." But which of (2)–(4) he counts as a defining feature must take a back seat here to the question to what extent he takes (1) to be satisfied in friendships based on pleasure and utility. For he clearly takes (1) to be a defining feature.

7. DIGRESSION ON *DIA*: EFFICIENT CAUSAL, FINAL CAUSAL, OR BOTH?

Much of the dispute about whether friendships based on utility and pleasure satisfy (1) has focused on the question of how to understand the preposition '*dia*' in Aristotle's talk of "friendships *dia* virtue, pleasure, and utility." This could refer simply to what causes the parties to have the relevant attitudes toward one another in an efficient causal sense; or it could refer to the final cause, i.e., to the end or purpose for the sake of which their relationship exists; or it could refer to both. Irwin 1999, at 274 argues that the '*dia*' expresses both efficient causal and final causal relations. On his account, those who love *dia* pleasure (or *dia* utility) love each other not simply as a result of the pleasure (or utility) each has received from the other, but also for the sake of such pleasure (or utility) as each expects to receive from the other.

Cooper 1999 argues, against this, that '*dia*' is primarily (efficient) causal and "at least as much retrospective as prospective." He reads Aristotle as

> making, in effect, the psychological claim that those who have enjoyed one another's company or have been mutually benefited through their common association, will, as a result of the benefits or the pleasures they receive, tend to wish for and be willing to act in the interest of the other person's good, independently of consideration of their *own* welfare or pleasure. [Cooper 1999, 323]

Cooper says it is "compatible" with this that each party should *expect* the friendship to yield pleasure (or utility) for himself. But pleasure (or utility) is nevertheless the "cause, not the goal, of the well-wishing" (1999, 324).

As we shall see below, Aristotle himself takes his account of *philia* to rely on the sort of psychological tendencies on which Cooper's reading of it relies. So it is plausible to read Aristotle as claiming that people tend, as a matter of psychological fact, to become fond of those they find pleasant or those who have been useful to them; and as claiming that people tend, as a matter of psychological fact, to wish goods to those of whom they are fond and to do so for the latter's sake (as distinct from their own). But we cannot read Aristotle this way if we are *required* to read his talk of friendship *dia* pleasure (or *dia* utility) as expressing final (as well as efficient) causal relations.

Irwin 1999 at 274 cites two passages that he takes to "associate '*dia*' clearly with the final cause." His *translation* of the second [*EN* X.2, 1172b21] associates them clearly: "What is most choiceworthy is what we choose not because of, or for the sake of, something else." But in suggesting that "for the sake of" explicates "because of" Irwin ignores the clear "neither/nor" structure of Aristotle's sentence, which (nontendentiously translated) reads as follows: "what is most choiceworthy is what we choose *neither* on account of something else *nor* for the sake of something else [*mê di' heteron mêd' heterou charin*]." Properly translated, this sentence tells more against than for the association of '*dia*' with the final cause.

And this is just what we should expect, given the prominence of Plato's *Lysis* in the background. For Socrates clearly distinguishes that *dia*-which (or on account of which) *A* is friend to *B* from that *heneka*-which (or for the sake of which) *A* is friend to *B*: it is *dia* something bad (namely, disease), but *heneka* something good (namely, health), that the sick person loves or is friend to the doctor [217–19]. And Socrates explicitly *rejects* the idea that we should equate loving *B heneka* some good with loving *B dia* some bad: he argues that even if all the bad things *dia* which *A* is friend to *B* were abolished, *A* might still be friend to *B heneka* some good [220c–d]. Aristotle might, of course, reject the Socratic distinction. But in that case, we should expect him to call attention (as he does elsewhere) to his disagreement with Socrates.

So Irwin's case rests primarily on *EN* VIII.3, 1156a31. But this, when read in context, provides at most weak support:

> The *philia* of young people seems to be *di' hêdonên*. For they live in accordance with their passion, and pursue above all what is pleasant for themselves and what is present [*to paron*]. Since they are of a volatile age, their pleasures are different <at different times>. Hence they become friends quickly and stop <quickly>. [1156a31–35]

This is compatible with Cooper's view: because young folk tend to pursue what is pleasant, they may (as a matter of psychological fact) tend to wish and do goods to those they find pleasant, and they may do so at least as much for the sake of those they find pleasant as for their own sakes (though they may do so only as long as they continue to find one another pleasant). Aristotle may simply be citing the common tendency of young folk to do all sorts of crazy things for their friends, without much regard for their *own* interests. This seems, in fact, to be the point of his reference to "what is present": young folk act according to their present passions without regard to their own future interests (including their own future passions). This is why, as Aristotle explains in *Rhetoric* II.12–13, it is so much easier to take advantage of young than of old folk, who tend to be so jealous of their own interests that they do not even enjoy one another's company. These chapters explicitly oppose the sort of calculating attention to one's own advantage that Aristotle takes to be characteristic of old age to the sort of non-calculating attitude he takes to be characteristic of youth; and they explicitly associate the latter with preferring what is *kalon* to what is advantageous.

Note, moreover, that even if we accept Irwin's association of '*dia*' with the final cause, *Politics* (*Pol.*) I.2 shows that we cannot move immediately from the claim that a relationship *comes to be* for the sake of some end to the conclusion that the relationship *continues to exist* for the sake of that end. After explaining that man and woman couple to produce offspring, and that the resulting families (*oikoi*, which exist in order to serve daily needs) form villages for the sake of satisfying other (not merely daily) needs, and that villages come together to form the polis, Aristotle says that the polis is the first community that is virtually self-sufficient and that it "*comes to be* for the sake of living, but *exists* for the sake of living well" [*Pol.* I.2, 1252b29–30]. Moreover, Aristotle explicitly allows some such phenomenon in the case of *philia*: some friendships that come to be for the sake of pleasure later exist in the absence of the relevant sort of pleasure if, from the friends' association with one another, they have become fond of one another's characters [*EN* VIII.4, 1157a7–12].

Still, Aristotle's claim that friendships based on pleasure and utility tend to dissolve when the parties cease to find one another pleasant or useful seems to support Irwin's general view. For even if, as a result of the pleasure or utility I have received from my friend, I wish well to her, and seek occasion by occasion to benefit her *without* an eye to my own pleasure or utility, the fact that I would *not* continue to do so if I ceased to expect pleasure or utility from the relationship seems good reason to say that my primary goal is *my* pleasure or *my* utility. And Aristotle himself seems to agree when he says that those who love on account of what is useful or pleasant love one another not "in themselves" [*kath' hautous*]—nor "for being persons of a certain sort" [*tô(i) poious tinas einai*] or "insofar as each is who he is" [*hê(i)] estin hosper estin]*—but rather insofar as the other is pleasant or useful to themselves [*EN* VIII.3, 1156a10–16].

But *why* does Aristotle introduce the technical language he typically uses to characterize the distinction between a thing's essence and its accidents? Why does he not say simply that those who love on account of utility (or pleasure) love only themselves and not the other—full stop? One (I think good) way to explain this is to read him as allowing that those who are friends on account of pleasure or utility really *do* wish one another well for the *other's* sake, and so satisfy the most important condition for being friends, with the result that he needs to explain what is *special* about the sort of wishing-well-for-the-other's-sake we find in character-friendship. So he appeals to the idea that *this* wishing-well-for-the-other's-sake is based on something essential to who the *other* is, and not simply on accidental features of her that might change with time, including the relationships in which she stands to the agent's own contingent tastes and/or needs. By focusing on essential features of the object, he minimizes the role played by the merely accidental tastes and needs of the agent as things *dia* which she might come to be fond of the other and so to wish him well for *his* sake. But in cases where accidental features of the parties *do* result in each being fond of the other and wishing the other well for her sake, Aristotle seems to allow that (1) *is* satisfied, even if only accidentally and only temporarily: that is why these cases fail to exhibit *all* the features (such as durability) that should *ideally* belong to friendship.

8. *NICOMACHEAN ETHICS* IX.7 (VIII.8 AND 12): BENEFACTORS, POETS, AND PARENTS

We can now begin to see the role played in Aristotle's account by facts about what people tend, as a matter of psychological fact, to love and cherish. Aristotle makes prominent use of such facts in *EN* IX.7, where he seeks to explain why benefactors seem to love their beneficiaries more than their beneficiaries love them. People find this puzzling because they expect beneficiaries to love their benefactors, on account of the benefits received from them, *more* than their benefactors love them. Aristotle rejects the common attempt to explain this by comparing benefactors to creditors and beneficiaries to debtors, and then claiming that debtors wish their creditors did not exist while creditors actually wish for the preservation of their debtors. For he denies that benefactors resemble creditors, who wish their debtors to be preserved for the sake of [*heneka*] recovering what they themselves are owed and so fail to satisfy (2): benefactors often love and cherish [*philousi kai agapôsi*] those whom they have benefited even if the latter are in no way useful to them and unlikely to become so later [*EN* IX.7, 1167b28–33]. The true explanation, he says, seems to be "more natural":[13]

> It is just what happens in the case of artists. For every <artist> loves and cherishes his own work [*to oikeion ergon*] more than he would be cherished by the work if it came to be ensouled. This happens especially perhaps in the case of poets; for they over-cherish their own poems [*ta oikeia poiêmata*], being fond of them as if they were their <own> children. And the case of benefactors seems to be like this. For the one benefited is their work, and they cherish this more than the work cherishes the one having produced it. The explanation of this is that being is choiceworthy[14] and lovable for all; and we exist in <our> activity, for to live is to act; and in activity, the producer is in a way the work <itself>; indeed he is fond of the work because <he is fond> also of <his own> being. And this is natural. [*EN* IX.7, 1167b33–1168a8]

This explanation appeals to human nature: to facts about what people, as a matter of psychological fact, tend to love and cherish and not (as the explanation that Aristotle seeks to supplant) to the specific motives of particular sorts of agents.

Aristotle cites several other such facts: for the benefactor, the beneficent activities are *kalon*, but for the beneficiary, they are merely advantageous, which is less pleasant and lovable than what is *kalon* [*EN* IX.7.1168a9–12]; everyone is fonder of the things that come about as a result of their own labor, which is why those who have earned their money are fonder of it than those who have inherited it [a21–23]. The points have little to do with the ends for the sake of which particular individuals act: people *just do* tend to find what is *kalon* more pleasant and more lovable than what is merely advantageous; and they *just do* tend to be fonder of things that have come about as a result of their own labor than of things that have not. Moreover, Aristotle's appeal to what is *kalon* may signal the *lack* of any ulterior motive: for he routinely associates the virtuous agent's choice of virtuous actions *for themselves* with acting for the sake of *to kalon*.

The chapter concludes, "And it seems that receiving benefit is effortless, while doing benefit involves work. On account of these things, mothers are more child-loving [*philoteknoterai*] <than fathers are>. For the genesis involves more labor on their part, and they know better <than fathers do> that the children come from themselves" [1168a23–27]. This should be compared with two other passages where motherly love is cited as paradigmatic. The first is in *EN* VIII.8, where—after arguing that being loved is better than being honored because being loved is enjoyed for itself in a way that

---

[13] [For further discussion of Aristotle's distinction between investigating things *phusikôs* and investigating things *logikôs*, see sec. 6 of "*Nicomachean Ethics* 7.3 on Akratic Ignorance" (III.7) (co-authored with Martin Pickavé).]

[14] [The Greek is '*haireton*,' which I have elsewhere rendered 'such-as-to-be-chosen' (on which see note 12 of "Self-Love and Authoritative Virtue" (Chapter 4, this volume). But see "The Pleasures of Thinking Together" (Chapter 7, this volume) for qualifications of the claim that being (or life) is *always* such-as-to-be-chosen.]

being honored is not—Aristotle claims that *philia* consists even more in loving than in being loved. He cites as evidence the fact that some mothers give up their own children to be raised by others and then love their children without seeking to be loved in return (if they cannot have both), it being sufficient for them to see the children doing well [*EN* VIII.8, 1159a16–34].

The second appears in *EN* VIII.12:

> Parents are fond of their children as being something of themselves [*hôs heautôn ti onta*], and children <are fond of> their parents as <themselves> being something from them [viz., the parents]. But parents know the things coming from themselves more than their offspring know that they are from them [viz., the parents]; and the one *from which* is more familiar with [*sunôkeiôtai*] the *one generated* than the one coming to be is with its producer. For what comes from oneself is *oikeion* to the one from which it comes . . . but the one from which <the latter comes> is in no way <*oikeion*> to it, or <at least> less so. And <these phenomena vary> with the length of time <involved>. For <parents> are fond of <their children> immediately upon their <children's> coming to be, while children <are fond of> their parents only after some time, when they have acquired comprehension [*sunesis*][15] or perception. From these things it is clear why *mothers love <their children> more <than their children love them>*.[16] Parents, then, love their children as themselves [*hôs heautous*], for the ones coming to be from them are like other selves [*hoion heteroi autoi*], by being separated <from them>). [1161b18–29]

Please note the role played here not just by what is *oikeion* to a subject, but also by the subject's *recognition* of it as such: this is supposed to help explain the kind of affection people tend as a matter of fact to have. Note especially my rendering of '*sunôkeiôtai*' as "familiar with." Ross (1980) has "attached to," which is good insofar as it suggests some sort of emotional bond; Irwin (1999) has "regards . . . as more his own," which is less good insofar as it suggests something primarily cognitive. I prefer "familiar with" both because it preserves the etymological connections with '*sun*' (meaning "with") and '*oikos*' (whose focal referent is the family), and because it has both cognitive and affective aspects: it suggests not only *recognizing that* something is *oikeion* to one, but also the sort of *emotional affiliation* people tend to have with those with whom they have lived. It suggests a bond requiring a certain kind of perception or understanding, which is why it takes time for children to achieve it.

---

[15] *Sunesis* is what *Republic* 376 says dogs have when they recognize people as *oikeion* [familiar] or *allotrion* [alien]: it is a kind of *comprehending perception*, which is what is needed to engender a child's fondness for its parents. [For related points, see sec. 6 of "The Lockeanism of Aristotle" [III.8].]

[16] The point here is *not* (as Ross and Irwin render it) that mothers tend to love their children *more than fathers do*: the thrust of this argument (as distinct from the one in *EN* IX.7) is that parents (at least initially) tend to love their children *more than their children love them*. If mothers are suddenly singled out here, that may be because Aristotle thinks (for reasons cited in IX.7) that mothers tend to love their children more than fathers do.

Aristotle is preparing here for his account of character-friendship, which is also a developmental achievement: it takes time and intimacy for the parties to become familiar with one another in ways such that they are "other selves" to each other, each appreciating and enjoying the other's activities in something like the way she appreciates and enjoys her own. But the apparent assimilation of character-friendship to the attitude of parents toward their children may give us pause. For this makes it seem as if Aristotle's account of character-friendship is grounded in the sort of egocentric bias on which ethnocentric and other objectionable forms of bias are based. So we must pause to see that this is not the case.

The first step is to see that *even* in the case of relations among kin, Aristotle treats character-friendship as the ideal. He compares *philia* between brothers to that between companions, especially to that between companions who are decent (presumably character-friends or those on the way to becoming so) but more generally to that between companions who resemble one another (presumably pleasure-friends, who tend to enjoy the same things, rather than utility-friends, who tend to differ in ways that allow each to provide the other with things he cannot provide for himself) [*EN* VIII.12, 1162a9–15]. I think it significant that Aristotle runs the comparison this way, rather than the other way around: pleasure-friendships are his most common paradigm, and character-friendships his most esteemed paradigm, so he points to ways in which *philia* between brothers is similar to these, not to the ways in which these are similar to it. And as he goes on to say, relations among family members—particularly between husband and wife—typically involve a mix of pleasure and utility, but they *can* also be "*dia* virtue *if* the parties are decent, for there is a virtue <characteristic> of each, and <each> will delight in such <virtue as the other has>" [VIII.12, 1162a25–27].

Aristotle clearly represents character-friendship as the ideal toward which even blood relations should aspire. This suggests that his appeal to psychological facts about whom and how we *do* love is not a crude attempt to justify conclusions about whom and how we *ought* to love, but rather a strategy for establishing the *possibility* of attitudes he seeks eventually to *recommend*. Given the prevalence of skepticism about the very *possibility* of these attitudes—the sort of skepticism betrayed, for example, in the common attempt to assimilate benefactors to creditors—Aristotle seeks to show how the attitudes he would recommend are made *possible* by *natural* human tendencies (such as parents' affection for their children and artists' affection for their work).

9. ETHNOCENTRISM AND ARISTOTLE'S ETHOCENTRIC IDEAL[17]

We may better appreciate Aristotle's strategy once we have noted a common error in recent translations of *EN* VIII.1. After saying that *philia* seems to belong by nature to

[17] [Please pay attention here. The copy-editor for my "Impersonal Friends" once failed to do so and substituted 'ethnocentric' for every occurrence of 'ethocentric' in that paper, thus rendering nonsense my claim that the point of ethocentric reasons is to combat the vices associated with ethnocentric

parents in relation to their offspring, and to offspring in relation to their parents, Aristotle says that such *philia* (perhaps including natural *philia* more generally) occurs

> not only among human beings, but also among birds and most animals, and among those belonging to the same clan [*tois homoethnesi*], especially human beings; whence we praise those who are lovers of humankind [*philanthrôpous*]; for one might see in traveling widely that every human is *oikeion* to every other and [likewise] dear [*philon*] <to every other>. [*EN* VIII.1, 1155a14–22]

Ross 1980 renders '*tois homoethnesi*,' correctly enough, "members of the same *race*."[18] Irwin and Rowe have each recently replaced this with talk of "belonging to the same *species*." Irwin defends "species" by saying that "the rest of the paragraph shows that Aristotle has species in mind (i.e., friendship among dogs or human beings, rather than friendship among greyhounds or Greeks)" (1999: 273). But this misses Aristotle's point, which is that human beings stand out among animals as especially *clannish*. We are the most *ethnocentric—or*, as Aristotle puts it, the most *homoethnic—of* animals. That is why we *praise* those who are (simply) *philanthrôpoi*: they have managed to overcome this common but regrettable tendency.

Those who take Aristotle's conception of the friend as an "other self" as endorsing bias toward those similar to oneself may be tempted to dismiss the point about praising those who are simply *philanthrôpoi* as mere endoxic chatter. But that would be rash. For taking Aristotle to *endorse* such bias rests on the mistaken view that he takes *similarity as such* not simply to *explain* but also to *justify* partiality toward those similar to oneself. But part of his point in recommending the character-friendship ideal is to precisely reject such egocentric views.[19]

Instead of taking the legitimacy of brute self-love for granted and seeking—as on rational egoist readings—to extend it to others, Aristotle argues in IX.8 that brute

ties. Writing as I do in the wake of the acquittal of George Zimmerman for the murder of Trayvon Martin, to mention just one of all too many such acquittals, I cannot overemphasize the importance of *ethocentric*—as distinct from *ethnocentric*—reasons.]

[18] [I have added "correctly enough" to prevent the mistake made by Michael Pakaluk in his Blog (http://dissoiblogoi.blogspot.ca/2006/10/whiting-on-philanthropia.html) of taking me to include Ross among the "recent commentators" whose mistake I seek to expose. I suspect, from the more general remarks preceding his criticism, that Pakaluk was seeking grounds on which to reject my views because he thinks they are inconsistent with the sort of emphasis on blood relations that figure in the Stoic theory of *oikeiôsis*. He wrote as though I had been unaware of the reasons for which some scholars see that theory as having roots in Aristotle. So just for the record, I actually had the Stoic theory of *oikeiôsis* in mind when writing. But rather than emphasizing its roots in blood relations, I tend to emphasize the ways in which the Stoic theory aimed to extend to other the kind of concern we have for our blood relations. For some attempt on my part to present the roots of the Stoic theory in Aristotle (and Plato), see secs. 5 and 6 of "The Lockeanism of Aristotle" (III.8).]

[19] I do *not* take the fact that Aristotle sometimes *expresses* ethnocentric (and other) biases to show that he *endorses* such bias as such. He may simply fail (like most of us) to recognize his own biases for what they are. For more on the ethocentric—or character-centered—ideal, see Whiting 1991 ["Impersonal Friends" (I.2). For more on the dangers of these biases, see "Trusting 'First' and 'Second' Selves" (I.3).]

self-love is *not* justified.[20] As the *Magna Moralia* puts it, "[the good man] is a lover-of-good [*philagathos*], not a lover-of-self [*philautos*]; for he loves himself only, if at all, because he is good" [II.14, 1212b18–20]. So if, as *EN* IX.4 suggests, the virtuous agent's attitudes toward his friends derives from his attitudes toward himself, he will not love his friends because they are his "other selves" in the sense that they are simply *like* him: he will love them, as he loves *himself*, because they are *good*. Any likeness they bear to him is a mere sign of what really matters—namely, their respective goodness.[21]

Note, in support of this, that in listing what seem to be the constitutive conditions of *philia*, the closest Aristotle comes to mentioning sameness or even similarity of character is in (3), when he speaks of friends "choosing the same things." But this does not require friends to be the same or even similar in character. People who are radically different may choose the same objects—perhaps because they agree (in spite of their differences) on the goodness of those objects, or perhaps because (as we tend to think characteristic of friendship) each chooses some objects for the sake of the other in the sense that she chooses these objects primarily because they are what the *other* wants.

Nor does Aristotle mention *homonoia* among the candidates for constitutive conditions. He no doubt thinks that character-friends are both similar in character and like-minded. But he may think that such similarity and like-mindedness count more as productive of *philia* than as constitutive of it. Such similarity and agreement may also result from or be reinforced by the relationship. There is clearly a complicated nexus here. But let us recall the *Lysis*, where Socrates and his interlocutors failed to account for *philia either* in terms of similarities between the parties *or* in terms of dissimilarities: Socrates then suggests that they appeal instead to the idea of what is *oikeion* to the parties, but insists that they refuse to *reduce* talk of what is *oikeion* to talk of what is *similar*.

Let us turn, keeping this in mind, to Aristotle's initial description of character-friendship:

> Each <friend> is good both *haplôs* and *for his friend*. For good people are both good *haplôs* and beneficial to one another. And they are similarly pleasant. For good people are pleasant both *haplôs* and *to one another*. For each finds his own actions [*hai oikeiai praxeis*] and such actions <in general> [*hai toiautai*] pleasant, and <the actions> of good people are the same or similar [*hai autai ê homoiai*]. [*EN* VIII.3, 1156b12–17].

We are now in a position to see that "his own" may not quite capture what Aristotle intends: '*oikeiai*' might mean not (or not simply) that the actions are strictly speaking

[20] For detailed analysis of *EN* IX.8, which I cannot provide here, see "Self-Love and Authoritative Virtue" (Chapter 4, this volume)].

[21] [See also "Love: Self-Propagation, Self-Preservation, or Ekstasis?" (I.7).]

the agent's *own*, but rather (or also) that they are somehow *familiar* or even *appropriate* to him.

It is clear from Aristotle's reference to the proverbial potters that he does not think that everyone finds actions *like* her own pleasant [*EE* VII.1, 1235a18–19]. Those who compete in some domain are often *pained* when they see *others* performing the sort of actions they *enjoy* seeing *themselves* perform. Whether one is pained or pleased depends on whether one values the actions in question *for themselves*, in which case one is likely to take pleasure in such actions simply as such; or whether one values the actions *as means to some further end* (such as wealth or honor) for the sake of which one competes with others. The point about good agents is that they value virtuous action *for itself* and *not* (either not simply or not primarily) *insofar as it is their own*. So virtuous agents tend, as a matter of psychological fact, to be similarly pleased by their own and others' virtuous actions.

This is part of the point of *EN* IX.4's talk of the way in which the virtuous person's attitudes toward others are derived from her attitudes toward herself. Some would take Aristotle's derivation in a more linguistic way, as saying that we *call* a relationship *philia* whenever two parties exhibit toward one another the sort of attitudes that each of us, given our natural tendency to *self*-love, takes toward him- or herself. But we can make better sense of the overall argument if we read IX.4 as making instead (or perhaps in addition) a somewhat different and primarily psychological point: namely, that the attitudes constitutive of *philia* are derived, as a matter of psychological fact, from the attitudes constitutive of the virtuous person's love for herself. For much of the surrounding argument appeals to such psychological facts. And Aristotle's point seems to be (at least partly) that insofar as a genuinely virtuous person loves and values virtue simply as such, and so loves and values herself (at least partly) insofar as she is virtuous, the virtuous person will as a matter of psychological fact be disposed to love other virtuous persons on account of *their* virtues. This contributes to a puzzle that Aristotle goes on to discuss in *EN* IX.8—namely, whether one should [*dei*] love oneself, or someone else, most of all.[22]

Aristotle resolves this puzzle by rejecting the dichotomous assumption on which it turns: that one must *either* love oneself most of all *or* love someone else most of all. Once we accept his distinction between self-love properly construed and self-love as it is usually (but mistakenly) understood, we are supposed to see an important sense in which self-love properly construed is impartial: insofar as self-love properly construed involves the virtuous person's love for herself qua virtuous, and insofar as a genuinely virtuous agent will value virtue as such, the virtuous agent should love other virtuous agents in much the same way that she loves herself (i.e., qua virtuous). By the end of IX.8 the "most of all" has dropped out: Aristotle concludes by saying simply that one should love oneself in the proper sense but not in the vulgar sense. It is compatible

[22] Please note (for future reference) that '*dei*' is here rendered "should" by Ross and Rowe, and "ought to" by Irwin.

with this that one should also love others in the proper sense, and even that one should love at least some others equally with oneself: perhaps this is how one should love one's "other selves."

This might be taken to suggest that the pleasure virtuous agents take in the virtuous actions of their friends (and perhaps even in the virtuous actions of strangers) is at least potentially equal to the pleasure they take in their own virtuous actions. But this does not follow. The point is that virtuous agents can sometimes take the same *kind* of pleasure in their own and others' virtuous actions. Other factors, especially epistemological ones, may limit the *extent* to which virtuous agents can appreciate (and so enjoy) the actions of others in the same way that they can appreciate (and so enjoy) their own. That Aristotle is aware of such factors is clear from his emphasis on the need for time and intimacy [*sunêtheia*].

Aristotle has two related reasons for requiring intimacy—one epistemological and one hedonic. Their relation is clear from *Poetics* 4, where Aristotle calls humans the "most mimetic of animals" and says that all enjoy imitations. Even in cases where seeing the objects themselves is painful—for example, with disgusting creatures or corpses—we enjoy viewing images of them because understanding is most pleasant, and in contemplating [*theôrountas*] such images we understand or work out what each is [*Poetics* 4, 1448b5–17]. Aristotle speaks here of the sheer joy of recognition, which increases when the object is *kalon*—as, for example, when we witness virtuous actions and recognize them as such.[23]

But matters are more complicated when it comes to observing *actions*. For superficially similar behaviors can result from radically different motives and can thus constitute radically different sorts of action. So we must know something about the *reasons* for which another acts, which involves having some knowledge of her *character*, before we are in a position to understand (and so enjoy) her actions in ways like those in which we typically understand (and so enjoy) our own (which is not to say that we are not sometimes more prone to error with regard to our own). There are thus *epistemological* constraints on the extent to which a virtuous agent can *enjoy* the virtuous actions of others. But we should not forget that these are constraints on a kind of *enjoyment*. For this gets lost in Cooper's interpretation of *EN* IX.9, which emphasizes epistemological aspects of the character-friends' contemplation of one another's actions at the expense of hedonic ones. Let me explain.

10. *NICOMACHEAN ETHICS* IX.9: THE *LYSIS* PUZZLE REVISITED

EN IX.9 begins with a puzzle:

> <On the one hand> people say that those who are blessed and self-sufficient have no need of friends. For the good things <in life> belong to them, and being

[23] [This point lies at the heart of "The Pleasures of Thinking Together" (Chapter 7, this volume).]

> self-sufficient they will need nothing in addition. But the friend, being another self, <is one who> provides the things one is unable to get on one's own . . .
>
> <On the other hand> it seems strange, when assigning all good things to one who is *eudaimôn*, not to grant him friends, which seem to be the greatest of external goods . . . And it is strange to make the blessed person solitary. For no one would choose to have all good things by himself [*kath' hauton*]. For man is political and by nature such as to live with others. So this [i.e., living together with others] will belong to one who is *eudaimôn*. For he has all the things that are good by nature. [*EN* IX.9, 1169b3–20]

Aristotle proceeds to diagnose the error behind the first view while preserving the element of truth contained in it. Its proponents are right, he thinks, that the friend is an "other self." But they have the wrong conception of this: they think it means someone who provides one with goods one *cannot* provide for oneself. This is largely because they think of friends as *useful*. So they move illegitimately from the claim that the blessed person has no need of *such* friends (i.e., *utility* friends) to the conclusion that she has no need of *any* friends [*EN* IX.9, 1169b23–28].[24]

The rest of IX.9 aims to clarify the "other self" doctrine with a view to elucidating the sense in which (as the final sentence says) one who is going to be *eudaimôn* will need [*deêsei*] to have excellent friends. Many commentators have found Aristotle's arguments for this disappointing. But that may stem more from their failure to understand his intended conclusion than from his failure to provide adequate arguments for it.

Consider, for example, Cooper. Like others, he takes Aristotle to be asking a *justificatory* question analogous to the familiar "why be moral?" question. In his view, Aristotle seeks to provide reasons why someone who aims to flourish *should* arrange things "so that he becomes attached to certain people in the ways characteristic of friendship" (1999, 337). Cooper is thus troubled by the fact that the arguments Aristotle actually gives seem to answer a different and less interesting question: namely, why will someone who already has friends "need or want to do things for them or with them?" Cooper thinks the answer, which is primarily *explanatory* of the actual attitudes and tendencies of friends, is less interesting in two ways. First, it is too easy: for it simply follows from what it *means* to be a friend that one who has a friend will, as a matter of psychological fact, want to do things with and for her friend. Second, and more importantly, the answer begs the question of why one who aims to flourish should have friends in the *first* place. So Cooper seeks to tease out of Aristotle's explicit arguments two implicit arguments that *justify* having friends in the first place.

Cooper turns for help to the *Magna Moralia*. For he takes *Magna Moralia* II.15, 1213a7–26 to argue that self-knowledge is *necessary* for eudaimonia and that character-friendship is the only (or at least the best) way to achieve self-knowledge. The idea

[24] I take "such friends" [*tôn toioutôn philôn*] in b27 to pick up '*tôn toioutôn*' in b24, and I read the intervening remarks about pleasure-friendship as parenthetical.

there is that bias toward oneself prevents one from seeing clearly what one is really like, and that just as one needs to look into a mirror to see one's own face, so too one needs to look upon someone similar in character to oneself in order to study one's own character. Cooper thinks the argument at *EN* IX.9, 1169b18–1170a4 is similar insofar as it claims first "that the good and flourishing man wants to study [*theôrein, EN* IX.9, 1169b33, 1170a2; *theasasthai, MM* II.15, 1213a16] good actions"; and second "that one cannot, or cannot so easily, study one's own actions as those of another."

But it may be significant that Aristotle describes the object of the virtuous agent's choice as, simply, to contemplate decent and appropriate actions [*EN* IX.9, 1170a1–3]: he does not suggest that the agent seeks primarily to contemplate her *own* actions. When he says that the virtuous agent will need virtuous friends if she chooses to study such actions (i.e., decent and appropriate ones), his point may be simply that she cannot (or cannot easily) contemplate her own actions, and so will have to get her *contemplative* pleasures (as distinct from her *engaged* pleasures) from observing the actions of others whose actions she is in a position to appreciate. His point need not concern her pursuit of self-knowledge.

The main obstacle to finding the *Magna Moralia* argument in the *Nicomachean Ethics* is that where the *Magna Moralia* talks about coming to know [*gnônai*] oneself, the *Nicomachean Ethics* speaks of perception or awareness [*aisthêsis* or *sunaisthêsis*] of oneself.[25] And one might be aware of oneself and one's own activities without knowing what they are really like. Cooper attempts to bridge the gap partly by rendering '*theôrein*' as "to study" rather than (as often appropriate) "to contemplate" or "to observe" (1999, 344 n. 13). He is effectively providing the contemplation of virtuous actions with an *end*: namely, the subject's acquisition of the kind of self-knowledge he takes Aristotle to treat as a "prerequisite of flourishing" (1999, 345). But this makes the reason Aristotle gives for having friends more instrumental than I think Aristotle wants to allow. For it assimilates the value of having friends to the value of being honored.

On Cooper's account, we value decent friends insofar as they serve, like honor from decent people, to confirm our sense of our own worth. But Aristotle regards the value even of such honor as "more superficial" than the value he seeks in would-be components of *eudaimonia* [*EN* I.5, 1095b22–26]. He explicitly contrasts the instrumental value of honor with the intrinsic value of both loving and being loved when he says that being loved is valued for itself in a way that being honored is not, and then cites the joy mothers take in loving *even when their love is not returned* as evidence that loving is even *more* valuable than being loved. So it seems unlikely that Aristotle would assimilate the value of having friends to the value of honor.

The second argument that Cooper teases out of *EN* IX.9 (from 1170a4–11) is similar to the first: he takes Aristotle's claim that it is easier to be continuously active in the company of friends than by oneself as resting partly on claims about the ways in which

---

[25] [For more on *sunaisthêsis*, see "The Lockeanism of Aristotle" (III.8).]

activities engaged in with those we respect provide "concrete and immediate" "confirmation of the worth" of our own pursuits (Cooper 1999, 346–48). But *EN* IX.9 seems to point in the opposite direction: its point is that contemplating the virtuous activity of one's character-friend is something good and pleasant *in itself*.[26] And Aristotle may well have used '*theôrein*' precisely to capture the *intrinsic* value of the activity in question, as distinct from any instrumental value it might have. For *theôria* is his paradigm of an activity engaged in for itself.

Cooper mentions other ways in which Aristotle may think that sharing in activities with others serves to augment one's own activity. For example, the agent "can be said to be active—indirectly—whenever and wherever any of the group is at work." But this approximates Irwin's suggestion that Aristotle regards the activity of one's friend as an "extension" of one's own: where Irwin speaks of the ways in which having friends allows an agent "to realize *himself* more fully than [he would] if he had no friend" (1988, 393),[27] Cooper speaks of shared activities as "expand[ing] the scope of one's activity by enabling one to participate, through membership in a group of jointly active persons, in the actions of others" (1999, 349). So Cooper and Irwin seem in the end to share the same fundamental outlook. Each takes Aristotle to be concerned primarily with the *justificatory* question: why have friends in the *first* place?

Aristotle no doubt believes that someone who has good friends will realize herself more fully than she would if she had no friends. But if he allows this to serve as the agent's reason for having friends in the first place, he threatens to undermine the primacy of wishing and doing well to another for the *other's* sake. For even if having friends involves some sort of wishing them well for *their* sakes, it is problematic for the agent to take as her reason for having friends the fact that doing so is the only (or the best) way to achieve the sort of self-knowledge or self-realization in which *her eudaimonia* consists. But we *need not* read Aristotle as arguing in this way.

We could resolve Cooper's original problem by reading Aristotle *either* as less concerned with the justificatory project than Cooper takes him to be *or* as concerned with a somewhat weaker justificatory project than the one Cooper has in mind. For the explanatory arguments that Aristotle gives may be more interesting than Cooper allows. Consider a context in which it is *assumed* that friendship involves conditions like wishing good to another for the other's sake but there are people who doubt that such conditions are ever—or *can* ever—be satisfied. In such contexts, there might be some point to explaining how it is *possible* for someone to take the same sort of intrinsic interest in another's good (or to derive the same sort of intrinsic enjoyment from another's activity) as she takes in her own good (or derives from her own activity). There might even be some point in arguing that virtuous agents are, as a matter of psychological fact, disposed to take this sort of interest in the good of other virtuous

---

[26] [This is pretty clearly the point in the Eudemian version of this chapter, discussed in detail in "The Pleasures of Thinking Together" (Chapter 7, this volume).]

[27] See, more generally, secs. 197–215 of Irwin 1988.

agents with whom they are acquainted and to derive this sort of enjoyment from the virtuous activities of those with whom they are intimate. For one could then argue that, given this tendency, a virtuous person who aims to flourish not only *will* have friends but *should* have virtuous friends in the sense that there is *good reason* for her to do so: such friends are pleasant (and in that sense goods) for her. This provides a kind of justification for having friends that does not threaten the self-sufficiency of the would-be eudaimôn.

Note that the conclusion of *EN* IX.9 is open to stronger and weaker interpretations. For '*deêsei*' can be taken either (as Cooper and Irwin take it) as expressing a hard 'must' or (as I suggest) as expressing a somewhat softer 'should' (as forms of '*dei*' are often taken in surrounding contexts).[28] If Aristotle is following Socrates' lead, and seeking to establish the *possibility* of a kind of love that is based not in the subject's needs but rather in her appreciation of the object's positive qualities, then 'should' may better capture his thought than does 'must' or 'needs.'

11. CONTEMPLATIVE (VERSUS ENGAGED) PLEASURES

The eudaimôn agent *should* have excellent friends, but not because she *needs* to. She *should* have them in the same sense in which she *should* contemplate or engage in virtuous action. Each of these activities is an *appropriate* response to ways the world is: contemplation is an appropriate response to the wonders of nature or the beauty of mathematical truth; and virtuous action is an appropriate response to (for example) the needs of others. Similarly, wishing another's good for her sake is an *appropriate* response to the recognized virtues of another, a response that is (as a matter of psychological fact) characteristic of virtuous agents and that tends (as a matter of psychological fact) to lead—with time, intimacy, and mutual recognition—to character-friendship.

In saying that such activities—i.e., friendship, contemplation, and virtuous action—are *appropriate* responses to ways the world is, I aim to challenge the tendency of some commentators to represent the would-be eudaimôn as engaging in these activities primarily qua forms of *self*-realization. For even if the agent's self-realization (or eudaimonia) consists in engaging in such activities, the nature of these activities may be such that an agent can engage in them and so realize herself (or achieve eudaimonia) *only if* she engages in them *for themselves* and *not* qua forms of self-realization.[29] The idea that I should wish-well-to-another-for-*her*-sake qua form of my *own* self-realization—or *because* doing so is a component of *my* eudaimonia—is not only morally but also conceptually problematic. For to the extent that I do what I do qua form of self-realization, it seems that I fail to do it *for itself*. And I take Aristotle's requirement

---

[28] See above, note 22.

[29] For more detailed argument on this point, see Whiting 2002 ["*Eudaimonia*, External Results, and Choosing Virtuous Actions for Themselves" (Chapter 3, this volume)].

that we choose virtuous actions *for themselves*, along with his requirement that we wish our friends well for *their* sakes, to be incompatible with the view that our primary reason for engaging in such activities is that doing so is a form of self-realization.

But some commentators seem to read the following lines as saying that the activities in which my friend's being consists are choiceworthy for me in the same way that the activities in which my own being consists are choiceworthy for me—i.e., as forms of my own self-realization:

> As the excellent person stands to himself, so he stands to his friend, for his friend is another himself.[30] So just as his own being is choiceworthy for each, so also (or nearly so) is the being of his friend <choiceworthy for him>. [*EN* IX.9, 1170b5–8]

So we need to examine these lines in context. These lines state the conclusion of an argument that runs from 1170a25 to 1170b8. But we should begin back at 1170a13, where Aristotle makes it clear that he is once again arguing *phusikôteron*—i.e., by appeal to natural (including psychological) facts. Aristotle then identifies the activities in which human *life*, and so human *being*, consists (i.e., perceiving and thinking) and goes on to explain that he is talking about the life of someone who is *good*, since such a life is determinate [*hôrismenon*], and not about the life of the vicious or corrupted person, or a life full of pain, since such lives are indeterminate [*ahoristos*].[31] We shall return shortly to these puzzling remarks. We must first survey the argument they introduce.

> *If* [a] [such] living[32] is itself good and pleasant . . . and [b] the one seeing perceives [*aisthanetai*] that he sees, and the one hearing <perceives> that he hears, and the one walking <perceives> that he walks, and similarly in the case of other activities there is something perceiving that we are acting, so that if we perceive, we perceive that we perceive, and if we think, <we perceive> that we think; and [c] <perceiving> that we perceive or think is perceiving that we exist . . . and [d] to perceive that one lives is one of the things pleasant in itself (for living is by nature good, and to perceive what is good belonging in oneself is pleasant); and [e] living is choiceworthy above all to good people, because being is good for them and pleasant <as well> (for they are pleased when they are aware of [*sunaisthanomenoi*] what is good in itself); and [f] as the excellent person stands to himself, so he stands to his friend (for his friend is another self), *then* [g] just as his own being is choiceworthy for each, so also (or nearly so) is the being of his friend <choiceworthy for him>. [*EN* IX.9, 1170a25–b8][33]

---

30 "Another himself" is Irwin's rendering of '*heteros . . . autos*'; Ross and Rowe each say "another self."

31 [For more on this, see "The Pleasures of Thinking Together" (Chapter 7, this volume).]

32 That is, the sort he has just specified, not that of someone who is corrupted or whose life is full of pain.

33 [For extended discussion of the Eudemian parallel to this passage, see "The Pleasures of Thinking Together" (Chapter 7, this volume).]

Hardie—presumably relying on Cartesian assumptions about the privacy of our own thoughts—objects that "the weak link in the argument (of IX.9) lies in the claim that a friend is an *alter ego* in the sense that we can be aware of his thoughts as we can be aware of our own" (1980, 332). But even were it obligatory for Aristotle to grant Cartesian assumptions, there is no reason to suppose that he is flouting them here. For he says at 1170b10 that awareness [*sunaisthêsis*] of the life-constituting activities of one's friend requires living together and *sharing in conversation and thought*, and he may well require conversation precisely *because* he recognizes that we do not have the sort of privileged access to the thoughts of another that we have to our own. But Aristotle is not a Cartesian, so he may even think that a person can come to know what she *herself* thinks only through sharing in conversation and thought with others. If so, he may well assimilate a person's awareness of what her friend thinks to her awareness of what she herself thinks, which would yield something like the *Magna Moralia* argument for the role of friends in achieving self-knowledge.

But Aristotle's point in IX.9 is different. What he emphasizes here is the *pleasure* taken both in our awareness of our own activities and in our awareness of our friend's activities. The key to understanding this lies in seeing that his puzzling remarks about determinacy and indeterminacy point (as *EN* X.3's discussion of pleasure points) to views expressed in Plato's *Philebus*. The relevance of the *Philebus* should be clear. For the *Philebus* is structured around questions about the sufficiency of various candidates for eudaimonia or "the (human) good." Socrates' argument is, roughly, that neither pleasure by itself nor intelligence by itself can be *the* (human) *good*, since the conjunction of pleasure and intelligence is better than either of these taken alone, whereas *the good* is supposed to be *teleion* and sufficient in the sense that it cannot be improved—as either pleasure or intelligence can be improved—by the addition of other goods. Aristotle is running a similar argument about having friends: if an otherwise happy life can be improved by the addition of friends, then a life without friends cannot be *the good*.

But the relevance of the *Philebus* extends far beyond this. "Intelligence" stands there for a range of cognitive capacities or states, including memory, knowledge, and opinion. And Socrates argues there that a life of pleasure without any of these cognitive states is less good than a life of pleasure that involves these states:

> without memory, it would be impossible for you to remember that you had ever enjoyed yourself or for any pleasure to survive from one moment to the next . . . and without true opinion, you would not realize that you were enjoying yourself even when you were; and being deprived of reasoning, you would not be able to reason about how you might enjoy the future; [you would be] living a life not of a human being but of a jellyfish or some one of the encrusted creatures living in the sea. [21c][34]

[34] The translation is by Dorothea Frede, in *Plato: Philebus*. Indianapolis: Hackett Publishing, 1993.

Socrates' point is not simply that (as with rudimentary somatic pleasures) pleasure *plus* awareness of it is better than pleasure taken alone. There are (at least) two further points.[35]

First, in the case of more sophisticated pleasures—such as those involved in writing a poem, doing a mathematical proof, or helping a friend—the first-order activities in which the pleasure is taken themselves involve cognition, typically of things apart from the agent's activity and the pleasure taken in it, things such as the meanings, sounds, and rhythms of words, the nature of mathematical truth, or the needs of others. It follows from this, in a way that is important to Aristotle's argument, that these activities require the agent's attention to be directed *outward*, toward *such things*.[36]

Second, a subject's higher-order awareness of these activities and their value is *itself* pleasant in ways that depend on the subject's cognitively loaded appreciation of them: she must *recognize* what is being done and *appreciate* the value of doing *that*. Suppose, for example, that I talk in my sleep, always in verse, and my partner records and publishes my poems under a pseudonym. Suppose further that I do not recognize the products as my own or have any independent appreciation of them. (Perhaps I was punished for versifying as a child and have, consciously at least, forsworn all such activity. And now, having been to college, I regard such verse as an objectionably anachronistic genre, so I write reviews attacking these very poems.) Suppose further that these poems are in fact great works, so widely appreciated that the Nobel Prize committee would like to be able to identify their author. Now compare the value *to me* of the mere activity of producing these poems to the value *to me* of the activity of producing the same poems in full awareness of what I am doing and with appreciation of the value of doing *that*: however good these poems are, and however good *haplôs* their production is, the activity of producing them will *not* be a good *to me* if I am neither aware of what I am doing nor appreciative of its value.

Or suppose that I am depressed and operating on "automatic pilot." Because I have promised to teach a disadvantaged child to read, I go through the motions, showing up weekly and contributing (as a matter of fact) greatly to her progress, all the while thinking how pointless the whole business is and wishing I had not made the promise in the first place. Here again, what I am doing may be good *for her*, and even good *haplôs*; but it will not have the sort of value *to me* that it would have if I were *both* aware of what I was doing—namely, opening up new worlds for her—and appreciative of the value of doing that. We can, of course, distinguish *awareness* of what I am doing from *appreciation* of it: I may be aware that I am writing rock music, but (having read Allan Bloom) am ashamed of what I am doing. The point here is that awareness *without* appreciation is less good *to me* than awareness *with* appreciation (justified, of course, by the value of my activity).

---

[35] I am much indebted, throughout this section, to the second chapter of Bobonich 2002.

[36] [This is one of many places where my debts to the work of Richard Moran should be clear.]

These two points apply as much, via memory and anticipation, to past and future activities as to present ones; and (as I take Aristotle to be arguing in *EN* IX.9) as much, via intimacy, to the appreciation of my friend's activities as to my own. For the argument quoted above is roughly that my appreciative awareness of my *friend's* activity serves (if my friend's activity is good) to *make* my friend's activity a good *to me* in much the same way that my appreciative awareness of my *own* activity serves (if my activity is good) to *make* my own activity a good *to me*. The two are not exactly alike, since my own activities would not in general *be* the kinds of activities they are, nor have the kinds of value they have, independently of *my* appreciation of them as such, whereas my friend's activities may *be* the kinds of activities they are, and have the kinds of value they have, independently of *my* appreciation of them as such (though *not* independently of *her* appreciation of them as such). But the point remains that there is a distinction between the value *haplôs* of an activity, and the value of that activity *to* (or *for*) any given subject, including its agent but not necessarily limited to its agent. To the extent that intimacy allows me to appreciate another's activity in something like the way I appreciate my own, her activity can come to have *to* (or *for*) me some of the kind of value that my own activity typically has *to* (or *for*) *me* in virtue of my own (admittedly constitutive) appreciation of it.[37]

The pleasures associated with such appreciation depend on their subject's beliefs about the value of their objects and are a sign of what their subject values. And while we can (and often do) take pleasure in the sight of things that we take to be instrumental means to things we value for themselves, Aristotle's point in *EN* IX.9 seems to be about the sort of intrinsic pleasure we take in the sight of things we value *for themselves*. This is the sort of pleasure the genuinely virtuous agent experiences both when she performs virtuous actions and when she sees others performing virtuous actions and recognizes them as such.

But Aristotle seems to think that there are special difficulties involved in contemplating one's *own* activities. His point may be partly that one can no more readily observe oneself engaging in virtuous action than one could before the rise of video cameras observe oneself wrestling. So his point may be partly that one can get the sort of pleasure involved in *observing* virtuous actions only where the virtuous actions of *others* are in play. But he may also be thinking of a deeper problem here, one not so amenable to technological resolution.

He may be thinking about the ways in which contemplating one's own virtuous activity can *impede* that activity. Contemplating one's own activity in progress may prevent one from focusing outward in ways required by such activity, and so prevent one from seeing and doing what one *ought* to do. And even contemplation after the fact—if, for example, one were to watch videos of oneself performing virtuous actions—might reflect a kind of self-indulgence that is incompatible with genuine virtue. But there is

[37] The depression example shows that there may be cases where my intimate friend can have the relevant sort of awareness even when I do not. But that is not a problem for Aristotle, who surely takes himself to rely on premises that hold only "for the most part."

no such problem in contemplating, even with great admiration, the virtuous actions of *others*. For my admiration of another's activity need not interfere with her activity nor undermine *its* status as virtuous.

I say "need not" because the other's desire for admiration *might* tempt her to do the sorts of things virtuous persons do, but not *as* the virtuous person does them—i.e., not for themselves and with her attention focused, as it should be, on the needs of others or on what justice requires et cetera.[38] That is why I must *really* know her, in order to know *what* she is doing, if I am to appreciate (and so enjoy) her actions in anything like the way I can (absent self-deception) appreciate (and so enjoy) my own actions. But if I *do* know her, it may be far easier to achieve contemplative enjoyment of her actions than to achieve contemplative enjoyment of my own. So Aristotle's point may have less to do with the difficulty of self-knowledge than with the difficulty of finding *contemplative enjoyment* in one's own actions, which typically require one's attention to be focused elsewhere.

Reading Aristotle this way allows us to explain his emphasis on pleasure in ways that Cooper's interpretation does not. It also helps to explain why Aristotle associates pleasure-friendship so closely with character-friendship. For even in relationships where virtuous activity is not the principal source of the pleasure the parties find in one another's company, each party may be disposed to take some of the same sort of pleasure in the other's activities as she takes in her own. Each may be disposed, for example, to enjoy the other's athletic victories, or the other's musical accomplishments, *for themselves*. And this may lead each to promote the *other's* activities *not* as extensions of her own, or as forms of (her own) *self*-realization, but rather *for themselves*.

12. CONCLUSION: EUDAIMONISM REVISITED

Insofar as my friend's activities are constitutive of her eudaimonia, I am of course—in promoting her activities *for themselves*—promoting her eudaimonia for *itself*. And while it may also be true that I am, in doing so, *realizing* my own eudaimonia, this is *not* the reason *why* I promote her activities, at least not if I am a genuine friend: I do so simply because I value her activities *for themselves*. So the fact that I am *realizing* my own eudaimonia does *not* require us to say that I am acting for the *sake* of my eudaimonia.

In sum, we need not read the "eudaimonist axiom" as requiring that all actions be performed ultimately for the sake of the agent's *own* eudaimonia: for Aristotle's account of *philia* shows how, given human nature, it is *possible* to act directly for the sake of *another's* eudaimonia. His account of *philia* thus serves to rescue the ethical credentials of his eudaimonism: there is no need to read it as a form of rational egoism. As Aristotle himself says of those who would assimilate the motivations of benefactors

---

[38] [See again "*Eudaimonia*, External Results, and Choosing Virtuous Actions for Themselves" (Chapter 3, this volume).]

to those of creditors, "Epicharmus would perhaps say" that those who read Aristotle as a rational egoist may do so because they read him "from a base point of view" [*EN* IX.7, 1167b25–27].

REFERENCES

Bobonich, C. 2002. *Plato's Utopia Recast: His Later Ethics and Politics*. Oxford: Oxford University Press.

Broadie, S. and Rowe, C. 2002. *Aristotle: Nicomachean Ethics*. Introduction and Commentary by S. Broadie and translation by C. Rowe. Oxford: Oxford University Press.

Cooper, J. 1977a. "Aristotle on the Forms of Friendship." *Review of Metaphysics* 30: 619–48; reprinted in J. Cooper 1999. *Reason and Emotion: Essays on Ancient Moral Psychology and Ethical Theory*. Princeton, NJ: Princeton University Press, 312–35. All citations follow pagination of reprint.

Cooper, J. 1977b. "Friendship and the Good in Aristotle" *Philosophical Review* 86: 290–315; reprinted in J. Cooper 1999. *Reason and Emotion: Essays on Ancient Moral Psychology and Ethical Theory*. Princeton, NJ: Princeton University Press, 336–55. All citations follow pagination of reprint.

Cooper, J. 1980. "Aristotle on Friendship." In A. O. Rorty (ed.), *Essays on Aristotle's "Ethics."* Berkeley: University of California Press, 301–40.

Cooper, J. 1999. *Reason and Emotion: Essays on Ancient Moral Psychology and Ethical Theory*. Princeton, NJ: Princeton University Press.

Hardie, W. F. R. 1980. *Aristotle's Ethical Theory*, 2nd edn. Oxford: Clarendon Press.

Irwin, T. 1988. *Aristotle's First Principles*. Oxford: Oxford University Press.

Irwin, T. 1999. *Aristotle: Nicomachean Ethics*, 2nd edn. Indianapolis, IN: Hackett.

Konstan, D. 1997. *Friendship in the Classical World*. Cambridge: Cambridge University Press.

Kraut, R. 1989. *Aristotle on the Human Good*. Princeton, NJ: Princeton University Press.

Pickavé, M. and Whiting, J. 2008. "*Nicomachean Ethics* VII.3 on Akratic Ignorance." *Oxford Studies in Ancient Philosophy* 34: 321–72. [Chapter 7, this volume]

Ross, W. D. 1980. *The Nicomachean Ethics*. Oxford: Oxford University Press. This is a revised version of Ross's translation, originally published in 1908. The revised version is also available in Vol. 2 of J. Barnes (ed.). 1984. *The Complete Works of Aristotle*. Princeton, NJ: Princeton University Press.

Vlastos, G. 1991. *Socrates: Ironist and Moral Philosopher*. Ithaca, NY: Cornell University Press.

Whiting, J. 1991. "Impersonal Friends." *The Monist* 74: 3–29. [I.2]

Whiting, J. 1996. "Self-Love and Authoritative Virtue: A Prolegomenon to a Kantian Reading of *Eudemian Ethics* VIII.3." In S. Engstrom and J. Whiting (eds.), *Aristotle, Kant, and the Stoics: Rethinking Happiness and Duty*. Cambridge: Cambridge University Press, 162–99. [Chapter 4, this volume]

Whiting, J. 2002. "Eudaimonia, External Results, and Choosing Virtuous Actions for Themselves." *Philosophy and Phenomenological Research* 65: 270–90. [Chapter 3, this volume]

Whiting, J. 2005. "Trusting 'First' and 'Second' Selves: Reflections on Virginia Woolf and Annette Baier." In J. Jenkins, J. Whiting, and C. Williams (eds.), *Persons and Passions: Essays in Honor of Annette Baier*. South Bend, IN: Notre Dame Press, 329–64. [I.3]

Whiting, J. 2008. "The Lockeanism of Aristotle." *Antiquorum Philosophia*, no. 2: 101–36. [III.8].

Whiting, J. 2013a. "Love: Self-Propagation, Self-Preservation, or Ekstasis?" *Canadian Journal of Philosophy* 43: 403–29. [I.7]

Whiting, J. 2013b. "The Pleasures of Thinking Together: Prolegomenon to a Complete Reading of *EE* 7.12." In F. Leigh (ed.), *The "Eudemian Ethics" on the Voluntary, Friendship, and Luck*. Leiden: Brill, 78–154. [Chapter 7, this volume]

FURTHER READING

Cooper, J. 1990. "Political Animals and Civic Friendship." In G. Patzig (ed.), *Aristoteles "Politik."* Göttingen: Vandenhoeck and Ruprecht, 221–41; reprinted in J. Cooper 1999. *Reason and Emotion: Essays on Ancient Moral Psychology and Ethical Theory*. Princeton, NJ: Princeton University Press, 356–77.

Pakaluk, M. 1998. *Aristotle: Nicomachean Ethics Books VIII and IX*. Oxford: Clarendon Press.

Price, A. W. 1989. *Love and Friendship in Plato and Aristotle*. Oxford: Clarendon Press.

Stern-Gillet, S. 1995. *Aristotle's Philosophy of Friendship*. Albany: State University of New York Press.

7

The Pleasures of Thinking Together

PROLEGOMENON TO A COMPLETE READING OF *EE* VII.12

1. INTRODUCTION

The first two thirds of *Eudemian Ethics* (*EE*) VII.12 correspond closely to *Nicomachean Ethics* (*EN*) IX.9. Each seeks to resolve a version of the same aporia, about whether someone who is self-sufficient (or *autarkês*) will have friends. Each relies on an argument from the value of perceiving one's own activities to the value of perceiving the activities of one's friend. And each reaches the same conclusion: the self-sufficient person will have friends. But there is a striking difference: whereas the Eudemian discussion explicitly compares the self-sufficient person to God, and is in fact organized around this comparison, the Nicomachean discussion does not even mention God.

M. M. McCabe's reading of the Eudemian chapter suggests a way to explain this.[1] She reads this chapter as discussing two versions of the aporia, the first invoking the comparison with God and the second dropping this comparison because (as Aristotle himself suggests) it somehow misleads us. McCabe thus reads the Eudemian chapter as responding primarily to what she views as the second version of the aporia. This suggests the following possibility (which, however, McCabe does not herself articulate): assuming (with most commentators) that Aristotle wrote the Eudemian books before he wrote the Nicomachean ones, Aristotle may have come to see—perhaps as a result of writing the Eudemian chapter—that the comparison with God was not just

[1] M. M. McCabe, "With Mirrors or Without? Self-Perception in *Eudemian Ethics* VII.12" ("Mirrors"), which appeared together with the present essay in Leigh 2012, *The Eudemian Ethics on the Voluntary, Friendship and Luck*.

Living Together. Jennifer Whiting, Oxford University Press. © Oxford University Press 2023.
DOI: 10.1093/oso/9780199969678.003.0008

potentially misleading but also unnecessary, so that the Nicomachean chapter could do without it.

But even granting the plausibility of this general line of thought, there are drawbacks to McCabe's reading of the Eudemian chapter. First, McCabe's reading emphasizes the second half of Aristotle's discussion at the expense of the first, and so fails to do justice to the way in which the comparison with God reappears in the conclusion of the Eudemian discussion. And many features of Aristotle's reply to what McCabe regards as the first version of the aporia reappear in the Nicomachean chapter—most notably, the crucial move from the value of perceiving one's own activities to the value of perceiving the activities of one's friend. So it is difficult to read *Aristotle* as thinking in terms of two versions of a single aporia, with the second version superseding the first.

Second, and more importantly, McCabe reads Aristotle's reply to the second (and in her view less misleading) version of the aporia as involving a major concession to the sort of incompleteness of human beings that is stressed in the Aristophanes speech in Plato's *Symposium*. But the effect of this is to remove—rather than to resolve—the aporia. Man, as McCabe puts it, "*spectacularly fails* to be like god" [my italics]. So there should be no problem understanding the evident fact that even the best and most self-sufficient among us *do* have friends: this is all too intelligible, given that (on her reading) we *need* friends in order to *complete ourselves*. But this stress on what we *need* not only threatens to remove the aporia; it also makes it difficult to see why Aristotle should regard the primary sort of friendship—namely, the friendship of virtuous agents with one another—as a paradigm of wishing and doing well for the friend for the *friend's* sake (as distinct from one's *own*). For it is hard to see how allowing the virtuous agent to have friends because she *needs* them in order to *complete herself* can satisfy Aristotle's persistent requirement that we wish and do well for our friends for *their* sakes (as distinct from our *own*).

McCabe seeks of course to explain how on her reading this requirement is satisfied. And like Aryeh Kosman, whose reading she in other respects opposes, she emphasizes the "joint activity" of the friends.[2] On her reading of the Eudemian chapter,

[2] See Kosman, "Aristotle on the Desirability of Friends" ("Desirability"). The main issue between Kosman and McCabe is, very roughly, whether the sort of self-perception of which Aristotle speaks in *EE* VII.12 and *EN* IX.9 is (as Kosman thinks) the sort of awareness of what one is experiencing and doing that we ordinarily take to be "built in" to the first-order experience and action not just of human beings but also of other animals; or whether such self-perception is (as McCabe thinks) not merely "reflexive" but in fact "reflective" in a way that involves a kind of stepping back and reflecting on one's experiences and actions, and that (far from being relatively automatic) involves effort and is open only to rational animals. My own view is that Aristotle is interested in both sorts of self-consciousness, but that it is the relatively automatic built-in sort that plays the most important role in these chapters, where the idea seems to be that in living together with one's friend, one can come to have something like the sort of relatively constant and unmediated (though not non-conceptual) awareness of the friend's experiences and actions that one has of one's own, which awareness gives rise *in turn* to something like the sorts of pleasure and pain associated with awareness of one's own good and bad experiences and actions as such (i.e., as good and bad). Of course, this sort of relatively immediate awareness may lead to the sort of individual and joint reflection of which McCabe speaks and may be informed in turn by previous activities of

> . . . the joint functioning of friendship is the way to fulfill *my* function; so that—as Aristophanes would have construed it—*the self is a composite entity, made up of the two of us*, engaged on the joint enterprise of self-perception and self-knowledge. I do not exploit [my friend] nor is my functioning along with him egocentric from my own point of view; instead, *we* function together for our *joint* benefit. [my italics][3]

Kosman too emphasizes joint—or, as he puts it, "shared"—activity. He places more emphasis than McCabe does on the individual subjectivities of the friends, but then speaks of "refiguring [the] separate I's as a common we." He goes on to say,

> . . . since we are engaged in shared perception, what my friend perceives is in a sense what I perceive, since it is what we perceive, *and his consciousness is mine, since it is ours.* The force of the conclusion that "the perceiving of one's friend is in a sense necessarily the perceiving of oneself, and his knowing in a sense one's own knowing" [*EE* 1245a35–37] now needs to be understood in light of this. I take Aristotle to mean here, as an important step in the argument, that one's friend's perception and cognitive awareness is in a sense one's *own.* [my italics][4]

But Kosman's construal of the passage quoted is (as we shall see below) controversial: Aristotle's point may be *not* (as Kosman takes it) that my friend's perceiving is in a sense my *own* perceiving, but *rather* (as it is most often taken) that perceiving my friend is in a sense perceiving *myself.*

Kosman seems to me to err here in a way that many readers err—namely, by taking Aristotle's talk of the friend as an "other self" to involve treating the friend as a kind of extension of oneself or at least as a part of some larger self of which one is oneself a part. But I do not think this does justice to the *independent* value of my *friend's* activities of perceiving and knowing, a value these have regardless of any relationship in which my friend happens to stand to me or to some larger self of which I am myself a

individual and joint reflection. For it may be in virtue of a kind of mutual understanding that is acquired only through conversation about their respective activities and the value of these activities that friends come to have the sort of relatively immediate comprehension of one another's experiences and actions that gives rise to each taking in the *other's* experiences and actions a kind of pleasure (or pain) that is not unlike the pleasure (or pain) each takes in his or her *own* experiences and actions. But my point here is that neither McCabe nor Kosman does justice to the role played by *pleasure* in *EE* VII.12; their disagreement with each other is thus largely tangential to my main argument.

[3] McCabe, "Mirrors," 73. Note the move from "*my* function" (which seems both inapt and insufficient to answer the moral concerns in play here) to "*our* joint benefit" (which seems more appropriate, given McCabe's general picture, and is arguably better able to address the moral concerns). One might, however, wonder whether Aristotle thinks that non-instrumental concern for another can be explained *only* by positing some larger self of which the agent is herself a part; or whether he thinks it possible to explain in some other way how an agent might come to take in the activities of another, *conceived as other*, something *like* the sort of *interest* she takes—and thus something *like* the sort of *pleasure* she takes—in her own activities. It is the second possibility that I want to explore here.

[4] Kosman, "Desirability," 149.

part. Nor do I think Aristotle would allow that this account does justice to that independence. For his strategy for explaining why the self-sufficient person has friends seems to rest not so much on establishing a sense in which her friend's perceiving and knowing are her *own* as on showing how she can come to stand to the experiences and actions of her friend in something *like* the relationships—both epistemic and hedonic—in which she stands to her own experiences and actions.[5] The crucial factor, I think, is the *pleasure* the self-sufficient person takes in the experiences and activities of her friend. The idea, very roughly, is that standing to one's friend and his activities in something like the *epistemic relationship* in which one stands to oneself and one's own activities gives rise to *pleasures* like those taken in one's own activities.[6]

The role played by pleasure seems to me to be missed not only by McCabe and Kosman, but also by the common reading of Aristotle that is Kosman's main target, a reading based as much on the *Nicomachean* chapter as on the *Eudemian* one. This is the reading according to which otherwise self-sufficient agents need friends in order to achieve a kind of *self*-knowledge or *self*-awareness. On this reading, awareness of one's friend either is or enables a kind of *self*-awareness because the friend—at least if she is a character-friend—is, as Aristotle puts it, an "other self."[7] But here again we face the question whether this reading respects Aristotle's view that the best sort of friendship involves concern for the friend for the *friend's* sake (as distinct from the agent's *own*). There is also a question whether this reading does justice to the role that Aristotle assigns to pleasure.

On my account, the pleasure a self-sufficient agent takes in the experiences and actions of her friend is part of what explains why she wants to live and act together with her friend, but the pleasure explains this in a way that does not involve satisfying any bona fide *need* on the part of the self-sufficient agent. Nor does the explanation involve pleasure's being the *end* for the sake of which the friendship and the sort of

---

[5] I continue here to challenge what I elsewhere call "colonizing ego" readings of Aristotle's conception of the friend as an "other self." See my "Impersonal Friends" [I.2] and "The Nicomachean Account of *Philia*" ("*NAP*") [Chapter 6, this volume]. But these papers were aimed primarily against treating the friend and her good as parts of the *agent's* good. My concern here is more with treating the friend and his good—together with the agent and her good—as parts of some *larger entity* and *its* good. I do not mean to suggest that Aristotle never has anything like this in mind: but I think that this reading misses an important way in which he thinks it possible for an individual agent, as such, to take in the activities *of her friend* something like the pleasure she takes in her *own* activities.

[6] The point of speaking of an *epistemic* relationship is to distinguish the sort of relationship in question from the sort of *ownership* of which Kosman speaks. But the issue is complicated if (as on Lockean views) the epistemic relationship is part of what constitutes the subject's ownership of its own experiences and activities. See my "The Lockeanism of Aristotle," *Antiquorum Philosophia*, 101–36 ("Lockeanism") [III.8]. I believe, however, that Aristotle's view can accommodate the relevant complications.

[7] The well-established talk of those who are friends on account of virtue as "character-friends" comes from John Cooper, "Aristotle on Friendship." Kosman ascribes the common reading to Stern-Gillet, *Aristotle's Philosophy of Friendship*, especially chaps. 2 and 6. For more on the idea of the friend as an "other self" or (as Aristotle sometimes says) "another this <so and so>," see my discussion of [6](A) below. [For criticism of Cooper's view that Aristotle ties the value of character-friendship to the difficulty of achieving self-knowledge, see "*NAP*" (Chapter 6, this volume).]

living and acting together that are involved in it either come to be or are sustained once they have come to be. So although pleasure is a factor that helps to render *intelligible* the evident but allegedly puzzling fact that the self-sufficient person *does* have friends, the friendship in question is not the sort of friendship that Aristotle speaks of as being on account of pleasure [*dia hêdonên*]; it is rather the sort of friendship that he speaks of as being on account of virtue [*di' aretên*].[8] For the pleasure that a virtuous agent takes in her *friend's* experiences and activities is—like the pleasure she takes in her *own* experiences and activities—taken in them *because they are good*. The pleasure thus supervenes on what self-sufficient agents *really* care about—namely, the goodness of their experiences and activities.[9] This is a point I think *EE* VII.12 goes out of its way to make. But the point tends to be missed because of the general obscurity of the section in which it is made. This is sec. 4 of the text as I divide it, a section whose obscurity is due as much to that of the apparently Pythagorean views on which it draws as to any indeterminacy in the text. It is here that I hope to make my most distinctive contribution to a proper reading of *EE* VII.12.

In sec. 4, as elsewhere in the chapter, the manuscripts are sufficiently corrupt that it is difficult to determine with confidence what exactly to read. And what it makes sense to read depends in each case not just on controversial decisions about what to read elsewhere in our text, but also on the reader's potentially question-begging sense of the overall argument and how exactly it works. It is thus impossible to separate completely the two tasks I undertake in what follows: that of establishing what text to read and that of making sense of this portion of text as a whole. The best I can do is to indicate where my sense of the argument has influenced my decisions about what to read, so that my readers can decide for themselves whether I have allowed such considerations to weigh too heavily in resolving textual issues.[10]

---

[8] For Aristotle's general accounts of the forms of *philia*, see *EE* VII.2 and *EN* VIII.3.

[9] This is confirmed in the very interesting passage at *EE* 1237a23ff. (where the point of *prosphatoi* is pretty clearly about what is *recent* in the sense of *most advanced*). Please note that my point in using "supervene" is not to suggest that the pleasure is always distinct from some activity: even if—as the treatment of pleasure in *EE* VI.13 (aka *EN* VII.13) suggests—the pleasure *is* in a sense the unimpeded activity of a subject in good condition in relation to good objects, the point remains that the pleasure is dependent on the *goodness* of the activity. Note: I think it pretty clear (pace Kenny, *The Aristotelian Ethics*) that the "common books" were originally Eudemian, though they may well have been revised (perhaps even by Aristotle) for inclusion in *EN*. Whether they were, as Hendrik Lorenz has suggested in conversation, so heavily revised that they might as well be counted as Nicomachean is another question. For a more cautious statement of his view, see Lorenz, "Virtue of Character in Aristotle's *Nicomachean Ethics*," 178–79. For more general discussion, see Rowe, *The Eudemian and Nicomachean Ethics*.

[10] That such considerations must be given *some* weight seems clear. Otherwise we must fall back on the sort of divination of which Harlfinger spoke in his study of the manuscript tradition: "*Mag auch die recensio in manch einem Punkt den bislang vorliegenden Text der EE verbessern helfen, die Hauptarbeit bei der constitution textus dieser so korrupten Schrift obliegt letzten Endes doch der divination*" ("Die Überlieferungsgeschichte der *Eudemischen Ethik*," 29). I am grateful to Brad Inwood for calling this passage to my attention during one of my many moments of despair over a textual issue. I am also grateful to him for constant advice and for sharing with me drafts of the complete translation of the *EE* (including the common books) that he and Rafael Woolf have now published: Inwood and Woolf (Cambridge: Cambridge University Press, 2012).

Even so, it will be difficult at points to see how decisions about particular bits of text are related to my overall argument. So I propose, before engaging with textual details, to outline in a relatively dogmatic way what I take to be going on in each section of the text as I divide it, and to explain very roughly how I take these sections to add up. But let me first introduce two texts that—especially when they are read together—provide important background.

2. IMPORTANT PLATONIC AND ARISTOTELIAN BACKGROUND

The first text is *Metaphysics* (*Met.*) XII, chaps. 7 and 9, where Aristotle compares the activities of human and divine thought [*nous*]. The relevance of these chapters to our text tends to be more widely acknowledged than it is adequately explained. This may be in part because the prior relevance of the second text is not viewed as part of the overall equation: this is Plato's *Philebus* (to which the *Metaphysics* chapters seem to respond). Once we see the relevance of the *Philebus* to the *Metaphysics* chapters, we shall be in a better position to see the relevance of the *Metaphysics* chapters to our Eudemian text.

The relevance of the *Philebus* to our text should be obvious, if only because both involve an explicit comparison [*parabolê*] of the best sort of human life to the life of God.[11] The *Philebus* is also the source of the requirements that structure not just the discussions of friendship and self-sufficiency in *EE* VII.12 and *EN* IX.9 but also Aristotle's overall discussion of the human good: namely, the requirements that the human good be *teleion* [complete] and *hikanon* [sufficient] in the sense that nothing further can be added to it to yield something even more desirable or worthy of choice—i.e., even more *haireton*—than it is when taken by itself.[12] Moreover, the *Philebus* and *EE* VII.12 offer parallel arguments: each argues that a certain life is not the human good because something further can be added to it to yield a life that is even more *haireton* for a human being than the relevant life taken *without* whatever is added. In the *Philebus* Socrates argues that the life of pure thought is not the human good because there are some pleasures such that their being added to a life of pure thought renders that life *even more haireton* for a human being than it would be in the absence of such pleasures; in *EE* VII.12, Aristotle argues that a solitary life, no matter how good in all other respects, fails to satisfy these criteria because there are pleasures to be had in the company of others such that the addition of these pleasures renders a life even more *haireton* for a human being than it would be in the absence of such pleasures.

Here, however, it is important to note the qualification "for a human being." This is crucial to the *Philebus* argument. For Socrates tends to identify pleasures with fillings

---

[11] Socrates speaks of a *parabolê* of lives at *Philebus* 33b2.

[12] Compare *Philebus* 20dff. with *EN* 1097a22–b21. I discuss these requirements at length in the Introduction to this volume.

of the sort of bodily lacks and social deficiencies that gods, unlike human beings, do not suffer.[13] So although Socrates thinks that a god lives the very best sort of life that *any* being can live, he does *not* allow that this sort of life includes any *pleasure*: a god's life is, as Plato might put it, "beyond pleasure."[14] But Socrates argues that it does *not follow* from this that the best sort of life *for a human being* consists exclusively in the godlike activity of contemplation. For he takes human life to admit pleasures of a sort that, when added to a life of pure thought, yield a life that is even more desirable *for a human being* than that life would be in the absence of such pleasures. If, per impossible, such pleasures *could* be added to a life of divine thought, then God's life *could* perhaps be improved by the company of others; but as things stand it *cannot*.

Aristotle, however, takes a different tack, one that shows why it would be too quick to conclude from the similarities between *EE* VII.12 and the *Philebus* that VII.12 worries that the comparison with God misleads us by leading us to forget about pleasure altogether. For Aristotle is not as inclined as Socrates is to identify pleasure with the filling of some lack or deficiency. So in spite of agreeing with Socrates that god is lacking in *nothing*, Aristotle is free to treat divine contemplation not simply as pleasant but as *itself* a pleasure [*hêdonê*]. He makes this point in the following passage about the first mover, which is a being that is supposed to move other things without itself moving, a being that Aristotle sometimes calls "God."

[ST1] [b]–[e] *Metaphysics* XII.7 [1072b14–28][15]

[b] . . . its <the unmoved mover's> career [*diagôgê*] is such as the best we have for a short time—for that one is always <engaged> in this way, but for us it is impossible <always to be so engaged>—since the activity of this <sc., the unmoved mover> is also <a> pleasure [*hêdonê*]. And on account of this,

[13] I say "tends" here so as to bracket questions about the extent to which the second form [*eidos*] of pleasure recognized in the *Philebus*—the form said at 31b–c to belong to the soul itself in itself—involves the filling of lacks. The talk at 51b of unperceived lacks suggests that it may. But the issue is complicated and I cannot discuss it here. The main point is that Aristotle, unlike Socrates in the *Philebus*, does not *frame* his discussion of pleasure in terms of the filling of lacks: in fact, he explicitly criticizes the *Philebus* view in *EE* VI (aka *EN* VII) 13.

[14] See *Philebus* 33a–b.

[15] "ST1" for "Supplementary Text 1," so as to distinguish the supplementary texts from the consecutive sections of *EE* VII.12 (which I have labeled simply [1]–[7], with subsections indicated by uppercase letters). I use lowercase letters (as here) to indicate subsections of the supplementary texts and start here with [b] so as to make it clear when I eventually introduce [a] that I am quoting from an earlier portion of the text. See [ST1][a] below.

Except where noted, translations are my own. I use square brackets, as with [*diagôgê*], to indicate the Greek for what precedes them; and angular brackets, as with <engaged>, to indicate what I understand in spite of its not being explicitly stated. In some cases what I understand is implicit in the text, but this is not always the case. I make liberal use of angular brackets so as to make it clear exactly how *I* fill in various gaps that one must *somehow or other* fill in. I am *not* thereby claiming that my way is the *only* way to fill them. My aim is twofold: to make it clear how as a matter of fact I understand what is to be filled in and to flag my interpretive decisions for the reader to make of what she will.

waking and perceiving and thinking are most pleasant, and hopes and memories <are pleasant> on account of these.[16]

[c] And the thinking that is in itself <thinking> is of that which is in itself best [*tou kath' hautou aristou*], and the <thinking that is> most of all <thinking> is of what is best of all.

[d] And nous thinks itself by partaking of the object of thought [*kata metalêpsin tou noêtou*].[17] For in grasping <the *noêtou*> and thinking, it <sc., nous> comes to be an object of thought, with the result that *nous* and *noêton* are the same. For that which is capable of receiving the object of thought and the substance <of what is thought> is nous, and having this <sc., the object> it <sc., nous> acts, with the result that it is this <sc., acting> more than that <sc., being capable of receiving> that divine nous seems to have, and contemplation is the most pleasant and best.

[e] If, then, God is *always* in this way <i.e., actively> well disposed [*houtôs eu echei*],[18] as we *sometimes* are, it is amazing. And if God is <always> better disposed <than we sometimes are> that is still more amazing. And God *is* <always> thus disposed. And life also belongs <to God>, for the activity of nous is life, and that one <sc., God> is the activity. And the life of that one is *in itself* activity, best and eternal <activity>.

I have quoted at length here because this passage will prove relevant in various ways as we proceed. The point at present is simply that Aristotle treats divine contemplation as involving—indeed *being*—a pleasure, albeit a pleasure of a sort that does not presuppose any sort of lack or deficiency on the part of its subject.[19]

So if we are to understand the God with which the self-sufficient person is compared in *EE* VII.12 as *Aristotle* understands his God, we cannot take the point to be that the comparison with God misleads by leading us to forget entirely about pleasure. For the comparison with God—at least as *Aristotle* conceives of God—should render the pleasures of contemplation *salient*. Aristotle's point—if it is a

[16] The reference to hopes and memories is reminiscent of *Philebus* 32b–39e. It seems pretty clear that Aristotle wrote *Met.* XII.7, especially this bit, in opposition to the *Philebus'* denial of pleasure to gods. But this bit also points to *EE* VII.12, which I read (together with *Met.* XII.7 and 9) as part of Aristotle's response to the *Philebus*.

[17] This section is clearly relevant to the interpretation of *EE* VII.12. See especially [4](C) below, where Aristotle also uses the language of *metalêpsis* and speaks of human perceivers and thinkers as in some sense becoming—like the divine thinkers here—objects of their *own* cognitive activities.

[18] Here again the language is very close to that used in *EE* VII.12. See [7](B) below, where Aristotle says that "for it is not in this way <sc., by thinking something else> that the god has his well <being / doing> [οὐ γὰρ οὕτως ὁ θεὸς εὖ ἔχει] but he is better than to think something else besides himself <thinking> himself."

[19] Cf. *EE* VI (aka *EN* VII) 13: 1153b9–12. Aristotle makes a parallel point about human contemplation at *EN* 1152b36ff., where he recognizes the existence of human pleasures that involve neither any pain or appetite, nor any defective nature, and cites the pleasures of contemplation as an example.

point about pleasure—is presumably that the comparison with God leads us to overlook a distinctively *human* sort of pleasure, one that (unlike the pleasures of food, drink, and sex) does not presuppose *any* sort of lack or deficiency on the part of its subject (not even, as we shall see in [5](B), the sort of deficiency of knowledge associated with the pleasures of learning). This distinctively human sort of pleasure is the sort of pleasure we *all* take in doing our favorite things in the company of others, even those of us whose favorite thing is contemplating purely theoretical truths.[20]

Here, however, it is still an open question whether the respect in which Aristotle takes the comparison with God to mislead is its leading us to forget about such distinctively human pleasures. For *Metaphysics* XII.9 (to be discussed below) highlights an important respect in which human thought differs from divine thought: namely, in requiring an object *distinct* from itself. So we might well suppose that Aristotle takes the comparison with God to mislead by leading us to forget about *this* difference. We might even suppose that he takes the comparison to mislead us in both ways: by leading us to overlook the dependence of human thought on an object distinct from itself *and* by leading us to overlook distinctively human forms of pleasure. In that case, we might even hypothesize that the two oversights are related: it may be that we overlook distinctively human forms of pleasure *precisely because* the comparison with God leads us to overlook our need for objects of thought distinct from ourselves.[21] For not only are our friends and their activities among the objects contemplation of which we find pleasant: it is also true that we sometimes find the contemplation of other things more pleasant when we contemplate them together with our friends than when we contemplate them alone. And in this we seem to differ from God—at least as *Aristotle* conceives of God.

Let us turn then, with this background in mind, to our text.

---

[20] It is possible that Aristotle thinks the comparison with God misleads his audience because *they* are operating with the *Philebus* conception of God as "beyond pleasure." That might well be the case if, for example, the Eudemian chapter was a very early text, preceding *Met.* XII; or if the Eudemian chapter was simply part of a lecture course responding to the *Philebus* view without assuming familiarity with or acceptance of the views advanced in *Met.* XII.7. But the clear affinities between these Eudemian and *Metaphysics* chapters seem to me to render this possibility less likely than those I suggest in the paragraph to which this note is attached and the paragraph that follows it.

[21] [Max Tegtmeyer has pointed out that I have moved in this paragraph from speaking about cognitive activities as either requiring (or not requiring) objects distinct from *themselves* to speaking about cognitive activities as either requiring (or not requiring) objects distinct from their *subjects*. In the divine case, where the distinction between the subject and object breaks down, there is no distinction. In the human case, Aristotle wants a parallel identification of the thinking subject with its activity. But human thinking requires an object distinct from itself. So even if human thinkers are in some sense identified with their activities of thought, their status as thinking subjects depends on there being some distinction between themselves as subjects of thought and the objects (including themselves, even if only peripherally) of their thoughts. The issues here are extremely difficult, so I want simply to call attention to the fact that I make this move and to set the issues aside for further reflection: I leave the original text more or less as it stands (though see note 26 below). I invite readers to reflect on these issues for themselves.]

3. Dogmatic Preview[22]

The relevant portion of *EE* VII.12 runs from 1244b1 through 1245b19. There is controversy about how exactly this discussion is structured, but I divide it as follows:

[1] Initial statement of the aporia [1244b1–21]
[2] Diagnostic hunch and *the basic logos*: to live is to perceive and to know [1244b21–26]
[3] First step: the value of one's *own* perceiving and knowing [1244b26–33]
[4] Second step: the importance of perceiving and knowing *good objects* (*oneself included*) [1244b33–45a10]
[5] Third step: a possible objection and two purported facts about human nature that point the way to a resolution of the aporia [1245a11–29]
[6] The culmination of the main argument: making sense of the purported facts [1245a29–b9]
[7] Recapitulation [1245b9–19][23]

The general shape of this division is supported by the manifest relation between [2] and [7]. [2] suggests that the initial statement of the aporia that was provided in [1] may mislead us insofar as its comparison of the maximally self-sufficient person to God leads us to overlook something important. And [7] returns to this point, suggesting (I submit) that what is overlooked has at least something to do with the way in which human thought, unlike divine thought, requires an object distinct from itself.

My reading of [7] is based partly on its acknowledged affinity (in both language and dogma) with the argument of *Metaphysics* XII.9, from which I quote at length below because of the role it plays in my overall account. The topic of this chapter is the nature of nous (in particular divine nous) and how it must be disposed if it is to be—as it is

[22] Though much of what follows this preview will be accessible only to specialist readers, nonspecialists should be able, with the preview in hand, to follow the main lines of argument. I shall try to facilitate this in what follows by mentioning only the most important philological details in the main text and subordinating the discussion of other details as much as possible to footnotes. I shall also try to explain the crucial philological points in ways such that nonspecialists can at least see what the basic questions are.

[23] Kosman and McCabe each divide things differently. McCabe sees a second version of the aporia, one meant to supersede the first, being introduced in [5] and answered in what follows. And Kosman, who sees only one version of the aporia, sees [2]–[5] as providing further elaboration of it, with the resolution starting only in [6]. (Sorabji, in his *Self: Ancient and Modern Insights about Individuality, Life and Death*, 234–35, seems to follow Kosman in this.) I agree with Kosman that there is only one version of the aporia and that its resolution comes in [6]. But I read [6] as *completing* an argument begun back in [3] and continued in [4] and [5]. And I read [5] as introducing friends into what has up to that point been an argument about the value to a subject, first of her *own* perceiving and knowing (this is in [3]), and then of her perceiving and knowing *good* things, *herself included* (this is in [4]). It is the introduction of friends in [5] that provides the crucial link between these earlier steps and the culmination of the argument in [6], where perceiving and knowing one's *friend* (assuming *she* is good) is supposed to have a value like that ascribed in [4] to perceiving and knowing *oneself* (assuming one is *oneself* good), the value in question being at least partly hedonic.

assumed to be—most divine among the things that appear. Aristotle suggests first that divine nous must actually think,[24] and that nothing else (besides itself) can be in control of its thinking. The idea here seems to be that the actualization of divine nous does not depend, as the actualization of perception depends, on objects distinct from itself, objects that serve as the contents and/or efficient causes of that activity. Aristotle then asks *what* divine nous thinks, whether something different from itself or not; and if something different, whether it always thinks the same thing or different things (presumably at different times). He continues as follows (with my bold highlighting the main ideas):

[ST2] *Metaphysics* XII.9 [1074b23–36]

[a] Does it make any difference, then, or none at all, whether the thinking is of what is fine or of any random thing?[25] Or is it out of place for it <sc., divine nous> to think about some things? It is clear then that it thinks the most divine and most honorable <thing>, and that it does not change. For the change <would be> to <something> worse, and such would in fact be a kind of movement.

πότερον οὖν διαφέρει τι ἢ οὐδὲν τὸ νοεῖν τὸ καλὸν ἢ τὸ τυχόν; ἢ καὶ ἄτοπον τὸ διανοεῖσθαι περὶ ἐνίων; δῆλον τοίνυν ὅτι τὸ θειότατον καὶ τιμιώτατον νοεῖ, καὶ οὐ μεταβάλλει· εἰς χεῖρον γὰρ ἡ μεταβολή, καὶ κίνησίς τις ἤδη τὸ τοιοῦτον. [1074b23–7]

[b] First, then, if it is not <actual> thinking but a capacity <to think>, it is plausible to suppose that the continuity of thinking would be toilsome for it. Next it is clear that something else would be <in this case> more honorable than nous, <namely, the thing being thought>. **For to think—i.e., <actual> thinking—will belong even to one thinking the worst thing, so that if this is to be avoided (for some things it is better not to see than to see), the <actual> thinking would not be the best <activity>.** Therefore, it thinks itself, since it is the best thing, and the thinking is <in its case> a thinking of thinking.

---

[24] 1074b17–18, taking 'μηδὲν' adverbially.

[25] Note once again the similarity in language with *EE* VII.12, especially in [5] below, where Aristotle suggests that the mere addition of speech, if it is simply participation in random speech [τοῦ λόγου κοινωνεῖν τοῦ τυχόντος], does *not* suffice to explain the preference of human beings—or at of least self-sufficient ones—for eating and drinking *together.* (I assume that by "random speech" he means what we call "small talk" or "chit-chat.") Aristotle goes on to reject the hypothesis that we can explain the preference of maximally self-sufficient agents for one another's company by appeal to the idea that they might *learn* from talking to one another, since this presupposes a defect incompatible with their self-sufficiency; and he suggests instead that we should explain this preference by appeal to (a) the *value* of the activities in which self-sufficient agents engage together and (b) the *pleasures* to which their mutual appreciation of this value gives rise. His examples are activities such as artistic contemplation and philosophy, each of which presumably involves not merely random speech but talk about something *kalon*.

πρῶτον μὲν οὖν εἰ μὴ νόησίς ἐστιν ἀλλὰ δύναμις, εὔλογον ἐπίπονον εἶναι τὸ συνεχὲς αὐτῷ τῆς νοήσεως· ἔπειτα δῆλον ὅτι ἄλλο τι ἂν εἴη τὸ τιμιώτερον ἢ ὁ νοῦς, τὸ νοούμενον. **καὶ γὰρ τὸ νοεῖν καὶ ἡ νόησις ὑπάρξει καὶ τὸ χείριστον νοοῦντι, ὥστ' εἰ φευκτὸν τοῦτο (καὶ γὰρ μὴ ὁρᾶν ἔνια κρεῖττον ἢ ὁρᾶν), οὐκ ἂν εἴη τὸ ἄριστον ἡ νόησις.** αὑτὸν ἄρα νοεῖ, εἴπερ ἐστὶ τὸ κράτιστον, καὶ ἔστιν ἡ νόησις νοήσεως νόησις. [1074b28–35]

[c] But it appears that knowledge and perception and opinion and thought are <each> always of something else, being of itself <only> peripherally.

φαίνεται δ' ἀεὶ ἄλλου ἡ ἐπιστήμη καὶ ἡ αἴσθησις καὶ ἡ δόξα καὶ ἡ διάνοια, αὑτῆς δ' ἐν παρέργῳ. [1074b35–6]

I shall return in due course to [a] and [b], especially the bit of [b] in bold. It is sufficient for present purposes to note the way in which [c] contrasts human forms of cognition—such as *epistêmê* and *aisthêsis*—with the divine form of cognition on which *Metaphysics* XII.9 is focused. For unlike the divine form, which is primarily and indeed only of itself, each of the human forms is always of some object distinct from itself and apparently only "peripherally" of itself. My suggestion is that understanding this will eventually help us to see why even the maximally self-sufficient person will have friends.

The idea, very roughly, is that among the objects of human thought and perception are other human beings, who can of course be thought of and perceived *as good*. And when a human being thinks of or perceives another *as good*, she herself in some sense takes on the form of the other, including the other's goodness, which is *pleasant* for her in a way that renders it intelligible that she—even if she is generally self-sufficient—wants to live and act together with the other. But this sort of pleasure is not available to a divine thinker, whose *own* activity of thought is according to Aristotle its *only* object of thought. So even if Aristotle allows, as Plato does not, that God's thinking is pleasant, Aristotle does not allow that the pleasure of God's thought can be increased by God's thinking *in the company of others*. So the comparison of the self-sufficient person with God may lead us to overlook the ways in which the pleasures of *human thinking* can—like the pleasures of human eating, drinking, and making merry—be increased by *thinking together* with others.

All of this fits the emphasis found in the culmination of the Eudemian argument on the way in which the pleasures of thought and perception are—like the pleasures of wining and dining (not to mention sex)—increased by our engaging in the relevant activities in the company of others; the higher pleasures may even be *more increased* by the company of others than the lower pleasures tend (at least for the most part) to be. The idea, again roughly, is that to the extent that it is more pleasant to perceive *oneself* enjoying a bit of contemplation than to perceive oneself enjoying a good meal, so too it is more pleasant to perceive one's *friend* enjoying a bit of contemplation than to perceive him enjoying a good meal. So if we take the pleasure involved in perceiving oneself enjoying a good meal to be increased by perceiving one's friend enjoying it too, we should be able to see how the pleasure involved in perceiving oneself enjoying contemplation of the starry skies above may be increased by perceiving one's friend enjoying it too. And we should be able to see this without needing to attribute any sort of lack or deficiency to a subject whose pleasure is thus increased by contemplating the starry skies above in the company of his friend. So we should be able to see this without impugning the self-sufficiency of the subject whose pleasures are increased in this way.

This no doubt makes it sound as if Aristotle's argument and the texts that present it are far more straightforward than they actually are. But it will help to have this general picture in mind as we approach a dizzying array of textual possibilities. It may also help, if one loses one's bearings at any point, to be able to refer back to the following, admittedly dogmatic, outline.

[1] presents what is effectively one side of an aporia both sides of which are presented in the Nicomachean chapter. It presents an argument, completed in [1](D), for thinking that the maximally self-sufficient person will *not need*—*and* so will *not have*—a friend. (Aristotle's general strategy is to deny the inference, familiar to readers of the *Philebus*, from a subject's *not needing* some thing to the subject's *not having* that thing. Aristotle aims to show that there are *reasons* for the maximally self-sufficient agent to keep company with others *even if she has no need* for such company. And the reasons to which he appeals will prove in the end to be largely hedonic.) [1](E) then makes some points about what must be true of any friend the maximally self-sufficient agent in fact has (assuming she has one). So the contrast that becomes explicit in [5](D)—between the *argument* according to which the self-sufficient person *should not* have friends and the *evident fact* that such persons *do* have friends—is already implicit in [1].

[2] suggests that the comparison with God may mislead us and that the key to resolving the aporia lies in understanding that what it is for a human being "to live *in activity and as an end*" is to perceive and to know. This suggests that certain features of human perceiving and knowing—at least when these things are construed *as activities and ends*—play a crucial role here, so that when we come to understand human perceiving and knowing qua activities and ends, we should be able to understand why an otherwise self-sufficient agent will want to live *together* with friends.

It will turn out that one of the things Aristotle thinks we must come to see about human perceiving and knowing is the way in which these activities—unlike divine knowing—require objects *distinct* from themselves and their respective subjects.[26] For attending to some of the most characteristic objects of human perceiving and knowing—namely, our friends and their activities—reveals a form of pleasure that will allow us to make sense of the evident fact that even maximally self-sufficient human beings do have friends. The relevant form of pleasure is the form that each human being seems to take in engaging together with like-minded others in the *best* activities of which she is capable. Since the relevant activities in the case of maximally

[26] [I have added "and their respective subjects" to accommodate the point made in note 21 above.]

self-sufficient agents are forms of perceiving and knowing that are chosen *for themselves* and not simply as means to further ends, the pleasures that will allow us to make sense of this evident fact will be the pleasures that such agents take in engaging, together with like-minded others, in the forms of perceiving and knowing that they value not as means to further ends *but for themselves.*

[3] is where Aristotle's main argument begins. It is also where the serious textual difficulties begin, in part no doubt because of the ways in which indeterminacies in the original manuscripts gave rise to different determinations in the hands of different copyists. The problems stem from the fact that what originally appeared in majuscule as AYTO and its various forms could be read in any of the following ways, depending on various factors (including not just its position but also each individual reader's sense of the overall argument). It could be read (and thus copied into miniscule) as αὐτό, which could be either (a) an *intensive pronoun* (as in "Beauty *itself*" or "the animal *itself*") or (b) a *definite adjective* meaning "same" (as in "the *same* beauty" or "the *same* animal"). Or it could (at least in oblique cases) be read (and so copied into miniscule) as αὑτό, which is a *reflexive pronoun* (as in "the animal perceives *itself*"). The problems here are compounded by the frequency with which AYTO and its various forms are scattered throughout the text. And I suspect that the problems have been exacerbated by a tendency on the part of copyists, editors, and commentators to assume that Aristotle is making more or less the same point in the different places where AYTO appears, when Aristotle may in fact be making different points in what are different stages of an evolving argument.

Resuming now my dogmatic outline, I read the controversial occurrences of AYTO in [3] as forms of the *intensive* pronoun. So I read [3] as making a point about the identity of the *subjects* of the perceivings and knowings in which human living was said back in [2] to consist. The point here is that what is most *haireton* for each person is that she *herself* should perceive and that she *herself* should know; it is *not* (as commentators who see a *reflexive* pronoun here take it) that she should perceive and know *herself*. But it is compatible with this that AYTO and its various forms should be read differently elsewhere in the argument: it may be, for example, that they function in [4] as *reflexive* pronouns used to make a somewhat different point about the *objects* of perceiving and knowing.

[4] is exceptionally difficult, even given the extent to which [3] raises the bar. But I take Aristotle to be turning from the point made in [3], about the *subjects* of the relevant perceivings and knowings, to some point or points about the *objects* of these perceivings and knowings. I say "point or points" because what I see here is a combination of two points whose relations to one another are not entirely clear to me. The first is that it is generally more *haireton* for a subject to perceive and know *herself* than to perceive and know *others*. I take this point to rest largely on the value of self-awareness both as it is presented in Plato's *Philebus* (where those activities in which the agent is *aware* of what she is doing are generally taken to be *more haireton* than those in which she is *not aware* of what she is doing) and as it is understood by Aristotle (who takes a certain kind of awareness of what one is doing to be required for responsible agency and for the sorts of activities, including distinctively human forms of friendship, that

are made possible by such agency).[27] The second point is a version of one made in [ST2][b]—namely, that the value of any given *activity* of perceiving or knowing depends at least in part on the value of the *object* that is perceived or known. Hence the better the *objects* of any given subject's perceiving and knowing, the better (at least for the most part) that subject's *perceiving and knowing*, and so the better the *life* that consists in this perceiving and knowing.

How exactly these points are combined in [4] is hard to say. But the combination may turn on two features of human perception and knowledge as Aristotle presents these elsewhere: first, the way in which (as he explains in *De Anima*) the subject, in perceiving and knowing, becomes in some sense *like* the object perceived or known; and second, the way in which (as he explains in *Metaphysics* XII.9) the subject, in perceiving and knowing *other* things, comes to perceive and know *herself*, at least "peripherally." The upshot is roughly that in perceiving and knowing *good* objects, the subject herself becomes in some sense *like* those objects, and so in a *better* state than she would have been in had she perceived and known inferior objects instead.

This, I think, prepares the way for Aristotle's central point, which comes in [6](B) and (C), where Aristotle argues that to perceive one's *friend* is in a way to perceive *oneself*. It will follow, given what he has argued in [4], that the better the activity in which an agent perceives *her friend* engaged, the better the condition in which *she herself* not only *comes to be* but also *perceives herself* being. And this will allow Aristotle to argue in [6](C) that the better the activity in which an agent perceives her friend engaged, the more pleasant her own *self*-perception. As he says in [6](C), "it is always more pleasant to perceive oneself in the better <of two> good <conditions>." But before Aristotle can connect the pleasures of perceiving and knowing oneself with those of perceiving and knowing one's friend, he must reintroduce the friend, who has been offstage since the argument began back in [3](A). This is the function of [5].

Aristotle concedes in [5] that choosing to live together with others may seem foolish to those who begin by considering activities that we share in common with other animals—for example, eating and drinking. For in the case of other animals, who engage in such activities without sharing in conversation, it seems to make no difference whether they engage in these activities side by side or in separate fields. So it might seem that in our case too the value of such activities is not increased by our engaging in them in the company of others—unless perhaps these activities are accompanied by conversation that somehow enhances their value.

At this point Aristotle seems to suggest—in a way reminiscent of the question posed in [ST2][a]—that partaking of random speech *cannot* be such as to make a significant difference. But he proceeds in [5](C) to introduce two alleged facts of human nature, one of which casts doubt on this and serves together with the other to challenge the initial argument against supposing that the self-sufficient person will have a friend. The first is that *everyone*—including, therefore, those engaged in mundane activities

[27] For more on this, see Whiting, "Lockeanism" [III.8] 115–18.

like wining and dining—finds it *more pleasant* to enjoy goods together with friends than to enjoy them alone. This idea here, I think, is that random speech *does* make a difference to *some* agents—namely, those who find that even "small talk" or "chit-chat" increases the pleasure of such activities. The second alleged fact to which Aristotle appeals is that it is especially the *best* activities of which a person is capable that she *most* enjoys doing with others, with the result that different people tend, according to differences in their abilities, to enjoy doing different things together. Aristotle is clearly working towards the idea that a self-sufficient agent, for whom the attractions of "small-talk" or "chit-chat" are not enough to draw her to others, will nonetheless get *more enjoyment* from engaging with others in the *best* activities of which she is capable than she does from engaging in them on her own.

I think Aristotle regards these facts in something like the way he elsewhere regards facts about what people tend as a matter of psychological fact to love and cherish—namely, as facts about human nature that pack a kind of explanatory punch.[28] And I think it the task of [6] to *make sense* of these facts in a way that shows what is wrong with the *argument* against supposing that the self-sufficient person will have a friend. The basic idea is this: the "higher" the activity, the greater the pleasure to be had in engaging in it with others. So to the extent that we think it makes sense—as we clearly think it does—for people who pursue "mundane" pleasures to prefer pursuing them with friends to pursuing them alone, we should think that it *makes sense* (perhaps even *more sense*) for people who pursue "higher" pleasures to prefer pursuing them with friends to pursuing them alone.

The explanation for this turns at least in part on points established back in [4]: the "higher" the activity in which I perceive my friend engaging, the better the condition in which I myself both come to be and perceive myself being; so the "higher" the activity in which I perceive my friend engaging, the more pleasant my *self*-perception. Here, however, it is important to see that this pleasure does not function as the end for the sake of which I value perception of myself or others: it is the goodness of the *object* perceived that makes the *activity* of perceiving that object good and so *haireton*. The pleasure taken in perceiving a good object is thus a byproduct of what is truly *haireton*. But it is a byproduct that allows us to *make sense* of the fact that self-sufficient agents *do* have friends. For given the completeness criterion presented in the *Philebus* and taken over by Aristotle himself, a life *with* these pleasures is more *haireton* for a human being than a life *without* them.

But it is precisely such pleasures that the comparison with God may lead us to overlook. For even if we allow (as Aristotle himself allows) that the activity of God is pleasant, the comparison with God may lead us to overlook the way in which human forms of cognition, in requiring objects distinct from their subjects, give rise to the distinctively human form of pleasure involved in engaging together with others in the best activities of which we are capable. But we cannot afford to ignore the way in which human forms of cognition depend on objects distinct from their subjects. For, as Aristotle says in [7], ignoring that may lead us to conclude that the self-sufficient agent will not even think! Aristotle's argument is thus a kind of *reductio* of taking the comparison with God too far.

---

[28] See *EN* IX.7 and sec. 8 of Whiting, "*NAP*" [Chapter 6, this volume].

Many important points have been omitted from this preview. But I hope I have said enough to convey what I take to be Aristotle's main line of argument. Let us turn then to the nitty-gritty of the text to see whether there are independent grounds for taking it to convey something like the line of argument suggested here.

4. THE EUDEMIAN TEXT AS I DIVIDE IT: [1]–[3]

The Eudemian chapter begins, like its Nicomachean counterpart, with a presentation of the fundamental aporia. But the Eudemian presentation is one-sided in a way the Nicomachean presentation is not. The Eudemian chapter focuses from the outset on the reasons for thinking that the self-sufficient person will *not* have friends, while the Nicomachean chapter starts in the same place but quickly introduces the other side, saying (only seven lines in) that it seems strange to attribute all goods to someone who is eudaimôn (and thus *autarkês*) but to deny that he has friends, given that a friend seems to be the greatest of external goods [*EN* 1169b8–10]. What generates the sense of aporia in the Eudemian chapter is the way in which, as [5](D) explicitly says, some *argument* to the effect that a self-sufficient person will *not* have friends is contradicted by the *obvious fact* that such agents *do* have friends, a fact at which [1](E) hints.

I take the argument in question to be presented in [1](B)–(D): (B) introduces the initial argument in the form of a rhetorical question; (C) reinforces the expected answer by drawing the comparison between the self-sufficient person and God; and (D) draws the general conclusion. [1](E) then hints at the fact that self-sufficient agents *do* have friends and says something about what sorts of friends such an agent seems likely to have. [2] then suggests not only that the comparison of the self-sufficient person with God misleads us but also that we might come to see why self-sufficient agents have friends if we attend to what it means to live "in activity *and as an end*," a point to which Aristotle returns in [6](C). But let us move one step at time. The chapter begins as follows.

[1] Initial presentation of the aporia [1244b1–21]

(A) We must also consider self-sufficiency and *philia*, and how their fundamental characters stand in relation to one another. For someone might puzzle whether, if someone were self-sufficient in all respects, he will have . . . a friend—*if a friend is sought according to need*. Or <is this> not <so>?[29]

σκεπτέον δὲ καὶ περὶ αὐταρκείας καὶ φιλίας, πῶς ἔχουσι πρὸς τὰς ἀλλήλων δυνάμεις. ἀπορήσειε γὰρ ἄν τις πότερον, εἴ τις εἴη κατὰ πάντα αὐτάρκης, ἔσται τούτῳ < . . . >[30] φίλος, εἰ κατ' ἔνδειαν ζητεῖται φίλος. ἢ οὔ; [1244b1–4]

[29] It is impossible, given the preceding lacuna, to determine the content of the negation whose possibility is being considered. I like to think that it is the claim that the friend is sought according to need. But there is no clear justification for this. So I leave this open.

[30] There is a lacuna in the manuscripts here (twelve spaces in C and L; nineteen in P).

(B) Or will the good person be most self-sufficient? If the person with virtue is eudaimôn, why would <such a person> need a friend? For it is characteristic of one who is self-sufficient to need neither useful <friends> nor ones who cheer <him>, nor <generally> living together <with others>.[31] For he is adequate company for himself.

ἢ ἔσται ⟨ὁ⟩[32] ἀγαθὸς αὐταρκέστατος; εἰ ὁ μετ' ἀρετῆς εὐδαίμων, τί ἂν δέοι φίλου; οὔτε γὰρ τῶν χρησίμων δεῖσθαι αὐτάρκους οὔτε τῶν εὐφρανούντων οὔτε τοῦ συζῆν· αὐτὸς γὰρ αὑτῷ ἱκανὸς συνεῖναι. [1244b4–7]

(C) This is especially clear in the case of God. For it is obvious that needing nothing in addition <to himself>,[33] he will not need a friend, nor will he have <a friend>, nor <indeed> anything characteristic of a master.[34]

μάλιστα δὲ τοῦτο φανερὸν ἐπὶ θεοῦ· δῆλον γὰρ ὡς οὐδενὸς προσδεόμενος οὐδὲ φίλου δεήσεται, οὐδ' ἔσται αὐτῷ οὔ[τε μη]θὲν δεσπότου.[35] [1244b7–10]

---

31 One might be tempted to see [1](B) as referring seriatim to each of Aristotle's three canonical forms of friendship and so to take the reference to συζῆν to refer simply to friendship on account of *virtue*. But [1](D)'s talk of friendships with a view to συζῆν seems (given the contrast with friends who are useful) to include those who are friends on account of pleasure; hence my insertion of <generally>, which seems justified given that the association of pleasure-friendship with συζῆν is confirmed elsewhere. Aristotle takes friendships based on pleasure to resemble—and sometimes to morph into—friendships based on virtue (which are often associated with the value of συζῆν). See, e.g., *EN* 1157a10–12 together with section 7 of my "*NAP*" [Chapter 6, this volume]. For these reasons, I take [1](B)'s reference to συζῆν as covering *both* friendships on account of pleasure *and* friendships on account of virtue.

32 Following Ross, "Emendations in the *Nicomachean Ethics*."

33 The "in addition" is meant to represent the 'προσ' in 'προσδεόμενος'. See also *EN* 1098a8–16; 1099a15; 1155a26–28. Here again, the *Philebus* is in the background: see 20e5, where Socrates says that if either φρόνησις or ἡδονή is <the> good, "it must need nothing further in addition" (**προσδεῖσθαι**)."

34 Although *all* the manuscripts agree in reading οὐδ' ἔσται αὐτῷ οὔτε **μηθὲν δεσπότου** (where my translation runs "nor will he have <a friend>, nor <indeed> anything characteristic of a master"), many modern texts and translations (especially in English) read some form of 'δέομαι' (connoting *need* or *want*) in place of 'δεσπότου.' Décarie, *Aristote* (whom I follow) is the main exception. The Revised Oxford translation thus runs, "nor will [a God] have [a friend], supposing that he does *not need* one" (reading οὐδ' ἔσται αὐτῷ **μηθενὸς δεομένῳ**). And Rackham's *Aristotle* (Loeb) has "that inasmuch as [God] has *no need of* [a friend] he will not have one" (reading οὐδ' ἔσται αὐτῷ εἴ γε **μηθὲν δέοιτ ὅτου**). But such radical change seems to me unwarranted, given both the frequent talk of despots in surrounding chapters and the availability of Décarie's relatively simple emendation.

For talk of the *despotês* in surrounding chapters, see VII.5 1239b10–29 (arguably relevant here); VII.6 1240a33–b1 and VII.9 1241b11–24 (both quoted in the discussion of [6](A) below); VII.10 1242a26–35; and especially VII.15/VIII.3 1249a12–b23. These passages suggest various points Aristotle might be making here, including one suggested by the last mentioned text: namely, that God does not need even the sort of internal master we have in phronêsis, for God's *only* activity is *itself* his end. But there is no need to appeal to anything so speculative. Aristotle could simply be calling attention to the fact that even the most self-sufficient men—namely, masters—need (in the sense that they have a *use* for) things (such as slaves) for which God has *no* use whatsoever. This would set us up nicely for the point that that it does not follow from the fact that God will not have a friend that the maximally self-sufficient person will not. For God no more has slaves than he has friends; but it is precisely self-sufficient men who have slaves. This may even help to explain why they do not need the sort of *utility* friends that less self-sufficient agents might be thought to need! But we need not resolve this here. For nothing in my interpretation of the main argument depends on this.

35 Following Décarie, *Aristote*, 194 n. 222.

(D) *So also* a human being who is most eudaimôn will be least of all in need of a friend, except insofar as it is impossible for him to be self-sufficient. It is *therefore necessary*[36] that the fewest friends belong to the one who lives <the> best <life> and that they are always becoming fewer, and that he will not take trouble in order that <they> should be <his> friends, but will look down not only on those <friends> who are useful but even on those who are such-as-to-be-chosen with a view to living together.[37]

ὥστε καὶ ἄνθρωπος ὁ εὐδαιμονέστατος ἥκιστα δεήσεται φίλου, ἀλλ' ᾗ καθ' ὅσον ἀδύνατον εἶναι αὐτάρκη. ἀνάγκη ἄρα ἐλαχίστους εἶναι φίλους τῷ ἄριστα ζῶντι, καὶ ἀεὶ ἐλάττους γίνεσθαι, καὶ μὴ σπουδάζειν ὅπως ὦσι φίλοι, ἀλλ' ὀλιγωρεῖν μὴ μόνον τῶν χρησίμων, ἀλλὰ καὶ <τῶν>[38] εἰς τὸ συζῆν αἱρετῶν. [1244b10–15]

(E) But surely in that case it would seem clear that the friend <sc., any friend the self-sufficient person does have> will be neither for the sake of use nor for the sake of <any> benefit. But <his friend is> not a friend on account of virtue alone. For whenever we are in need of nothing, it is then that all seek companions in enjoying <things>, and those who will receive benefits rather than bestow them. And we have better judgment when we are self-sufficient (than when in need), when above all we should have[39] friends **worthy** of living together <with us>.[40]

ἀλλὰ μὴν καὶ τότε φανερὸν ἂν εἶναι δόξειεν ὡς οὐ χρήσεως ἕνεκα ὁ φίλος οὐδ' ὠφελείας. ἀλλ' οὐ δι' ἀρετὴν φίλος μόνον.[41] ὅταν γὰρ μηθενὸς ἐνδεεῖς

---

[36] I have italicized this and the preceding "so also" in order to highlight what I take to be the conclusion of the argument to which Aristotle refers back both in [5](D) and again in [7](A).

[37] I shall return shortly to my reasons for adopting the "such-as-to-be-chosen" locution, which is intended to capture possibilities ranging from "*can* be chosen," through "is the sort of thing that *tends* to be chosen," to "what is *worthy* of being chosen" (and which will play an important role in what follows). See note 12 of my "Self-Love and Authoritative Virtue" [Chapter 4, this volume].

[38] Following Spengel, *Über die unter dem Namen des Aristoteles* (with Walzer and Mingay's Oxford Classical Texts (OCT), *Ethica Eudemia*).

[39] On the reasonableness of understanding 'δεῖσθαι' sometimes as "ought" rather than a hard "must," see section 10 of my "*NAP*" [Chapter 6, this volume].

[40] The idea here is that the self-sufficient agent's judgment is not distorted by her own needs, or even (when it comes to pleasure) her own mere tastes. So she can focus on the features of her friend that make the friend *worthy* of living together with her. For more on the way Aristotle seeks focus on features of the *object*, as distinct from needs and mere tastes of the *subject*, see my "*NAP*" [Chapter 6, this volume].

[41] Reading ἀλλ' οὐ at the start of the second sentence with all manuscripts (instead of ἀλλ' ὁ, which is adopted following the Codex Oxoniensis by Bekker, *Aristotelis Opera*, and Solomon, *Works of Aristotle*); but rejecting the manuscripts' μόνος in favor of the OCT's μόνον (due to D. B. Robinson). Solomon (followed by Rackham) reads ἀλλ' ὁ δι' ἀρετὴν φίλος μόνος and translates "but the friend through virtue is the only friend." This leaves it open that the point here is that the friend on account of virtue is the only friend that a *self-sufficient* person will have. Rackham's translation, on the other hand, supplies a general point that is often ascribed to Aristotle: "the only real friend is one loved on account of goodness." But this seems misguided: Aristotle explicitly denies this general point back in VII.2 (at 1236a23–32, which is discussed in section 5 of my "*NAP*" [Chapter 6, this volume]). For a very different reading, see McCabe, "Mirrors."

ὦμεν, τότε τοὺς συναπλαυσομένους ζητοῦσι πάντες, καὶ τοὺς εὖ πεισομένους μᾶλλον ἢ τοὺς ποιήσοντας. ἀμείνω δ' ἔχομεν κρίσιν αὐτάρκεις ὄντες ἢ μετ' ἐνδείας, ὅτε μάλιστα τῶν συζῆν ἀξίων δεόμεθα φίλων. [1244b15–21]

[2] Diagnostic hunch and the basic logos [1244b21–26]

(A) We must consider this puzzle, lest something in it be well said, while something escapes our notice on account of the comparison <to God>.

περὶ δὲ τῆς ἀπορίας ταύτης σκεπτέον, μή ποτε τὸ μέν τι λέγεται καλῶς, τὸ δὲ λανθάνει διὰ τὴν παραβολήν. [1244b21–22]

(B) The matter is plain when we have grasped what it is to live *in activity and as an end*. It is clear then that it <to live *in activity and as an end*> is to perceive and to know, and so also that to live together <presumably in activity and as an end> is to perceive together and to know together.

δῆλον δὲ λαβοῦσι τί τὸ ζῆν τὸ κατ' ἐνέργειαν καὶ ὡς τέλος. φανερὸν οὖν ὅτι τὸ αἰσθάνεσθαι καὶ τὸ γνωρίζειν, ὥστε καὶ τὸ συζῆν τὸ συναισθάνεσθαι καὶ τὸ συγγνωρίζειν ἐστίν. [1244b22–26]

There is a lacuna in [1] (A) such that it is impossible to tell what exactly the point there is. But little if anything in the interpretation of what follows depends on this: the gist of the puzzle is reasonably clear. I have italicized the last bit of (A) so as to call attention to the assumption that I think Aristotle means to challenge—namely, that it is only in accordance with some *need* that a person seeks a friend. For I think it pretty clear from what follows that Aristotle's solution to the puzzle consists largely in denying this. He argues, very roughly, that there are activities such that although an agent can successfully engage in them on her own, the pleasure she takes in them is increased by engaging in them together with a friend. So although the self-sufficient agent has no *needs* that a friend might fill, it *makes sense* that such agents have friends with whom they engage in such activities (since such activities are more pleasant engaged in with friends than engaged in alone).

It is clear from [2](A) that Aristotle takes the puzzle in question to have been presented in [1], in spite of the fact that there is no explicit presentation there of the case *for* the self-sufficient person's *having* friends: there is simply the suggestion in the first sentence of [1](E) that any friend the self-sufficient agent does have—assuming he has one—will not be for the sake of use or any benefit. Readers recalling the three forms of friendship that were introduced in *EE* VII.2 and employed in subsequent chapters will at this point be inclined to suppose that any friend the self-sufficient agent has must be *either* on account of virtue *or* on account of pleasure. So it is no surprise that Aristotle turns immediately to friendship on account of virtue and then makes indirect reference to the issue of pleasure.

But there is a question about the second sentence of [1](E). Is the point that any friend the self-sufficient person does have is a friend *only* on account of virtue? Or is the point rather that any friend the self-sufficient person does have is a friend *not only* on account of virtue *but also* on account of something else? I have opted for the latter because of the way in which the next sentence, like the rest of the chapter as I read it, points to the alleged fact that *all* people tend in the absence of need to enjoy doing with others the sorts of things they *most* enjoy doing. So I take the next sentence to suggest that even if self-sufficient agents are friends *primarily* on account of virtue, it is *not only* on account of virtue that they are friends: they are *also* friends on account of the *pleasure* they take in doing things *together*.

There is a subtle but important shift here, from the talk at the end of [1](D) of friends who are such-as-to-be-chosen [*haireton*] with a view to living together, to the talk at the end of [1](E) of friends who are worthy [*axion*] of living together. We have already encountered talk of what is *haireton*—and of what is *more haireton* than what—in Plato's *Philebus*, and I have so far represented this (following many commentators) by talk of "what is desirable or worthy of choice." But there is a multivocity in the -τός/-τόν suffix that plays an important role throughout what follows. So let me pause here to explain the possibilities.

We have seen this suffix in the *Metaphysics* XII use of '*to noêton*,' which is cognate with the verb '*noein*' (meaning "to think") and is used to refer to the *object* of thought. And we shall encounter this suffix repeatedly in our Eudemian text, both in talk of the objects of perception and knowledge and in talk of the objects of choice. In some cases, the suffix bears the meaning of the passive participle, so that '*to aisthêton*' (which is cognate with the verb '*aisthanesthai*,' meaning "to perceive") means "what is perceived" in the sense that it is *actually* perceived; and '*to gnôston*' (which is cognate with the verb '*gignôskein*,' meaning "to know") means "what is known" in the sense of what is *actually* known. But the suffix often indicates *possibility*, so that '*to aisthêton*' and '*to gnôston*' are often used in the sense of "what *can* be perceived" and "what *can* be known"; and '*to haireton*' (which is cognate with '*hairesthai*,' meaning "to choose") often means "what *can* be chosen" or—as I render it in my translations—"what is *such-as-to-be*-chosen." This translation is intended to reflect a complication that arises especially in the case of '*to haireton*,' which can be used to mean not simply "what *can* be chosen" or even "the sort of thing people *tend* to choose," but sometimes means "what is *worthy* of choice."[42]

It may be on account of the ambiguity of '*haireton*' that Aristotle shifts from his talk (at the end of [1](D)) of friends that are "*such-as-to-be-chosen* with a view to living together" to his talk (at the end of [1](E)) of friends that are "*worthy* of living together <with us>." For he may want to make it clear that the self-sufficient person is likely to have only the latter sort of friend: the sort *worthy* of the kind of living together of which Aristotle goes on to speak in [2](B), where he identifies living (in the case of a human being) with perceiving and knowing. That Aristotle's point is about a friend

[42] The range of possibilities is clearly exemplified by '*to philêton*' (which is cognate with the verb '*philein*,' meaning "to love"): this can be used to refer to what is *actually loved* or to what is *lovable* (where this in turn may be *either* the sort of thing that people are *in fact* disposed to love *or* the sort of thing that is *worthy* of being loved).

worthy of sharing one's perceptions and thoughts is borne out in what follows, especially [4], where Aristotle turns his attention to the way in which the value of the *activities* of perceiving and knowing depends on the value of the *objects* perceived and known: the better the objects, the better the subject's perceiving and knowing. But the argument does not end there: the crucial step involves the connection with pleasure that is made in [6]: the better the perceiving and knowing, the *more pleasant* the perceiving and knowing; so the better the perceiving and knowing *together*, the more pleasant the perceiving and knowing *together*.

The argument for this is prefaced in [2](B) with what (for reasons to be explained below) I call "the basic *logos*": namely, that what it is (for a human being) to live, *in activity and as an end,* is to perceive and know. The talk of living *in activity* also appears in *EN* IX.9; but the talk of living *as an end* appears only in the Eudemian chapter, where it seems to play an important role in the culmination of the main argument. This is [6](C), where Aristotle says that the activities that self-sufficient agents most enjoy doing together with friends are those belonging "in the end." The idea is no doubt that the activities that self-sufficient agents most enjoy doing together are the ones that *constitute* their eudaimonia, the ones for the sake of which they would (as Aristotle puts it in *EE* I.5) choose to come to be rather than not come to be.

It is worth pausing here to note that the idea of something for the sake of which one would choose to come to be rather than not figures prominently in the *Eudemian Ethics* in a way it does not in the *Nicomachean*. Aristotle tells a story in *EE* I.5 about Anaxagoras answering a question about that for the sake of which he would choose to come to be by saying, "for the sake of contemplating the heaven and the order of the whole cosmos." Aristotle contrasts this raison d'être with the ones given by those who would choose to live for the sake of sensual pleasure and those who would choose to live for the sake of performing virtuous actions [1216a10–27]. The idea reappears in VII.12, where Aristotle commences the main argument. For it is clear from the first step that the argument takes the desire to live not as primitive but as something to be explained by the value of the activities in which our living consists.

[3] First step: what is most *haireton* for each subject is to perceive and to know [1244b26–33]

(A) For each <human being> what is most such-as-to-be-chosen is that **he himself** perceive and that **he himself** know. And on account of this the desire for living is innate to all <human beings>. For one should take living as a kind of knowledge.

ἔστι δὲ τὸ **αὐτὸν** αἰσθάνεσθαι καὶ τὸ **αὐτὸν** γνωρίζειν αἱρετώτατον ἑκάστῳ, καὶ διὰ τοῦτο τοῦ ζῆν πᾶσιν ἔμφυτος ἡ ὄρεξις· τὸ γὰρ ζῆν δεῖ τιθέναι[43] γνῶσιν τινά. [1244b26–29]

[43] Following Bonitz: the manuscripts have διατιθέναι (retained by Osborne, "Selves and Other Selves").

(B) If, then, someone should cut off <?> and should make the knowing itself in itself or not[44] <knowing itself in itself> (but this <sc., that something is cut off> escapes notice, just as it was written in the *logos*, though in actual fact it is possible for it not to escape notice)[45] there would be no difference between another knowing and oneself <knowing>. It would be similar to another *living* instead of oneself.

εἰ οὖν τις ἀποτέμοι καὶ ποιήσειε τὸ γινώσκειν αὐτὸ καθ' αὐτὸ καὶ μὴ (ἀλλὰ τοῦτο μὲν λανθάνει, ὥσπερ ἐν τῷ λόγῳ γέγραπται, τῷ μέντοι πράγματι ἔστι μὴ λανθάνειν), οὐθὲν ἂν διαφέροι ἢ τὸ γινώσκειν ἄλλον ἀνθ' αὐτοῦ· τὸ δ' ὅμοιον τῷ ζῆν ἀνθ' αὐτοῦ ἄλλον. [1244b29–33]

There is much controversy about how exactly to read (A), but however we do so the following seems clear: (A) states a premise in Aristotle's own voice, one about what is most *haireton* for each individual; and (B) speaks of someone who "cuts off" or ignores an important aspect of what is claimed in (A) without realizing that he is doing so (or without realizing what he cuts off), with the result that he makes—or at least risks making—a claim on a par with the claim that it makes no difference whether it is oneself or someone else who *lives*. It seems to be assumed in (B) that this is ridiculous and that what is most *haireton* for each individual is *of course* that he *himself* should live. And the point there seems to be that someone who treats the sort of knowing in which our living consists as knowing *itself in itself* risks losing sight of this obvious truth: he ends up speaking as if it makes no evaluative difference to a subject, *whose* knowing is at issue, his own or that of someone else.[46]

---

[44] It seems to me most natural to take this μὴ as introducing the complement of the immediately preceding talk of "the knowing itself in itself"—i.e., to take this as referring, within the realm of knowing, to the knowing that is *not* itself in itself. This leaves it open in what respect the knowing in question is *not* itself in itself, whether for example it is the subjects or the objects of the knowing—or perhaps both—that are now part of the mix. The alternative, I suppose, is to take it to negate whatever sort of knowing was in play back in [3](A): either the subject's *own* knowing (if we follow Kosman, "Desirability") or the subject's knowledge *of himself* (if we follow the OCT). In this case, the subsequent comparison with another's *living* instead of oneself would seem to favor taking it Kosman's way (i.e., as indicating that the *subject* has been cut off and is now being thrown back into the mix). But the comparison with living does *not require* us to take the initial point to be that the subject *alone* is cut off or ignored: someone who makes claims about knowledge itself in itself ignores *both* the subject *and* the object. And while Aristotle may start here in [3](B) by noting a problem he sees in ignoring the *subject* of the relevant knowing, he may go on (as I think he does in [4]) to raise problems he sees in ignoring the *object*. So it seems best in the end—and grammatically most natural—to take μὴ to introduce the complement of τὸ γινώσκειν αὐτὸ καθ' αὐτὸ.

[45] It is tempting to suppose that the idea here is of something that an abstract *logos* might lead us to overlook even though it is something that is—either in our actual experience or if we look closely at the matter [τὸ πράγμα] in question—fairly obvious, something we could hardly fail to notice. This is presumably why Richards, *Aristotelica*, wants to understand ἀνάγκη ἐστί. I am sympathetic to understanding the passage this way, but read and translate only the weaker claim (which appears in all the manuscripts): namely, that "it is in actual fact *possible* for it *not* to escape notice." I wonder, however, whether a τι might have dropped out after ἐστί, due to haplography, so that the claim was originally "though in actual fact it is *something* that does not escape notice."

[46] For a recent translation and interpretation of this passage that seems (as many do) to miss this point, see Sorabji, *Self*, 234–39.

Of course the talk of "knowing itself in itself" leaves out *both* the subject *and* the object of the relevant knowing, but the comparison with another *living* instead of oneself places the emphasis squarely on the problem with cutting off or ignoring the *subject* of the relevant knowledge. For "to live" does not take an object (except perhaps an internal accusative). So this comparison seems to rule out one common way (adopted in Walzer and Mingay's OCT) of resolving disputes about how to read [3](A), the one according to which [3](A) specifies the *objects* of the perceiving and knowing in which our living is supposed to consist (namely, *ourselves*).

What we find in all the manuscripts—except the second hand of the Marcianus (henceforth: Marcianus$_2$)—is "τὸ αὐτὸ αἰσθάνεσθαι καὶ τὸ αὐτὸ γνωρίζειν" (which is most naturally rendered "the **same** perceiving and the **same** knowing").[47] But it is difficult to make sense of this in context.[48] So many readers—including, I assume Marcianus$_2$—have sought an alternative reading.

Marcianus$_2$ has τὸ **αὑτοῦ** αἰσθάνεσθαι καὶ τὸ **αὑτὸν** γνωρίζειν (i.e., "to perceive and to know **oneself**"), which is adopted in the OCT, perhaps because the editors think it likely that Marcianus$_2$ was correcting Marcianus$_1$ by appeal to some more authoritative

[47] Jakub Krajczynski suggested (in conversation) taking αὐτὸ as an accusative pronoun in the *neuter*, intended to make the point that for each *animal* its *own* perceiving and its *own* knowing are most *haireton*. But this seems to me difficult, given the combination of the overall context (which is clearly about human subjects) and (B)'s immediate use of the masculine in its talk of *another* knowing and *another* living (instead of oneself). Perhaps, however, as Pieter Sjoerd Hasper suggested (in conversation), the αὐτὸ is used more abstractly to refer to *any x* in *whatever* domain is relevant, the talk being of *x* itself perceiving or *x* itself knowing. If the relevant domain is that of human subjects, then this is much the same as what I propose.

[48] The most plausible ways of construing the received text seem to me as follows.

(a) *numerically the same* perceivings and knowings are most choiceworthy *for each of two friends* in the sense that each friend values the other's perceivings and knowings in the same way that she values her own—i.e., above the perceivings and knowings of all others;

(b) *specifically the same* perceivings and knowings are most choiceworthy *for each of two friends* in the sense that friends value the same *kinds* of perceivings and knowings—i.e., they like perceiving and knowing the same sorts of things;

(c) *specifically the same* perceivings and knowings are most choiceworthy *for each person* (or perhaps *for each animal*).

And while (b) might conceivably be a premise in an argument for having friends, it is hard to see how (a) could be construed as anything other than what the argument aims to *prove*. But (b) fails to explain—as the διὰ τοῦτο in the second part of the sentence requires it to do—why the desire for living is innate to all, whether we take this (as the context suggests) as referring to all *persons* or (as it might conceivably be taken) as referring to all *animals*. Only (c) seems capable of explaining this. According to (c), the same *kinds* of perceivings and knowings are most choiceworthy for each person (or perhaps each animal); hence the desire to live—which is necessary if one is to experience such perceivings and knowings—is innate to all. In other words, each person (or perhaps animal) wants to live because each wants above all the sort of perceivings and knowings for which living is requisite. Aristotle may well think this: in fact, he probably does. But I do not see—either on my own or in the extant literature—how this might serve as the first step in any argument for having friends as coherent as the argument afforded (in ways to be explained below) by starting with the premise embodied in Kosman's relatively conservative proposal. Nor does (c) allow us to make good sense of the comparison with another *living* instead of oneself. For an alternative attempt to make sense (though somewhat far-out sense) of the manuscript reading, see Catherine Osborne, "Selves and Other Selves."

manuscript. But it seems to me more probable that Marcianus$_2$, unable to make sense of τὸ **αὐτὸ** αἰσθάνεσθαι καὶ τὸ **αὐτὸ** γνωρίζειν in this context, looked ahead to [4](A)'s talk of τὸ **ἑαυτοῦ** αἰσθάνεσθαι καὶ γνωρίζειν (i.e., "to perceive and to know **oneself**") for signs of the point here in [3](A). This would explain his converting the first αὐτὸ to αὐτοῦ and the second to αὐτὸν (because αἰσθάνεσθαι requires a genitive object and γνωρίζειν an accusative one). But this assimilates the point of [3](A) to that of [4](A), which is pretty clearly a point about the objects (as distinct from the subjects) of the relevant perceiving and knowing. And [4](A) may well be intended to make a *distinct* point, one representing a separate stage in Aristotle's argument. For the emphasis in [3](B) is clearly on the danger of cutting off or ignoring the *subjects* of the relevant perceiving and knowing. So we cannot simply read the point of [3](A) off the text of [4](A), which is most naturally read as concerned with the *objects* of the relevant perceiving and knowing.

It makes more sense of what we find in [3](B)—and is no less conservative than what we find in Marcianus$_2$—to follow Kosman in adding "ν" at the end of *each* αὐτὸ and reading τὸ **αὐτὸν** αἰσθάνεσθαι καὶ τὸ **αὐτὸν** γνωρίζειν (i.e., that he **himself** perceive and that he **himself** know).[49] But Kosman, I think, then makes the converse of the mistake of which I suspect Marcianus$_2$: instead of assimilating [3](A) to [4](A), Kosman takes his reading of [3](A) to require him to read the genitive ἑαυτοῦ in [4](A) in what he admits is not the most natural way—namely, as a genitive of subject indicating the subject's *own* perceiving. But if [3] and [4] represent different stages in Aristotle's argument, it is no more legitimate to take [3](A) as a guide to what [4](A) must be saying than to reason the other way around—though Kosman's mistake is potentially more dangerous insofar as he proposes to read [4](A) in light of his *emended* version of [3](A) (which could lead him to miss the mark in *both* cases). Still, I think Kosman's reading of [3](A) the best on offer and I propose to accept it without, however, accepting the unnatural interpretation of [4](A) that Kosman seems to think required by it. For I think it relatively clear, in ways to be explained below, that [3] and [4] are supposed to make *distinct* contributions to Aristotle's overall argument.[50]

---

[49] This is plausible, given that one can imagine a scribe failing to understand the somewhat unusual construction τὸ **αὐτὸν** αἰσθάνεσθαι καὶ τὸ **αὐτὸν** γνωρίζειν—or failing to understand how a claim that sounds so egoistic could figure in a discussion of friendship while thinking that it would make sense in a discussion of friendship to claim that the same perceiving and knowing are choiceworthy to each of two friends—and so dropping the two *ν*s. But this would (as I explain in the preceding note) leave us with something that does not make clear sense in this context.

[50] It is worth noting here another more radical (but not unreasonable) proposal due to Solomon and adopted in Rackham's Loeb edition. Solomon proposes to reverse the τὸ and the αὐτὸ in both occurrences of τὸ αὐτὸ and to take αὐτὸ as an intensive pronoun. This yields αὐτὸ τὸ αἰσθάνεσθαι καὶ αὐτὸ τὸ γνωρίζειν, which Solomon renders "mere perception and mere knowledge." Solomon's Greek fits well enough with what we find in [3](B), which is what makes his proposal reasonable. But his translation suggests he was looking ahead to [3](B), where he renders the talk of τὸ γινώσκειν αὐτὸ καθ' αὐτὸ as "mere knowledge." But this seems to me misleading, and I myself would render this "the perceiving *itself* and the knowing *itself*" (as in Platonic talk of "Beauty *itself*"). For "mere perceiving and mere knowing" is highly misleading if I am right that Aristotle's point in [4] is to contrast objects *worthy* of being perceived and known with objects not so worthy, and to insist that living well is a matter of perceiving and knowing *worthy* objects: it is precisely *mere* perceiving and *mere* knowing (as we use the term "mere") that *fail* to characterize the sort of life Aristotle thinks we all desire.

It is worth pausing here to note one further reason for following Kosman in putting the emphasis in [3](A) on the identity of the *subject*: however obvious it is that what is most choiceworthy for each subject is that he *himself* should know, it is nowhere near as obvious *what object* it is *most haireton* for him to know—namely, himself or someone (or something) else. So it would make sense for Aristotle to start with the former, more obvious point and to turn only after he has established that to the latter, more controversial one. And the latter *is* controversial. For why should it not in fact be *more haireton* for a subject to know someone or something *superior to himself*—for example, God or the starry skies above—than to know *himself*? We shall return to this question, for it is part of what Aristotle himself seems to address in [4].

I am now in a position to explain how I understand [3](B)'s reference to what was written in some *logos*, which might be either an argument or simply an account of some phenomenon (hence my transliteration throughout what follows). The idea seems to be that some written *logos* leads us to claim that what is most *haireton* for each subject is "knowing itself in itself" without, however, attending to *whose* knowing is supposed to be *most haireton* for each, her own or that of someone else. And this is supposed to be like saying that living is most *haireton* for each subject without attending to *whose* living is supposed to be most *haireton* for each, her own or someone else's. But the fact that what is most *haireton* for each subject is his or her *own* living is the sort of thing that only an abstract *logos* could lead one to overlook.

But what exactly *is* the *logos* that might lead one to overlook this? I assume both that the burden of proof is on anyone who proposes (as Dirlmeier does in *Eudemische Ethik*) to read this as referring to something written elsewhere and that the burden is even higher if we can make sense of this as referring to something written here. And there seem to me two candidates here: *either* what was written in [2](B), where Aristotle identifies living with perceiving and knowing, without specifying *whose* perceiving or knowing he is talking about; *or* what was written in [3](A), assuming that we read it (with Kosman) as concerned with the subject's *own* perceiving and knowing.

But if we take what was written in the *logos* to be what was written in Kosman's version of [3](A), then the rest of [3](B) makes no sense.[51] For the rest seems to assume that what was written *fails* to mention the subject, which is precisely what Kosman's version mentions. And though one might think this a reason for following Marcianus$_2$ and taking [3](A) to identify only the *object* of the relevant perceiving and knowing, this would be misguided—and not simply for the reasons already mentioned. For insofar as the object mentioned in Marcianus$_2$ is the *subject himself*, reference to the subject is *built into* Marcianus$_2$'s version of [3](A). So what is written there is unlikely to lead the reader to forget that it is the subject's *own* perceiving and knowing that is supposed to be most *haireton* for him.[52]

[51] Reference to the subject is not built into Solomon's reading, so if we follow Solomon we could take the argument referred to in [3](B) to be the one written in [3](A). But Solomon's emendation is the most radical on offer and there is (even apart from that) good reason to reject it: see note 50.

[52] This might seem to us so obvious that not even an abstract *logos* could lead one to forget it: but it may not have gone without saying in Aristotelian circles, where it was sometimes claimed that the lives of

For these reasons, I take "what was written in the *logos*" to refer back to what was written in [2](B), where Aristotle identifies living with perceiving and knowing without mentioning *either* the subject *or* the object of the relevant perceiving and knowing. (This is why I call what we find there "the basic *logos*.") And I read the μή that precedes the parenthesis in [3](B) as negating "the knowing itself in itself" rather than "the subject's *own* knowing" or (as the OCT has it) "the subject's knowing *himself*." In other words, I take what escapes notice to *include* the fact that it is the subject's *own* knowing that is in question, which is what the comparison with talk of another's *living* is supposed to make clear. But what escapes notice need not be *limited* to this fact: it remains open to Aristotle to make an *additional* point about the relevance of the *object* to the value of any given *activity* of knowing. And this is precisely what I take him to do in [4]. But before turning to that, let me summarize briefly how I read [3] and say a few words about the role I think it plays in the ensuing argument.

[3] calls to our attention something that the *logos* written in [2](B) might lead us to forget—namely, that what is most *haireton* for each subject is not simply that there should *be* perceiving *itself in itself* and that there should *be* knowing *itself in itself*; what is most *haireton* for each subject is that she *herself* should perceive and that she *herself* should know. And this is crucial to showing, in the end, why the subject should (as the basic *logos* claims) value perceiving *together with* and knowing *together with* her friend. For it is only if she is *present with* her friend *when* her friend is perceiving and knowing that her friend's perceiving and knowing enter the sphere of what is most *haireton* for *her*—namely, her *own* perceiving and knowing. In other words, it is only if she is *conscious of* her friend's perceiving and knowing that her friend's perceiving and knowing become, so to speak, part of *her life*.

Note, however, that I do not think that the friend's perceiving and knowing become part of the subject's life in the way Kosman suggests—i.e., by becoming in some sense her *own* perceiving and her *own* knowing: they do *not* become part of her life in the sense that *she* becomes in some way *their* subject. Rather, they become part of her life in something like the way her own first-order perceiving and knowing become part of her life: namely, by coming to be among the *objects* perceived and known by her, objects that help *if they are good* to make her second-order activities of perceiving and knowing not simply good but also pleasant, and indeed pleasant *because* they are *good*. In other words, just as perceiving and knowing her *own* perceiving and knowing is pleasant *if* her own perceiving and knowing are *good*, so too perceiving and knowing *her friend's* perceiving and knowing is pleasant *if* her friend's perceiving and knowing are *good*.

---

some subjects—for example, slaves—should be devoted to facilitating the perceiving and thinking done by others (something Aristotle himself is not beyond saying). See. for example, *EE* 1241b17–22, quoted in the discussion of [6](A) below, where Aristotle denies that there is any *koinônia* between master and slave because (at least in the context of this relationship) the slave has no independent good of his own.

5. INTERLUDE: THE *PHILEBUS* BACKGROUND AND METHODOLOGICAL REMARKS ON THE RELATION BETWEEN [3] AND [4]

It will be easier to appreciate all of this if we keep the *Philebus* background firmly in mind. So let us recall the passage early on where Socrates asks Protarchus whether he would be content to go through life enjoying the greatest pleasures without, however, *any* form of nous, and Protarchus replies that he most certainly would. Socrates then presses Protarchus to concede that without nous he would not only fail to remember past pleasures and to anticipate future ones: he would also fail to *recognize that he was enjoying himself at the time when he was actually doing so.* He would—as Socrates puts it and Protarchus immediately agrees—be living "the life of a jellyfish or one of those encrusted creatures that lives in the sea." And this—like the converse life of pure nous without any pleasure—is something they agree is *not haireton* for a human being.[53]

The basic idea here is that just as a life of pure thought fails to count as *the* good for a human being because there are forms of pleasure such that adding them to a life of pure thought makes that life *more haireton* for its subject than it would otherwise be, so too a life of pure pleasure fails to count as *the* good for a human being because there is a form of nous such that adding this form of nous to a life of pure pleasure makes that life *more haireton* for its subject than it would otherwise be. The relevant form of nous seems to be a form of self-awareness or what we might call "self-consciousness." So the idea seems to be that adding self-awareness (or self-consciousness) to a life makes that life *more haireton* for its subject than it would be in the absence of such awareness (or consciousness).[54]

---

[53] The points made here, in 21a–d, are restated in 60a–c, where Socrates speaks explicitly (in a way whose relevance will become clearer in my discussion of [4]) about the nature of the good [τὴν τἀγαθοῦ . . . φύσιν] and says that "any creature that was in permanent possession of it <sc., the good>, entirely and in every way, would never be in need of anything else [μηδενὸς ἑτέρου ποτὲ ἔτι προσδεῖσθαι] but would live in perfect self-sufficiency [τὸ δὲ ἱκανὸν τελεώτατον ἔχειν]" (*Philebus* translation by D. Frede). The language in both places is similar to the language used by Aristotle in the initial presentation of our aporia. See the talk in [1](B) of the good person being "adequate company for himself" [αὐτὸς γὰρ αὑτῷ ἱκανὸς συνεῖναι] and in [1](C) of God "needing nothing <in addition to himself>" [οὐδενὸς προσδεόμενος]. So there should be little doubt about the relevance of these passages to the argument of *EE* VII.12.

[54] It is not entirely clear whether this is supposed to be at least partly because of the way in which adding self-awareness is taken to add new forms of pleasure or whether that is excluded by the terms of the thought experiment. For the life of pure pleasure is supposed to be imbued throughout with "the greatest pleasures." But even if the terms of Socrates' thought experiment are supposed to rule out the possibility that self-consciousness might increase the subject's pleasure, Protarchus may not fully appreciate these terms. So even if *Socrates* takes self-awareness to make a non-hedonic contribution to the value of any life involving it, *Protarchus* may accept Socrates' point because he takes the addition of self-awareness to yield new forms of pleasure and so greater pleasure overall. And Plato may well intend for his readers to conclude that self-awareness can make both hedonic and non-hedonic contributions to the value of a life. So we should keep both sorts of contribution in mind as we return to VII.12. For further discussion of this point, see Cooper, "Plato and Aristotle on 'Finality' and '(Self-) Sufficiency," sec. II.

Aristotle, I think, makes use of this basic idea in *EE* VII.12 when he argues that the self-sufficient agent does not simply want it to be the case *that her friend perceives and knows*. The idea, as we shall see in [5](C), is that the self-sufficient agent wants to be *present with* her friend *when her friend is perceiving and knowing* and to be present with her friend in something like the way in which she is typically present with *herself* when *she herself* is perceiving and knowing. For just as her *own* perceiving and knowing, when they are good, make her *awareness of* her own perceiving and knowing not just good but also pleasant (and pleasant because its *objects* are good), so too her *friend's* perceiving and knowing, when *they* are good, make her *awareness of* her friend's perceiving and knowing not just good but also pleasant (and pleasant because *its* objects are good).

This, I think, is why Aristotle shifts in [4] to a point about the *objects* of the perceiving and knowing in which the subject's life is supposed to consist. [4] begins—in *all* the manuscripts—as follows:

> εὐλόγως δὲ τὸ ἑαυτοῦ αἰσθάνεσθαι καὶ γνωρίζειν αἱρετώτερον.

I render this (as it is mostly naturally taken):

> it is plausible that to perceive *oneself* and to know <*oneself*> is <for each> *more* such-as-to-be-chosen <than to perceive and to know another>.[55]

Many commentators fail to see any shift here, perhaps because they assume that Aristotle's use of εὐλόγως at the start of [4] is meant to indicate that he is simply confirming the point made in [3], however exactly one takes that point. But there are good reasons for supposing that [3] and [4] represent distinct stages in Aristotle's argument and that we should neither assimilate [3] to [4] (as Marcianus$_2$ does) nor assimilate [4] to [3] (as Kosman does). For the assumption that Aristotle is making the same point in both places is problematic whichever direction one moves. And it is problematic for two reasons, each of which applies on its own but is reinforced by the other.

First, taking Aristotle to have the *same* focus in both [3] and [4]—whether that focus is on the subjects or on the objects of the relevant perceivings and knowings—requires us to read Aristotle as moving from the superlative claim that the relevant perceivings and knowings are *most haireton* for each person, to the comparative claim that these same perceivings and knowings are *more haireton* for each person than some other unspecified perceivings and knowings (which they must of course be if they are for her the *most haireton* ones). But it is difficult to see what point would be served by making such a move. There might, however, be some point to

[55] This is probably intended to refer to other persons; but it could perhaps be intended to refer simply to other objects, whether persons or not.

moving from the claim (i) that each person's *own* perceivings and knowings are for her *most haireton* in the sense that they are generally *more haireton* for her than *anyone else's* perceivings and knowings, to the claim (ii) that *among her own* perceivings and knowings, *some* are *more haireton* than *others*. For this would shift the focus from the special sort of value that resides for each person in her own perceivings and knowings to the sorts of differences in value *among* her own perceivings and knowings that might stem (for example) from the differences in value of their respective *objects*. In other words, even if a person's own perceiving is always *more haireton* for her than anyone else's is, it is surely *more haireton* for her to perceive herself in a *good* condition than to perceive herself in a *bad* condition; and it may well be *more haireton* for her to perceive a *friend* in a good condition than to perceive a *stranger* in the same condition. These, I think, are the sorts of points Aristotle seeks to make in [4], where I read him as finally—after reintroducing in [3] the *subjects* that were left out of the *logos* written in [2](B)—reintroducing the *objects* that were likewise left out of that *logos*.

Second, the idea that [4](A) simply confirms the point made in [3] is clearly undermined by the conjunction of two things: namely, the naturalness of taking [4](A)'s universally attested ἑαυτοῦ as referring to the *object* of perception, and the difficulty (given the parallel with living) of taking the point back in [3] to be about the identity of the *objects* of the relevant perceivings and knowings. This conjunction makes it natural to read Aristotle as turning from the point in [3], about the *subjects* of the relevant perceivings and knowings, to some point in [4] about the *objects* of these perceivings and knowings. And this natural reading is supported by what follows the εὐλόγως claim. For the next sentence (δεῖ γὰρ . . .) is clearly meant to introduce the reason for accepting the εὐλόγως claim. And it is pretty clear that the reason Aristotle goes on to give, in the remainder of [4], has something to do with *objects* of the perceivings and knowings in which the subject's living is supposed to consist.

But the reason given is obscure and the remainder of [4] exceptionally difficult. So I shall present and discuss [4] one stage at a time. First, however, I want to note some *general* reasons Aristotle might have for thinking it plausible to suppose that it is *more haireton* for a subject to perceive and know *herself* than to perceive and know *others*, reasons best approached once again through the *Philebus*, with its discussion of the value of nous construed as a form of self-awareness.

The *Philebus* suggests two ways in which self-awareness might contribute to the value of its subject's life, thus suggesting two ways in which it may be *more haireton* for a subject to perceive and know *herself* than to perceive and know *others*. For readers may reasonably take *Protarchus* to think that nous makes a subject's life more haireton by adding new kinds of *pleasure* while taking *Socrates* to mean that nous makes a life more haireton in some *non-hedonic* way. Readers may, for example, take Socrates to think that performing a stereotypically virtuous action *with* a certain kind of awareness of what one is doing has a kind of *moral* value that is lacking in the performance of such an action *without* such awareness of what one is doing.[56] And this example suggests that the two kinds of value may even complement each other: an agent's awareness of the moral value of her action may give rise to the distinctive sort of pleasure that Aristotle thinks virtuous agents take in virtuous activity. And the same goes for any other sorts of value there prove to be: for example, aesthetic value.[57] So the *Philebus* can be read as suggesting *both* hedonic *and* non-hedonic ways in which subject's perceiving and knowing herself and her own activities make her life *more haireton* than it would otherwise be.

But most pertinent here is the kind of non-hedonic value that Aristotle himself sees in self-awareness and associates with intentional action and so (in his view) with the sort of behavior that is the appropriate object of praise and blame. In many cases, *what* I am doing is partly a function of what I *take* myself to be doing, where this in turn is partly a function of what I am *aiming* to do.[58] In this sense, a certain kind of self-awareness is partly *constitutive* of the kind of agency that Aristotle takes to be distinctive of rational animals. And this yields a sense in which it is in fact reasonable to say that it is *more haireton* for a human subject to perceive and know herself than to perceive and know others. For an agent's awareness of herself and what she is doing is partly constitutive of what *she* is doing in a way in which her awareness of others and what they are doing is *not* generally speaking even partly constitutive of what *they* are doing: it is *their* awareness of themselves and what *they* are doing that is partly constitutive of *that*. In this sense an agent's awareness of herself and what she is doing is partly constitutive of rational (and so responsible) agency. So there is an important sense in which it is in fact *more haireton* for each human being to perceive and know *herself* than to perceive and know *others*. For without such perception and knowledge, she would not *be* a rational agent: she would not be able to engage in any sort of *prohairesis* at all.

Here, however, it is important to note two ways in which Aristotle may limit the priority he assigns to perceiving and knowing oneself. First, there are some activities in which perceiving and knowing others, and being perceived and known in turn by them, are partly constitutive of *what* one is *oneself* doing: for example, having a conversation or playing a game of squash. And second, even apart from such "joint activities," the claim that it is *more haireton* to perceive and know oneself than to perceive and know others may well be one that Aristotle thinks true (as he thinks most claims about sublunary phenomena are true) only "for the most part." So Aristotle's point in what follows may well be that although this claim is *for the most part* true, the activities of one's *friend* may in some sense constitute an important *exception* (at least if he is a character-friend). In that case there may be respects in which it is *as haireton*—or at

[56] For the talk of stereotypically virtuous actions, see my "*Eudaimonia*, External Results, and Choosing Virtuous Actions" [Chapter 3, this volume].

[57] See *EN* X.5. For an example involving awareness of aesthetic value, see section 11 of my "*NAP*" [Chapter 6, this volume].

[58] For more on this, see my "Lockeanism" [III.8].

least nearly so—for an individual to perceive and know her friend's activities as it is for her to perceive and know her own.[59]

6. THE EUDEMIAN TEXT CONTINUED: [4] IN THE LIGHT OF *METAPHYSICS* XII.7 AND 9

Let us turn then to [4], keeping these points in mind. It will also help if we keep in mind what has been claimed so far: namely, that what is generally *most haireton* for each human being is the perceiving and knowing in which its *own* living consists: i.e., its *own* perceiving and knowing.

[4] Second step: to perceive oneself and to know oneself is for each subject more *haireton* <than to perceive or know another> [1244b33–45a10]

(A) And it is plausible that to perceive oneself and to know <oneself> is <for each> more such-as-to-be-chosen <than to perceive and to know another>. For it is necessary at the same time (a) to posit two things together in the argument—**both** [τε] that the living is **actually**[60] such-as-to-be-chosen **and** [καὶ] that <it is> the good <of its subject>—**and** [καὶ] from these <claims> (b) for the same thing—i.e., such a nature[61]—to belong to **them.**

εὐλόγως δὲ τὸ ἑαυτοῦ αἰσθάνεσθαι καὶ γνωρίζειν αἱρετώτερον. δεῖ γὰρ ἅμα συνθεῖναι δύο ἐν τῷ λόγῳ, ὅτι τε τὸ ζῆν **καὶ** αἱρετόν, **καὶ** ὅτι τὸ ἀγαθόν, **καὶ** ἐκ τούτων [ὅτι] τὸ αὐτὸ **αὐτοῖς** ὑπάρχειν[62] τὴν τοιαύτην φύσιν. [1244b33–45a1]

---

[59] For the "nearly so" claim, see the parallel passage in *EN* IX.9, regarding the way in which the *existence* of the friend is *haireton* in the same way—or nearly so [παραπλησίως]—as one's *own* existence [1170b8]. If the *EN* parallel is (as I think) later, then this qualification may suggest increasing theoretical caution and/or increasing psychological realism on Aristotle's part.

[60] For καὶ, going with what follows it, as "actually," see Denniston, *The Greek Particles* 316–17.

[61] It is not necessary to my argument to take τὴν τοιαύτην φύσιν to refer to the nature of the good, but I think it plausible, especially given *EN* IX.9, 1170a20–21 (where Aristotle speaks of the determinate as being of the nature of the good) together with *Philebus* 60b10. I am, on the other hand, somewhat tempted to suppose that the nature in question is that of being an object of self-perception and self-knowledge, which would make the point here a version of the *Philebus* point that self-aware activities are *more haireton* than their non-self-aware analogues. This would afford a clearer connection with the shift here to perceiving and knowing *oneself*. Still, it seems easier to connect what follows, especially in [4](B), with *Metaphysics* XII.7's emphasis on the goodness of the objects of perception (whether the objects are one's own activities or not). For the connections with *Metaphysics* XII.7 are clear, especially given the talk there of the column of what is *haireton*. So I am on the whole somewhat more inclined to take τὴν τοιαύτην φύσιν to refer to the nature of the good than to refer to being an object of self-perception and self-knowledge. But see note 68 below.

[62] I suggest deleting the third ὅτι so as to make sense of the infinitive ὑπάρχειν, which I take to be governed (together with the συνθεῖναι δύο clause) by the initial δεῖ. And I read τὸ αὐτὸ **αὐτοῖς** ὑπάρχειν where the manuscripts have τὸ **αὐτὸ τοῖς** ὑπάρχειν. The fact that deleting the third ὅτι helps with the infinitive is a reason for deleting it rather than the second, as Solomon's original translation seems to do (see my next note). For one can see how the third ὅτι might have been added by someone puzzled about what follows from putting the first two together and so *both* looking to (b) for the content of the second of

I have put 'them [αὐτοῖς] in bold because one of the problems here is to determine its referent. But this problem is best treated in the context of two more fundamental problems posed by the text as I have chosen to read it.

The first is the problem of determining what two things must be put together in the argument. The second is that of determining what is supposed to follow from putting them together (which subsumes the problem of determining the referent of 'them'). Let me begin with the first. Since I take the burden of proof to fall on any reading that declines to take the first two ὅτι (or "that") clauses as specifying the two things that must be put together, I shall start from this assumption and turn immediately to the question of how to understand these two clauses.

It is syntactically most natural to take τὸ ἀγαθόν as the subject of the second ὅτι clause while understanding αἱρετόν (from the first) as its implicit predicate, thus yielding "that living is *haireton* and that the good <is *haireton*>."[63] Each conjunct is no doubt something Aristotle believes, though he may in the end accept only a qualified version of the first.[64] But the second conjunct would seem to go without saying and to

---

the two claims that must be put together *and* expecting this content to be signaled by ὅτι. One can perhaps imagine a scenario in which it was the second ὅτι that was inserted, but this would require one to posit an original with ὅτι plus the infinitive. So it seems better to suppose that it was the third, not the second, that was mistakenly introduced.

Please note that I follow Dirlmeier ad loc in adding the letters (a) and (b) so as to indicate how I now take the ἅμα—namely, with δεῖ γὰρ and as joining (a) and (b)—and not (as I once took it and as Décarie takes it) with συνθεῖναι and as joining the two ὅτι clauses internal to (a). In other words, I take the basic structure of the sentence to be δεῖ γὰρ ἅμα (a) συνθεῖναι δύο . . . καὶ (b) τὸ αὐτὸ αὐτοῖς ὑπάρχειν. . . .

Décarie (who takes τὴν τοιαύτην φύσιν to refer to "*une nature bonne ou une vie bonne*") has ad loc the following:

> *Car il faut poser ensemble deux points présentés dans le discours: que la vie est desirable et que le bien l'est aussi, et en consequence, qu'il est desirable qu'une telle nature appartienne à tous deux pour la même raison.*

Dirlmeier gets the basic structure right but takes τὸ ἀγαθόν as the *subject* of the second ὅτι clause rather than—as I argue it should be taken—as the *predicate*. So he ends up with the following claim, which is true but too trivial to advance the argument:

> *Man muß nämlich zwei in dem Buch enthaltene Dinge vereinigen: (a) daß das Leben und daß das Gute wählenswert ist, und (b)—was daraus folgt—daß sie wählenswert sind, weil ihnen jene bekannte Werthaftigkeit eigen ist.*

[63] This is how almost all commentators and translators seem to take it: but I now wonder about Solomon, whose original translation (as distinct from the version in Barnes' Revised Oxford translation, Volume II) seems to leave open the possibility for which I argue. He has the following: "Naturally, perception and knowledge of oneself is more desirable. For we must take two things into consideration, *that life is desirable and also the good*, and thence that it is desirable that such a nature should belong to oneself as belongs to *them*." The revised Oxford text disambiguates, saying, ". . . *that life is desirable and also that the good is*, . . ." This has the virtue of translating the second ὅτι, but I think it possible (in the way my translation indicates) to translate that without losing the point that Solomon's original translation leaves open—namely, that the life in question is not only *haireton* but also *the good* of its subject. It is also worth noting that Solomon's translation (both original and revised) seems to read the δεῖ γὰρ ἅμα as I read it—namely, as applying to (a) and (b). So Solomon's original seems to me the best anyone has done so far to get this bit right.

[64] The claim that Aristotle accepts only a qualified version of the first conjunct receives some support from the Nicomachean parallel to [4], where Aristotle says,

contribute little if anything toward a conclusion worth establishing: what follows from *these* two claims is simply that *both* living *and* the good are *haireton*. And while we could perhaps construe what follows the two ὅτι clauses as telling us something like that—namely, that being *haireton* must belong *both* to living *and* to the good—it is hard to see what point would be served by saying that.

So I think it better to take τὸ ἀγαθόν as the predicate of the second ὅτι clause, with τὸ ζῆν as its implicit subject. This is syntactically less natural but grammatically possible.[65] On this account, Aristotle's argument is a variation on an argument of the *Philebus*. Aristotle first says that the living in question—the one that [3](A) takes to be *most haireton* for its subject—is not just *any old* living: it must be *haireton,* presumably in the sense of being *worthy* of being chosen. Aristotle then adds—again in accordance with [3](A)'s claim that the living in question is *most haireton* for its subject—that the living in question is in fact *the good* of its subject, where this means that nothing further can be added to it to yield a life that would be even better for that subject.[66]

It is easy to see the remainder of the sentence (καὶ ἐκ τούτων . . .) as spelling out something that follows from this. There are in fact multiple possibilities here. The first and most common is to take αὑτοῖς in the final sentence to refer to the *subjects*

To live is defined for animals by the capacity for perceiving, and for human beings <by the capacity for> perceiving or thinking. But the capacity is referred back to the activity, and the real <living> is in the activity. It seems then that to live is really to perceive or to think. For <to live in this sense > is determinate, **and the determinate is <characteristic> of the nature of the good**. But what is good by nature is also <good> for the decent person. Whence <to perceive or to think> seems to all <humans> to be pleasant. But we should not take a wicked life or a corrupt one, nor <one lived> in pains, for such <a life> is indeterminate, just like the things belonging to it.

τὸ δὲ ζῆν ὁρίζονται τοῖς ζῴοις δυνάμει αἰσθήσεως, ἀνθρώποις δ' αἰσθήσεως ἢ νοήσεως· ἡ δὲ δύναμις εἰς τὴν ἐνέργειαν ἀνάγεται, τὸ δὲ κύριον ἐν τῇ ἐνεργείᾳ· ἔοικε δὴ τὸ ζῆν εἶναι κυρίως τὸ αἰσθάνεσθαι ἢ νοεῖν. τὸ δὲ ζῆν τῶν καθ' αὑτὸ ἀγαθῶν καὶ ἡδέων· ὡρισμένον γάρ, **τὸ δ' ὡρισμένον τῆς τἀγαθοῦ φύσεως**· τὸ δὲ τῇ φύσει ἀγαθὸν καὶ τῷ ἐπιεικεῖ· διόπερ ἔοικε πᾶσιν ἡδὺ εἶναι· οὐ δεῖ δὲ λαμβάνειν μοχθηρὰν ζωὴν καὶ διεφθαρμένην, οὐδ' ἐν λύπαις· ἀόριστος γὰρ ἡ τοιαύτη, καθάπερ τὰ ὑπάρχοντα αὐτῇ. [1170a16–24]

I read the argument of *EE* VII.12 as aimed at making much the same point. So I take argument there to be not about *mere life*, but about the sort of life that is not only *haireton* for its subject but in fact *the good* of that subject. And I take Aristotle to be talking about the conditions a life *must* satisfy *if* it is to count as such (i.e., as *the* good of its subject).

[65] See Smyth, *Greek Grammar* §1152: "Even in the predicate the article is used with a noun referring to a definite object . . . that is [i] well known, [ii] previously mentioned or hinted at, or [iii] identical with the subject." (I have added the labels [i]–[iii] for clarity of exposition.) τὸ ἀγαθόν clearly satisfies the first two conditions: it refers to an idea that is [i] familiar from *Philebus* 20b–d and that [ii] Aristotle has previously mentioned (at the start of *EE*). My claim here is that τὸ ἀγαθόν also satisfies the third condition: Aristotle is [iii] *identifying* the sort of living he is talking about with *the good* of its subject.

[66] I think this explains the first καὶ (rendered "actually"; cf. note 60 above) in the second sentence of [4](A). The idea (with each of the three instances of 'καὶ' indicated in bold) is that we must at the same time (a) put together that the living in question is ***actually*** choiceworthy ***and*** that it <sc., the living in question> is in fact *the good* of the relevant creature; ***and*** (b) recognize that it follows from putting these together that something (probably the nature of the good) must belong to the perceivings and knowings in which the living has been said back in [2](B) to consist. If this is right, then there is no need to bracket (or delete) the first 'καὶ.'

of the relevant perceiving and knowing. On this reading, it is supposed to follow from the conjunction of the first two ὅτι clauses that something or other must belong to these subjects. The idea would then be that *if* their living is to be not only *haireton* for them but in fact *the good* for them, *then* something or other *must* belong to these *subjects themselves*. The something or other is whatever it is to which τὴν τοιαύτην φύσιν (taken in apposition to τὸ αὐτὸ) refers, probably the nature of the good, perhaps the nature of what is *haireton*, and just maybe the nature of the sort of self-awareness introduced in the initial εὐλόγως claim. So Aristotle may be saying that the nature of the good (or perhaps of the *haireton*) must belong to the subjects themselves if their lives are to count as *the good* for them; or he may be saying, as Socrates in the *Philebus* says, that self-awareness must belong to these subjects if their lives are to count as *the good* for them. But either reading is awkward, given that Aristotle has hitherto spoken of the subject in the singular.[67]

The second line of interpretation, which I prefer, involves taking αὐτοῖς to refer to the perceiving and the knowing in which a subject's living is supposed to consist. We can then read the remainder of the sentence as saying that it follows from putting the first two claims together that something or other must belong *to the perceivings and knowings* in which the subject's life consists. Once again, the 'δεῖ' should be understood as referring to a condition that *must* be satisfied *if* the subject's life is to be not only *haireton* for it but in fact *the good* for it. And the condition seems once again to be *either* (i) that the nature of the good (or perhaps the nature of the *haireton*) should belong to the perceivings and knowings in which the subject's living consists *or* (ii) that the sort of self-awareness mentioned in the εὐλόγως claim should belong to these perceivings and knowings. And while I cannot rule (ii) out, I am inclined to prefer (i) because of the way in which it receives support from the previously quoted portion of *Metaphysics* XII.9, which is clearly related—in ways I shall now explain—to [4] as a whole.[68]

Recall [ST2][b], where Aristotle makes it clear that he does not think that all perceivings and knowings are in themselves good and such-as-to-be-chosen: "some things," he says, "it is better *not* to see than to see." Aristotle makes this point in support of his conclusion that it is not *actual* thinking, simply as such, that is the best activity, since *actual* thinking "belongs even to one thinking the worst <object>": it is only thinking

[67] It must be conceded that [4](C) shifts quickly to the plural ("*we* are not each of these things in ourselves") and then back again to the singular ("but the one perceiving comes to be such-as-to-be-perceived . . ."). So we cannot rule this line out. But if one adopts this line, it seems best to take what is supposed to belong to the subjects themselves to be not the nature of the good or the *haireton*, but rather the sort of self-awareness mentioned in the initial εὐλόγως claim. Still, the second line of interpretation (to which I now turn) seems to me to provide a smoother argument: it *assumes* self-awareness and *then* says what *else* is required if the subject's life is to satisfy the conditions for being its good.

[68] I am, however, reluctant to dismiss entirely the latter possibility because it might shed light on what remains for me the most difficult point in all of this—namely, to see how the point about the value of perceiving and knowing *oneself* is supposed to be connected with the point about the way in which the value of the *activities* of perceiving and knowing is supposed to depend on the value of the *objects* perceived and known (where these objects include but are not limited to the subject herself, who is presumably perceived only peripherally [ἐν παρέργῳ]). See note 61.

the *best object* that is the *best activity*. Aristotle clearly takes perceiving and thinking to be similar in that the value of either is partly a function of the value of its *object*. And he does not simply think it *better* to perceive and/or know good objects than to perceive and/or know bad ones; he thinks some objects are so bad that seeing (and presumably also knowing) them is itself *to be avoided*. So even if perceiving and knowing *oneself* are *generally* more *haireton* than perceiving and knowing *others*, this claim may not hold without qualification: it is surely not more *haireton* to perceive or know oneself to be doing something *shameful* than to perceive or know another—especially if the other is one's friend—to be doing something *kalon*. For whatever sort of constitutive and/or hedonic value we assign to self-awareness, it is surely a bad thing—and painful for anyone who is not altogether corrupt—to perceive herself to be doing the sort of thing that Aristotle says one should rather die, after the most horrid suffering, than do: for example, slaying one's mother [*EN* 1110a25–29].

The remainder of [4] confirms the relevance of these points from *Metaphysics* XII.9 to our chapter. For [4](B)'s puzzling talk of the column [*sustoichia*] of what is *haireton* is best understood by appeal to the similar talk in *Metaphysics* XII.7, which is where the argument of *Metaphysics* XII.9 is launched. XII.7 is about the need (if we are to explain the range of movements we see in both superlunary and sublunary spheres) for the least one being that moves other things without itself moving. Aristotle begins by suggesting that we know from our experience that there can be such things, since objects of thought and objects of desire both move other things without themselves moving. He continues as follows:

[ST1] [a] *Metaphysics* XII.7 [1072a29–b1]

[a] . . . it is more the case that we desire <things> because they seem <*kalon*> than that they seem <*kalon*> because we desire <them>. For thinking is a source <of desire>. And **nous** is moved by the object of thought, and one column is <of that which is> **in itself an object of thought** [νοητὴ δὲ ἡ ἑτέρα συστοιχία **καθ' αὑτήν**]. And in the case of this <column> substance is first, and in the case of this <sc., substance> the one that is simple and in activity <is first>.[69] ... But surely also what is fine and what is **on account of itself such-as-to-be-chosen** are in the same column [ἀλλὰ μὴν καὶ τὸ καλὸν καὶ **τὸ δι' αὑτὸ αἱρετὸν** ἐν τῇ αὐτῇ συστοιχίᾳ]. And the first <in each column?> is always the best or analogous <to the best>.

As we saw in [ST1][b]–[e], Aristotle proceeds from [a] to speak of divine nous and to identify it with an *activity* of thought, as distinct from any receptivity to objects of thought. He says that this activity is in fact a form of life—indeed the best and *most pleasant* life there is. And in *Metaphysics* XII.9, he explicitly contrasts this activity with

[69] The idea, I think, is that the primary object of thought (which has been said to be the *same* as the primary object of desire) is that substance which is here said to be "simple and in activity" (namely, God).

human forms of cognition: divine noetic activity, which is eternal, is such as the best of which we are capable for only a short time, only better [1072b18–28].

Let us turn, then, with these passages from *Metaphysics* XII in mind, to the remainder of [4]:

[4](B) If, then, in such a pair of columns one <member> is always in the column of what is such-as-to-be-chosen, both what is such-as-to-be-known and what is such-as-to-be-perceived are generally speaking <in that column> by partaking of some determinate nature. So, to wish to perceive oneself is to wish oneself to be such <sc., partaking of some determinate nature>.

εἰ οὖν ἐστιν ἀεὶ τῆς τοιαύτης συστοιχίας ἡ ἑτέρα ἐν τῇ τοῦ αἱρετοῦ τάξει, καὶ τὸ γνωστὸν καὶ τὸ αἰσθητόν ἐστιν ὡς ὅλως εἰπεῖν τῷ κοινωνεῖν τῆς ὡρισμένης φύσεως·[70] ὥστε τὸ αὑτοῦ βούλεσθαι αἰσθάνεσθαι τὸ αὑτὸν εἶναι τοιονδὶ βούλεσθαι ἐστίν. [1245a1–5]

I think most commentators take the columns referred to here as opposing living, perceiving and knowing (qua *haireton*) to not-living, not-perceiving and not-knowing (qua not *haireton*). But the talk in *Metaphysics* XII.7 of what is "*in itself* such-as-to-be-thought/known" and "what is *on account of itself* such-as-to-be-chosen" suggests that the distinction is instead between *different sorts of objects* of thought and choice: those that are *in themselves* such-as-to-be-thought or chosen and those that are *not in themselves* such-as-to-be-thought or chosen. And the *Metaphysics*' association of the former with what is *kalon* is significant.

The idea there, I think, is that one column contains objects that are *in themselves worthy* of being thought and chosen, while the other contains objects that are such-as-to-be-thought or chosen *only (if at all) on account of other things*.[71] So it seems best to take the columns referred to in the Eudemian chapter not as opposing the activities of living, perceiving, and knowing to the absence of these activities, but rather as opposing the sorts of living, perceiving, and knowing that are *in themselves worthy of choice* to the sorts of living, perceiving, and knowing that are *not in themselves worthy of choice* (where these include but are not limited to the sorts of living, perceiving, and knowing that are, as *Metaphysics* XII.9 puts it, *pheukton*).[72]

70 This seems to me to provide some support for taking τὴν τοιαύτην φύσιν in [4](A) as referring to the nature of the good. The idea here, I think, is that the wish to perceive oneself is implicitly a wish to perceive oneself in a *good*—and so a *determinate—condition*.

71 It is worth noting here that "pure" and "impure" (or more and less "theoretical") forms of inquiry are contrasted both at the end of *Metaphysics* XII.9 (1075a1–5) and toward the end of the *Philebus* (55dff.).

72 This fits *both* the question in *Metaphysics* XII.9 about whether it makes any difference (presumably to the value of thinking) *what* divine nous thinks (i.e., whether the object must be *kalon* or whether any random object will do); *and* the question in *EE* I.5 about that for the sake of which one would choose to live rather than not. The affinities of *EE* with *Met.* XII clearly extend well beyond *EE* VII.12.

The point of [4](B), then, is to signal that however *haireton* it may be for a subject to perceive herself, she does not wish to perceive herself in any old condition: she wishes to perceive herself in a *good* condition, which involves partaking of some determinate nature. This suggests that it is not enough for the subject to perceive herself engaged in activities (such as contemplation or virtuous action) that are *in fact* good; she must perceive herself engaged in activities the goodness of which she herself *recognizes as such*. These activities will, moreover, always involve some object or objects distinct from herself—for example, the starry skies above or the needs of those around her. In this respect, even the most self-sufficient human being differs from God. As Aristotle says in *Metaphysics* XII.9, we do not perceive or know ourselves except "peripherally," i.e., in perceiving and knowing *other* things.

Aristotle makes this point from the *Metaphysics* somewhat differently in [4], where he seems to draw on the accounts of perception and thought presented in his *De Anima*. [4] continues as follows (with the main sentence bolded, so that it can be taken in at a glance without the parenthetical interruption):

[4](C) **Since, then, we are not in ourselves each of these things <sc., *to gnôston* and *to aisthêton*[73]>, but <we become each of these things> by partaking of the powers <of things> in the <activity of> perceiving and knowing <them>** (for when perceiving one becomes *aisthêtos* in this way and in accordance with this: <namely,> just as the things one perceives prior <to perceiving oneself> are, one becomes <such> according to the way in which <one perceives these things> and what <one perceives>; and when knowing <one becomes> such-as-to-be-known <in the same ways>, **so on account of this, too, one wishes always to live because one wishes always to know, and <one wishes> this because one <wishes> oneself to be *to gnôston*.**

ἐπεὶ οὖν οὐ κατ' αὐτούς ἐσμεν ἕκαστον τούτων, ἀλλὰ κατὰ μετάληψιν τῶν δυνάμεων ἐν τῷ αἰσθάνεσθαι ἢ γνωρίζειν (αἰσθανόμενος μὲν γὰρ αἰσθητὸς γίνεται ταύτῃ καὶ κατὰ τοῦτο, καθὰ πρότερον αἰσθάνεται, καὶ ᾗ καὶ οὗ, γνωστὸς δὲ γινώσκων)· **ὥστε διὰ τοῦτο καὶ ζῆν ἀεὶ βούλεται, ὅτι βούλεται ἀεὶ γνωρίζειν, τοῦτο δὲ ὅτι αὐτὸς εἶναι τὸ γνωστόν.** [1245a5–10]

I have simply transliterated forms of 'γνωστός' and 'αἰσθητός' because there are serious questions about how exactly they should be understood here, in particular about how 'γνωστόν' is used at the very end.

The idea in the parenthesis can be understood in two ways, each corresponding to a common way of taking the *-tos /-ton* suffix. The idea may be that the subject is not in

[73] Supplied from 1245a2, as supported by the parenthetical remark that follows here (about becoming *aisthêtos* when perceiving and *gnôstos* when knowing).

herself such that she *can be* perceived or known (presumably by herself), but comes to be a *possible* object of (her own) perceiving and knowing only in the act of perceiving and knowing *other* things. Or the idea may be that the subject is not in herself *actually* perceived or known (again, I assume, by herself), but comes to be an *actual* object of (her own) perceiving or knowing only in the act of perceiving and knowing *other* things. The latter seems to me more likely, given that the sort of pleasure on which the argument will ultimately turn is something that comes about only when the subject is *actually* perceiving or knowing. But this is not decisive, since the point here could be that it is only in *actually* perceiving or knowing *other* things that the subject becomes a *possible* object of her *own* perceiving or knowing. Still, to the extent that the argument turns in the end on the net pleasure a subject derives from perceiving or knowing herself to be in the better of two conditions, the argument seems in the end to require that the subject be an *actual* (even if only peripheral) object of her own perceiving or knowing.[74]

In sum, I am inclined to take the idea in the parenthesis to involve the subject's being an *actual* object of her own perceiving and knowing. But whichever way we go here, it will be in accordance with the *other* things perceived and known, and with the *way* in which the subject perceives and knows these other things, that the subject *herself* comes to be an object (whether possible or actual) of her own perceiving and knowing. And either way, it is important that the other things perceived and known be *good* things, since there is a sense in which the subject becomes *like* the objects perceived and known: the better the objects she perceives, the better in some sense the condition in which she can or does perceive herself, even if only "peripherally." And, as we shall soon see, the better the condition in which a subject perceives herself, the *more pleasant* her concomitant self-perception. But this idea is yet to come: it is articulated only in [6](C).

Still, anticipating the connection with pleasure may help to explain the emphasis I see in [4](C) on *actual* perceiving and knowing; for it is only when there is actual perceiving and knowing that the relevant pleasure occurs. And if the connection with pleasure is what explains the emphasis on actual perceiving and knowing, then we should perhaps be thinking of the talk of "living *in activity and as an end*" (back in the basic *logos*) as involving a genuine conjunction and not simply epexegesis. For the emphasis in [4](B) is on a distinction between objects that are *in themselves* worthy of being perceived and known and objects that are *not in themselves* worthy of being perceived and known, which suggests a distinction between perceivings and knowings that are *in themselves* such-as-to-be-chosen and perceivings and knowing that are *not in themselves* such-as-to-be-chosen. So there seem to be two distinct points in [4], one corresponding to κατ' ἐνέργειαν and the other to καὶ ὡς τέλος: if living is supposed to

[74] See *EN* IX.12: περὶ αὑτὸν δ' ἡ αἴσθησις ὅτι ἔστιν αἱρετή, καὶ περὶ τὸν φίλον δή· ἡ δ' ἐνέργεια γίνεται αὐτῆς ἐν τῷ συζῆν, ὥστ' εἰκότως τούτου ἐφίενται. [1171b35–72a1] "Concerning oneself, the perception that one exists is *haireton*, and concerning one's friend, too <the perception that he exists is *haireton*>; and the actuality of this <perception> comes to be in living together <with the friend>, so that friends reasonably aim for this <sc., living together>."

constitute *the good* of its subject, then it must involve perceiving and knowing that is not only (as (C) tells us) *actual* but also (as (B) tells us) *in itself* such-as-to-be-chosen. The emphasis here in [4] seems to be on the κατ' ἐνέργειαν; Aristotle will make more of the ὡς τέλος in [6](C), where he argues that the association of self-sufficient agents is above all of things ἐν τέλει. But more about that later.

We must at this point return to the question how 'τὸ γνωστόν' is used at the end of [4](C). Is Aristotle saying that each human being wishes always to know because she wishes to be *an object of her own knowledge*? Or could he be saying that each human being wishes always to know because she wishes in some sense to be *the object known* where this object is *something distinct from herself*? In other words, could Aristotle be saying that each ultimately wishes to *be*—perhaps in the sense of *being like*—whatever object it is she knows (assuming of course that the object is *good*)?

The chapter so far supports only the first interpretation. The latter possibility arises mainly because of what is yet to come: it arises in light of [6](A's) talk of the friend wishing to be "another Heracles," where this seems to embody a wish on the part of Heracles' friend to be, if not Heracles himself then, at least *like* Heracles. But to the extent that the default reading of our chapter should be forward, not backward, we should at present stick with the first interpretation and take the point to be that the subject wishes to be the object—or at least an object—of her own knowledge.

It is important to see that any knowledge in question here *must* be the subject's *own*. For it is sometimes supposed that the final sentence refers instead to the subject's desire to be known or (in the Hegelian terms that are sometimes used) "recognized" *by others*. But however one resolves the issues about [3], the only perceiving and knowing thus far mentioned are the subject's *own*. There is nothing so far about her being an object of anyone else's perceiving and knowing. In fact there has been no mention since the argument was launched in [3](A) of the friend (or anyone else) perceiving or knowing. So *if* Aristotle *is* concerned with a wish for recognition, it must be a wish for *self*-recognition, the wish to be an object of one's *own* knowledge.[75]

But it is not obvious that the passage is concerned with the subject's wish to be known or recognized, either by herself or by anyone else. For the subject's wish to be *to gnôston* seems to me to be related to the way in which the subject, in knowing some object, in some sense *becomes*—or *becomes like*—*the object known*. That is why the focus in [4] is on the *object's* being in the column of what is *haireton:* because the subject becomes *like* the object, it is important that the object be *kalon* and not just any random thing.

I realize that VII.12 is often read as arguing that the self-sufficient agent *needs* a friend in order to achieve *self*-knowledge. But this sort of reading—which seems to be based primarily on a dubious assimilation of VII.12 to the famous mirror passage in

[75] Unless Aristotle simply introduces the talk of another's perceiving and knowing here out of the blue. But given that he presents what he is saying as following from what precedes (ὥστε διὰ τοῦτο . . .), it would be uncharitable to accuse him of doing so as long as there is *some* way (as I think there is) to construe this as following from what precedes.

Magna Moralia II.15—fails to do justice to the role played by pleasure throughout the Eudemian argument, from the talk in [1](E) of the virtuous agent's seeking *companions in enjoyment* to the talk in [6](B) of its being *even more pleasant* to enjoy divine pleasures with others than it is to enjoy "lower" pleasures with them.[76] Consider, moreover, how puzzling it would be if the idea in [4](C) were that the subject comes to know *herself* by coming to know another who is *like* herself. For—to steal a line from Plato's *Meno*—how will she recognize the other's likeness to herself if she does not *already* recognize that she herself possesses those characteristics in respect of which the other is supposed to resemble her?

It is also worth noting here how dubious it would be to rely at this point in the chapter on the general idea of the friend as an "other self," an idea that appears in this chapter *if at all* only when we get to [6](A). I say "if at all" because the versions of "another self" (e.g., "second self" and "*ein zweites Ich*") that are found in virtually all modern translations of this passage are based on an emendation that substitutes **ἄλλος αὐτός** for **ἄλλος οὗτος** (which is found in *all* extant manuscripts of our chapter). We shall return to this issue when we reach [6](A). But however we resolve it there, the point here in [4] concerns the objects of some *generic* subject's perceiving and knowing. And the subject is now being singled out (after [3]'s silence on this point) as among the objects—indeed one of the more *haireton* objects—of her own perceiving and knowing. There has been no explicit mention—at least not since the argument proper was launched in [3](A)—of *friends* as objects of perceiving and knowing. The talk so far has been entirely general: the better the object, *whatever it is*, the better the perceiving or knowing of it. And thus far, the only human object of perceiving and knowing that has been explicitly identified is the subject herself.

It is of course true, given [ST2][c], that Aristotle's introduction of the subject as an object of its own perceiving and knowing presupposes objects of perception and knowledge that are *prior* (logically if not temporally) to the subject herself. For it is perception and knowledge of these objects that renders the subject herself an actual (or at least possible) object of her own perceiving and knowing. But nothing has been said so far about the *identity* of these prior objects. We know that they must be *kalon*;

---

[76] Another reason for doubting that Aristotle speaks here of a desire to be known is the fact that he elsewhere belittles the desire to be known, comparing it—together with the desire to be loved—to the desire to be honored, which (being honored) seems to be chosen not for its own sake but only incidentally (in order, for example, we might be assured of our own goodness or to receive the sorts of favors that tend to be attached to honor) [*EN* 1159a15–27]. In the same passage—which claims (in a way relevant to *EE* VII.12) that *philia* is *in itself haireton*—Aristotle goes on to say that *philia* consists more in loving than in being loved and to cite in support of this the *enjoyment* mothers take in loving: some mothers, in cases where it is not possible for them both to love and to be loved in turn, give up their children to be raised by others, it being enough for them to *see* their children doing well even if the children fail on account of not knowing their mothers to give to their mothers the sort of things (including, no doubt, love) that are due to a mother [*EN* 1159a27–33]. I emphasize the *seeing* here because Aristotle presumably thinks it important for reasons similar to those for which it is important to live together with one's friend—namely, because the seeing, like the sort of awareness of the friend provided by living together, gives rise to *pleasure*.

but that is entirely compatible with their being strangers, works of art, or the starry skies above.

Friends are of course common objects of human perceiving and knowing. But Aristotle cannot without begging the question take it for granted that friends *must* count among the objects of the *self-sufficient* person's perceiving and knowing. For if a human subject becomes better to the extent that the objects she perceives and knows are better, why suppose that the best human subject will want to perceive and know *friends*, however good they may be? Will she not prefer to contemplate something even better—for example, *God*? And if that is what she prefers, what reason will she have to do *that* in the company of a friend?

7. THE EUDEMIAN TEXT CONTINUED: [5]'S REINTRODUCTION OF THE FRIEND

The point of [5], I think, is to raise such questions and then to hint at their answer, which turns—as [5](C) suggests and [6] confirms—on the role played, even in the best sort of friendship, by *pleasure*.

[5] Step three: a possible objection and two purported facts about human nature that point the way to a resolution of the aporia [1245a11–a29]

(A) Now choosing to live together might seem to those considering <the matter> in a certain way foolish, <starting> first in the case of things <we share> in common also with the other animals, such as eating together and drinking together. For what difference does it make if these things <i.e., eating and drinking> occur among those who are near <to one another> or separate <from one another>, if one takes away speech? But surely also to partake of random speech is <yet> another such activity <as merely eating and drinking together without speech>.

τὸ δὴ συζῆν αἱρεῖσθαι δόξειε μὲν ἂν εἶναι σκοπουμένοις πως εὔηθες· ἐπὶ τῶν κοινῶν[77] πρῶτον καὶ τοῖς ἄλλοις ζῴοις, οἷον τοῦ συνεσθίειν ἢ τοῦ συμπίνειν· τί γὰρ διαφέρει τὸ πλησίον οὖσι ταῦτα συμβαίνειν ἢ χωρίς, ἂν ἀφέλῃς[78] τὸν λόγον; ἀλλὰ μὴν καὶ τοῦ λόγου κοινωνεῖν τοῦ τυχόντος ἕτερον τοιοῦτον· [1245a11–16]

[77] Although I once thought that the frequent use of κοινωνία in surrounding chapters and even three lines hence provided reason to resist following the OCT in adopting τῶν κοινῶν (suggested by Bonitz), I now think the opposite. For the difficulty of understanding κοινωνία here—especially the implausibility of taking the point to be about our wining and dining with the other animals—persuades me that that a scribe who was thinking along the same lines I myself once thought must mistakenly have decided that κοινωνία belonged here as well. Still, for a great scene of a man dining with other animals, see chap. 43 of Trojanow, *Der Weltensammler*.

[78] P has ἂν ἀφέλεις; C ἀναφέρεις; and L ἀναφέρει.

(B) (At the same time it is not possible for friends who are self-sufficient either to teach <one another> or to learn <from one another>. For if one is learning, then *he* is not in the condition he should be in, while if he is teaching, his friend <is not>. And the similarity <between them> *is philia*.)[79]

(ἅμα τε οὔτε διδάσκειν οὔτε μανθάνειν τοῖς αὐταρκέσι φίλοις οἷόν τε· μανθάνων μὲν γὰρ αὐτὸς οὐκ ἔχει ὡς δεῖ, διδάσκοντος δ' ὁ φίλος, ἡ δ' ὁμοιότης φιλία). [1245a16–18]

(C) But surely it at least appears <to make a difference to do these things together> and we all partake of goods more pleasantly with friends <than apart from them>, insofar as <these goods> belong to each and <are the> best <good> of which <each> is capable. But of these <best goods>, it belongs to one person <to partake> of pleasure, to another <to partake> of artistic contemplation, and to <yet> another <to partake> of philosophy. It is also necessary to be together with[80] the friend <when partaking of these things>—whence the saying "distant friends are trouble." So <friends> ought not be apart from one another when this <sc., partaking of the relevant good> is happening. (Whence *erôs* too seems to be similar to *philia*. For the lover desires **living well**,[81] but not in that respect in which he should most <desire this> but according to perception.)

ἀλλὰ μὴν φαίνεταί γε, καὶ πάντες ἥδιον τῶν ἀγαθῶν μετὰ τῶν φίλων κοινωνοῦμεν, καθ' ὅσον ἐπιβάλλει ἑκάστῳ καὶ οὗ δύναται ἀρίστου, ἀλλὰ τούτων τῷ μὲν ἡδονῆς σωματικῆς τῷ δὲ θεωρίας μουσικῆς, τῷ δὲ φιλοσοφίας. καὶ τὸ ἅμα δεῖ εἶναι τῷ φίλῳ. διό φησι 'μόχθος οἱ τηλοῦ φίλοι', ὥστ' οὐ δεῖ γενέσθαι ἀπ' ἀλλήλων τούτου γινομένου. ὅθεν καὶ ὁ ἔρως δοκεῖ φιλίᾳ ὅμοιον εἶναι· τοῦ γὰρ **εὖ ζῆν** ὀρέγεται ὁ ἐρῶν, ἀλλ' οὐχ ᾗ μάλιστα δεῖ, ἀλλὰ κατ' αἴσθησιν. [1245a18–26]

[79] Cf. *EN* 1159b13ff., where Aristotle associates teaching and learning with friendship *for advantage*.

[80] ἅμα does not apply only to simultaneity; it can also (as *Metaphysics* 1068b26 makes clear) connote being in the same place (presumably at the same time), which is clearly Aristotle's point here.

[81] Though my overall line of interpretation does not depend on this, I follow the manuscripts here in reading εὖ ζῆν rather than συζῆν, which is due to Casaubon (cited in Susemihl, *Eudemi Rhodii Ethica*) and is followed in all of the editions and translations I have consulted—presumably on the basis of the two occurrences of συζῆν coming up in [6](C). But this seems to me both unnecessary and to miss the flow of the argument, which moves, in a way that [6](C) makes clear, from a point about the agent's own εὖ ζῆν to a point about the intelligibility of the agent's desire for συζῆν. So we might well *expect* [5](C) to make points about εὖ ζῆν that prepare the way for the argument of [6](C). And it is a virtue of my interpretation and the emphasis that it places on living *well* (as distinct from *mere* living) that it accommodates the phrase found here in *all* the manuscripts.

The general point in [5](C), which is picked up again in [6](C), is about the different sorts of activities in which differently abled subjects take their εὖ ζῆν to consist: each subject will (at least for the most part) take his or her εὖ ζῆν to consist primarily in the *best* sort of activity of which he or she is capable, and each will find it especially pleasant—and so especially *haireton*—to engage in the relevant activity together with one or more like-minded (and similarly abled) others. What we find at the end of [5](C) (ὅθεν καὶ ὁ ἔρως . . . ἀλλὰ κατ' αἴσθησιν) is best construed as parenthetical remark—made in the context

(D) **The argument**[82] then says those things, raising puzzles. But **the fact** is evidently thus <sc., as we have just said>. So it is clear that the <argument> raising these puzzles leads us somehow astray.

ὁ μὲν τοίνυν **λόγος** ἐκεῖνά φησι διαπορῶν, τὸ δ' **ἔργον** οὕτω φαίνεται γινόμενον, ὥστε δῆλον ὅτι παρακρούεταί πως ἡμᾶς ὁ διαπορῶν. [1245a16–29]

I do not think that [5] simply reformulates the initial aporia, this time without the potentially misleading comparison with God. For the problem raised here is raised midstream, so to speak, in the course of Aristotle's response to the initial aporia. In rejecting the idea that the value of eating or drinking together can be increased by adding random speech, [5](A) seems to assume the point of view established in [4]: the value of speech is partly a function of the value of its *subject matter*. So adding random speech cannot explain the preference of *self-sufficient* agents for sharing meals with one another: *such* agents may well prefer eating alone to eating in the company of idle chatter.[83]

It is clear from [5](B) that Aristotle is searching here for what would serve to explain why *even self-sufficient* agents prefer—like other human beings—eating and drinking with their friends to eating and drinking alone. The point in (A) is *not* that conversation can make *no* difference to such agents: it is simply that random speech—i.e., small talk or chit-chat—is not of sufficient value to explain the preference of these agents for eating and drinking together. In other words, it is from the point of view

of this *general* point about the pleasures of engaging together with friends in whatever activities one takes to constitute one's εὖ ζῆν—about the way in which ἔρως is like φιλία. Like the friend, the lover desires εὖ ζῆν; but the lover has a fundamentally sensual conception of this and so fails in fact to desire the sort of perceiving *and knowing*—and so the sort of perceiving *and knowing together*—that is proper to a *human* being. Taken parenthetically, this point makes perfect sense, both in the immediate context and in the broader context, which is ultimately about εὖ ζῆν. For Aristotle concludes in [7](B) by saying that for us—unlike God—τὸ εὖ is in relation to another. And although Aristotle speaks there simply of τὸ εὖ and not of εὖ ζῆν, this may be on account of the comparison with God. For though [ST1][e] speaks of God's noetic activity as itself a kind of life, Aristotle may think that this involves extending the use of the term ζωή in a way that requires precisely the sort of argument he gives in that passage. For Aristotle often associates life with the sort of nutritive and reproductive activities from which gods (as he conceives of them) are excluded. So [7](B) may be one among other places where he uses a vaguer term than he might otherwise have used—in this case τὸ εὖ instead of τὸ εὖ ζῆν—because the more specific term is too heavily biased toward one of two things he is comparing or contrasting with one another. For discussion of another case of such (arguably deliberate) vagueness, see Pickavé and Whiting "*Nicomachean Ethics* VII.3 on Akratic Ignorance," 362 [III.7].

[82] The argument is most plausibly taken to be the one presented in [1], perhaps together with the one presented in [5](A) and (B) to the extent that they restate the argument of [1]. It is different from what I am calling "the basic logos" of [2](B), referred to in [3](B). But there is nothing untoward about this, given the frequency with which Aristotle (like other authors) uses '*logos*' in different ways in different sentences within relatively short stretches of text.

[83] I take the talk of "random speech" to be an echo of the talk in *Metaphysics* XII.7 of a random object of thought, though the latter may well be an echo of the former if *EE* VII.12 is earlier than *Metaphysics* XII.7. I do not myself have a view about which is earlier; nor do I think that anything in my argument depends on assuming either order.

of *self-sufficient* agents that adding random speech yields simply "another such thing" as the sort of speechless eating and drinking together that Aristotle has just mentioned. But it does *not* follow from this that there is *no* form of speech whose addition would explain a preference on the part of self-sufficient agents for wining and dining together; perhaps edifying conversation would do the trick.

This proposal is taken up and rejected in [5](B). The preference of self-sufficient agents for eating and drinking together *cannot* be explained by appeal to what either might thereby *learn* from the other. For the assumption that either one stands to learn from the other conflicts with the sort of self-sufficiency that each is supposed, by hypothesis, to display. The hypothesis makes these agents as godlike as possible in what seems to be a *Philebus*-influenced way: neither is supposed to have any (perceived) epistemic deficiency that might be remedied by her association with the other.[84] In this sense, the hypothesis itself speaks against common interpretations according to which the relationship allows each agent to achieve a kind of self-knowledge she would otherwise lack. Aristotle's point has more to do, in ways that [5](C) begins to reveal, with *pleasure*. But not with the pleasures of eating and drinking, where these are associated with the filling of some bodily lack. Nor even with the pleasures of learning, where these are associated with remedying some epistemic deficiency. Aristotle is working here toward the sort of "pure" pleasures that the *Philebus* grants to human—as distinct from divine—subjects.

What [5] contributes to the positive argument comes in [5](C), where Aristotle prepares to show why it is not in fact foolish (as [5](A) concedes it may *seem*) for self-sufficient agents to prefer living together to living alone. [5](C) prepares the way for this by introducing purported facts about human nature, starting with the fact that we all—I suppose this is "for the most part"—find it *more pleasant* to partake of good activities together with friends than to partake of them alone, especially when these activities are the best of which we are capable.[85] Aristotle is building here, even if only implicitly, on another purported fact: namely, that each of us tends—again, I suppose, "for the most part"—to get *more enjoyment* from engaging in the more rather than the less challenging activities of which we are capable.[86] That Aristotle is building on some such fact is suggested by the way he allows that differently abled individuals will have different preferences here, each wanting (at least for the most part) to engage together

---

[84] See *Philebus* 52, but note the way in which Socrates there seeks to allow *some* ignorance, provided that its subject is *not aware* of it (since such awareness would be painful). The Socrates of the *Philebus* seems to be moving away from a general account of pleasure according to which all pleasures are remedial, but he has not yet freed himself entirely from this account; so it is important to him that the pleasures of learning involve only such epistemic deficiencies as are imperceptible to their subject. Still, he is moving in the direction of the Aristotelian view found in *EE* VI (aka *EN* VII) 13.

[85] Aristotle makes similar appeals to facts about human nature in the Nicomachean discussion of *philia*. For more on this see section 8 of my "*NAP*" [Chapter 6, this volume].

[86] Something like this was actually dubbed "the Aristotelian principle" by John Rawls in *A Theory of Justice* (Cambridge, MA: Harvard University Press), 426 n. 20. As Rawls puts it, "the more enjoyable activities and the more desirable and enduring pleasures spring from the exercise of greater abilities involving more complex discriminations." Rawls also notes that J. S. Mill "comes very close to stating [this principle] in *Utilitarianism*, Ch. II, pars. 4–8." See J. S. Mill, *Utilitarianism*, 1863.

with friends in the *best* activities of which he or she is capable: for some it will be bodily pleasure that will prove more enjoyable when they pursue it with others; for others it will be artistic contemplation or philosophy.

Aristotle is alluding here to the different activities that differently disposed and differently abled individuals take as their respective ends—the activities for the sake of which they would choose to be born rather than not. If this is not yet clear, it becomes clear when Aristotle speaks in [6](C) of the association of self-sufficient agents as being "most of all" an association of unspecified things (probably activities) "in the end." For the relevant end appears to be either eudaimonia itself or (what comes to much the same thing) whatever specific activity the parties take to constitute their eudaimonia. But here in [5](C) Aristotle is simply presenting what he takes to be widely acknowledged tendencies of human nature: first, the tendency of each to get more pleasure from the "higher" activities of which he or she is capable than from the "lower" ones; and second, the tendency of each to find the pleasure he or she takes in these "higher" activities to be increased by engaging in them together with friends. It remains for [6] to *make sense* of these tendencies.

Unfortunately, the relevance of these points to the overall argument tends to get lost in the interpretive fuss about how to understand [6](A)'s reference to the friend as "another Heracles, another *this*." The problem is not simply that some editors emend [6](A) so that it reads (like *EN* 1166a32) ἄλλος αὐτός instead of ἄλλος οὗτος. The problem is mainly that readers—including those who do not emend—fail to read [6](A) in its proper context, which is the context provided earlier in *EE* VII, especially in VII.6.

8. THE EUDEMIAN TEXT CONTINUED: READING [6] *IN CONTEXT*

Aristotle's argument in *EE* VII.6 is that so-called friendship with oneself is not *without qualification* a form of friendship, but *only analogous* to the form of friendship that obtains between virtuous agents. The reason for this is that in friendship strictly so-called, the loving and the being loved belong to *distinct subjects* each of which is *divided from the other*. So it is only insofar as a person is in some sense *two* that he can be called a friend to himself and said to exhibit in relationship to himself any of the attitudes characteristic of friendship strictly so-called. These attitudes include (i) wishing goods (or what one believes to be goods) to another not on account of oneself but for the sake of *that* person [ἐκείνου ἕνεκα]; (ii) wishing existence for another on account of *that* person [δι' ἐκεῖνον] and not on account of oneself; and (iii) choosing to live together with the other on account of the association itself [δι'αὐτὴν τὴν ὁμιλίαν] and not on account of some other thing.[87] Aristotle clarifies the last point by saying that fathers

[87] I have italicized *'that'* [ἐκεῖνον] here to highlight the way in which Aristotle often uses it (not just here but elsewhere) to refer to the friend in the sense of the one who is loved as distinct from the one who does the loving. This is relevant to the interpretation of [6](B).

choose existence for their children but prefer the company of others [1240a29–20]. He continues a few lines later as follows:

[ST3] *Eudemian Ethics* VII.6 [1240a33–b37]

[a] Further, we shall count it as loving to feel pain together with the one who is pained, not on account of some other thing (as slaves <feel pain> in relation to their masters because <the masters> are harsh <with the slaves> when they are in pain) but on account of <the ones being pained> themselves, as mothers <feel pain together> with their children and the birds that suffer together <feel pain with one another>. For the friend *wishes above all* [βούλεται γὰρ μάλιστά] not just to feel pain together with his friend but in fact <to feel> the same pain (e.g., to thirst together with the <friend who is> thirsty) if this is possible, and if not <to feel a pain> as close as possible to it. And the same account applies in the case of enjoyment. <For to enjoy> not on account of some other thing, but on account of *that* person, because *he* enjoys [ἀλλὰ **δι' ἐκεῖνον**, ὅτι χαίρει], is *philikon*.[88] [1240a33–b1]

[b] . . . All of these <characteristics>[89] refer to the individual [πρὸς τὸν ἕνα]. For he wishes goods to himself in this way <sc., on account of himself and not on account of something else>. For no one does well to himself on account of some other thing . . .[90] And existing together and living together, and enjoying together and being pained together, and indeed <being> one soul, and not being able even to live without one another but to die together <all refer to the individual>. For the individual [ὁ εἷς] is like this, and presumably keeps company himself with himself [ὁμιλεῖ αὐτὸς αὑτῷ]. [b3–11]

[c] And all these <characteristics> belong to the good person in relation to himself. For in the bad person there is a discrepancy, as, for example, in the *akratês*. And on account of this, it seems possible for him to be an object of hate to himself. But insofar as <the individual> is one and undivided [ᾗ δ' εἷς καὶ ἀδιαίρετος] he is himself to himself such-as-to-be-desired [ὀρεκτὸς αὐτὸς αὑτῷ]. Such is the good person and the friend in accordance with virtue, since the bad person at any rate is not one but many, and even on the same day different <from himself> and unstable <from one moment to the next>. So the friendship of oneself in relation to oneself boils down to the friendship of the good person <in relation to himself>. For because <the good person> is in a way similar and one and himself in relation to himself

[88] On '*philikon*' as "characteristic of or productive of *philia*," see section 6 of my "*NAP*" [Chapter 6, this volume].

[89] Starting with (i)–(iii) in my paraphrase of what precedes this passage.

[90] The text is corrupt here, but the crucial point is clear enough in what follows the ellipsis.

good [ὅτι γάρ πῃ ὅμοιοῖ καὶ εἷς καὶ αὐτὸς αὑτῷ ἀγαθός], in this way he is himself to himself a friend and such-as-to-be-desired [ταύτῃ αὐτὸς αὑτῷ φίλος καὶ ὀρεκτός] [b11–20] . . .[91]

[d] But everyone *seems* himself to himself good. And the person who is good without qualification seeks *to be* <good> and <*to be*> himself to himself a friend, just as was said, because there are two <things> in him that by nature wish to be friends and that it is impossible to separate [ὅτι δύ' ἔχει ἐν αὑτῷ ἃ φύσει βούλεται εἶναι φίλα καὶ **διασπάσαι** ἀδύνατον].[92] Wherefore in the case of man each seems to be a friend to himself, while in the case of the other animals <this does not seem to be the case>; for example, a horse <does not seem to be a friend> itself in relation to itself, nor therefore is it a friend <to itself >. But neither are children <friends themselves in relation to themselves>. But <friendship with oneself arises> whenever one is actually capable of *prohairesis*. For it is only then that nous disagrees with appetite. And friendship in relation to oneself seems to be like the <sort of *philia* spoken of> according to kinship [κατὰ συγγένειαν]. For it is not up to the parties themselves to dissolve either <sort of relation>; but if they disagree with one another, nevertheless in the one case they are still kin [ἔτι συγγενεῖς], and in the other case the <the man> is still one individual [ἔτι εἷς] as long as he lives. [b27–37]

It should be clear from a quick comparison of the language used here with that used in [6](A) that this passage sets the stage for [6](A). For there too Aristotle speaks of what the friend "wishes" [βούλεται]; of the friend as "separated" [διέσπασται] from his friend; of things in some sense coming to be in one thing or a single individual [ἐφ' ἑνὸς]; of the friend as the one who is "most akin" [τὸ συγγενέστατον]; of the friends as "similar" [ὅμοιος] in some respect to one another; and of the individual as in some sense "divisible" [διαιρετὸς]. So let us turn at last to the culmination of Aristotle's argument.

---

[91] This talk of an individual being *orektos* himself to himself may sound odd. But it should be clear from my earlier remarks about the multivocity of the -τός/-τόν suffix that this may mean simply that he sees the sort of person he is as a *desirable* sort of person to be. One may of course find such self-admiration morally dangerous. For more on this, see my "Eudaimonia, External Results, and Choosing Virtuous Actions for Themselves" [Chapter 3, this volume]; "Impersonal Friends" [I.2]; and "Self-Love and Authoritative Virtue" [Chapter 4, this volume]. But the point here is simply that it is not unlike the sort of admiration one might have for one's friend.

[92] The idea is apparently that because a human being has parts that are "inseparable" from one another, each human being *seems* to be a friend "himself in relation to himself" even when this is not in fact the case (as, for example, with the *akratês*, whose parts struggle against one another); but the soul of a non-rational animal does not admit the sort of duality required even for the illusion of its being a friend "itself in relation to itself." The text here, especially in the following lines, is uncertain, but the basic idea seems relatively clear.

[6] The pleasures of perceiving and knowing together with friends [1245a29–b9]

(A) We must consider whence the truth <emerges >. For **the friend wishes** to be, as the proverb says, *another Heracles, another this* <so and so>.[93] **But he is separated** <from his friend>[94] and it is difficult for all <?> **to come to be in <a single> individual**.[95] But <the friend is> by nature what is **most akin** <to oneself>, and one person is **similar** <to oneself> in body, another <is similar to oneself> in soul, and with respect to these <sc., body and soul> different individuals <are similar to one another> in different parts. But nonetheless the friend **wishes** <the two of them to be> **divisible** just as he himself is.

σκεπτέον ἔνθεν τἀληθές. ὁ γὰρ φίλος **βούλεται** εἶναι, ὥσπερ ἡ παροιμία φησίν, ἄλλος Ἡρακλῆς, ἄλλος οὗτος. **διέσπασται δὲ** καὶ χαλεπὸν πάντα[96] **ἐφ'**

---

[93] Dirlmeier, who reads ἄλλος Ἡρακλῆς, ἄλλος αὐτός, actually translates "*ein* zweiter *Heracles, ein* zweites *Ich*," which (in introducing the "Ich") pulls in two different directions. This is puzzling: if the initial idea is that *Heracles' friend* wants to be another Heracles and in that sense more *like* Heracles, then what are we to make of the idea that he wants to be "another himself" (or as Dirlmeier puts it "another I")? The point here does not seem to be a point about what is required for self-knowledge: it seems to be about what *Heracles' friend* wishes—namely, to be *another* Heracles (presumably in the sense that he wants to be *like* Heracles). So looking at Heracles is far less like looking in a mirror than like looking to a role model. For this and other reasons, I do not think we should read this passage in light of the mirror passage at *Magna Moralia* II 15.5: what is going on there may be either some later author's confused presentation of Aristotle or (as Brad Inwood suggests) a later author presenting what he himself takes to be a *revised* Aristotelian view, one that incorporates Platonic elements (in this case the mirror image from *Alcibiades I* 132d–33b, though it is also worth keeping *Phaedrus* 252d–253c in mind in this context). See Inwood, *Ethics after Aristotle*, for this idea about what later Peripatetics are up to.

[94] See *Rhetoric* 1386a10 for this sense: . . . διὸ καὶ τὸ διασπᾶσθαι ἀπὸ φίλων καὶ συνήθων ἐλεεινόν.

[95] I take this to be justified by the fact that Aristotle has been using εἷς (as we saw in [ST3]) to refer to the individual as such.

[96] It is difficult to know what to read here. All but the Marcianus have χαλεπὸν τὰ ἐφ' ἑνὸς γενέσθαι, leaving the subject of γενέσθαι unclear. The Marcianus has χαλεπὸν τὰ ἀφ' ἑνὸς γενέσθαι, perhaps because the scribe took the point to be about the difficulty of getting everything one *needs* or at least *wants* from a single individual. But that would be misguided if (as I argue here) Aristotle's point is that the self-sufficient person neither needs nor wants things from her friend, but simply takes a kind of pleasure in perceiving the good activities of her friend that is like the kind of pleasure she takes in perceiving good activities of her own.

Both the OCT (citing Richards) and Rackham's Loeb read πάντα instead of τὰ, and so print χαλεπὸν **πάντα** ἐφ' ἑνὸς γενέσθαι. But this does not provide much guidance as to the sense: it is difficult for *all* the *whats* to come to be in one *what*? Many assume (in a way that is perhaps suggested by what follows) that the point is about the bodily and psychic *characteristics* of the friends, and that the idea is that not all of the characteristics of one's friend can come to be in one individual. But I wonder whether the point could be picking up on the point of [ST3][a] and so concern the difficulty of having *all* of the experiences that one's friend has—i.e., to thirst (in some sense) when he thirsts, to have one's thirst quenched (in some sense) when his thirst is quenched, etc. For even if we take this (as I think we should) to involve having numerically distinct experiences of the same kind, we might reasonably think it "difficult" for even the best of friends always to share token experiences of the same kind in this way. It is here that I am most tempted to reconsider the manuscript reading τὸ αὐτὸ αἰσθάνεσθαι καὶ τὸ αὐτὸ γνωρίζειν back at [3](A); but I still do not know how to make sense of that in context.

ἑνὸς γενέσθαι· ἀλλὰ κατὰ μὲν τὴν φύσιν ὃ **συγγενέστατον**, κατὰ δὲ τὸ σῶμα **ὅμοιος** ἕτερος, ἄλλος δὲ κατὰ τὴν ψυχήν, καὶ τούτων κατὰ μόριον ἕτερος ἕτερον. ἀλλ' οὐθέν τε ἧττον **βούλεται** ὥσπερ αὐτὸς **διαιρετὸς** εἶναι ὁ φίλος. [1245a29–35]

Although ὁ γὰρ φίλος βούλεται at the start of the second sentence is sometimes taken as a claim about what the *term* φίλος *means*, I think it pretty clear that βούλεται is used here to pick up the thread from *EE* VII.6 about what a *friend* characteristically *wishes* or *wants*. But there is disagreement about *what* it is she is supposed to wish or want. For as noted above, virtually all modern translators read ἄλλος **αὐτός** here in place of ἄλλος **οὗτος**. Instead of "another this" or "another this <so-and-so>," we find "another self" (Rackham; Kosman; Sorabji; Osborne; Kenny [2011]; Inwood and Woolf); "a second self" (Solomon); "*un autre soi-même*" (Décarie); and "*ein zweites Ich*" (Dirlmeier). But *all* the manuscripts have ἄλλος **οὗτος**, which is *also* what we find in all ostensible occurrences of the proverb [*paroimia*] to which the text alludes.[97] Especially in the light of this last point, about ostensible occurrences of the proverb, I think it best to follow the manuscripts, *if* we can make sense of what they say. For I find it easier to imagine someone recalling the Nicomachean talk of the friend as ἄλλος **αὐτός**, and supplying that here, than to imagine someone seeing that here and changing it to ἄλλος **οὗτος**.[98]

Moreover, I think we *can* make sense—indeed good sense—of what the manuscripts say. The idea seems to be that *Heracles*' friend wishes to be "*another* Heracles" in the sense that she wishes to be, if not Heracles himself, at least *like* Heracles. And the reason for this seems to be that being *like* Heracles is a *good way to be* (which means it is *a good way to perceive oneself*, even if only peripherally, *being*). The point of the οὗτος may

[97] For general discussion of the *paroimia*, see Dirlmeier, *Magna Moralia*, 470–77 (ad 1213a10ff.). Both Aelian 12.22 and Plutarch *Theseus* 29.3–4 have (in very different contexts) ἄλλος οὗτος Ἡρακλῆς. Kosman, "Desirability," discusses the Plutarch passage, where he suggests something like the idea I see in [6](A)—namely, that Heracles is someone *worth* emulating. But the point in Plutarch is not the one I see here: namely, that *Heracles' friend* wants to be like Heracles because that is a good way to be; the point is rather that Theseus sees his friend Meleager *not* as another *Theseus* (i.e., another *himself*), but as another *Heracles*: i.e., as someone who can help Meleager do the sort of things that Heracles could help him do. (Kosman suggests translating "a regular Heracles.") And Kosman takes the application to [6](A) to lie in the fact that friends are supposed to *do* things *together* (which of course involves perceiving and thinking *together*) in a way such that what each does (and perceives and thinks) forms part of what *they*—*as* a *pair*—do (and perceive and think). And Kosman—who, somewhat mysteriously in light of his discussion of Plutarch, follows tradition in substituting αὐτός for οὗτος in [6](A)—takes the point in [6](B) to be not (as it is most naturally taken) that perceiving one's friend is in a way perceiving oneself, but rather that one's friend's perceiving is in a way one's own since it is part of what the two, as a *pair*, perceive. See sec. VI of Kosman, "Desirability."

[98] This argument is not decisive, since someone thinking of the *paroimia* might substitute οὗτος for αὐτός, as ὥσπερ ἡ παροιμία φησὶν would in fact seem to *license*. But ὥσπερ ἡ παροιμία φησὶν, unless it too was a later insertion, suggests that οὗτος is what *belongs* here. So it is *possible* that αὐτός was intended but "corrected" early on, thus explaining the fact that it appears in none of the extant manuscripts. But that seems to me very unlikely.

be simply to invite generalization by encouraging the reader to substitute for Heracles his or her *own* friend (i.e., the person he or she most wishes to be *like*) or the friend of whomever he or she takes the primary subject of the argument to be (i.e., whomever *that* subject most wishes to be *like*).[99]

Why *exactly* the friend wants this is not entirely clear. It is possible that she wants this at least partly because she wants to have the sort of powers that enable *her* to come to the aid of *Heracles* in the way that *he* can come to the aid of *his* friends. But the way in which Aristotle describes the giving and receiving of benefits at the end of [6](C)—i.e., as what people fall back on when they cannot live together sharing in the best activity or activities of which they are capable—casts doubt on the idea that this is the friend's main reason for wanting to be "another Heracles." For it seems pretty clear that Aristotle introduces the wish to be "another Heracles" as part of his explanation of why self-sufficient agents will want to *live together*. So let us assume for the moment that the friend *admires* Heracles and wants at the very least to be *like* Heracles because that is a *good way* to be (and so of course a *pleasant* way to perceive *oneself* being). Does this allow us to make sense of what comes next?

Aristotle's next claim is that the friend is separated from what I shall henceforth call "her Heracles" and that this makes something or other difficult. But what exactly is the difficulty supposed to be? Is Aristotle alluding, as McCabe suggests, to the lamentable fact—at least according to Plato's Aristophanes—that the friend and "her Heracles" are separate individuals and so cannot strictly speaking *become one*?

I doubt this for two reasons. First, the language used here is far closer to the language of *EE* VII.6 than to that of the *Symposium*, where Aristophanes uses the verbs χωρίζω (at 192c1–2) and διασχίζω (at 193a5), instead of διασπάω, and speaks explicitly (as Aristotle does not) of halves and wholes and of things growing together (see, e.g., συμφυσῆσαι at 192e1). Second, and more importantly, I find it hard to believe that becoming one with her friend is what the friend is supposed to want, since it would in that case be a grotesque understatement to describe what she wants as "difficult" [χαλεπὸν]. Moreover, there are other things, more aptly described as "difficult," that I *can* imagine Aristotle supposing the friend wants, including coming to be *exactly like* "her Heracles." For (as the text goes on to say) different people resemble an individual in different respects: some resemble her in body, some in soul, and even with regard to these two things, different people resemble different parts or aspects of her body or soul. In other words, the fact that any similarity there is between friends tends to be only partial limits the extent to which one can come to be exactly like "one's Heracles" (or exactly like whoever it is the subject most wants to be like).

[99] I am grateful to Jakub Krajczynski for discussion of this point. He suggests, quite plausibly, that the οὗτος in ἄλλος οὗτος may be meant to connect with [4](B)'s point about wanting to be of some *determinate* nature. Unfortunately, there is not space here to explore this promising suggestion, which, however, seems to me compatible with taking the οὗτος to invite generalization: the friend wants to be another *this determinate character* (for *whatever* determinate character it is she herself admires and wants to be like).

This is the best I can do to make sense of the difficulty to which Aristotle refers in the third sentence of [6](A). So I interpret [6](A) as first conceding, in light of the fact that the friends are separate from each other, that "it is difficult for all <aspects of the friend> to come to be in a single individual"; and as then pointing to various respects in which friends, though being separate individuals, can nevertheless be *sungeneis*. The point here, I think, is the one stressed in *EE* VII.6 and elsewhere: namely, that friendship strictly speaking *presupposes* the *separateness* of the friends. So while I am happy to see here some allusion to Aristophanes' suggestion (in Plato's *Symposium*) that the friends' literally becoming one is the ideal, it seems to me that any such allusion is at least as likely to be *rejecting* Aristophanes' suggestion as to be *endorsing* it.

Let me note in support of this claim another passage, even closer to *EE* VII.12, where Aristotle emphasizes the separateness of friends: namely, the following passage from *EE* VII.9.

> **[ST4]** Since in similar ways soul stands to body and craftsperson to tool and master to slave, there is no *koinônia* of these with one another, for they are not two <individuals> but the one is an individual and the other is something belonging to the individual. *Nor <in these relationships> is the good divided between each, but the <good> of both is for the sake of the individual.* (οὐδὲ διαιρετὸν τὸ ἀγαθὸν ἑκατέρῳ, ἀλλὰ τὸ ἀμφοτέρων τοῦ ἑνὸς οὗ ἕνεκα ἐστίν.) [1241b17–22, my italics]

The point here seems to be that a *koinônia* involves *two distinct* goods, one for *each* of the individuals involved. If there is to be a *genuine koinônia*, then neither party's good can be subsumed by the other's in anything like the way the slave's good is subsumed by the master's. Nor, I think, can either's good be subsumed by the good of some *composite* entity in the ways that Kosman and McCabe suggest. For we should recall here the criticisms leveled in Aristotle's *Politics* (*Pol.*) against the sort of community of women, children, and property that is proposed by Socrates in Plato's *Republic:* Aristotle objects that a polis—which he calls a *koinônia*—is by nature a *multitude* and so something destroyed by excessive unity [*Pol.* 1261a16–22]. And Aristotle explicitly compares what Socrates proposes in the *Republic* to the desire that Aristophanes ascribes to lovers in Plato's *Symposium*: the desire "to grow together and from being two to become one": this, Aristotle objects, would spell the destruction of both (or at least of one of them) [*Pol.* 1262b10–14].

We should thus take the emphasis in the phrase *allos Heraklês* to be on the *allos*. The friend does not want to *become* Heracles, nor even to become *one with* Heracles. He wants to become *another* Heracles: "*ein zweiter Heracles,*" as Dirlmeier actually renders it. For as we saw in *EE* VII.6, friendship strictly so-called requires the existence of *two* parties: the loving and the being loved *must* be in things that are divided from one another, and divided in a more literal way than the parts of a person (or her soul) are divided from one another. So it seems plausible to interpret the wish expressed in the last sentence of [6](A) as assuming the sort of duality that is presupposed by friendship while seeking forms of epistemic and hedonic intimacy with the other that might be viewed as analogous to the forms of epistemic and hedonic intimacy that Aristotle takes to hold among the parts of a virtuous agent's soul.

By "epistemic intimacy," I mean more than the interpersonal analogue of the sort of *relatively constant* awareness that a rational agent has of what she herself is doing and experiencing. I mean also the sort of *comprehending* awareness of what the other is doing that is—like the comprehending awareness of what oneself is doing—based on a grasp of the agent's *prohairesis*. And I mean further the kind of *openness and transparency* that is afforded by absence of conflict: that there be no need or incentive in the intrapersonal case for repression or self-deception and no need or incentive in the interpersonal case for any analogues of these. This sort of epistemic intimacy is connected with what I call "hedonic intimacy." Because there is no conflict among the parts of the virtuous agent's soul, it does not happen that one part reproaches another part for what it does or feels, or that one part is embarrassed by or regrets behavior driven by another part. And so too in the interpersonal case, at least where the friends are good: each approves of the other's attitudes and actions and so is pleased by the other's attitudes and actions in much the same way that each approves of and is pleased by her own. In this sense, each takes in the attitudes and actions of the other, something *like* the sort of pleasure she takes in her own. But the kind of pleasure she takes requires her to have a relatively immediate understanding of the attitudes and actions of the other: the two must have achieved the sort of epistemic intimacy (including perception of one another's *prohairesis*[100]) mentioned above. This helps to explain why we cannot, in perceiving or contemplating the attitudes and actions of strangers (however good they may be) take anything like the sort of pleasure we can take in perceiving and contemplating the attitudes and actions of our friends: we are not epistemically related to them in the right way.[101]

In sum, I read the last sentence of [6](A) as saying that the friend, while recognizing the sort of duality that is presupposed by friendship, nevertheless seeks a kind of epistemic and hedonic intimacy that can be attained only if the friends live together. For only then can each have the sort of more or less immediate, constant, and comprehending awareness of the other's activities and experiences that is analogous to her more or less immediate, constant, and comprehending awareness of her own.[102] But the wish characteristic of the friend is for far more than this: it is for reciprocal *understanding* and reciprocal *appreciation*, for the sort of *harmony* involved in hedonic intimacy, where each *approves of* and so is *pleased by* the *other's* activities and experiences

[100] See *EE* VII.2, especially 1236b2–6.

[101] For more on this, see sections 9 and 11 of my "*NAP*" [Chapter 6, this volume].

[102] Two important facts make the analogies between self-consciousness and consciousness of one's friend and her activities closer than it might at first seem: (1) the fact that there can be lapses of self-awareness (as, for example, when one acts mindlessly); and (2) the fact that the proper interpretation of one's own behavior is not always transparent to oneself.

in something like the way that each, being by hypothesis virtuous, *approves of* and so is *pleased by* her *own*.

This allows us to make sense of [6](B) without having to suppose (as Kosman supposes) that my *friend's* activity of perceiving *is* in some sense my *own*. The point in [6](B) is that perceiving *my friend*, where this involves perceiving her activities and experiences, necessarily occurs *together with* perceiving *myself* in some way and with knowing *myself* in some way. The relevant way may well be the one mentioned in *Metaphysics* XII.9, where Aristotle speaks of the way in which human beings, in perceiving and knowing other things, perceive and know themselves peripherally [*en parergô(i)*]. In that case, the main idea is the one articulated above: that in perceiving some object I in some sense take on the form of that object, so that the better the objects I perceive, the better the condition in which I perceive *myself* (even if only peripherally) *being*. And the better the condition in which I perceive myself being, the *more pleasant* my *self*-perception.

So in cases where the object is my friend successfully engaged in some activity, the better the activity in which I perceive *her* engaged, the better (ceteris paribus) the condition in which I perceive *myself* (even if only peripherally) being, and (as a result) the more pleasant my *self*-perception. And in cases where I *myself* am enjoying the *same* good, perceiving my friend enjoying that good together with me is pleasant in ways such that I come to be (and so perceive myself being) in an *even better* condition than I would be in were I enjoying that good on my own. This, I take it, is what is going on in [6](B) and (C), which are (as I have said) the culmination of Aristotle's argument.

[6](B) To perceive one's friend, then, is necessarily to perceive oneself in some way and to know oneself in some way. So *it makes sense*[103] that enjoying even mundane[104] things together and living together with the friend <in the enjoyment of such things> is pleasant (for the perception of **that one** always happens at the same time with <?>[105]); and even more so in the case of the more divine pleasures.

---

[103] Here, Aristotle aims to make sense of the purported facts cited back in [5](C).

[104] τὰ φορτικά is generally taken as referring to pleasures (which, as neuter, it cannot strictly do) and is often rendered in ways that have negative connotations: "vulgar/vulgaire" (Solomon, Rackham, Décarie); "base" (Inwood and Woolf); "crude" (Osborne). There is little problem with taking it to refer to pleasures (as the contrast with τὰς θειοτέρας ἡδονάς suggests) if we understand "pleasures" in the sense of the things or activities *in which* pleasure is taken (a distinction often made in discussions of the *Philebus*). But it is problematic to take τὰ φορτικά as having negative connotations, since the argument seems to assume that the things one perceives the friend enjoying are in some sense good: the idea is that seeing one's friend enjoy some good is pleasant in something like the way that seeing oneself enjoy some good is pleasant. The goods may be small and relatively trivial (so Dirlmeier's "trivial" is not bad); or they may be very important but ultimately instrumental goods, as, for example, eating construed as providing the nourishment required to engage in the sort of activities in which one takes one's living to consist. Hence my choice of "mundane."

[105] There are two ways to fill this out: perception of that one (i.e., the friend) is simultaneous (a) with *perception of oneself*; or (in cases where the friends live together) (b) with *the friend's enjoyment* of the mundane things just mentioned. See below, note 111.

τὸ οὖν τοῦ φίλου αἰσθάνεσθαι τὸ αὐτοῦ πως ἀνάγκη αἰσθάνεσθαι εἶναι, καὶ τὸ αὐτόν πως γνωρίζειν. ὥστε καὶ τὰ φορτικὰ μὲν συνήδεσθαι καὶ συζῆν τῷ φίλῳ ἡδὺ εὐλόγως (συμβαίνει γὰρ **ἐκείνου**[106] ἅμα αἴσθησις ἀεί), μᾶλλον δὲ τὰς θειοτέρας ἡδονάς. [1245a35–39]

(C) The reason for this <viz., its being more pleasant to enjoy more *divine* pleasures with friends than to enjoy mundane ones with friends> is that it is always more pleasant to observe oneself <being> in the better <of two> good <conditions>. (And this <sc., the better condition> is sometimes an affection, sometimes an action, and sometimes something else.) But if <________> himself to live well and in the same way also <______> his friend <to live well>, and <if _____ > to act together in living together, then their communion will be above all of the <activities belonging> in the end; whence <it will be> to contemplate together and to feast together. But such associations seem not to be on account of nourishment or necessary things, but rather <to be> enjoyments.[107] But each wishes to live together <with another> in <the pursuit of> whatever end he is capable of attaining. If this <living together in the pursuit of whatever end each is capable of attaining> is not possible, people choose above all to do well and to be <well> treated by their friends.[108]

αἴτιον δ' ὅτι ἀεὶ ἥδιον ἑαυτὸν θεωρεῖν ἐν τῷ βελτίονι ἀγαθῷ. (τοῦτο δ' ἐστὶν ὁτὲ μὲν πάθος, ὁτὲ δὲ πρᾶξις, ὁτὲ δὲ ἕτερόν τι.) εἰ δ' αὐτὸν εὖ ζῆν, καὶ οὕτω καὶ τὸν φίλον, ἐν δὲ τῷ συζῆν συνεργεῖν, ἡ κοινωνία τῶν ἐν τέλει μάλιστά γε. διὸ συνθεωρεῖν καὶ συνευωχεῖσθαι. οὐ < δὲ>[109] διὰ τροφὴν καὶ τὰ ἀναγκαῖα αἱ τοιαῦται ὁμιλίαι δοκοῦσιν εἶναι, ἀλλὰ ἀπολαύσεις. ἀλλ' ἕκαστος οὗ δύναται

---

[106] I follow *all* the manuscripts here in reading ἐκείνου (which, though it often refers to the remoter of two antecedents, is also used regularly in Aristotle's discussions of friendship to refer to the object as distinct from the subject of *philein*). I am not sure that I fully understand the difficulties commentators have had understanding this, difficulties that have led them to propose sometimes to understand ἐκείνου as referring not to the one loved but to the one who loves (which *is* the more distant term: see Dirlmeier ad loc., followed by Décarie); and sometimes (more radically) to substitute αὑτοῦ for ἐκείνου (Robinson, reported by Walzer and Mingay). But the difficulties seem to stem from taking the simultaneity in question (as it is traditionally taken) to be that of perceiving oneself and perceiving one's friend, and these difficulties can be avoided (in a way I explain in the main text) by taking the simultaneity in question to be that of (1) the *subject's perception* of her friend enjoying mundane pleasures and (2) the *friend's enjoyment* of those pleasures. For more on the difficulties of taking the simultaneity in the traditional way, see note 111 below.

[107] Taking ἀπολαύσεις to be nominative, rather than accusative with διὰ understood.

[108] This is one of many points where we can see that friendships based on pleasure are—contrary to what is often supposed—closer to friendships based on character than to those based on advantage. The point here is that when people cannot live together with their friends, sharing in the pursuit of whatever activities each takes to be part of his or her end, they fall back on friendships of advantage.

[109] The manuscripts have οὐ τὰ διὰ τροφὴν. Walzer and Mingay insert γὰρ and bracket τὰ: οὐ γὰρ {τὰ} διὰ τροφὴν. Others make adjustments in the text that follows: see below, note 116. I see no reason to insert γὰρ and suggest instead a weakly adversative δὲ in place of τὰ: the idea is to make it clear what sort of contemplating and feasting together he does *not* mean.

τυγχάνειν τέλους, ἐν τούτῳ βούλεται συζῆν· εἰ δὲ μή, καὶ ποιεῖν εὖ καὶ πάσχειν ὑπὸ τῶν φίλων αἱροῦνται μάλιστα. [1245a39–b9]

I assume that each of the blanks left in (C) should be filled in the same way, but find it difficult to decide between what seem to me the two most plausible ways (to which I shall return). But we need to start with (B), where I have also left a blank that remains to be filled in.

The claim that to perceive (or to know) one's friend is *necessarily* in some way to perceive (or to know) oneself is puzzling, but it is intelligible if we suppose that one cannot perceive (or know) one's friend without in some way—perhaps peripherally—perceiving (or knowing) oneself.[110] And the idea seems to be that whatever sort of self-perception is involved here helps to make sense of the fact that it is *pleasant* to perceive a friend enjoying even mundane things and to live together with him in the enjoyment of such things. But how exactly is this supposed to make sense?

As explained in note 104 above, I prefer "mundane" to "vulgar," "base," and other common ways of rendering φορτικός that have negative connotations. For the argument assumes that the things one perceives one's friend enjoying are in some sense *good:* that is part of the point of the talk of "the better good" at the start of (C). The idea is that the divine pleasures (perhaps in the sense of the activities in which pleasure is taken) are not just better, but better *goods,* than mundane pleasures are. This allows us to explain the pleasure that is associated with whatever sort of self-perception necessarily accompanies the perception of one's friend enjoying some good: because it is some *good* the subject sees her friend enjoying, a good by the subject's *own* lights, the subject herself is pleased by the image of her *friend* enjoying this in something like the way the subject would be pleased by seeing an image of *herself* enjoying it. And insofar as the image of her friend enjoying this good is the subject's own, the subject's perception of the friend's enjoying this good involves a kind of *self*-perception: awareness of some form that she herself has in some sense taken on in a way such that her own condition is (ceteris paribus) better than it would have been had she not taken on this form. So the self-perception that necessarily accompanies perception of her friend yields *some* pleasure (however great or small). And in cases where this pleasure is *added* to the pleasure of seeing herself enjoy the same activity, the subject's pleasure is *even greater* than it would be if she perceived herself enjoying that activity on her own.

The simplest and least theory-laden way to take the parenthetical remark that follows (συμβαίνει γὰρ . . .), and so to fill in the blank in [B], is to take the point to be that when one lives together with a friend one's own perception of the friend's enjoyments is simultaneous *with those enjoyments* in a way that helps to explain why living together with one's friend is *pleasant*: to see in real time (so to speak) one's friend

[110] If the point is about *comprehending* perception, then it may even be something like D. Davidson's point about the problem of radical interpretation (which is, very roughly, that it is difficult if not impossible to make sense of another except by one's *own* lights). See Davidson, "Radical Interpretation."

enjoying things—even relatively mundane things—is *pleasant*. But this way of filling in the blank threatens to render idle the premise according to which it is more pleasant to perceive *oneself* being in the better of two good conditions. For so construed, the parenthetical remark appeals primarily to the pleasure associated with witnessing the friend's enjoyment *in action*. But it may be that the point about *self*-perception being involved—presumably in the way indicated in [4](C)—is now taken for granted and the point here is indeed to explain the friends' desire to live together by appeal to the fact that it is especially pleasant for each to witness *firsthand* the other's enjoyments *in action*.[111]

My "even more so" at the end of [6](B) is deliberately ambiguous. For it is not clear whether the μᾶλλον is meant to pick up ἡδὺ or εὐλόγως. Given what Aristotle has just said, the point may be *either* that it is *even more pleasant* to enjoy divine pleasures with friends than to enjoy mundane ones with them; *or* that it *makes even more sense* that enjoying divine pleasures with friends is pleasant than that enjoying mundane pleasures with friends is. But given that Aristotle speaks immediately at the start of [6](C) of what is *more pleasant*, I think it best to read (B) as claiming that it is even *more pleasant* to enjoy divine pleasures with a friend and to live with a friend in the enjoyment of such pleasures than to enjoy mundane things together with a friend and to live together with a friend in the enjoyment of them.

This could be for either of two reasons. The point could be simply that divine pleasures (construed perhaps as activities in which pleasure is taken) are more pleasant than mundane ones, so that even if divine ones are no more increased than mundane ones are by being shared with friends, sharing divine pleasures is on the whole more pleasant than sharing mundane pleasures. Or the point could be that divine pleasures

[111] The alternative (which I cannot rule out) is to take the parenthetical point (as most commentators seem to take it) to concern the simultaneity of *perceiving the friend* and *perceiving oneself*. But this makes it more difficult to understand how the point about simultaneity is supposed to help explain the preceding claim about enjoying mundane things together (as the initial γὰρ demands it to). This helps, I think, to explain why commentators tend either to take ἐκείνου to refer to the *subject* of the perception (rather than the friend who is perceived) or to substitute αὑτοῦ for ἐκείνου: they think it obvious that self-perception is pleasant in a way it is not obvious that perception of the friend is pleasant. But given that we *can* understand the simultaneity claim in the way afforded by the first sentence of [6](B) (i.e., as saying that *whenever* one perceives the friend, one also in some way—perhaps peripherally—perceives oneself) there is no problem here, especially not if we invoke the *De Anima* view that seems to lie behind [4](B): i.e., the theory according to which perceiving some object involves in some sense becoming *like* the object. In this case, there is little rationale for the proposed substitution. Either way—whether we take the point to be that perception of the friend is simultaneous with perception of oneself or vice versa—we must suppose that the subject of both sorts of perception takes whatever she sees her friend enjoying to be *good*, with the result that she takes pleasure in perceiving her friend enjoying it. And this pleasure is presumably due to the way in which the subject, in becoming *like* the object perceived, comes to be (and so perceives herself being) in a better condition than she would otherwise be in, with the result that she enjoys *some* pleasure she would not enjoy were she not perceiving this object. So provided that we are willing to appeal to the *De Anima*, there is little (if any) explanatory advantage to substituting αὑτοῦ for ἐκείνου. And it may be best in the end to go for the simpler explanation set out in my main text. The primary question is whether that explanation allows us to explain the crucial role that *self*-perception seems to play in Aristotle's overall argument.

are increased *even more* than mundane pleasures are by being shared with friends. The latter would of course provide a stronger explanation of the fact that self-sufficient agents *do* have friends. But Aristotle does *not need* so strong a claim: even if divine pleasures are increased to the same extent as vulgar pleasures by being shared with friends, it would still make sense that people who enjoy divine pleasures choose to enjoy them together with friends.

Aristotle may nevertheless accept the stronger claim. For he seems to think that however much most folk take "random speech" to increase the pleasures of dining together, self-sufficient agents do not share their sentiments. The pleasures of "random speech" are too trivial to bring such agents together; they may even prefer dining in contemplative silence to dining in the company of idle chatter. But self-sufficient agents do in fact choose to dine with other such agents, which suggests that the pleasures of dining in conversation with like-minded others about things that are *kalon* are weighty enough to tempt them away from dining in contemplative silence.

One reason for thinking that the "more divine" pleasures tend to be *disproportionately* increased by being shared with others may be tied to the claim back in [4](A) that it is plausible that perceiving and knowing oneself is more *haireton* than perceiving and knowing another. Let me start with that claim. On the *Philebus*-inspired story we have seen so far, self-perception and self-knowledge are pleasant partly on account of the value the subject sees in the first-order activities in which she perceives herself engaging. The idea is roughly that however good it is to lose oneself in contemplation of the starry skies above, it is *even better* to contemplate the starry skies above with some sort of awareness (even if only peripheral) that *that* valuable activity is precisely the activity in which one is engaged, where such awareness involves some *appreciation of the value* of doing *that*. And part of what makes self-conscious enjoyment of any worthwhile activity, however mundane, better than self-blind enjoyment of the same activity (assuming that is possible) may be the increased pleasure the subject gets when she enjoys that activity in full realization that she is doing so (as compared, for example, with cases where she engages in that activity in the way a depressed person, operating on something like "automatic pilot," might engage in it).[112]

This yields another sense in which—as [4](A) suggests—it is reasonable that it should be *more haireton* to perceive and know oneself than to perceive and know another. For there is a special sort of enjoyment that comes with *self-conscious* activity, a kind of enjoyment that kicks in even at the lowest level, where the activities are ones we share with other animals. This kind of enjoyment may even seem *peculiar* to the perception of one's *own* activities.[113] For however much one might enjoy perceiving a *friend* enjoying a good meal, there is a special sort of pleasure involved in perceiving

---

[112] For more on this, see section 11 of my "*NAP*" [Chapter 6, this volume], a section much indebted to chapter 2 of C. Bobonich *Plato's Utopia Recast*.

[113] I think we can see here the seeds of the Stoic theory of *oikeiôsis*, discussed in my "Lockeanism" [III.8].

oneself enjoying a good meal, a pleasure to which the actual having of a good meal (with the first-order pleasures that involves) is arguably internal.[114]

But the prevalence of this sort of pleasure, which is bodily-based and to that extent difficult (if not impossible) to share, may recede as one moves from the mundane to the more divine pleasures. In perceiving one's *friend* performing a virtuous action or working out a mathematical proof one may experience something *more like* the sort of pleasure the *friend himself* experiences in doing these things than one experiences in perceiving one's friend enjoying a good meal. For in the comprehending perception of one's friend working out a mathematical proof, one takes on the form of what the friend is doing in a more literal way than one does in the comprehending perception of the friend enjoying a good meal: really following someone doing a proof is arguably much closer to actually doing a proof than watching one's friend eat a fine meal (or engage in some especially satisfying sex) is to eating that meal (or engaging in such sex) oneself. And though an abstract argument written *here* might obscure the difference between the comprehending perception of one's friend doing *such* things and the comprehending perception of one's friend doing *proving a mathematical theorem* or *performing a virtuous action*, the difference is harder to deny when it comes to actual experience.

In sum, it is plausible to suppose that the enjoyment of divine pleasures is increased *even more* than the enjoyment of mundane pleasures is by their being shared with friends, and that [6](B) is making this point, which [6](C) goes on to explain. The first part of [6](C) is relatively clear. The problem is to see how the first step—i.e., the claim that it is more pleasant to perceive oneself being in the better of two good conditions—is connected with what follows.

It is not entirely clear whether the unusual phrase ἐν τῷ βελτίονι ἀγαθῷ is predicative and so part of the content of what it is more pleasant for the subject to contemplate (i.e., *himself being in the better good*); or whether it is adverbial and so telling us something about the condition the subject is in when he contemplates himself. One (by no means decisive) reason to prefer the former is that the closely parallel passage in *EN* IX.9 speaks clearly of a case in which *oneself being good* is part of the content of what is perceived [τὸ αἰσθάνεσθαι **αὑτοῦ ἀγαθοῦ ὄντος**], and this content is supposed to explain why the perception is pleasant in itself.[115] The idea there is surely that

---

[114] One might object here that one can get the same sort of pleasure from hallucinating that one is having a good meal, but one can equally well hallucinate one's friend enjoying a good meal. And in the case where I hallucinate that I am enjoying a fine meal, I am not really having the pleasure of *having a fine meal*: I am merely hallucinating having such a pleasure, which hallucination may itself be pleasant even if it is *not* the pleasure *of having a fine meal*. (I am somewhat tempted to see disjunctivist views in Plato's and Aristotle's treatments of pleasure, which is according to each of them a form of *aisthêsis*: but I cannot discuss this here.) For more on these issues, see my "Fools Pleasures in Plato's *Philebus*."

[115] See *EN* 1170b7–14:

> Then just as his own being is *haireton* for each, in the same way also—or nearly so—his friend's being <is *haireton* for each>. But <his> being was <said to be> *haireton* on account of perceiving himself being good, and such perception is pleasant in itself. He must therefore *sunaisthanesthai*

one is pleased *because* one sees one's own condition *as good*. And that seems to be the idea here as well, especially given the insistence back in [4](A) that the objects of our perceiving and knowing *be good*. But even if we adopt the second, adverbial reading, we seem to be moved in the direction of the first. At least, this is so if contemplating oneself when one is in a certain condition is supposed to involve awareness of that condition (whether, as the immediately following parenthetical remark tells us, the condition is one of being affected, of acting, or of something else). So there is little to be gained by insisting on the first reading.

The crucial point is that the "better good" is meant to contrast more with less divine pleasures. The parenthetical remark may even be meant to suggest a hierarchy, with πάθος pointing to bodily pleasures, πρᾶξις pointing to the psychic pleasures afforded by virtuous (and other such worthwhile) activities, and ἕτερόν τι hinting at the pleasures of contemplation. But however exactly we take the parenthetical remark, the idea is surely that it is more pleasant to contemplate or see oneself—even if only peripherally—when one is enjoying the pleasures of contemplation than when one is enjoying mundane pleasures. The challenge is to construe the conditional claim that follows this remark in a way such that it connects the initial point about perceiving oneself in the "better good" with the apparently straightforward conclusion that the association of self-sufficient agents will involve contemplating together and feasting together. In other words, the challenge is to fill in the blanks in [6](C) in a way that yields a coherent train of thought, preferably a coherent argument.

Dirlmeier supplies 'δεῖ,' suggesting some sort of conditional or deontic necessity, tied perhaps to the assumption that the self-sufficient person is maximally godlike. This yields something like "if he [viz., the self-sufficient person] *is assumed* to live well, and in the same way also his friend *is assumed* to live well, and if they *are assumed* to act together in living together, then their association will be above all of things in the end, whence it will be to contemplate together and to feast together." But there is nothing in the context to suggest 'δεῖ' and reading the conditional this way leaves the initial claim—about its being more pleasant to observe oneself in the better good—out of the argumentative loop. So Collingwood's suggestion (cited in critical apparatus of the OCT) is better. He suggests that we understand ἐστι, *subaudiendum*, with ἡδὺ (from 1245a38): "if <*it is pleasant*> for him to live well, and in the same way also for his friend to live well, and if <*it is pleasant*> for them to act together in living together, then their association. . . ."

---

his friend as well, that he is <or is good?>; and this would come about in living together and sharing speech and thought. For this is what living together would seem to mean in the case of human beings and not simply, as in the case of cattle, that they feed in the same place.

καθάπερ οὖν τὸ αὐτὸν εἶναι αἱρετόν ἐστιν ἑκάστῳ, οὕτω καὶ τὸ τὸν φίλον, ἢ παραπλησίως. τὸ δ' εἶναι ἦν αἱρετὸν διὰ τὸ αἰσθάνεσθαι αὑτοῦ ἀγαθοῦ ὄντος, ἡ δὲ τοιαύτη αἴσθησις ἡδεῖα καθ' ἑαυτήν. συναισθάνεσθαι ἄρα δεῖ καὶ τοῦ φίλου ὅτι ἔστιν, τοῦτο δὲ γίνοιτ' ἂν ἐν τῷ συζῆν καὶ κοινωνεῖν λόγων καὶ διανοίας· οὕτω γὰρ ἂν δόξειε τὸ συζῆν ἐπὶ τῶν ἀνθρώπων λέγεσθαι, καὶ οὐχ ὥσπερ ἐπὶ τῶν βοσκημάτων τὸ ἐν τῷ αὐτῷ νέμεσθαι.

A promising alternative to this is to supply either (i) ἥδιον θεωρεῖν or (ii) simply θεωρεῖν (both from the more immediate 1245b1) and to read αὑτὸν instead of αὐτὸν (which we are free to do without argument, since this distinction would not have been marked in the original manuscripts). This yields either

(i) if it is <*more pleasant to observe*> himself living well <than merely living> and in the same way also <*more pleasant to observe*> his friend <living well than merely living>, and <if it is *more pleasant to observe*> their acting together in living together <than to *observe* their acting apart in living apart>, then their association will be above all of activities in their end.

or

(ii) if <he *observes*> himself living well and in the same way also <*observes*> his friend <living well>, and <if he *observes* their> acting together in living together, then their association will be above all of activities in the end.

But (ii) shares the disadvantage of Dirlmeier's 'δεῖ': it leaves the claims about pleasure out of the argumentative loop. On his reading, the idea seems to be that living *well* (as distinct from merely living) involves activities in the end (as distinct from things that contribute to the end) so that what self-sufficient agents observe when they observe themselves living well (and doing so together) is their sharing activities in the end. This is no doubt true, but it depends in no way on the points about pleasure that are labored in the surrounding context. So it seems better to take the conjunctive antecedent to make claims about pleasure that are explained by the truth of the consequent. The idea will then be that *because* self-sufficient agents share above all things in the end, self-sufficient agents will get whatever kind or degree of pleasure is implicitly referred to in the antecedent.

The end is presumably eudaimonia itself or (what comes to much the same) the activity or activities in which their eudaimonia consists. The point of the μάλιστά γε seems to be that their association consists primarily in sharing things in the end as distinct from things that contribute to this end, which are no doubt taken care of by others. There is of course an implicit contrast here with the associations of less self-sufficient agents, which may be devoted, to greater and lesser degrees, to things in the ends of these agents: friendships based on pleasure will presumably be more devoted to sharing things in the respective ends of the friends, and friendships based on advantage presumably less devoted to such things. So it will also be true that the association of self-sufficient agents is—above *all other associations*—devoted to activities in the end whose pursuit these agents share. But this is a consequence of what the μάλιστά γε seems aimed to capture—namely, that their association consists *to the highest degree possible* in sharing things in the end. These are things like *contemplating* together and *feasting* together, activities whose goodness is *maximally non-instrumental*.

In other words, the more self-sufficient the friends are, the more their association can be devoted to such activities, with the result that in living together and perceiving one another engaged in such activities, they perceive one another (their selves included) in *better* conditions than those in which they would perceive one another (their selves included) if the activities they shared were *more instrumental*. So the more self-sufficient the friends are, the more pleasant it is for *them* to perceive one another engaged (and engaged *together*) in the sort of activities they share. The association of maximally self-sufficient agents is thus *maximally* pleasant. This is *not* to say that pleasure is the end for the sake of which self-sufficient agents associate with one another—unless perhaps the pleasure in question is to be *identified* with the activity (unimpeded of course) in question.

It is here that the advantages of (i) over Collingwood's (ἐστι) ἡδὺ become clear. For (i) gives a role in a way (ἐστι) ἡδὺ does not to the initial claim that it is more pleasant to observe oneself in the better of two good conditions. The idea is not—as (ἐστι) ἡδὺ suggests—that two individuals each of whom lives well will thereby live pleasantly, both individually and together. For this, though no doubt true, does not guarantee that their association will be *above all* of things in the end. The idea is rather that each party gets a degree of pleasure not just from *observing* both himself and his friend living well, but from *observing* their acting together in a shared life: and the degree of pleasure each gets from *observing* this acting together in a shared life is supposed to be *greater* than the degree of pleasure each would get if he did *not* observe their acting together in a shared life. But in order for that to be true, it must *not* be possible for either to get *more* pleasure from living well, and observing himself living well, *on his own*. And the only way for that to be true is for the activities they share to be above all activities in the end. Otherwise, either *might* get more pleasure by pursuing on his own activities even more in the end than the ones he pursues together with his friend.

This way of understanding the argument gives roles both to the *comparative* claims about pleasure and to apparent basis of these comparative claims in the friends' *observation* of one another's individual and joint activities. It is the *greater pleasure* experienced by friends who perceive one another living *well* and who share together in *that* sort of living—as compared with the lesser pleasure experienced by friends who perceive one another merely living or living less well—that drives the argument: and the greater pleasure ascribed to maximally self-sufficient friends is tied to the fact that they *observe* themselves engaged *together* in activities that are *maximally non-instrumental*.

I think that the role played by pleasure here has been missed in part because editors have taken ἀπολαύσεις in *EE* 1245b6–7 in a pejorative sense (as Dirlmeier explicitly does) and so associated the ἀπολαύσεις in question not with the activities characteristic of self-sufficient friends but rather with mundane forms of social intercourse engaged in for the sake of nourishment and other necessities. But it is difficult to make sense of what we find in the manuscripts—οὐ τὰ διὰ τροφὴν καὶ τὰ ἀναγκαῖα αἱ τοιαῦται ὁμιλίαι δοκοῦσιν εἶναι, ἀλλὰ ἀπολαύσεις—if we take ἀπολαύσεις in a pejorative sense. For the text appears to be saying that the association of self-sufficient agents involves not the pleasures of nourishment and other necessities, but rather ἀπολαύσεις. And the assumption that ἀπολαύσεις are base has led to various proposals, all involving the insertion (based on speculation about the sense of the passage) of some negation.[116]

But the problem dissolves if we take ἀπολαύσεις in a positive sense: the claim will then be that the affiliations of self-sufficient agents seem not to be on account of nourishment and other necessities, but rather to *be enjoyments*.[117] And this reading receives support from what Aristotle said back in [1](E): namely, that it is whenever we lack nothing that we all seek companions in enjoyment [**τοὺς συναπλαυσομένους**] and people who receive benefits rather than bestow them. For the bit about people who receive benefits rather than bestow them suggests that [1](E) is closely related to [6](C), which ends with a similar claim: namely, that those who are unable to live together with friends in pursuit of whatever end they are capable of attaining choose (clearly as a kind of second best) benefiting and being benefited by their friends.[118]

In sum, the idea of [6](C) is that everyone wants to live together with friends in pursuit of whatever end he or she is capable of attaining because living together with one's friend in the pursuit of this end is *more pleasant* than living alone in the pursuit of this end. Implicit in this is a hierarchy of ends such that the association of maximally self-sufficient agents will be *maximally pleasant* not just because their association consists above all in the pursuit of the relevant end but because this end is itself maximally pleasant. But these agents do not pursue this end because it is pleasant: they pursue it because it is *good*—indeed *better* than any other good.[119] That is why observing themselves enjoying it and enjoying it *together* is more pleasant than observing themselves enjoying (indeed enjoying together) any other good. But not everyone can enjoy what *they* enjoy. So others will aim to enjoy—and to enjoy together with friends—the best activities of which they are capable, activities the successful pursuit of which will yield the most pleasant lives available to *them*. And failing that, people will fall back on the sort of friendship based on advantage that

[116] Fritzsche took οὐ τὰ διὰ τροφὴν καὶ τὰ ἀναγκαῖα with the preceding διὸ συνθεωρεῖν καὶ συνευωχεῖσθαι and proposed to read αἱ <γὰρ> τοιαῦται ὁμιλίαι <**οὐχ** ὁμιλίαι> ἀλλὰ ἀπολαύσεις, yielding something like "for such affiliations <as those involving the pleasures of nourishment and other necessities> are <**not** true affiliations> but <mere> pleasures." Susemihl (who also takes οὐ τὰ διὰ τροφὴν καὶ τὰ ἀναγκαῖα with the preceding διὸ συνθεωρεῖν καὶ συνευωχεῖσθαι) posits a lacuna after αἱ τοιαῦται and speculates that it should be filled in either with ὁμιλίαι γὰρ **οὐχ** ("for such affiliations are **not** <true> affiliations") or with γὰρ **οὐχ** ("for such are **not** affiliations but <mere> pleasures"). Rackham follows suit, inserting γὰρ κοινωνίαι **οὐχ**, and translates, "for such partnerships do **not** seem to be real social intercourse but mere enjoyment."

[117] I am agreeing here with Kosman 148–49. Osborne's reading is similar, though she follows the OCT in adopting Collingwood's γὰρ.

[118] That this is a kind of second best is clear from *Rhetoric* II.12–13, where Aristotle contrasts the friendships of younger people (which seem to be more on account of pleasure) with those of older people (which seem to be more on account of advantage): younger people enjoy one another's company and sometimes even pursue it to their own detriment. Cf. *EN* 1156a31–35.

[119] Here again the relevance of *Metaphysics* XII should be clear. See, for example [ST1], especially [ST1][a].

Aristotle clearly regards as inferior not just to friendship based on character but also to friendship based on pleasure.[120]

Another (perhaps surprising) reason for taking ἀπολαύσεις in a positive sense is that doing so will make the maximally self-sufficient agent even more like God, but in a way that will allow us to see why the comparison with God might nevertheless mislead us into thinking that the maximally self-sufficient agent will not have a friend. Recall [ST1][b], where Aristotle says that the unmoved mover's *diagôgê* is like the best of which we are capable for a short time, since it is also a pleasure [*hêdonê*], and then goes on to say (in a way that should call the *Philebus* to mind) that on account of this—i.e., the unmoved mover's *diagôgê* being a pleasure—waking, perceiving, and thinking are most pleasant (presumably for us), while hopes and memories are pleasant on account of these things (namely, the perceivings and thinkings we either hope to have or remember having had in our waking moments).

I mention the connection with the *Philebus* simply to reinforce the connections I have been seeking to establish between our text, *Metaphysics* XII, and that work. But my focus here is on the way in which [6](C) as I read it involves a claim parallel to the claim that the *diagôgê* of Aristotle's God is *a pleasure*—namely, that the associations of self-sufficient agents are themselves *enjoyments*. In other words, contemplating together and feasting together are themselves enjoyments. But such forms of enjoyment are not available to an unmoved mover, whose only so-called object of thought is its own thinking, which helps to explain why assimilating the self-sufficient agent too closely to God may lead us to overlook the sort of enjoyment that allows us to make sense of the fact that self-sufficient persons, *unlike* Aristotle's divine thinkers, have friends.

Forget for now the enjoyment of feasting together, for which there seems to be no parallel in the case of unmoved movers. Let us focus simply on the enjoyment of contemplating together. This enjoyment depends on the conjunction of several facts explained in the preceding argument: first, the fact that perceiving one's friend necessarily involves a kind of self-perception; second, the fact that perceiving oneself in a good condition is pleasant—indeed the better one's condition, the more pleasant one's self-perception; and third, the fact that in perceiving good objects (including one's *friend* enjoying some good) one thereby comes to be in a better condition, ceteris paribus, than one would be in if one were not perceiving such objects. It follows from the conjunction of these facts that perceiving one's friend enjoying goods is itself pleasant in ways such that we can *make sense* of the fact that people—including self-sufficient people—want to live together with their friends in the enjoyment of the best goods they are capable of attaining. For it is only if they perceive themselves living together with a friend and engaged together with a friend in the best activities of which they are capable that they will experience the pleasures (a) of perceiving their

[120] This is one of several texts showing that—contrary to what is often supposed—Aristotle takes friendships based on pleasure to be more closely associated with friendships based on character than with friendships based on advantage. See also *EN* VIII.4.

friend enjoying that good and (b) perceiving themselves (even if only peripherally) in a better condition than they would perceive themselves in were they enjoying that good on their own.

But it is easy to forget about such pleasures if we assimilate the self-sufficient agent too closely to a divine thinker whose only object (as it were) of thought is its own activity of thinking. For in this case, we risk forgetting about the way in which contemplating *other* things—our friends and their activities included—can, when these things are *good*, bring it about that our self-perception is more pleasant (and to that extent more *haireton*) than it would otherwise be. It does *not follow* that the self-sufficient agent *needs* friends: there are other possible objects of contemplation, such as the starry skies above, he can contemplate on his own. But insofar as contemplating such things is itself more pleasant when he does it—and sees himself doing it—together with friends, it *makes sense* that he will want to do it together with friends, a kind of sense which the comparison with God may render obscure. For such pleasure is not available to Aristotle's God, whose contemplative activity is not made more pleasant by the company of others.

We are now in a position to understand the final stage of Aristotle's argument and to do so without introducing the gratuitous negation that commentators sometimes introduce.

[7] Recapitulation [1245b9–19]

(A) One the one hand, it is clear that we ought to live together <with others> and that that everyone wishes for this above all, especially the most eudaimôn and best person. But this did not appear <to be the case> according to the <initial argument, and this happened, reasonably rough, although <the argument> says <something> true. For although the comparison <with God> is true, the solution is in accordance with the synthesis <sc., the one introduced in [4](A)>.

ὅτι μὲν τοίνυν καὶ δεῖ συζῆν, καὶ ὅτι μάλιστα βούλονται πάντες, καὶ ὅτι ὁ εὐδαιμονέστατος καὶ ἄριστος μάλιστα τοιοῦτος, φανερόν· ὅτι δὲ κατὰ τὸν λόγον οὐκ ἐφαίνετο, καὶ τοῦτ' εὐλόγως συνέβαινε λέγοντος ἀληθῆ. κατὰ τὴν σύνθεσιν γὰρ τῆς παραβολῆς ἀληθοῦς οὔσης ἡ λύσις[121] ἔστιν. [1245b9–14]

(B) For because <as the argument says truly> God is not such as to have need of a friend, we think the one who is similar <does not need a friend>. Yet according to this argument the excellent person will not even think. For it is not in this way <by thinking something *else* besides himself thinking himself> that the God is <being/doing> well, but he is better than to think something else besides himself <thinking?> himself. The reason is that for

[121] The OCT supplies οὐκ here, following Rieckher. But this seems to me, for reasons explained below, both unnecessary and misguided.

us <doing> well is in relation to <something> different, but for that one <sc., God> he himself is his own <doing> well.[122]

> ὅτι γὰρ ὁ θεὸς οὐ τοιοῦτος οἷος δεῖσθαι φίλου, καὶ τὸν ὅμοιον ἀξιοῦμεν. καίτοι κατὰ τοῦτον τὸν λόγον οὐδὲ[123] νοήσει ὁ σπουδαῖος· οὐ γὰρ οὕτως ὁ θεὸς εὖ ἔχει, ἀλλὰ βέλτιον ἢ ὥστε ἄλλο τι[124] νοεῖν παρ' αὐτὸς αὐτόν. αἴτιον δ' ὅτι ἡμῖν μὲν τὸ εὖ καθ' ἕτερον, ἐκείνῳ δὲ αὐτὸς αὐτοῦ τὸ εὖ ἐστίν. [1245b14–19]

The manuscripts all say that the solution, presumably to the initial aporia, is in accordance with the *sunthesis*. But the OCT, following Rieckher, inserts 'οὐκ' in the last clause of (A), supposing perhaps that the *sunthesis* in question is of the self-sufficient man with God. But the term Aristotle uses in referring to the comparison of the self-sufficient person with God is '*parabolê*.' So it seems more reasonable to take the talk of the *sunthesis* as referring back to [4](A), where Aristotle speaks of the need to *suntheinai* two things—namely, that the living in question be *haireton* and that the living in question be *the good* of its subject. We can then dispense with the gratuitous 'οὐκ'.

What the *sunthesis* in [4](A) tells us is that the sort of perceiving and knowing in which the self-sufficient agent's life consists must be not only *haireton* but also in fact *the good* of their subject in the sense that nothing can be added to these things to yield something even more *haireton* for her. It follows from this not only (as [4](A) tells us) that the objects of the self-sufficient subject's perceiving and knowing must be the best possible ones, but also (as [5] and [6] go on to explain) that she must perceive and know these objects *together with a friend*. For insofar as perceiving and knowing such objects together with a friend is *more pleasant* than perceiving and knowing such objects on her own, the solitary contemplation of such objects *cannot* be *the good* for her: for such contemplation *can* be improved by engaging in it with like-minded others. But the activity of Aristotle's God admits of no such improvement: divine thinkers are *completely* self-sufficient, requiring nothing else—not even an object of thought distinct from themselves—for their activity, which *is* their pleasure.

So there are at least two ways in which the comparison of the self-sufficient agent with God threatens to mislead us. It can lead us to forget the need for objects of perception and thought distinct from ourselves, objects without which we would not even perceive or think, let alone perceive or think ourselves. And even if we do not forget the need for such objects, the comparison may lead us to forget about the way in which our thinking, unlike that of Aristotle's divine intellects, can be improved by the

---

[122] Cf. *De Motu Animalium* 700b32–35: "But the eternally noble and that which is truly and primarily good, and not good at one time but not at another, is too divine and too honorable to be relative to anything else [πρὸς ἕτερον]" (translation by Nussbaum).

[123] Rackham prints 'οὐδὲν' and translates "will not think of anything"; Dirlmeier thinks 'οὐδὲ νοήσει' requires an object and suggests that 'τι' has fallen out due to haplography. But this seems to me to miss Aristotle's point, which is that without objects distinct from themselves human subjects will *not even think*!

[124] P and C have ἀλλότριον.

company of others. Most of VII.12 seems to me concerned to make the second point, about the way in which contemplating together with our friends is more pleasant—and so more *haireton*—than contemplating on our own. In [7](B) Aristotle simply adds the final twist, so to speak, of his knife: if we forget about the self-sufficient subject's need for objects of thought distinct from herself, we end up with a subject that does *not even think*. And what could be *less* godlike than that?[125]

WORKS CITED

Barnes, J. (ed.) *The Complete Works of Aristotle*. Revised Oxford Translation. Princeton, NJ: Princeton University Press, 1984.

Bekker, I. 1831. *Aristotelis Opera*. Berlin: Academia Regia Borussica.

Bobonich, C. 2002. *Plato's Utopia Recast: His Later Ethics and Politics*. Oxford: Oxford University Press.

Bonitz, H. 1844. *Observationes Criticae in Aristotelis quae feruntur Magna Moralia et Ethica Eudemia*.

Cooper, J. 1980. "Aristotle on Friendship." In A. Rorty (ed.), *Essays on Aristotle's Ethics*. Berkeley: University of California Press, 301–40.

Cooper, J. 2003. "Plato and Aristotle on 'Finality' and '(Self-)Sufficiency.'" In R. Heinaman (ed.), *Plato and Aristotle's Ethics: Proceedings of the Fourth Keeling Colloquium in Ancient Philosophy*. London: Ashgate, 117–47.

Davidson, D. 1973. "Radical Interpretation." *Dialectica* 27: 314–28; reprinted in D. Davidson 2001. *Inquiries into Truth and Interpretation*. Oxford: Clarendon Press.

Décarie, V. 1997. *Aristote: Éthique à Eudème: Introduction, traduction, notes et indices*. Paris: Librairie J. Vrin.

Denniston, J. D. 1950. *The Greek Particles*, 2nd edn. Oxford: Oxford University Press.

Dirlmeier, F. 1958. *Aristoteles Werke in deutscher Übersetzung, Band 8, Magna Moralia*. Berlin: Akademie Verlag.

Dirlmeier, F. 1962. *Aristoteles Werke in deutscher Übersetzung, Band 7, Eudemische Ethik*. Berlin: Akademie Verlag.

[125] I have not yet reached reflective equilibrium on some of the points discussed here, but am letting this go because I promised it to Bob Heinaman, who has shown far more patience with me than even an old friend can be expected to show (for which I thank him). I also want to thank Fiona Leigh for taking over from Bob: she too has been a model of patience. Work on this essay has generally been an object lesson in the benefits—not to mention the pleasures—of thinking together. I have benefited over the years from discussions with audiences at the Keeling Colloquium (especially M. M. McCabe, who kindly shared with me her own work in progress); the Paris-Lille Aristotle seminar; the Centre for Advanced Study at the Norwegian Academy of Science and Letters; the ancient philosophy workshop in Toronto; and the classical philosophy group at Princeton (especially the temporally extended help of Hendrik Lorenz, who first pressed me to see the forest and later helped me to prune some of the trees). I also want to thank Aryeh Kosman and Joel Yurdin for a pleasant day at Haverford in discussing the material with Jacob Krajczynski (to whom I am indebted for extended conversation and written comments). And I want above all to thank Brad Inwood for his constant support and Charles Brittain for serving (once again) as a first-rate midwife (I just hope he hasn't let any wind-eggs slip by).

Fraisse, J. C. 1971. "AYTARKEIA ET ΦΙΛΙΑ en EE VII.12, 1244 b1–1245b19." In P. Moraux and D. Harlfinger (eds.), *Untersuchungen zur "Eudemischen Ethik": Akten des 5. Symposiums Aristotelicum*. Berlin: de Gruyter, 245–52.

Frede, D. 1993. *Plato: Philebus*. Indianapolis, IN: Hackett.

Fritzsche, A. 1851. *Eudemi Rhodii Ethica*. Regensburg.

Harlfinger, D. 1971. "Die Überlieferungsgeschichte der *Eudemischen Ethik*." In P. Moraux and D. Harlfinger (eds.), *Untersuchungen zur "Eudemischen Ethik": Akten des 5. Symposium Aristotelicum*. Berlin: de Gruyter, 1–50.

Inwood, B. 2014. *Ethics after Aristotle*. Cambridge, MA: Harvard University Press.

Inwood, B. and Woolf, R. 2012. *Aristotle: The Eudemian Ethics*, translation with commentary. Cambridge: Cambridge University Press.

Kenny, A. 1978. *The Aristotelian Ethics: A Study of the Relationship between the Eudemian and Nicomachean Ethics of Aristotle*. Oxford: Clarendon Press.

Kenny, A. 2011. *Aristotle: The Eudemian Ethics*. Oxford: Oxford University Press.

Kosman, A. 2004. "Aristotle on the Desirability of Friends." *Ancient Philosophy* 24: 135–54.

Lorenz, H. 2009. "Virtue of Character in Aristotle's *Nicomachean Ethics*." *Oxford Studies in Ancient Philosophy* 37: 177–212.

McCabe, M. M. 2012. "With Mirrors or Without? Self-Perception in *Eudemian Ethics* VII.12." In F. Leigh (ed.), *"The Eudemian Ethics" on the Voluntary, Friendship and Luck*. Leiden: Brill, 43–76.

Moraux, P. and Harlfinger, D. (eds.) 1971. *Untersuchungen zur "Eudemischen Ethik," Akten des 5. Symposiums Aristotelicum*. Berlin: de Gruyter.

Nussbaum, M. (ed. and trans.) 1978. *Aristotle's "De Motu Animalium."* Princeton, NJ: Princeton University Press.

Osborne, C. 2009. "Selves and Other Selves in Aristotle's *Eudemian Ethics* vii 12." *Ancient Philosophy* 29: 1–23.

Perrin, B. 1914. *Plutarch Lives: Vol. I. Loeb Classical Library 46*. London: Heinemann; Cambridge, MA: Harvard University Press.

Pickavé, M. and Whiting, J. 2008, "*Nicomachean Ethics* VII.3 on Akratic Ignorance." *Oxford Studies in Ancient Philosophy* 34: 323–71. [III.7]

Rackham, H. 1935. *Aristotle: The Eudemian Ethics*. Loeb Classical Library 285. London: Heinemann; Cambridge, MA: Harvard University Press.

Rawls, J. 1971. *A Theory of Justice*. Cambridge, MA: Harvard University Press.

Richards, H. 1915. *Aristotelica*. London: Grant Richards.

Rieckher, J. 1858. *Aristoteles, Werke, VI. Schriften zur praktischen Philosophie, 7 Bd. Eudemische Ethik*. Stuttgart.

Ross, W. D. 1918. "Emendations in the *Eudemian Ethics*." *Journal of Philology* 34: 155–58.

Rowe, C. J. 1971. *The Eudemian and Nicomachean Ethics: A Study in the Development of Aristotle's Thought*. Cambridge: Cambridge University Press.

Smyth, H. W. 1920. *Greek Grammar*. Cambridge, MA: Harvard University Press.

Solomon, J. 1925. *The Works of Aristotle, Translated under the Editorship of Sir David Ross, Volume IX*. Oxford: Oxford University Press.

Sorabji, R. 2006. *Self: Ancient and Modern Insights about Individuality, Life and Death*. Chicago: University of Chicago Press.

Spengel, L. 1841. *Über die unter dem Namen des Aristoteles erhaltenen ethischen Schriften*. Munich.

Stern Gillet, S. 2000. *Aristotle's Philosophy of Friendship*. Albany: SUNY Press.

Susemihl, F. 1884. *Eudemi Rhodii Ethica*. Teubner.

Trojanow, I. 2007. *Der Weltensammler*. München: Deutscher Taschenbuch Verlag.

Walzer, R. R. and Mingay, J. M. 1991 *Aristotelis: Ethica Eudemia*. Oxford: Oxford University Press.

Whiting, J. 1991. "Impersonal Friends." *The Monist* 74: 3–29. [I.2]

Whiting, J. 1996. "Self-Love and Authoritative Virtue: Prolegomenon to a Kantian Reading of *EE* VIII.3." In S. Engstrom and J. Whiting (eds.), *Aristotle, Kant and the Stoics, Rethinking Happiness and Duty*. Cambridge: Cambridge University Press, 162–99. [Chapter 4, this volume]

Whiting, J. 2002. "Eudaimonia, External Results, and Choosing Virtuous Actions for themselves." *Philosophy and Phenomenological Research* 65: 270–90. [Chapter 3, this volume]

Whiting, J. 2006. "The Nicomachean Account of Philia." In R. Kraut (ed.), *The Blackwell Guide to the Nicomachean Ethics*. Oxford: Wiley-Blackwell, 276–304. [Chapter 6, this volume]

Whiting, J. 2008. "The Lockeanism of Aristotle." *Antiquorum Philosophia* 2: 101–36. [III.8]

Whiting, J. 2014. "Fools Pleasures in Plato's *Philebus*." In M. Lee (ed.), *Strategies of Argument: Essays in Ancient Ethics, Epistemology, and Logic*. Oxford University Press, 21–59.

Widmann, G. 1969. *Autarkie und Philia in der aristotelischen Ethiken*. Tübingen: dissertation.

Wilson, N. G. 1997. *Aelian: A Historical Miscellany*. Loeb Classical Library 486. London: Heinemann; Cambridge, MA: Harvard University Press.

REPRINT INFORMATION

1. "Aristotle's Function Argument: A Defense." *Ancient Philosophy* 8 (1988): 33–48. All rights reserved. Reprinted by permission of the present editor.
2. "Human Nature and Intellectualism in Aristotle." *Archiv für Geschichte der Philosophie* 68 (1986): 70–95. All rights reserved. Reprinted by permission of the present editor.
3. "Eudaimonia, External Results, and Choosing Virtuous Actions for Themselves." *Philosophy and Phenomenological Research* LXV (2002): 270–90. All rights reserved. Reprinted by permission of *Wiley-Blackwell*. Permissions US@Wiley.com.
4. "Self-Love and Authoritative Virtue: Prolegomenon to a Kantian Reading of *Eudemian Ethics* VIII.3." In *Aristotle, Kant, and the Stoics: Rethinking Happiness and Duty*, edited by Stephen Engstrom and Jennifer Whiting. Cambridge: Cambridge University Press (1996), 162–99. Copyright © 1996 Cambridge University Press. Reprinted with permission.
5. "Strong Dialectic, Neurathian Reflection, and the Ascent of Desire: Irwin and McDowell on Aristotle's Methods of Ethics." *Proceedings of the Boston Area Colloquium of Ancient Philosophy* 17, no. 1 (2002): 61–122. All rights reserved. Reprinted by permission of *Brill*.
6. "The Nicomachean Account of Philia." In *The Blackwell Guide to the Nicomachean Ethics*, edited by Richard Kraut. Oxford: Wiley-Blackwell (2002), 276–304. All rights reserved. Reprinted by permission of *Wiley-Blackwell*. Permissions US@ Wiley.com.

7. "The Pleasures of Thinking Together: Prolegomenon to a Complete Reading of *Eudemian Ethics* VII.12." In *The Eudemian Ethics on the Voluntary, Friendship, and Luck*, edited by Fiona Leigh. Leiden: Brill (2012), 77–154.

INDEX LOCORUM

For the benefit of digital users, indexed terms that span two pages (e.g., 52–53) may, on occasion, appear on only one of those pages

This index includes citations from this and its companion volume (see Preface)

LT for *Living Together*

BS for *Body and Soul*

GENERAL INDEX

For the benefit of digital users, indexed terms that span two pages (e.g., 52–53) may, on occasion, appear on only one of those pages

This index includes citations from this and its companion volume (see Preface)

LT for *Living Together*

BS for *Body and Soul*